Tom Swan's
Code Secrets

Tom Swan's
Code Secrets

Tom Swan

SAMS
PUBLISHING

A Division of Prentice Hall Computer Publishing
11711 North College, Carmel, Indiana, 46032 USA

To G.V.

© **1993 by Tom Swan**

International Standard Book Number: 0-672-30287-X

Library of Congress Catalog Card Number: 93-83480

96   95   94   93   4   3   2   1

Interpretation of the printing code: the rightmost double-digit number is the year of the book's printing; the rightmost single-digit, the number of the book's printing. For example, a printing code of 93-1 shows that the first printing of the book occurred in 1993.

Trademarks

Screen reproductions in this book were created by means of the program Collage Plus from Inner Media, Inc., Hollis, NH.

Composed in AGaramond and MCPdigital by Prentice Hall Computer Publishing

Printed in the United States of America

Publisher
Richard K. Swadley

Acquisitions Manager
Jordan Gold

Acquisitions Editor
Gregory S. Croy

Development Editor
Phillip Paxton

Production Editor
Erik Dafforn

Editorial Coordinators
Rebecca S. Freeman
Bill Whitmer

Editorial Assistants
Rosemarie Graham
Sharon Cox

Technical Editor
Greg Guntle

Cover Designer
Tim Amrhein

**Director of Production
and Manufacturing**
Jeff Valler

Production Manager
Corinne Walls

Imprint Manager
Matthew Morrill

Book Designer
Michele Laseau

Production Analyst
Mary Beth Wakefield

**Proofreading/Indexing
Coordinator**
Joelynn Gifford

Graphics Image Specialists
Dennis Sheehan
Sue VandeWalle

Production
Lisa Daugherty, Terri Edwards,
Dennis Clay Hager, Carla Hall-Batton,
Howard Jones, John Kane, Sean Medlock,
Roger Morgan, Juli Pavey, Angela Pozdol,
Caroline Roop, Michelle Self, Susan Shepard,
Greg Simsic, Suzanne Tully, Alyssa Yesh

Indexer
John Sleeva

Overview

Contents

Part 2 Secrets of C++ Data Structures

7 Crafting Function Templates   141

8 Shaping Class Templates   163

12   Developing Abstract Container Classes   309

Part 3 Secrets of C++ Memory and Data Management

13   Managing Dynamic Memory   363

Preface

Imagine two computer science students of the same age and similar abilities. Teach them C++, give them the same textbooks, and equip them with identical state-of-the-art computers. One student writes an innovative software application, earning fame and fortune. The other student fails to complete a single working program.

Why? What's the secret? Why can some programmers write computer programs more easily than others? Are they more talented, more intelligent, or just plain lucky? While our first student relaxes poolside at a new mansion purchased with royalties, the second might wonder, "What am I doing wrong? How can *I* learn the secrets that will help me to write successful code?"

If I were selling snake oil in a sideshow, I might look you in the eye and suggest that, by reading *Code Secrets,* you too will reap untold rewards in the computer software business. But you know better. The truth is, I don't know the secret to success. Maybe there isn't one.

I have noticed, however, a common characteristic among successful programmers I've met in 15 years of programming and writing about programming topics. Despite having different abilities, top programmers share one unmistakable trait: *They are consumed by an insatiable desire to learn techniques not found in textbooks and rarely taught in schools.*

I've tried to fill *Code Secrets* with exactly that kind of information—tips and techniques that take most programmers years to acquire on their own. Nevertheless, this book doesn't have all the answers—only a snake oil charlatan would promise a cure to every ill. But if I've done my job, among this book's advanced C++ techniques, you will also find the motivation to discover your own solutions to future programming tasks. If there's a secret to success in software development, this has to be it.

Tom Swan
CompuServe ID 73627,3241

Acknowledgments

This book would not exist without the tireless efforts of many individuals at Sams Publishing. Erik Dafforn applied his well-honed editing skills to the manuscript and always saved the day. Richard Swadley, Greg Croy, and Jordan Gold took care of business concerns, giving me the time and peace of mind I needed to write. Wayne Blankenbeckler watched over disk production and scoured the earth for shareware bonus programs included on the accompanying disk. Dean Miller handled electronic mail and online transfers of edited chapters. I owe thanks also to Greg Gruntle, Becky Freeman, Bill Whitmer, Mary Beth Wakefield, Carla Hall-Batton, and an excellent proofreading and indexing staff at Sams.

Last but never least, I thank my wife and assistant Anne for reading the manuscript—finding many errors—and also brewing tea, keeping me fed, answering the phone, dragging me outside for fresh air, and making sense out of our wild and crazy schedule.

Writing a book is hard work. Many thanks to all who contributed for making the writing of *Code Secrets* a rewarding and fun experience as well.

Introduction

This mini chapter introduces *Code Secrets,* outlines the book's parts, lists requirements, and suggests ways to make the most of the chapters. You don't have to read this introduction word for word, but you should at least scan it to become familiar with the book's layout.

Hurry Up— I'm the Impatient Type!

Turn to *Installing the Disk,* then skip directly to Chapter 1, "Migrating to Streams." Go for it!

What, Me Hurry? I Want the Full Story!

Code Secrets covers a variety of programming topics, presented in the context of a tutorial on advanced C++ techniques. Read on for requirements and suggestions for using the book.

Requirements

You need an ANSI C++ draft-standard compiler and a computer on which to run it. If you can meet those two requirements, you should be able to use any computer or operating system to run the sample programs in this book.

Code Secrets does not teach the C++ programming language from scratch. To understand the chapters, you should already have completed a beginning course in C++ programming. You might also gain the required basics from a C++

tutorial such as one of my books, *Learning C++, Mastering Borland C++,* or *Tom Swan's C++ Primer.* You should be familiar with the concepts of object-oriented programming, but you don't have to be an OOP wizard.

> **Note:** If the terms *class, encapsulation, inheritance,* and *virtual member function* sound like Martian, you need to bone up on C++ fundamentals before this book will make any sense.

All listings and snippets of code conform to the currently available ANSI C++ draft-standard. I tested every listing with Borland C++ (version 3.1) and with Turbo C++ (version 3.0), but you should be able to use the programs with newer versions or with any up-to-date C++ compiler. If you run into trouble compiling programs, see Appendix A for help.

The disk bound into the back cover is formatted for a 100 percent compatible IBM PC. The listings are stored as 8-bit ASCII text. Each line ends with a carriage return and line feed. Except for those control codes, the files contain no formatting instructions or embedded tabs.

Installing the Disk

> **Note:** The files on the disk are compressed. Before you can use the files, you must decompress them by using the supplied utility, LHA.EXE. The disk is formatted for use in an IBM PC or 100 percent compatible.

1. Create a directory on your hard drive to hold the decompressed files. (I call my directory SECRETS, but you can use another name if you want.) To install the files on drive C:, enter the commands

```
c:
md \secrets
```

2. Copy all files from the disk to your newly created directory. With the disk in drive A: (or another floppy drive), enter the command

```
copy a:\*.* c:\secrets
```

3. Remove the floppy disk. You don't need it anymore, but it *does* make a rather expensive coaster, so you might want to store it safely away. Change to the newly created directory on your hard drive and run the supplied UNPACK.BAT program to complete the installation. Enter the commands

```
c:
cd \secrets
unpack
```

4. After you see the message "Done," delete the .LZH compressed files and the UNPACK.BAT batch file. Enter

```
del *.lzh
del unpack.bat
```

5. For additional notes and late breaking news, see the README.TXT file (load it into any ASCII text editor).

> **Note:** All programs are supplied on disk in text form as printed in this book. You must compile the programs before you can run them.

If you are rushing through this introduction, skip to Chapter 1, "Migrating to Streams." Otherwise, continue on for a description of the book's contents.

How to Use This Book

This book is not a crime novel—there's no butler or victim, and you won't ruin the ending by reading the chapters out of order. If you know C++ well, you can pick and choose the chapters you find interesting. If you are just getting started with C++, it's probably best to read the book from front to back, perhaps as you study a C++ tutorial.

Here are some other suggestions for getting the biggest bang from this book:

- Keep a C++ reference handy for looking up unfamiliar terms and constructions. I assume that you understand C++ fundamentals. To save time and space, I do not define terms and concepts that any good C++ tutorial should explain.

- Run the sample statements that demonstrate a chapter's concepts. You can't learn to swim without getting wet, and you can't learn C++ programming without running programs on a computer.

- If you don't understand the purpose of a statement, remove it and observe the effect when you compile and run the modified code. Removing a section of a program often reveals more about the statements than you would discover from pondering the text.

- Pose questions, and answer them by revising the sample listings. Use your compiler to play "what if" games. You might ask, for example, "What if I use a pointer in this position? What happens?" Don't ponder the question. Modify the code and get your answer from the result. Becoming expert at solving your own puzzles is one of the key secrets to expanding your programming knowledge.

- Insert output statements at strategic locations. A well-placed output statement that displays a string such as *Surprise!* might demonstrate a program's organization better than any explanation I could give in the text.

- Run compiled programs in a debugger. Use your debugger's commands to examine variables, to single-step program statements, and to halt programs at breakpoints. A debugger makes a great teacher—it's not only useful for chasing bugs. If you are not familar with your system's debugger, set aside an afternoon to learn its commands. You will thank yourself dozens of times in the future for spending this time now.

About the Chapters

Following are brief descriptions of the book's parts and chapters. Read this section to locate specific topics in the book. Also consult the table of contents, index, and *Classified Secrets* inside the front cover when you are on the prowl for a tip or fact.

Parts

Code Secrets is divided into three parts, each devoted to an advanced topic on C++ programming. I chose these topics for their practicality, and because they are glossed over in most beginning C++ tutorials. The parts are

- *Part 1. Secrets of C++ Streams.* The true power of I/O streams has yet to be realized in software development. Chapters in this part introduce C++ streams and show advanced uses for streams, overloaded operators, streamable classes, manipulators, and file-handling techniques.

- *Part 2. Secrets of C++ Data Structures.* The key to using C++ classes effectively is to understand them as new data types. Chapters in Part 2 demonstrate this concept with a variety of data types implemented as classes. Sample programs make extensive use of C++ templates—one of the newest features adopted into the ANSI C++ draft-standard. In Part 2, you develop a sophisticated String class along with a full-featured container class library, based entirely on templates.

- *Part 3. Secrets of C++ Memory and Data Management.* C++ gives programmers the option of controlling memory allocations. The chapters in this part explain how to overload the new and delete operators to take advantage of this capability. In Part 3, you learn how to construct a custom heap manager, deal with memory errors, use sparse and triangular matrices, and store "persistent" objects in object-oriented database files.

Chapters

Chapters in each part cover a range of related subjects. Following are brief descriptions of each chapter.

Part 1. Secrets of C++ Streams

- *1. Migrating to Streams.* Introduces C++ streams, lists advantages and disadvantages, and discusses how streams differ from standard I/O functions.

- *2. Understanding Sinks, Sources, and iostream Classes.* Paints the broad picture of the iostream class hierarchy, and shows how to make good use of the library's sink and source objects such as cout and cin.

- *3. Calling Stream Member Functions.* Travels deeper into C++ streams, examining iostream class member functions that you can use to configure input and output streams.

- *4. Molding Manipulators.* Shows how to use and program manipulators to shape input and output directly in stream statements.

- *5. Creating Streamable Classes.* Explains how to add "streamability" to C++ classes, in effect reprogramming input and output streams to recognize data types of your own making.

- *6. Reading and Writing File Streams.* Details the ins and outs of using file streams to read and write data stored in files. Includes instructions for expanding standard text-only streams to read and write binary objects in files.

Part 2. Secrets of C++ Data Structures

- *7. Crafting Function Templates.* Reveals how to use templates for creating functions that are automatically formed at compile time to accomodate objects of different data types.

- *8. Shaping Class Templates.* Continues the template story with details on creating and using class templates that the compiler remolds for use with objects and values of practically any type.

- *9. Vectoring in on Arrays.* Describes how to use class templates to create arrays, or *vectors,* that can hold any kind of values and class objects.

- *10. Constructing a String Class.* Follows the step-by-step development of a sophisticated `String` class—one of the controversial issues surrounding the formation of a future ANSI C++ standard.

- *11. Implementing Fundamental Data Structures.* Suggests ways to use templates and classes to develop object-oriented forms of common data structures such as lists and trees.

- *12. Developing Abstract Container Classes.* Demonstrates how to use fundamental data structures to implement higher-level abstract containers such as arrays, stacks, queues, deques, and sets.

Part 3. Secrets of C++ Memory and Data Management

- *13. Managing Dynamic Memory.* Reviews memory management techniques for storing C++ class objects and other data on the heap, and points out several tips for making good use of the C++ heap operators, `new` and `delete`.

- *14. Overloading `new` and `delete`.* Presents techniques for overloading `new` and `delete` to gain control over object-memory allocations. Explains how to construct a custom heap memory manager.

- *15. Storing Objects Efficiently.* Covers five techniques for improving object-storage efficiency, including pointers, clones, placement-syntax, variable-size objects, and duplicate object references.

- *16. Gaining Space with Sparse Matrices.* Considers memory conservation methods using sparse arrays, triangular sparse matrices, and rectangular sparse matrices. Sample programs show how to take advantage of these "holesome" techniques to create huge sparse structures in relatively small spaces.

- *17. Preserving Persistent Objects.* Discusses objects that survive, or *persist,* beyond the runtime lives of their programs in polymorphic database files. Shows how to store objects of different kinds in a file, then safely read the objects back into memory.

Final Words

Code Secrets covers a variety of programming topics in the context of a tutorial on advanced C++ techniques. The supplied disk provides all of the book's listings ready for use with any ANSI C++ draft-standard compiler. I tested all listings with Borland C++ and Turbo C++, but you should be able to use the programs with any conforming compiler.

After installing the disk and scanning this introduction for an overview of the book's chapters, turn to Part 1 for an introduction to input and output streams and how they differ from standard I/O functions.

Secrets of
C++ Streams

Migrating to Streams

S treams are the eyes and ears of a C++ program. With streams, programs can read and write data of any type, from simple lines of text on a terminal to complex structures stored in disk files.

Many C++ programmers won't try streams long enough to get their feet wet. Instead, they continue to swim with old I/O standards like `printf()` and `gets()`. There's nothing technically wrong with these C-style functions, but if you don't use streams, you are missing out on one of the top secrets in advanced C++ programming—how to create and use streamable data types.

This chapter introduces streams, and it compares them with standard I/O techniques. Other chapters in Part 1 explain how to overload stream operators, how to create streamable classes, how to use and create manipulators, and how to read and write disk files using streams.

The Dying Standard

Most C and C++ programmers learn to write output statements like this:

```
printf("What is your name? ");
```

The literal string passed to `printf()` can also contain embedded formatting instructions. If `char *p` addresses the string `"Item count"`, and if an integer `v` equals 5412, this statement:

```
printf("%s equals %d\n", p, v);
```

writes the following line to the standard output file:

```
Item count equals 5412
```

After you master `printf()`'s highly cryptic formatting rules, you can create tables, display floating point values, write integers in decimal, hex, and octal, and perform many other output formatting tricks. For input, you can use the similar (and equally cryptic) function, `scanf()`, or you might call functions like `getch()` and `gets()` to read characters and strings.

What's the problem with these I/O techniques? Nothing—as long as programs remain small and their I/O tasks are not too demanding. In larger, more complex programs, standard I/O functions create more barriers than bridges. Among the brick walls that C programmers keep beating their heads into, these are some of the most formidable:

● Standard I/O functions are not programmable—unless, that is, you have the original source code and you don't mind fiddling with files that are likely to be updated regularly, requiring you to refiddle with the updates again and again.

● You are forced to memorize dozens of inconsistent rules and function names. This isn't so terrible a problem with standard I/O, but in complex programs that use third-party I/O function libraries, new programmers waste too much time studying function references before they can write a single line of code. Old style function libraries make it difficult to get new programming projects under way.

● Standard I/O functions recognize only native data types. There is no easy way, for instance, to teach `printf()` how to format a structure or a class object. Old functions are like old dogs: you can't teach them new tricks. (I don't have anything against old dogs, though.)

● Using the standard I/O library is supposed to ensure portability, but exactly the opposite often happens. Because the standard library cannot accommodate new tasks, programmers frequently enhance the library by writing custom low-level functions or by employing a third-party toolkit. These approaches often make programs highly system-dependent and even more difficult to port to other operating environments.

A Stream of New Life

C++ classes give programmers the means to create new fundamental data types that behave much like built-in types such as int and char. Streams are natural extensions of this concept. With C++, you can create *streamable classes* that define their own I/O operations. Most C++ compilers come with an extensive example of this idea in the form of an *iostream library* that you can use for I/O instead of calling standard functions like `printf()` and `gets()`.

To introduce streams—and to help those who are having trouble getting up to speed with stream statements—the following sections list a couple of simple programs, one written with standard I/O techniques and one with streams.

Standard I/O

Even though the iostream library is available in most C++ installations, many C++ programmers continue to write C-style programs like Listing 1.1, OLDIO.CPP.

Listing 1.1. OLDIO.CPP.

```
#include <stdio.h>

void main()
{
  char name[128];

  printf("What's your name? ");
  gets(name);
  printf("Hello, %s.\n", name);
}
```

Running OLDIO.CPP and entering Rumplestiltskin produces the following display:

```
What's your name? Rumplestiltskin
Hello, Rumplestiltskin.
```

After printf() displays a prompt on the standard output, the gets() function reads input into a character array, name. A second printf() statement then displays name formatted with your response inserted in place of the embedded command, %s.

Stream I/O

Here's OLDIO.CPP written using C++ streams. Listing 1.2, NEWIO.CPP, generates results identical to those of the standard version.

Listing 1.2. NEWIO.CPP.

```cpp
#include <iostream.h>

void main()
{
  char name[128];

  cout << "What's your name? ";
  cin >> name;
  cout << "Hello, " << name << '.' << '\n';
}
```

The cout object is called a *sink,* a destination for data (see Figure 1.1). The data in this case is the string "What's your name?" The << *put-to* operator sends an object or a literal value (a string, a number, or whatever) to a sink. The cout sink object is usually attached to the standard output.

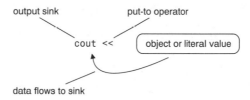

Figure 1.1. A sink object is a destination for data.

The cin object is called a *source*—a site from which data flows into a program (see Figure 1.2). To hold incoming data, an input statement requires a target address—in this example, the location of the char array name. The >> *get-from* operator extracts input from a source and deposits that input in an object, here the character array name. The cin source object is usually attached to the standard input.

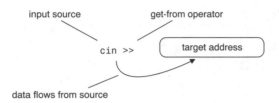

Figure 1.2. A source object is a site from which data flows.

As NEWIO.CPP demonstrates, you can combine multiple output stream expressions into a single statement. This statement:

```
cout << A << B << C;
```

is equivalent to the three separate statements:

```
cout << A;
cout << B;
cout << C;
```

You also can string together input stream statements, though not usually to any great advantage. The statement

```
cin >> A >> B >> C;   // ???
```

makes users enter three items separated by blanks or new lines. Unfortunately, on some systems, it's possible for users to keep pressing the Enter key, scrolling a prompt off screen, without satisfying the input statement's demand for information. You might use a multipart input statement to read data from a file, but it's not so good for prompting users interactively.

> **Note:** Throughout this book, I use three question marks in a C++ comment (`// ???`) to flag questionable lines and surefire bugs.

To avoid input-stream confusion, it's probably best to prompt for and input items individually:

```
cout << "\nEnter A: ";
cin >> A;
cout << "\nEnter B: ";
cin >> B;
cout << "\nEnter C: ";
cin >> C;
```

There's much more to streams, but for simple uses, that's all you need to know. In fact, if you need only a few input and output statements, you can use streams or standard functions as you choose—there's not much advantage of one technique over the other.

As programs grow larger, however, streams bring benefits that might not be obvious from simple examples such as OLDIO.CPP and NEWIO.CPP. The next two sections take a closer look at some of the potential advantages and disadvantages of streams.

Stream Advantages

Streams are especially useful for class-library designers. They provide a consistent style of I/O, helping programmers learn how to use a new library's tools. The statement

```
cout << "Value == " << value << '\n';
```

displays a labeled object value and starts a new line. Even when different kinds of data are involved, stream statements look much the same. There is nothing in this sample statement, for example, to indicate value's data type. If value is an integer, the statement might display

```
Value == 1234
```

If value is an object of a Complex class, *the same statement* might display something like this:

```
Value == (8.659275e-17, 1.414214)
```

"Aha!" you should say. The identical statement gives different results depending on the object's data type. And what a great advantage that is! Streams are object-oriented—they accommodate the types of objects you give them, and their results depend on the data objects used in the statements.

Tip: Think of an object—an integer, a string, or a class object, for example—as being able to read and write *itself* using iostreams. In this sense, an output stream statement doesn't actually write an object's value; rather, the object writes itself onto the stream—a notion that will become more important when you design your own streamable classes.

The iostream library supplied with most C++ compilers can convert all built-in data types to text for writing on the standard output file (see Figure 1.3). As in standard output functions, character symbols like '\n' are converted to control codes that start new lines when written to the terminal or printer. You can also teach streams to output new data types—a subject you'll meet again in Chapter 5, "Creating Streamable Classes."

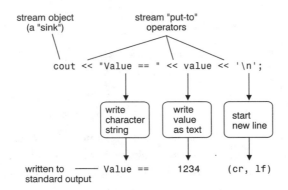

Figure 1.3. Streams are object oriented; they accommodate the types of objects you give them.

Another advantage of streams concerns type checking. The iostream library is strongly typed, a fact that helps the compiler catch many errors before they become serious. In the preceding output stream statement, if value happens to be an object of a class or a struct, unless you include the necessary statements to output objects of that type, *the program will not compile.*

Contrast this vital characteristic of C++ streams with the standard I/O approach. Suppose you have a structure named GrRectangle, declared as

```
struct GrRectangle {
  int left;
  int top;
  int right;
  int bottom;
};
```

You then define a variable of this structural type and display its `left` and `right` members in a `printf()` statement:

```
GrRectangle anyRect;
anyRect.left = 10;
anyRect.right = 20;
...
printf("left == %d, right == %d\n",
  anyRect.left, anyRect.right);
```

Someday in the future—most likely a few hours before you leave for a two-week vacation to the islands—management proclaims that henceforth (a good bureaucratic word) all `GrRectangle` members shall be represented in floating point. You now have until 5 pm today to rewrite that `printf()` statement and the hundreds like it strewn throughout your program. Don't expect any sympathy from the compiler—it can't verify the correctness or even the number of arguments passed to `printf()`. You have to locate by hand every statement that needs changing. Ugh.

The equivalent C++ stream statement adapts to the new requirements with no modifications:

```
cout << "left == " << anyRect.left << ", "
    << "right == " << anyRect.right << '\n';
```

Simply recompiling this statement updates the program to accommodate anyRect's floating point `left` and `right` data members. Furthermore, if `left` and `right` are redefined using a nonstandard data type—a structure, for example, or a class—the statement *will not compile* until you provide output stream services for the new type. The C++ compiler, in other words, helps you to locate incorrect statements in your code. Isn't that what compilers are supposed to do?

For my money, I need no further justifications to convince me to use C++ streams. But then, I also prefer the islands to the office. See you at the beach?

Stream Disadvantages

C++ streams have a few disadvantages. Just learning the new I/O syntax is a problem for C programmers who might find this:

```
puts("Search for? ");
gets(s);
```

to be clearer than this:

```
cout << "Search for? ";
cin >> s;
```

If you're a C programmer, give yourself time to get used to the new syntax. Don't be overly concerned by the new uses for the << and >> operators, which as you probably know, are already employed for left and right binary shifts. Despite the operators' new uses, they are still available for shifts as they always have been in C and C++.

Stream statements might often seem more *wordy* than *worthy*. Using the preceding declarations for struct GrRectangle, statements with many operands like this one:

```
cout << "anyRect.left == " << anyRect.left << ", "
  << "anyRect.right == " << anyRect.right << "\n";
```

might seem more concise when written the standard way, especially if you are familiar with the printf() function as used here:

```
printf("anyRect.left == %d, anyRect.right == %d\n",
  anyRect.right, anyRect.left);
```

The "bloated iostream statement criticism" is easily met by dividing and aligning the statement's elements:

```
cout << "anyRect.left == "    // Display label for left member
    << anyRect.left           // Show value of left member
    << ", "                   // Separate values with a comma
    << "anyRect.right == "    // Display label for right member
    << anyRect.right          // Show value of right member
    << "\n";                  // Start a new display line
```

Although typing statement elements on separate lines takes more work, the format increases the program's clarity. Besides, if you charge per line, think of the extra money you'll make.

Seriously, unlike `printf()` statement arguments, stream statement elements come out in the same order they appear in the program's text—a real help to making future adjustments. For example, you can easily insert a new value or label by using an editor's "insert line" command. You also can comment each element *inside the single statement* as I've done here, clarifying the program to a crystalline shine.

The iostream Library

Although C++ defines the operators << and >> used in stream statements, the iostream library is provided as an *extension* to the language. To use iostreams, you must include the iostream.h library header and link your program to the appropriate object-code modules (whatever they are and however that's done on your system). The key point to remember is that streams are not built into C++. Their use is strictly optional.

Note: Depending on which C++ compiler you have, the iostream.h header might be named iostream.hpp, iostream.hxx, or another filename.

After including the iostream.h header, you can then write input and output stream statements to prompt for and display values. You've already seen several examples. Here's one more:

```
#include <iostream.h>
...
double measurement;
cout << "Enter measurement: ";
cin >> measurement;
cout << "Measurement == " << measurement << '\n';
```

One of the iostream library's main purposes is to convert objects like measurement from binary to text—or in the case of an input statement, from text to binary. In fact, you might consider the iostream library to be primarily a text and binary data translator rather than simply a package of I/O subroutines.

But translation of binary objects to and from text is only part of the iostream equation. The iostream library also provides *sinks and sources* like `cout` and `cin` for writing and reading objects of standard data types, usually by calling operating system functions. These are the library's jobs because, like C, the C++ language does not provide any native I/O services. In fact, the << and >> symbols used in iostream statements are not new C++ operators at all; *they are simply the logical-shift operators from C overloaded by the iostream library to perform I/O.*

Reread that last sentence until it sticks in your mind like oatmeal clings to the bottom of a pot. Operator overloading and the iostream library's text and binary translation services make stream statements possible. "Streamability" is not a native C++ feature.

Final Words

C's standard I/O function library hasn't kept up with the modern world. Some C++ programmers, however, continue to use standard I/O techniques rather than migrate to C++ streams.

Don't be one of them. The C++ iostream library provides a consistent style of I/O, and as future chapters explain, the library's classes mesh well with the goals of object-oriented programming.

In the next chapter, you'll take a close look at the iostream library's sinks, sources, and classes. As you'll see, there's a lot more to streams than a couple of overloaded operators.

Understanding Sinks, Sources, and iostream Classes

Many newcomers to C++ streams are confused by the relationship between stream operators and the iostream library. As if joined in a secret marriage, the fundamental stream partners—operators, sinks, sources, and classes—are intimately connected, but their bounds are hidden from public view.

Sinks and Sources

In standard I/O, programs read and write data through files. A file is usually identified by a numeric handle, or in some cases, by the address of a data structure.

Though used differently, sinks and sources in the iostream library are roughly equivalent to conventional file handles. Most versions of the iostream library provide the sink and source objects discussed in the following sections.

cin

The cin object is the only source object in the iostream library. Typically, cin is tied to the standard input, which usually reads characters from the keyboard or some other default input device. On many operating systems, the standard input file can be redirected to read characters from another file or device—a text file, for instance.

The cin object supports all built-in data types. You can read floating point values from the standard input using statements like these:

```
float f;    // Define floating point variable
cin >> f;   // Read value into f from standard input
```

Or, you can read integers:

```
int k;      // Define integer variable
cin >> k;   // Read value into k from standard input
```

It's also possible to read strings from cin, but you might introduce a bug if you write statements such as

```
char array[80];  // Define a string
cin >> array;    // ???
```

The last statement can erode your program's integrity. In plain talk, it's a bug. If the standard input file can read more than 79 characters plus a null terminator, the statement can write data beyond array's last reserved byte. Don't input strings this way. Instead, call the cin object's getline() function like this:

```
cin.getline(array, sizeof(array) - 1);
```

I'm jumping the gun here. Chapter 3, "Calling Stream Member Functions," covers `getline()` and other iostream member functions.

> **Note:** To try out the programming fragments in this and the next several sections, create a test program (I always name my throw-away tests X.CPP). A simple test program could have these lines (you might have to change iostream.h to iostream.hpp or iostream.hxx):
>
> ```
> #include <iostream.h>
> #include <string.h>
> int main()
> {
> // Insert statements here
>   return 0;
> }
> ```
>
> Enter the fragment at "`// Insert statements here`," compile, and run. Delete each fragment before entering the next. You don't have to save these test programs. Consult the appendixes in this book for hints if you have trouble running your compiler.

cout

When you send any object of any built-in type (or a literal value) to `cout`, the iostream library translates the binary value to text and then sends that text to the standard output. (Character data is, of course, sent immediately on its way.) Normally, you can expect the standard output to be attached to the computer's display terminal, though it could be redirected by an operating system command to another device or a file.

Like `cin`, `cout` supports all native types. You can use `cout` to write integers, strings, floating point values, and so on. You also can combine multiple values in a single output statement:

```
double d = 3.14159;
int k = 1234;
cout << "k == " << k << ", d == " << d;
```

If output doesn't appear when you think it should, your version of the iostream library might be buffered. In that case, you should be able to *flush* the output stream by tacking on a newline character:

```
cout << "k == " << k << '\n';  // Write k and start a new line
```

It's not always convenient, however, to flush a stream with a new line. Consider the case where you need to prompt for input and have the cursor remain on the same line as the prompt:

```
cout << "Enter a value: ";
cin >> k;  // ???
```

If output is buffered, the prompt might not appear until *after* you respond to the input statement, a wacky situation that is sure to displease your program's users—except, perhaps, those who get a kick out of riding backwards in trains.

To avoid getting out of synch with buffered output, flush the output stream this way:

```
cout << "Enter a value: " << flush;
cin >> k;
```

If this doesn't compile, try including the iomanip.h header:

```
#include <iomanip.h>  // Sometimes named iomanip.hpp or iomanip.hxx
```

The flush object is called a *manipulator,* a subject I'll cover more fully in Chapter 4, "Molding Manipulators." You can use another manipulator, endl, in place of a literal newline character. The following two statements produce identical results:

```
cout << "The same old line." << '\n';  // Literal new line
cout << "The same old line." << endl;  // Manipulated new line
```

Of course, when writing strings, you can just as easily include the newline symbol directly in the quoted text:

```
cout << "The same old line.\n";
```

> **Note:** As a general rule, it's probably best to use the endl manipulator rather than '\n', which isn't as clear and can't be reprogrammed as endl can. On the other hand, it's perfectly acceptable to embed '\n' characters in strings.

cerr

The cerr sink is analogous to the standard error file. The only difference between cout and cerr is that cerr cannot be redirected. (Clever programmers tend to figure out tricky ways to redirect cerr, but I'll play by the rules here and assume that it's not possible to redirect the standard error file.) Also, cerr is unbuffered—its output always goes directly to the display terminal (or whatever happens to be the standard output device on your system).

Error messages are the logical items to write to cerr. In the midst of various other output statements, the following error message is practically guaranteed to show up on the terminal, even if the standard output is redirected:

```
cerr << "! This program is losing its mind." << endl;
```

clog

The clog sink is identical to cerr, except that clog is buffered. (Only in C++ can you be happy about having a clogged sink.) Like cerr, output to clog is not redirectable. On some systems, due to buffering, using clog instead of cerr might improve display speed:

```
clog << "! The program is fine. YOU are losing your mind." << endl;
```

Stream Ties

A sink and a source can be related, or *tied*. Like the two ends of a shoestring, tying a sink and a source knots the I/O lines together, intertwining their operations.

Reading from a source tied to a sink automatically flushes any buffered data previously written to the associated sink. If you write these statements:

```
int k;
cout << "Enter a value: ";
cin >> k;  // ???
```

when the program runs, if the prompt doesn't appear until after the input statement executes, the problem might be due to cout and cin becoming untied. (Or they might never have tied the knot in the first place.) To resolve the problem, tie the sink to the source:

```
cin.tie(&cout);
```

To untie a sink and a source, pass 0 (null) to tie():

```
cin.tie(0);
```

Classes

As you dig deeper into C++ streams, you'll probably itch to learn how the iostream library's classes are related. (You might want to print a copy of your system's iostream.h header file for reference.) Figure 2.1 shows a typical iostream library's class hierarchy.

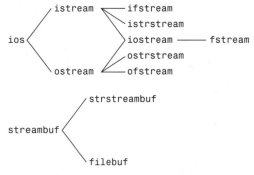

Figure 2.1. A typical iostream library's class hierarchy.

> **Note:** Classes `istream` and `ostream` inherit `ios` as a virtual base class. This means that in any other classes derived using multiple inheritance from *both* `ostream` and `istream`, only one instance of the `ios` base class will exist. In Figure 2.1, for example, an object of type `iostream` would have a single copy of the data members declared in `ios` even though this class appears to be inherited twice, via `istream` and `ostream`. (By the way, a current ANSI C++ draft-standard no longer includes the `iostream` class.)

C++ compiler vendors like to rearrange the iostream hierarchy, add extra classes, and take other liberties with the proposed standard. (So, what else is new?) Borland C++, for example, derives the class `ostream_withassign` from `ostream` in order to overload the = operator for the purpose of relating a `streambuf` object with an output stream.

Minor differences such as this among iostream library implementations probably won't cause much trouble. Most iostream implementations provide the classes in Table 2.1 arranged as in Figure 2.1. If your iostream library doesn't have at least these classes, get another compiler.

Table 2.1. Classes in a typical iostream library.

Class	*Description*
`filebuf`	Derived from `streambuf`. Provides a file-based sink or source of characters.
`fstream`	Derived from `iostream`. Used to construct file stream objects that can read and write data in disk files.
`ifstream`	Derived from `istream`. Provides formatted input from disk files using a `filebuf` object.

continues

Table 2.1. continued

Class	Description
ios	Base class for most iostream classes. Declares state variables and member functions for accessing and modifying those variables. Not necessarily abstract, but not intended to be instantiated as an object.
iostream	Derived via multiple inheritance from istream and ostream. Not present in current ANSI C++ draft-standard specifications. Formerly provided (and still available in many C++ compilers) for constructing objects to be used simultaneously as sinks and sources.
istream	Derived from ios. Serves as an interface for transferring formatted character data from a streambuf object. The cin source object is of type istream (or of a derived type in some libraries). Overloads the >> operator for all standard types.
istrstream	Derived from istream. Provides input operations for strstreambuf objects, used for in-memory formatting.
ofstream	Derived from ostream. Provides formatted output to disk files using a filebuf object.
ostream	Derived from ios. Serves as an interface for transferring formatted character data to a streambuf object. The cout, cerr, and clog sink objects are of type ostream (or of a derived type in some libraries). Overloads the << operator for all standard types.
ostrstream	Derived from ostream. Provides output operations for strstreambuf objects, used for in-memory formatting.

Class	*Description*
streambuf	Base class for filebuf and strstreambuf. Provides buffered I/O functions for reading ("get" operations) and writing ("put" operations). May or may not be implemented as an abstract class, but either way, should never be instantiated directly as an object in programs.
strstreambuf	Derived from streambuf. Literally a "string streambuf," this class operates as a character stream implemented as a pointer to an array of char. Used by the istrstream and ostrstream classes for in-memory formatting of character data.

Don't struggle to memorize the purpose of every class in the iostream hierarchy. For most programs, you can concentrate on the ios, ostream, and istream classes and ignore the others.

In-Memory Formatting

If software houses were theaters, all the programmers would be backstage pulling ropes and working the lights. The visible actions in many programs are supported by the efforts of programming that goes on behind the scenes.

In addition to their usual roles as input consumers and output producers, C++ streams can also work quietly in the background. Rather than output a value to the terminal or printer, for example, you can have the iostream library convert that value to text and store the characters in a buffer. You can then perform whatever other magic you want on that buffer's contents. (See Figure 2.2.)

Listing 2.1, STROUT.CPP, demonstrates this in-memory technique, also sometimes referred to as *incore formatting*.

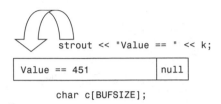

Figure 2.2. An output stream can write characters to an in-memory buffer.

Note: To use in-memory classes, include the strstrea.h header along with iostream.h. The header file might be named strstream.h (including *m*), strstrea.h (no *m*), or it might end in .hpp or .hxx, depending on your compiler and operating system.

Listing 2.1. STROUT.CPP.

```cpp
#include <iostream.h>
#include <strstrea.h>

#define BUFSIZE 256

char c[BUFSIZE];

void main()
{
  int k = 451;
  ostrstream strout(c, BUFSIZE); // Construct string sink
  strout << "Value == " << k;    // Store k as string in c
  cout << c << endl;             // Show result
}
```

The second statement inside function main() constructs an object, strout, of the ostrstream class. Object strout is an in-memory sink. To the class constructor, the program passes the address of a character buffer and the buffer's size.

The output stream statement inserts a literal string (`"Value =="`) and an integer value (`k`) into the in-memory sink, `strout`. The translated characters are deposited into the program's buffer, written to `cout` by the final statement. On-screen, this statement displays

```
Value == 451
```

Equally important is the technique of using an in-memory input stream to translate character data into binary. Listing 2.2, STRIN.CPP, demonstrates the method.

Listing 2.2. STRIN.CPP.

```
#include <iostream.h>
#include <strstrea.h>
#include <string.h>

#define BUFSIZE 256

char c[BUFSIZE];

void main()
{
  double d;
  strcpy(c, "3.14159");   // Copy string to c
  istrstream strin(c);    // Construct string source
  strin >> d;             // Input d from c
  cout << d << endl;      // Show result
}
```

Again, the program defines a global `char` buffer, `c`. Inside `main()`, function `strcpy()` from the string library copies a literal string, `"3.14159"`, into the buffer. In another program, the buffer's data might come from a file or some other source.

The third line inside `main()` constructs an in-memory source object, `strin`, of the `istrstream` class. A simple input stream statement, `strin >> d`, translates the characters stored in `c` into a `double` value, storing the results in variable `d`.

Notice how this statement automatically adapts to the correct data type, eliminating the need to call a "convert string to double" function. (I hate to think of the time I've wasted hunting through references for such functions because I can never remember whether they are spelled `str2dbl()`, `stringtodouble()`, `dblfromstr()`, or whatever. Probably none of these.)

After performing an input operation on an in-memory character array, to reuse that array, you need to reset the stream's internal "get pointer" to the array's beginning. After STRIN.CPP's last statement, for example, you might add the following lines to prompt for a string and translate the results to a binary floating-point value:

```
cout << "Enter value: ";        // Display prompt
cin.getline(c, BUFSIZE - 1);    // Read line into c
strin.seekg(ios::beg);          // Reset stream to beginning
strin >> d;                     // Translate input to a double value
cout << d << endl;              // Show result
```

The new programming calls the `cin` object's `getline()` member function to read a line of text into array c. The third statement is key: calling the `seekg()` function, which is inherited from class `ostream`, positions the input stream to take its input from the beginning of the source—here the start of the array. If you take out this statement, the program might no longer recognize the new information because the preceding use of the stream probably advanced the internal pointer somewhere beyond the buffer's beginning.

Similarly, to reset an in-memory output stream's "put pointer," call the `seekp()` function inherited from class `ostream`. Suppose, for instance, you want to format a second value for inserting into an output stream that you have already used. To demonstrate the solution to this problem, add these lines after the last statement in STROUT.CPP:

```
strout.seekp(ios::beg);         // Reset stream to beginning
k = 1234;                       // Assign value to k
strout << "Value == " << k;     // Translate value to text
cout << c << endl;             // Show result in buffer c
```

Calling `seekp()`, inherited from class `ostream`, with the argument `ios::beg` repositions the output stream's "put" pointer to the beginning of the character array c to which the stream was attached.

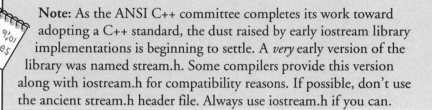

Note: As the ANSI C++ committee completes its work toward adopting a C++ standard, the dust raised by early iostream library implementations is beginning to settle. A *very* early version of the library was named stream.h. Some compilers provide this version along with iostream.h for compatibility reasons. If possible, don't use the ancient stream.h header file. Always use iostream.h if you can.

Final Words

The iostream library's sinks and sources are roughly analogous to a standard I/O library's file handles or references. Using stream statements, programs can read data from the cin source object and write data to the cout, cerr, or clog sinks.

Most iostream libraries should include at least the classes outlined in this chapter—if not, get a newer compiler. Minor differences in the class hierarchy, however, probably won't cause trouble.

Streams are also useful for in-memory formatting. Using the istrstream and ostrstream classes, you can translate a character array into a binary data type, and you can format binary values into text.

The sinks and sources discussed in this chapter—cin, cout, cerr, and clog—are objects of class data types declared in the iostream library. These classes include many public member functions that you can call in reference to sink and source objects. As you'll discover next, the iostream library's class member functions add a new dimension to C++ streams.

Calling Stream
Member Functions

When shopping for an automobile, you probably would not neglect to look under the hood. (With my mechanical skills, however, about the only fact this experiment determines is that indeed there *is* a motor inside.) Like engines the world over, the iostream library is powered by an assembly of parts. Fortunately, you can't bark your knuckles by taking the library apart and learning what makes it go.

Inside *iostream* Classes

Inside the three main iostream library classes—ios, ostream, and istream—are several member functions that you can call to perform a variety of I/O tasks. Because the cout, cerr, and clog objects are defined using the ostream class, you can use these objects to call any public member functions declared in ostream and inherited from the ios virtual base class. You can similarly call istream member functions for the cin source object.

Figure 3.1 illustrates this important concept. The statement cout.width(12) calls the width() member function declared in class ios and inherited by ostream. Because cout is an object of the ostream class, you can call this public member function and others in reference to the object.

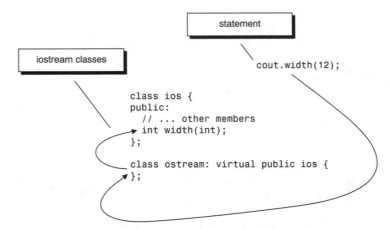

Figure 3.1. Using object cout, this sample statement calls the width() member function inherited from class ios by the ostream class.

Calling member functions for sink and source objects adds a new dimension to iostream statements. This chapter describes how to use some of the more useful member functions in the three main iostream classes. In addition, later in this chapter I'll cover (and, to some extent, complain about) *stream states,* the iostream library's unfortunately primitive (but at least usable) error handling mechanism.

ios **Member Functions**

To display an integer value in a 12-character column and fill white space with asterisks—something I just know you've been *dying* to do—call the ios class's width() and fill() member functions like this:

```
int k = 1234;        // Define and assign a sample value
cout << "k == ";     // Display a prompt
cout.fill('*');      // Set the fill character
cout.width(12);      // Set the output column width
cout << k << endl;   // Show result
```

The cout sink is an ostream object. The ostream class is derived from ios, so you can call public ios member functions like fill() and width() in reference to cout. Running a program with the preceding statements displays

```
k == ********1234
```

The fill() function sets the fill character for subsequent output, but width()'s effect is temporary. If you follow the above statements with

```
int i = 4321;
cout.width(8);
cout << i << endl;
```

the fill character remains set to an asterisk, but the width must be reset. The statements write this string to cout:

```
****4321
```

Because streams remember the character passed to fill(), it's probably best to preserve and restore the current fill character returned by the function. Do that by assigning fill() to a variable:

```
char oldFill = cout.fill('*');
...
cout.fill(oldFill);  // Reset fill character
```

It's usually okay, however, just to pass fill() a blank:

```
cout.fill(' ');  // Reset fill to blank (the default)
```

To get the current fill character, call `fill()` with no arguments:

```
char currentFill = cout.fill();
cout << "Fill character == " << currentFill << endl;
```

Call `eof()` to end an input loop upon reaching the end of the source. The following lines copy characters from the standard input to the standard output:

```
char c;
while (!cin.eof()) {  // While "not end of input"
  cin >> c;           // Read a character
  cout << c;          // Write a character
}
```

This isn't the best way to copy characters from one place to another (I'll show you a better method later), but it has the interesting effect of stripping the input naked of white space—blanks, tabs, and so on. "Running naked" is the default behaviour of input streams, a fact that, for one example, makes input statements automatically ignore blanks entered in front of numbers.

Set floating point output precision by calling `ios`'s `precision()` function, passing the desired number of significant digits as an argument:

```
cout.precision(12);
cout << PI;
```

This assumes your compiler defines a constant PI somewhere. (For Borland C++, include header math.h and use M_PI rather than PI.) The `precision()` function returns the current precision as an `int` value, and it's probably best to save and restore this value using an `int` variable:

```
int oldPrec = cout.precision(12);
...
cout.precision(oldPrec);  // Reset original precision
```

Finally in `ios` are three functions that inspect, set, and clear various *format flag settings* in `ios` objects. These settings might include options unique to your iostream library, but the ones described here should be widely available. The three `ios` class functions are:

- **long flags()** returns the current formatting flags as a long integer value.

- **long setf()** sets (enables) one or more formatting flags.

- **long unsetf()** clears (disables) one or more formatting flags.

Never mind how the flags are stored. Such low-level details are hidden for good reason, and they should remain out of sight. Ignore actual flag values—unless, that is, you don't care whether your code is portable. Internal flag values might differ greatly from one C++ implementation to another.

In order to provide a common interface, but still use efficient bit flags, the ios class declares enumerated symbols that control various formatting options. Borland C++, for example, includes the enum declaration in Figure 3.2 in class ios (the comments are mostly mine).

```
enum {
   skipws      = 0x0001,   // Skip white space on input
   left        = 0x0002,   // Left justify output
   right       = 0x0004,   // Right justify output
   internal    = 0x0008,   // Insert padding after sign or base (e.g. 0x)
   dec         = 0x0010,   // Convert integer values to decimal
   oct         = 0x0020,   // Convert integer values to octal
   hex         = 0x0040,   // Convert integer values to hexadecimal
   showbase    = 0x0080,   // Write numeric base indicator (e.g. 0x)
   showpoint   = 0x0100,   // Always output a decimal point
   uppercase   = 0x0200,   // Output uppercase hex digits (A to F)
   showpos     = 0x0400,   // Precede positive integers with +
   scientific  = 0x0800,   // Format floating point in scientific notation
   fixed       = 0x1000,   // Format floating point in decimal notation
   unitbuf     = 0x2000,   // Flush output after inserts into buffer
   stdio       = 0x4000    // Flush output after each character
};
```

Figure 3.2. The enum declaration from class ios.

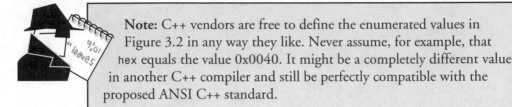

Note: C++ vendors are free to define the enumerated values in Figure 3.2 in any way they like. Never assume, for example, that hex equals the value 0x0040. It might be a completely different value in another C++ compiler and still be perfectly compatible with the proposed ANSI C++ standard.

If you haven't experimented with iostream flags, you'll be surprised how easy it is to use them for complex formatting. For example, you can use a single flag to construct a simple integer-to-hex converter:

```
int k;
cout << "Enter integer value: ";
cin >> k;
cout.setf(ios::hex);  // Set output format to hex
cout << "Value in hex == " << k << endl;
```

In calling setf(), you must completely qualify the enumerated hex symbol. This statement does not compile:

```
cout.setf(hex);  // ???
```

To pass flags to setf(), use qualified expressions such as ios::hex and ios::scientific, specifying the class (ios) that declares the enumerated symbols, a scope resolution operator (::), and the flag name. The enumerated symbols reside in the class, so you must use the class name to get to them.

To clear a flag, call unsetf():

```
cout.unsetf(ios::hex);
```

Both setf() and unsetf() return the current flag setting. Save and restore existing flags like this:

```
int k = 1234;
long oldFlags = cout.setf(ios::showbase | ios::hex);
cout << "k == " << k << endl;
cout.setf(oldFlags);
```

This fragment displays

```
k == 0x4d2
```

For uppercase hex letters, also pass the `ios::uppercase` flag to `setf()`. Change the assignment to `long oldFlags` in the preceding statements to

```
long oldFlags =
  cout.setf(ios::showbase | ios::hex | ios::uppercase);
```

The statement now writes

```
k == 0X4D2
```

The `setf()` and `unsetf()` functions change only the specified flags. Others remain unscathed. To retrieve the current set of flags, call `flags()` with no arguments:

```
long currentFlags = cout.flags();
```

You can also use an overloaded form of `flags()` to set flag values, but watch out. Calling `flags()` for this purpose does *not* preserve existing flag settings as do `setf()` and `unsetf()`. The statement

```
cout.flags(ios::hex);
```

sets the current flags *equal* to `ios::hex`, clearing all other settings and possibly causing chaos on-screen. The secret to using `flags()` correctly is to logically OR the function's return value with the flag you want, then pass the kit and kaboodle to another call to `flags()`:

```
cout.flags(cout.flags() | ios::hex);
```

There's little reason, however, to go to so much trouble. The following statement has the identical effect and is obviously the better choice:

```
cout.setf(ios::hex);
```

ostream Member Functions

The `ostream` class has only three functions that you are likely to need for most I/O operations. To force a buffered output stream to cough up its data, call `flush()` after any output statement. You might not have to do this, but depending on your version of the iostream library, if a prompt doesn't appear at the correct time, try calling `flush()` like this:

```
int k;
cout << "Enter a value: ";
cout.flush();  // Flush preceding output before continuing
cin >> k;
cout << "k == " << k << endl;
```

Remember that flush() is a member of the ostream class and is therefore available only for objects of that class—usually cout, cerr, and clog. This statement does not compile:

```
cin.flush();  // ???
```

The cin object is of the class istream, which does not have a flush() member function.

Two other useful ostream members are put() and write(). Use put() to write single characters to an output sink. The statements

```
cout.put('C');
cout.put('+');
cout.put('+');
cout.put('\n');
```

sputter out *C++* the hard way and start a new line on the standard output. Of course, it's easier just to write a literal string with an output stream statement:

```
cout << "C++\n";
```

More generally useful in ostream are the overloaded write() member functions. These are declared as

```
ostream& write(const signed char *, int n);
ostream& write(const unsigned char *, int n);
```

The only reason for overloading these functions is to accommodate pointers to signed and unsigned character strings. Except for that, the functions operate identically.

Use write() to output a specified number of characters to an output sink. Include the iostream.h and string.h headers, and then use write() like this:

```
#include <iostream.h>
#include <string.h>
...
char string[] = "The Cat in the Hat";
cout.write(string, strlen(string));
cout.put('\n');
```

The write() function in this sample writes all of the characters in string to the standard output. The put() function starts a new line. Together, the two last statements are equivalent to

```
cout << string << endl;
```

Obviously, this is more concise. You normally use write() to write only a limited number of characters from a string. When following the preceding declarations, for example, this statement displays *The Cat:*

```
cout.write(string, 7);
```

Be careful when specifying the number of characters. If you write too many characters, as in this faulty statement:

```
cout.write(string, 25);  // ???
```

the program writes any null plus other bytes beyond the end of the string, possibly leading to an exception on some operating systems.

istream Member Functions

The istream class offers several member functions that you can call for an input source object. There is only one such predefined object, cin. As you know, you can use cin in an input stream statement to read single characters:

```
char c;
cin >> c;  // Read character from standard input
```

You can do the same by calling the get() member function in reference to cin:

```
cin.get(c);
```

The get() member function is overloaded to the hilt. Here's the complete set:

```
int get();
istream& get(signed char *, int len, char = '\n');
istream& get(unsigned char *, int len, char = '\n');
istream& get(signed char&);
istream& get(unsigned char&);
istream& get(streambuf&, char = '\n');
```

If you can't get it with `get()`, it can't be gotten. The parameterless `get()` extracts a character or the end of file indicator from an input stream. Upon reaching the end of file, `get()` returns the predefined symbolic constant `EOF`. The other `get()` functions return `istream&`—in other words, a reference to an input stream object, usually `cin`.

You can use `get()` in a `while` loop to copy characters from the input to the output (`char c` can be signed or unsigned):

```
char c;
while (cin.get(c))
  cout.put(c);
```

This is preferable to the earlier copy loop (see the section in this chapter called "ios Member Functions"). Because `get()` does not eat white space, however, the following is *not* equivalent:

```
while (cin >> c)
  cout << c;
```

Expressions such as (`cin >> c`) have values, just as `get()` statements and other expressions do. The `while` statement uses this fact to read characters (but skip white space) until reaching the end of the standard input file, at which time the expression (`cin >> c`) becomes false, ending the loop.

To read a line of text, prepare a `char` buffer and call the overloaded `get()` with three parameters:

```
char buffer[80];
cout << "Enter a string: ";
cin.get(buffer, sizeof(buffer) - 1, '\n');  // Read line
cout << "String == " << buffer << endl;
```

Pass to `get()` the address of a `char` buffer, the size of the buffer in bytes minus one, and the character that ends input (usually `'\n'`). The function reads up to the specified number of characters or until receiving the specified terminating character, and then inserts a null byte after the last character in the buffer. The function does *not* insert the terminating character ('\n' here). This character is the default, so you can shorten the third line to

```
cin.get(buffer, sizeof(buffer) - 1);
```

To read only the first word of an input source—defining "word" as a sequence of nonblank characters—use a statement such as

```
cin.get(buffer, sizeof(buffer) - 1, ' ');
```

Be aware that these forms of get() do not extract the terminating character from the input source. If you use multiple get() statements like these:

```
char buffer[80];
cout << "Enter a string: ";
cin.get(buffer, sizeof(buffer) - 1);     // Read line
cout << "String == " << buffer << endl;
cout << "Enter another string: ";
cin.get(buffer, sizeof(buffer) - 1);     // ???
cout << "String == " << buffer << endl;
```

the program does not pause at the second get() statement as you might hope. Instead, the program continues past the second get() because the first get() leaves the newline character in the input. You can get rid of this nuisance character by inserting a call to the overloaded get(char &c) function before the second get() statement to read past the end of the line:

```
char c;
cin.get(c);
```

It's usually better, though, (and far easier) to call the istream class's getline() member function, which operates identically to get() but extracts the terminating input character from the input stream. This modified fragment prompts for and reads one line of text, then prompts and pauses for a second line:

```
char buffer[80];
cout << "Enter a string: ";
cin.getline(buffer, sizeof(buffer) - 1);  // Read line
cout << "String == " << buffer << endl;
cout << "Enter another string: ";
cin.getline(buffer, sizeof(buffer) - 1);  // Pause, read next line
cout << "String == " << buffer << endl;
```

That's much better. Now the program pauses at each call to `getline()`. Like `get()`, `getline()` reads a specified number of characters into a `char` buffer, appends a null terminator after the last character, and reads past a terminating character (`'\n'` by default). Though `getline()` does *not* insert that terminating character into the buffer, the function removes the terminating character from the input source. Always use `get()` or `getline()` to read strings safely.

Call the `ignore()` member function to read past a designated character. You might use this function to read some text and then skip characters up to the end of a line. For example, the next fragment prompts for a word, reads characters into a `char` buffer up to a blank, then ignores any other characters to the end of the line:

```cpp
char buffer[80];
cout << "Enter a word: ";
cin.get(buffer, sizeof(buffer) - 1, ' ');  // Read "word"
cout << buffer << endl;
cin.ignore(9999, '\n');  // Skip past end of line
```

Run these statements and enter a string such as Row Row Row Your Boat. Only the first *Row* is read into `buffer`. The `ignore()` member function skips the specified number of characters (9999 here), but stops upon reaching the designated terminator—a blank in this case. The default terminator is EOF (end of file).

Two other related functions peek ahead and return characters back to the input stream. I'm always using these functions (so call me a "peeking Tom"), especially in parsers that search for certain characters. Earlier, for instance, I suggested inserting a call to `cin.get()` to read a possible new line control code from the input stream:

```cpp
char c;
char buffer[80];
...
cin.get(buffer, sizeof(buffer) - 1);
cin.get(c);  // ???
```

This assumes, however, that the first call to `get()` *leaves* a newline character in the input stream. Assumptions like that are as dangerous as lightning. Use this alternative to prevent electrocuting the operating system:

```
if (cin.peek() == '\n')
  cin.get(c);
```

The `cin.get(c)` statement is called only if a newline character is waiting to be read from the input.

When parsing multicharacter symbols—C's beginning comment bracket `/*`, for example—the `istream` class's `putback()` member function comes in handy. The problem is simply stated: after reading a slash (`'/'`), you have to examine the *next* character to determine whether the parser has reached a comment. If not, you should put that character back where you found it. A possible solution follows:

```
char c;
if (cin.get(c) && c == '/')
  if (cin.get(c) && c == '*')
    cout << "Inside comment" << endl;
  else {
    cout << "Not a comment" << endl;
    cin.putback(c);
  }
cout << "Next character == " << (char)cin.peek() << endl;
```

The final statement displays the next character in the input stream. Run the fragment and enter `/*x`. The program displays

```
Inside comment
Next character == x
```

Run it again and enter `/vx` (simulating a possible division expression). This time the program displays

```
Not a comment
Next character == v
```

Because the character following the slash was not an asterisk, the `putback()` function returned the character to the input stream.

The `if` statements in this fragment use an interesting technique for reading and examining characters one-by-one from streams. The statement

```
if (cin.get(c) && c == '/')
  doSomething(c);
```

passes c to doSomething() if a character is successfully read from cin and if that character equals '/'. The if statement expression relies upon *short-circuit expression evaluation* in C++.

> **Note:** With short-circuit expression evaluation, if the first part of the logical expression, cin.get(c), is false, the second part, c == '/', is not evaluated. The multipart logical expression is short-circuited as soon as the outcome is certain.

You can often use peek() in place of putback(), though various circumstances might require either function. Here's the same comment detector written without putback().

```
if (cin.get(c) && c == '/')
  if (cin.peek() == '*') {
    cout << "Inside comment" << endl;
    cin.get(c);  // Read '*'
  } else
    cout << "Not a comment" << endl;
cout << "Next character == " << (char)cin.peek() << endl;
```

That leaves only one more istream member function to cover: read(). There are two overloaded versions:

```
istream& read(signed char *, int n);
istream& read(unsigned char *, int n);
```

As with ostream's write(), the only difference between the two functions is whether the first argument addresses signed or unsigned character strings. Use read() to extract a fixed number of characters from the input stream into a buffer (I intentionally disabled the commented statement in the middle of this sample):

```
char buffer[11] = "**********";  // 10 asterisks
cout << "Enter a string: ";
cin.read(buffer, 8);
// buffer[8] = 0;  // Intentionally disabled
cout << "Buffer == " << buffer << endl;
cout << "Length == " << strlen(buffer) << endl;
```

Running this fragment and entering abcdefghijklmnop displays

```
Enter a string: abcdefghijklmnop
Buffer == abcdefgh**
Length == 10
```

The read() member function does not end until it reads the specified number of characters or reaches the end of the input. The function also does not insert a null terminator after the last character read, leaving two extraneous asterisks in buffer. Enable the disabled statement to insert the null.

After calling read() (or any other input function), member function gcount() returns the number of characters actually read. It's probably best to call gcount() to determine where input stopped rather than assuming, as in the preceding sample, that read() actually extracted the expected number of characters. The assignment to buffer[8] is more safely written as

```
buffer[cin.gcount()] = 0;
```

Now, even if an error occurs or if read() reaches the end of the input file before reading the specified number of characters, the null is still inserted into buffer[] at the correct position.

Stream States

The ios class—the base class for most iostream library classes—defines a set of enumerated constants that indicate a stream object's state. These states are used for error handling.

Every such object—cin or cout, for example—has a state that indicates whether a preceding operation was successful. To identify various state values, the ios class defines these enumerated constants:

```
enum io_state {
  goodbit  = 0x00,    // No errors detected
  eofbit   = 0x01,    // End of file reached
  failbit  = 0x02,    // I/O formatting failure
  badbit   = 0x04,    // I/O buffer failure
};
```

Note: Compiler vendors are free to assign any values to the flags shown here for io_state, or to add new ones. Borland C++, for instance, adds hardfail = 0x80, which indicates an unrecoverable hardware error. Other compilers might not have a similar flag.

The exact values assigned to these constants are not guaranteed—don't write code that depends on them. To detect stream errors, use one of several ios member functions. For example, call bad() after any input or output statement to detect errors:

```
int k = 123;
cout << "k == " << k << endl;
if (cout.bad())
  cerr << "Error detected!" << endl;
```

Or, you can call fail(), much in the same way:

```
if (cout.fail())
  cerr << "Error detected!" << endl;
```

There's a lot of justified confusion over whether to call bad() or fail() to detect errors. The secret in choosing between these functions is to understand what they are technically supposed to do in response to certain state-flag settings. In short:

- The bad() function returns true if the stream's enumerated badbit flag is set.

- The fail() function returns true if the stream's failbit *or* badbit flag is set.

The failbit flag indicates a formatting problem—probably no big deal. The badbit flag is more serious. It tells you an error has occurred in the input or output buffer. Notice that the poorly named fail() function depends on both flags, not only on failbit, as the function's name implies. Confusing? Yes, so just follow these rules:

- Use the two-flag-sensitive fail() to cover most error conditions.

- Use the single-flag-sensitive bad() to detect only serious errors but ignore noncritical formatting difficulties flagged by failbit.

Alternatively, you can detect the success of an input or output operation by calling good(). Again, there's a lot of justified confusion over how to use good() properly. Reversing the logical sense of the preceding example, you might display a message that an output operation succeeded:

```
int k = 123;
cout << "k == " << k << endl;
if (cout.good())  // i.e. if no errors detected
  cout << "No error detected!" << endl;
```

The good() member function returns true (nonzero) if the stream's error state is zero—that is, *if no error bits are set.* Because of this fact, the following incredible expression might be true:

```
cout.good() != !cout.bad()  // ???
```

Putting that into English, in C++ streams, "not bad" is *not* always equivalent to "good." Run through the logic mentally a couple of times, and you will see that this fact must be so. As I mentioned before, bad() detects only badbit errors; it does not detect less serious failbit difficulties. Even if bad() returns false, then, an error might still have occurred! Conversely, good() returns true only if all state flags are in the off state, indicating no errors.

> **Hint:** Many programmers wrongly believe that good() and bad() are exact opposites, which might be true in the movies, but is not in C++ streams. Memorize that fact, and the foregoing discussion will make much more sense. With any luck, so will your programs.

Call the ios class's eof() function to detect the end of a file. Using eof(), here's yet another way to copy the standard input to the standard output:

```
char c;
while (!cin.eof()) {
  cin.get(c);
  cout.put(c);  // ???
}
```

This construction may or may not work in all cases, so it's best not to use it. C++ doesn't clearly define whether `eof()` becomes true before or after reading the final character from an input stream. Depending on the operating system's peculiarities, it might be necessary to change the call to `cout.put()` to

```
if (!cin.cof())
  cout.put(c);
```

The alternative copy loop presented earlier remains the superior choice. Here it is again for comparison:

```
char c;
while (cin.get(c))
  cout.put(c);
```

To access the stream's state, call `ios`'s `rdstate()`, which returns a value of type `iostate`. The exact nature of `iostate` is not defined, and it might differ from one compiler to the next. Change the current state by calling `ios::clear()`, passing an optional value as an argument. The statement

```
cout.clear();
```

resets the stream state to zero and is equivalent to

```
cout.clear(0);
```

> **Note:** As you might detect from this section, stream states are unsophisticated, quirky elements of the iostream library. We can only hope that this situation improves as the ANSI C++ draft-standard matures. *Exceptions,* mechanisms for dealing with errors, are expected to be incorporated into the iostream library, potentially improving error detection and response. Stream error handling as currently implemented is barely adequate, although it's at least as good as the error facilities in the standard I/O library.

Final Words

The iostream library classes declare many public member functions you can call in reference to sink and source objects such as cout and cin. Use these functions to perform a variety of formatting operations on input and output streams.

You can also use ios class state flags and related member functions such as fail(), good(), and bad() for error handling. Beware that good() and bad() are not exact opposites.

Calling member functions for iostream class objects adds a new dimension to C++ streams, but it also complicates programs by forcing you to write separate formatting statements. *Manipulators,* as you'll discover in the next chapter, neatly solve this problem.

Molding
Manipulators

S omebody once told me his job as a programmer was simply defined. "All I do," he said, pointing in the air left then right, "is read data from here, do *whatever* to it, and then write it back over there."

He could have used C++ *manipulators*. Employed in stream statements, manipulators mold and shape data on its way from one place to another. Manipulators can simplify formatting jobs, and they can add extra clarity to a program's source code. The iostream library comes with several built-in manipulators. You can also write your own. When you need to do *whatever* to some data, a manipulator might be the perfect solution.

Built-In Manipulators

Calling ios, istream, and ostream member functions can lead to awkward programming. Consider a typical case. Suppose you need to display two integer values, mask and count, the first in hexadecimal and the second in decimal. You also need to label these values. Using member functions, you might compose the code like this:

```
int mask = 8092;          // Define and assign mask value
int count = 123;          // Define and assign count value
cout << "mask == ";       // Display label
cout.setf(ios::hex);      // Set output formatting to hexadecimal
cout << mask;             // Display mask in hexadecimal
cout << ", count == ";    // Display second part of label
cout.setf(ios::dec);      // Reset output formatting to decimal
cout << count << endl;    // Display count in decimal; start new line
```

Running this fragment produces

```
mask == 1f9c, count == 123
```

That's a heavy load of statements just to produce one scrawny line of output. Isn't there a better way?

Yes, there is. Rather than dropping in and out of an output sequence to call member functions like setf(), you can instead include the iomanip.h header and use manipulators to select formatting options. With the help of manipulators, the preceding lines reduce to a single output stream statement:

```
#include <iomanip.h>
...
cout << "mask == "    << hex << mask
     << ", count == " << dec << count
     << endl;
```

> **Note:** If you are entering programming fragments into a test program, insert #include <iomanip.h> at the beginning of your test file. The header file might be named iomanip.hpp or iomanip.hxx on some systems.

Using manipulators such as hex and dec in a stream statement is exactly equivalent to calling a formatting function such as setf(). The endl manipulator is the same as writing the newline character '/n'.

Each manipulator affects formatting in a defined way. The hex manipulator, for example, selects hexadecimal formatting for integer values such as mask. The dec manipulator selects decimal formatting.

In past chapters, you used endl to start a new line. A similar manipulator, flush, flushes the output stream:

```
cout << "Enter a string: " << flush;
cin.getline(buffer, sizeof(buffer) - 1);
cout << buffer << endl;
```

Manipulators as Filters

You might think of manipulators as *filters* that configure input or output streams (see Figure 4.1). A value goes into the filter and comes out the other end formatted according to the filter's characteristics.

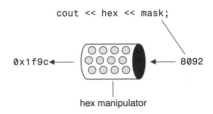

Figure 4.1. A manipulator like hex acts as a formatting filter.

Figure 4.1 is somewhat inaccurate because data doesn't actually flow *through* a manipulator, although it's useful to envision the effect this way. Technically speaking, a manipulator changes the way a sink object like cout formats data. A manipulator can also affect an input source object such as cin.

Whatever its purpose, a manipulator's sole advantage is simplicity. From a software developer's perspective, manipulators are safer to use than member functions like setf(), unsetf(), and flag(), none of which offers any protection against selecting improper or incompatible options. The purpose of the hex manipulator is plainly obvious—you would have to be half asleep to use it incorrectly. Whenever possible, use a manipulator rather than calling ios, ostream, or istream member functions. And if you design class libraries, provide manipulators for your customers to use.

Standard Manipulators

Table 4.1 lists the draft-standard ANSI C++ manipulators supplied with most C++ compilers. Input and output manipulators return a reference to an ios object. Input-only manipulators (there is only one) return a reference to an istream object. Output-only manipulators return a reference to an ostream object.

Table 4.1. Built-in iostream manipulators.

Manipulator without Parameters	Effect
dec	Select I/O decimal formatting flag
endl	Insert new line and flush output stream
ends	Insert null character
flush	Flush buffered output stream
hex	Select I/O hexadecimal formatting flag
oct	Select I/O octal formatting flag
ws	Extract whitespace characters from input

Manipulators with Parameters	Effect
resetiosflags(long n)	Clear formatting flags specified in n
setbase(int n)	Set integer radix to n (0 or 10 for decimal)
setfill(int c)	Set fill character to c
setiosflags(long n)	Set formatting flags to n
setprecision(int n)	Set floating-point precision to n
setw(int n)	Set I/O column width to n

Some manipulators require no arguments; others have one (they could have two or more). You must include the iomanip.h header before using manipulators with one or more arguments, but you don't have to include the header to use parameterless manipulators like endl and flush.

Because a manipulator returns a reference to an ios, istream, or ostream object, the manipulators can be used as elements of a multipart stream statement. You don't *call* manipulators as functions; you insert them directly into iostream statements.

Manipulators in Practice

Manipulators are easy to use. To set output column width, for example, rather than write multiple statements like these:

```
double distance = 87.695;  // Define and assign distance value
cout << "Distance == ";    // Display label
cout.width(12);            // Set the output width
cout.fill('#');            // Set the fill character
cout << distance << endl;  // Show formatted result
```

use manipulators to reduce the jumble to one relatively simple statement:

```
cout << "Distance == "
     << setw(12) << setfill('#')
     << distance << endl;
```

This fragment demonstrates how to use a manipulator that requires an argument—in this case, the character '#' passed to setfill(). The manipulator looks like a function call, but it might be compiled inline.

You can also use manipulators for input. To read a hexadecimal value from the standard input, add the hex manipulator to an input stream statement:

```
int value;
cout << "Enter value in hex: ";
cin >> hex >> value;  // Note hex manipulator!
cout << "Value in hex == " << hex << value << endl;
cout << "Value in decimal == " << dec << value << endl;
```

Running this fragment and entering f69c when prompted for a value produces these lines on-screen:

```
Enter value in hex: f69c
Value in hex == fffff69c
Value in decimal == -2404
```

As these samples show, it's possible for the *same* manipulator to configure input and output streams, a fact that can reduce code size and keep new symbols to a minimum. You don't necessarily have to write separate manipulators to handle input and output operations. You can write and use one manipulator to do both.

Parsing Input into Words

Listing 4.1, RWORDS.CPP, demonstrates how to use a manipulator to read characters safely into a limited-size buffer. The program reads and divides the standard input into words—character sequences, that is, delimited by white space. Run the program by entering a redirection command. For example, on MS-DOS systems, enter

```
rwords <rwords.cpp
```

This passes the contents of the file RWORDS.CPP to the program and writes the results on the standard output. On-screen, you should see a list of the file's words scroll by (probably too quickly to read). To store the results in a file named RESULT.TXT so you can inspect them, enter

```
rwords <rwords.cpp >result.txt
```

Note: On MS-DOS systems, type Ctrl+Z and press Enter to quit the following program if you accidentally run it without redirecting output to a file.

Listing 4.1. RWORDS.CPP.

```cpp
#include <iostream.h>
#include <iomanip.h>

const bufSize = 24;        // Maximum char buffer size
char buf[bufSize];         // Array of bufSize chars

int main()
{
  while (cin >> setw(bufSize) >> buf)
    cout << buf << endl;
  return 0;
}
```

Normally, using `cin` to read strings into a buffer is dangerous because you risk overwriting the end of the buffer's allotted memory. For example, the statement

```
cin >> buf;  // ???
```

is usually best rewritten as

```
cin.get(buf, sizeof(buf) - 1, ' ');
```

Even though that's the solution I recommended in Chapter 3, "Calling Stream Member Functions," I dislike having to pass so many arguments to the `get()` member function. In terms of object-orientation, the statement is out of character.

A better technique uses the `setw()` manipulator to specify the buffer's size. Insert the manipulator directly in the stream statement ahead of the reference to `buf`, conditioning the stream to limit input to a specified number of bytes:

```
cin >> setw(sizeof(buf)) >> buf;
```

Or, use a constant as I did in RWORDS.CPP. The result is concise, clear, and as neat as a paperclip:

```
cin >> setw(bufsize) >> buf;
```

Manipulators with Parameters

`setw()` is an example of a manipulator that requires an argument. Other manipulators also accept arguments. To set the fill character, for instance, use the `setfill()` manipulator as in this sample:

```
int k = 3412;
cout << setfill('#') << setw(12) << k << endl;
```

This output stream statement sets the fill character to `'#'` and the width to 12. It then writes the value of `k` and starts a new line on the standard output file.

Set floating point output precision with the `setprecision()` manipulator. Suppose you define a symbolic constant `PI` as

```
#define PI 3.14159265358979323846
```

If you write the value directly to cout using this statement, the results are formatted according to the default output precision:

```
cout << "pi == " << PI << endl;
```

On my system, running that statement produces the line

```
pi == 3.141593
```

To expand the precision to 12 digits, insert the setprecision() manipulator into the statement

```
cout << "pi == " << setprecision(12) << PI << endl;
```

Now, the output becomes

```
pi == 3.14159265359
```

The setprecision() manipulator must come immediately before the value to be written, PI in this case. The manipulator's effect lasts only for one object. If you place the manipulator before the literal string, the value would be written using the default precision.

Set the output radix, or base, using the setbase() manipulator. These lines write k's value in hexadecimal (base 16):

```
int k = 3412;
cout << setbase(16) << k << endl;
```

There's not much reason, however, to specify an output radix this way. It's easier just to use the hex manipulator:

```
cout << hex << k << endl;
```

Ideally, setbase() would do something logical for *any* number base. To output values in binary, for instance, I'd like to be able to use a statement such as

```
cout << setbase(2) << k << endl;   // ???
```

Unfortunately, this statement doesn't produce the desired binary output on my system. Depending on the compiler you have, perhaps it will on yours.

Finally, use the setiosflag() and resetiosflags() manipulators to set and restore ios class formatting flags, similar to calling setf() and unsetf() as described in Chapter 3. For example, to write a positive integer value k preceded by a plus sign, set the ios::showpos flag by calling setf() like this:

```
cout.setf(ios::showpos);
cout << "k == " << k << endl;
```

On-screen, if k equals 1234, this fragment displays

```
k == +1234
```

To reset to normal formatting—not prefacing positive values with plus—call unsetf():

```
cout.unsetf(ios::showpos);
```

You can select these and other formatting options directly in an output stream statement by using the setiosflags() and resetiosflags() manipulators. The following statement sets the ios::showpos flag and writes k prefaced with a plus sign if the value is positive:

```
cout << "k == "
    << setiosflags(ios::showpos)
    << k << endl;
```

Reset the flag to normal with a statement such as

```
cout << resetiosflags(ios::showpos);
```

Custom Manipulators

You are not restricted to using the supplied set of manipulators—you can also write your own. To understand the secret of a manipulator's construction, it's helpful to examine an existing manipulator. Here's how the hex manipulator is typically declared in iostream.h:

```
ios& hex(ios&);
```

Simply stated, hex is a function that returns a reference to an ios object and also requires an argument of that type. This design permits the function to be used in an input or an output stream statement. (The ios class is the base class for istream and ostream, so any manipulator designed like hex can be used in all streams.)

The hex manipulator might be implemented like this:

```
ios& hex(ios& io)
{
  io.setf(ios::hex);   // Set hex formatting flag
  return io;           // Return ios reference
}
```

The implemented manipulator calls the setf() member function for the io parameter, setting the stream's ios::hex formatting flag. The function then returns the ios reference so the manipulator can be used in a stream statement with multiple operators and elements.

Manipulators as Functions

Using hex as a guide, it's easy to construct your own manipulators. The technique is especially useful when you need to set a combination of formatting flags. Rather than call setf() directly in program statements, create a manipulator to set the flags, then use the manipulator in stream statements. If you later need to use a different set of flags, just revise the manipulator and recompile.

Listing 4.2, CMANIP.CPP, demonstrates how to write a parameterless manipulator. Run the program and enter a value in hexadecimal. On my system, entering 6f9c produces these lines on-screen:

```
Enter value in hex: 6f9c
Value in hex == 6f9c
Value in uhex == 0X6F9C
Value in decimal == 28572
```

Note: The manipulator's prototype would normally be placed in a header file, and the function's implementation would usually reside in a separate module. I included all these elements in CMANIP.CPP to simplify the example.

Listing 4.2. CMANIP.CPP.

```
#include <iostream.h>
#include <iomanip.h>

// Manipulator prototype
ios& uhex(ios &);

int main()
{
  int value;

  cout << "Enter value in hex: ";
  cin >> hex >> value;
  cout << "Value in hex == " << hex << value << endl;
  cout << "Value in uhex == " << uhex << value << endl;
  cout << "Value in decimal == " << dec << value << endl;
  return 0;
}

// Manipulator implementation
ios& uhex(ios &io)
{
  io.setf(ios::hex | ios::showbase | ios::uppercase);
  return io;
}
```

The program declares a parameterless manipulator named uhex (uppercase hexadecimal). Actually, the manipulator declares one parameter—a reference to an ios class object—but even so, it is called a *parameterless manipulator* because, when you use it, you don't pass the manipulator any arguments. The declared parameter simply enables the manipulator to be used in output and input stream statements.

The manipulator's implementation calls setf() to activate three ios formatting flags: hex, showbase, and uppercase. The manipulator returns the same ios reference passed as an argument.

Input and Output Manipulators

Write istream (input) and ostream (output) manipulators similarly. If you will use uhex only in output stream statements, you can change the manipulator prototype in CMANIP.CPP to

```
ostream& uhex(ostream &);
```

Then, implement the uhex manipulator like this:

```
ostream& uhex(ostream &os)
{
  os.setf(ios::hex | ios::showbase | ios::uppercase);
  return os;
}
```

The function's contents haven't changed, but uhex now uses and returns a reference to an ostream object rather than an ios object. Write istream input manipulators the same way, but use the istream class rather than ostream.

Manipulators as Objects

You can write sophisticated manipulators as class objects. Listing 4.3, REPEAT.CPP demonstrates the technique with a manipulator named repeat that inserts a specified number of characters into an output stream. The manipulator is useful for displaying dashed lines—I call them "cut lines" because they look like the dotted lines around a coupon in a newspaper. You can also use the repeat manipulator to insert a number of blanks into an output stream, perhaps to align data into columns.

Listing 4.3. REPEAT.CPP.

```cpp
#include <iostream.h>
#include <iomanip.h>

ostream& fnrepeat(ostream &os, char c, unsigned n);

class repeat {
  char theChar;        // Character to be inserted
  unsigned theCount;   // Number of characters to insert
public:
  repeat(char c, unsigned n)
    : theChar(c), theCount(n) {}
  friend ostream& operator<<(ostream& os, repeat &r)
    { return fnrepeat(os, r.theChar, r.theCount); }
};

int main()
{
  cout << repeat('-', 45) << endl;
  cout << "*** Cut on the dotted line" << endl;

  repeat dots45('.', 45);
  cout << dots45 << endl;

  cout << repeat(' ', 12) << "<-- 12 blanks" << endl;
  return 0;
}

ostream& fnrepeat(ostream &os, char c, unsigned n)
{
  while (n--) os.put(c);
  return os;
}
```

There are some new elements in this program that I'll discuss in the next chapter, "Streamable Classes." Rather than use a simple function, in this case I declared the manipulator as class repeat. In the class are two private data members—theChar (character to be repeated) and theCount (number of repetitions). These members save argument values passed to a repeat manipulator object when it is constructed.

An overloaded friend function, operator<<, overloads the << operator and returns a reference to an ostream object. The overloaded operator function requires two parameters: an ostream reference and a reference to an object of the repeat class. This second parameter is what makes an object of the class usable as a manipulator. The actual statements that perform the manipulator's activities—in this case, repeating a character a certain number of times—are found inside the fnrepeat() function, called by the overloaded operator.

The main program shows different ways to use the repeat manipulator. The first output statement constructs a temporary repeat object directly in an output stream statement to write 45 hyphens to cout. The second output statement writes a literal string. The last statement in the sample program constructs another temporary repeat object to write 12 blanks.

In the middle of the program, an object dots45 is constructed, specifying a period and 45 as arguments. Using the object in an output stream statement writes that many periods (dots) to an ostream object such as cout. The statement

```
cout << dots45 << endl;
```

completely hides the repeat manipulator's complexity, and it also shows how a manipulator appears to add new native capabilities to C++.

Final Words

Programmers spend a great deal of time manipulating data, a job that's tailor-made for C++ manipulators. But manipulators are not the only tools available for solving input and output problems. A more sophisticated technique overloads stream operators for a class, creating a *streamable class* that provides its own I/O services. If you still doubt the power of C++ streams, the next chapter should put any lingering reservations to rest.

Creating Streamable Classes

On their own, C++ streams are no more or less capable than standard I/O functions. By overloading stream operators, however, you can reprogram C++ streams to recognize objects of your own data types. You also can build *streamable classes* that provide for their own I/O. Rather than write functions to which you pass data—the old school of I/O thought—with streamable classes you invent new data types that have I/O capabilities built in. The resulting benefits make C++ streams practically irresistible.

Overloaded Stream Operators

Recall from Chapter 1, "Migrating to Streams," that the stream operators, << and >>, are simply the binary shift operators overloaded by the iostream library to perform input and output operations. Your own programs and library modules can also overload the operators to provide streamability for other data types such as structs.

> **Note:** Two files on disk, OVERIN.CPP and OVEROUT.CPP, in the PART1 directory, contain the programming listed in the next two sections.

Output Overloads

As nonmember functions (those not declared inside a class), overloaded stream operators can recognize nonclass data types. For example, consider the problem of writing a struct to an output stream. First, declare the struct:

```
struct TAnyStruct {
  int x;
  int y;
};
```

In a conventional C program, to write an object of type TAnyStruct to an output file, you would probably create a function, perhaps named WriteStruct(), to which you can pass a TAnyStruct pointer or reference. The function prototype might look like this:

```
void WriteStruct(TAnyStruct &s);
```

That harmless-looking line is a trap waiting to grab you by the ankles. These statements work well enough:

```
TAnyStruct v;
v.x = 123;
v.y = 321;
WriteStruct(v);
```

But a major problem in the WriteStruct() statement is the absence of an output destination. To where is v written? There's nothing in the code to answer that question, so you probably need to pass a nonportable file reference, or perhaps you should write separate functions to print, display, and write TAnyStruct values to specific output devices.

Conventional programs are filled with functions like that, needlessly complicating the program with a proliferation of function names (see Figure 5.1). Maybe two or three extra function names won't hurt, but what about two or three *hundred* names as found in many third-party subroutine libraries? Given the turnover rate in most programming shops, companies can no longer afford to train programmers to learn the ins and outs of extensive function libraries.

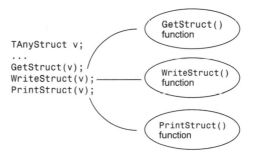

Figure 5.1. Conventional programs pass structures to functions, leading to a proliferation of new names.

With C++ you can do better. Rather than write new I/O functions, you can instead overload the stream operators for new data types. You and your fellow programmers already know how to use streams, so there are no new syntax rules to learn. Declare the overloaded function prototype *outside of any class declaration* as

```
ostream & operator<< (ostream &os, TAnyStruct &s);
```

Examine this prototype carefully. It's a concise package that provides all you need to output any data type (I'll get to overloaded input operators in a moment). The overloaded function's *name* is operator<<. This might not look exactly like a function name, but that's what it is. C++ recognizes operator<< as a special kind of identifier that can serve as a function name *and* as a new use for the << operator.

The overloaded `operator<<` function returns a reference to an `ostream` object—an output sink such as `cout`, for example, from the iostream library. Overloaded `<<` operators must return this reference so they can be used in stream statements. The overloaded `operator<<` function also must declare two parameters:

● `ostream &os` A reference to the `ostream` object to which the overloaded function should write its data. The function must return this *same* reference.

● `TAnyStruct &s` A reference to the data to be written to the output stream. You don't have to use a reference. You could also pass data by address or value. References are probably best, however, for large objects like `structs`.

The compiler enforces this format with the severity of a military drill sergeant. The following three incorrect declarations *are not allowed:*

```
ostream & operator<< (TAnyStruct &s);  // ???
ostream & operator<< (ostream &os, TAnyStruct &a, TAnyStruct &b);// ???
ostream & operator<< (ostream &os);  // ???
```

The first line neglects to include an `ostream` reference parameter, which must be first. The second attempts to declare two `TAnyStruct` parameters—only one is permitted. The third lacks a data parameter—it has nothing to do. Remember, operator functions of all kinds require exact numbers and types of parameters. You don't have as much freedom in their declarations as you do with common functions.

After defining a properly overloaded `operator<<` function, implement that function, either in the same module or in a separate file. Here's a sample implementation of the `TAnyStruct` overloaded `operator<<` function:

```
ostream & operator<< (ostream &os, TAnyStruct &s)
{
  os << "s.x == " << s.x << endl;  // Write to os, not to cout
  os << "s.y == " << s.y << endl;  // Write to os
  return os;  // Return output stream reference
}
```

Two key features demonstrated here are characteristic of all overloaded operator<< functions. One, output statements should refer to the function's ostream reference parameter, identified as os in this case. *Don't write to cout inside the function!* Instead, design your overloaded operator<< functions to refer to the ostream reference passed to the function (named os in this sample). Two, the function must return that same ostream reference passed as an argument, a rule that permits the overloaded operator to be cascaded in multipart output stream statements. The sample statements in this example are, of course, arbitrary. Your overloaded operator<< function can perform any actions you want.

With the prototype and function implementation in place, you can now write TAnyStruct variables using output stream statements. Try these lines on for size:

```
TAnyStruct v;    // Define a struct, v
v.x = 123;       // Assign value to a struct member
v.y = 321;       // Assign value to another struct member
cout << v;       // Write struct via overloaded operator!
```

The final statement writes v by calling the overloaded operator<< function (see Figure 5.2). The statement determines the correct output function to call based on the object's data type.

I can't understand why more C++ programmers don't take advantage of this simple technique! Best of all, if you have several TAnyStruct variables—A, B, and C—you can write them all using a single statement:

```
cout << A << B << C;
```

If there's anything simpler, package it and sell it. You'll make millions.

Figure 5.2. An output stream statement automatically calls TAnyStruct's overloaded operator<< function.

Input Overloads

Overloading the >> input-stream operator is equally easy. Take the output prototype from the preceding section, replace ostream with istream, name the function operator>>, and you've got it:

```
istream & operator>> (istream &is, TAnyStruct &s);
```

The prototype returns a reference to an istream object, similar to the way the output function returned an ostream reference. The new function requires two parameters:

- istream &is—A reference to the istream object from which the over-loaded function should read its data. The function must return this *same* reference.

- TAnyStruct &s—A reference to the data object that is to receive the information extracted from the stream. You must use a reference or pointer. Passing an input object by value would be senseless because the object would then be stored locally and discarded after the function returns.

Implement the function to read input into the data reference—the TAnyStruct reference named s in this case. Here's a sample implementation that prompts for two values and uses input stream statements to read responses directly into the struct's x and y members:

```
istream & operator>> (istream &is, TAnyStruct &s)
{
  cout << "Enter value for X: ";  // Display prompt
  is >> s.x;                      // Input member x
  cout << "Enter value for Y: ";  // Display prompt
  is >> s.y;                      // Input member y
  return is;  // Return input stream reference
}
```

The function includes output statements that write prompts to cout. The input statements, however, refer to the is parameter, not to a global source object such as cin. That way, the function can be used with any istream or derived input source object.

The function returns the *same* istream reference passed as a parameter, permitting the function to be used in cascaded multipart input stream statements. I mentioned in Chapter 1 that I don't recommend using multipart input statements because they tend to produce confusing interactions on-screen. They are useful, though, for reading data from files.

Combined with the overloaded output operator from before, a program can now define a variable of type TAnyStruct, prompt for and read values into the struct, and display the entire ball of wax with only a few deceptively simple statements (see Figure 5.3):

```
TAnyStruct v;   // Define a TAnyStruct variable
cin >> v;       // Read members via the overloaded input operator
cout << v;      // Write members via the overloaded output operator
```

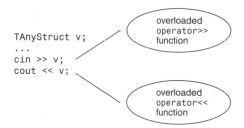

Figure 5.3. Overloaded << and >> operators lead to deceptively simple I/O statements.

Streamable Classes

Combining overloaded stream operators and classes creates data types that provide for their own I/O. Objects of *streamable classes* read and write themselves in streams—the perfect solution for getting all your data ducks in a row.

Almost everyone who creates a streamable class for the first time, however, ends up with more questions than answers. Some typical mysteries are "Why must overloaded operators be friends of a class?" "Why can't overloaded stream operators be class members?" And, "How can you create polymorphic overloaded operators that behave like virtual member functions?"

Many C++ tutorials tell you how to create streamable classes, but they don't bother explaining the reasons behind the rules and regulations. Learn these reasons well, and the rules of syntax will seem as natural as sunshine.

Overloaded Stream Operators

All streamable classes follow the same general layout. Here's a generic sample that you can use to build any streamable class:

```
class AnyClass {
  int anyData;   // Data member
  friend ostream & operator<< (ostream &, AnyClass &);
  friend istream & operator>> (istream &, AnyClass &);
public:
  AnyClass(): anyData(0) { }      // Constructor
  AnyClass(int n): anyData(n) { }  // Overloaded constructor
};
```

(See the Sidebar, "Initializing Class Data Members," If you are not familiar with the syntax used by the two AnyClass constructors in this sample.)

This version of AnyClass has one private data member, anyData, representing the data to be stored in objects of the class. The data doesn't have to be private, but it usually is. In the class's public section, a default constructor initializes anyData to zero. A second, overloaded constructor initializes anyData to an int value passed to the constructor as an argument.

That much of the class is de rigueur. But these two declarations might seem to be strange bedfellows:

```
friend ostream & operator<< (ostream &, AnyClass &);
friend istream & operator>> (istream &, AnyClass &);
```

These *friend functions* are *not* members of AnyClass, and they are *not* inherited by classes derived from AnyClass. By convention, overloaded stream operator functions are declared in a class's private section, but it actually doesn't matter where you declare them. Friends cross all class barriers. Like friend classes, friend functions can go anywhere.

Sidebar: Initializing Class Data Members

Be sure to understand the constructor form used in this sample class declaration:

```
class AnyClass {
  int anyData;    // Data member
public:
  AnyClass(): anyData(0) { }  // Constructor; initialize anyData
};
```

In the constructor, the expression after the colon, anyData(0), looks like a call to a base class constructor. Actually, this is just a substitute for an explicit assignment to the class's anyData member. Alternatively, you could write the constructor using an inline statement:

```
AnyClass() { anyData = 0; }  // Constructor; initialize anyData
```

Both constructors do the same job of initializing anyData to zero. When you have multiple data members, use the following form to initialize the members from arguments passed to a constructor:

```
class AnyClass {
  int a, b, c;    // Data members
public:
  AnyClass(int A, int B, int C)  // Constructor
    : a(A), b(B), c(C) { }        // Initialize data members
};
```

The constructor initializes data members a, b, and c using parameters A, B, and C. As a convention, I sometimes use uppercase for the parameters; lowercase for the data members—that way, I can spell the items the same but distinguish among them by case. The constructor operates as though it were written using inline statements:

```
AnyClass(int A, int B, int C)  // Constructor
  { a = A; b = B; c = C; }      // Initialize data members
```

C++ doesn't specify which method is better, though perhaps a smart compiler could generate more efficient code for the former syntax than it could for the inline statements. Even so, if a data member is an object of a class, you *must* initialize it using the former style. Check out this class:

```
class AnyClass {
  AnotherClass x;  // Data class object
public:
  AnyClass(): x(100) { }  // Initialize x object!
};
```

Here, member x is an object of class AnotherClass (not shown). Assuming that AnotherClass's constructor requires an integer argument, AnyClass's constructor must initialize x using the method demonstrated here. You can't directly assign 100 to x because x is not an integer variable. Even if AnotherClass overloads the assignment operator, you still couldn't assign 100 to x because an overloaded operator is not a constructor.

The overloaded operator functions declare two parameters: a reference to an ostream or istream object, and a reference to the class for which the functions are declared—in this case, AnyClass. In addition, the functions return the same reference to ostream or istream passed as the first argument to the functions. These rules are as rigid as cold steel. Except for the class name, overloaded operator<< and operator>> functions must be declared exactly as shown here.

Friends and Members

Turn back to the beginning of this chapter (see the "Output Overloads" section) and you'll see that an overloaded operator function for a struct is almost identical to the overloaded functions in the preceding section's AnyClass. There's only one significant difference. In a class, an overloaded stream operator *must be a friend function.*

If the purpose of this rule seems obscure, consider these two facts:

● The << and >> operators are binary in nature, so their overloaded functions must have two operands. (The same rule applies to other binary operators. An overloaded operator+ function also requires two operands.)

- The *first* of the two required `operator<<` parameters must be `ostream &`. Similarly, the first parameter to `operator>>` must be `istream &`.

Attempting to declare the overloaded stream operators as class members conflicts with those two rules:

```
class AnyClass {
  int anyData;   // Data member
  ostream & operator<< (ostream &);  // ???
  istream & operator>> (istream &);  // ???
public:
  // ...
};
```

The compiler accepts these declarations, but they don't work as expected because, as class members, the overloaded operators can't participate in stream statements written the usual way. For example, attempting to write an object X of type `AnyClass` causes the compiler to complain about an "Illegal structure operation" (or similar) and halt compilation:

```
cout << X;   // ???
```

The reason this statement doesn't hold water is because, like all member functions, overloaded operator member functions have a hidden `this` parameter secretly declared as a pointer to an object of the class (`AnyClass *` in this case.) The compiler "sees" the faulty functions as though you had declared them as in Figure 5.4.

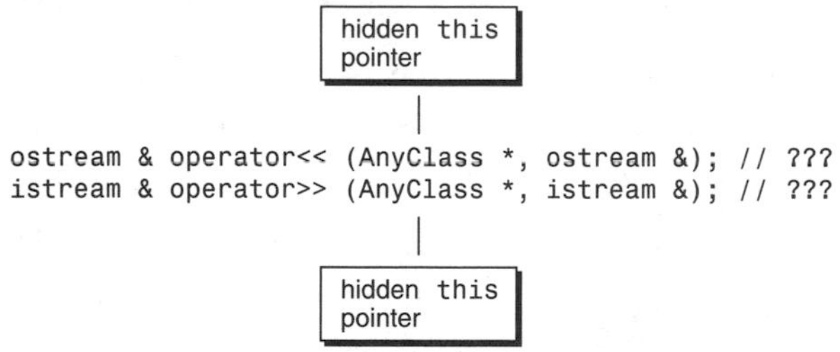

```
              hidden this
              pointer
                  |
  ostream & operator<< (AnyClass *, ostream &); // ???
  istream & operator>> (AnyClass *, istream &); // ???
                  |
              hidden this
              pointer
```

Figure 5.4. Like all member functions, these incorrectly declared stream operator functions have a hidden `this` parameter of type `AnyClass *`.

A revelation of heavenly proportions should appear when you compare the function parameters in Figure 5.4 with the parameters in these *correct* friend-function declarations:

```
friend ostream & operator<< (ostream &, AnyClass &);
friend istream & operator>> (istream &, AnyClass &);
```

These parameters are correct. The ones for the class member functions in Figure 5.4 *are in the wrong order!* Also, in the figure, the first parameter (the hidden this) is a pointer, not a reference.

These facts are significant because of the way stream statements are compiled. Using the correctly written friend functions in which the first parameter is a stream reference, you can use the overloaded operators in the familiar way:

```
cout << A << B << C;
```

The compiler translates that statement as though it were written

```
((cout << A) << B) << C;
```

Like all expressions, each parenthesized expression in this sample returns a value—in this case, a reference to cout. To see this concept more clearly, take the expression apart. The innermost expression,

```
(cout << A)   // Write A to cout; return cout
```

writes A to cout and *also returns a reference to* cout. That reference becomes the sink object for the *next* argument, in this case, object B. So, now we have

```
(cout << A) << B;   // Write B to result of expression at left
```

Object B is written to the ostream & reference returned by the parenthesized expression (cout << A). Object C is in turn written to the ostream & reference returned by *that* expression:

```
((cout << A) << B) << C;   // Write C to result of expression at left
```

Because expression evaluation proceeds from left to right for the << operator, you can discard the parentheses and simply write

```
cout << A << B << C;
```

None of this would work, however, if the overloaded operator functions were members of a class (see Figure 5.4). In that case, because the first parameter to operator<< is a this pointer to an object of the class and the second parameter is an ostream reference, you would have to write the stream statement backwards and include parentheses to force evaluation to proceed from right to left:

```
C << (B << (A << cout));  // !!!
```

That may look kooky, but it works when the overloaded operator<< function is a class member. The resulting backwards syntax, however, is too confusing to give the technique any practical value. What's more, the parentheses are required because expression evaluation normally goes from left to right.

The whole issue of using friends versus member functions is one of those rare cases where the end justifies the means. You declare operator<< and operator>> functions as friends so you can use them sensibly in stream statements, not because of any hard and fast rule of syntax in C++. Understanding this concept is key to creating useful streamable classes.

A Sample Streamable Class

Listing 5.1, PHONE.CPP, demonstrates how to create a complete streamable class that stores a telephone number.

Listing 5.1. PHONE.CPP.

```
#include <iostream.h>
#include <iomanip.h>

class Phone {
public:
  int area, exchange, number;
  friend ostream & operator<< (ostream &, Phone &);
  friend istream & operator>> (istream &, Phone &);
```

continues

Listing 5.1. continued

```cpp
public:
  Phone()
    : area(0), exchange(0), number(0) { }
  Phone(int a, int e, int n)
    : area(a), exchange(e), number(n) { }
};

int main()
{
  Phone p1(212, 555, 1212);
  cout << "p1 == " << p1 << endl;

  Phone p2;
  cin >> p2;
  cout << "p2 == " << p2 << endl;

  return 0;
}

// Overloaded output operator
ostream & operator<< (ostream &os, Phone &p)
{
  os << p.area << '/' << p.exchange << '-' << p.number;
  return os;
}

// Overloaded input operator
istream & operator>> (istream &is, Phone &p)
{
  cout << "Area code (ex. 717): ";
  is >> p.area;
  cout << "Exchange (ex. 555) : ";
  is >> p.exchange;
  cout << "Number (ex. 1212)  : ";
  is >> p.number;
  return is;
}
```

Though simplistic, class Phone is a classic example of a streamable class. To store a telephone number, the class declares three integer data members, area, exchange, and number. The two friend functions are declared as explained in the preceding sections, but the final parameter in each declaration is a reference to a Phone object.

Look at how the friends are implemented near the end of the listing. The operator<< function writes a telephone number in the following form:

aaa/eee-nnnn

Here, aaa is the area code, eee the exchange, and nnnn the number. To read a telephone number, operator>> prompts for each of the three values, then reads them into the Phone object referenced by p.

As the listing's main() function demonstrates, because the Phone class is streamable, you can read and write Phone objects exactly as you do objects of built-in types like int and char. In fact, that's the primary goal of a streamable class—to give you the means to construct new data types without requiring you to learn new skills.

Overloading Output (<<)

As a more practical example of streamable classes, in this and the next section, you'll develop two classes for creating data-entry screens, as you might use in a database system. Here are the basic goals:

- Develop a Label class that can display text at a certain position on-screen using an output stream operator.

- Test the Label class with a sample data-entry form.

- Develop a Field class that prompts for information at a certain screen position using an input stream operator.

- Combine the Label and Field classes to create a data-entry form that can label and prompt for multiple pieces of information.

Listing 5.2, label.h, lists the Label class declaration.

Listing 5.2. label.h.

```
#ifndef __LABEL_H
#define __LABEL_H        // Prevent multiple #includes

class Label {
  int x, y;     // Screen coordinate
  char *s;      // Label text
  friend ostream& operator<< (ostream &, Label &);
public:
  Label(int X, int Y, const char *S);
  ~Label();
  int getx() { return x; }
  int gety() { return y; }
};

#endif  // __LABEL_H
```

The Label class has three private data members: two integers representing a screen coordinate, and a char pointer to address the label's text. Friend function operator<< provides output-streamability for objects of the Label class. Programs don't input labels, so only the output operator is needed.

Listing 5.3, LABEL.CPP implements the Label class.

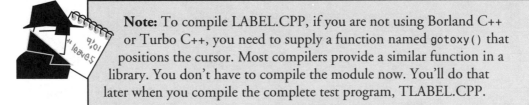

Note: To compile LABEL.CPP, if you are not using Borland C++ or Turbo C++, you need to supply a function named gotoxy() that positions the cursor. Most compilers provide a similar function in a library. You don't have to compile the module now. You'll do that later when you compile the complete test program, TLABEL.CPP.

Listing 5.3. LABEL.CPP.

```
#include <iostream.h>
#include <string.h>
#include <conio.h>        // Borland C++ screen functions
#include "label.h"

// Overloaded output stream operator
ostream & operator<< (ostream &os, Label &f)
{
  gotoxy(f.x, f.y);   // Position cursor
  os << f.s;          // Display label
  return os;          // Return ostream reference
}

// Construct Label objects
Label::Label(int X, int Y, const char *S)
  : x(X), y(Y)
{
  s = new char[strlen(S) + 1];  // Reserve memory for label
  if (s) strcpy(s, S);          // Copy Text to s
}

// Destroy Label objects
Label::~Label()
{
  delete s;
}
```

The overloaded operator<< function calls gotoxy() to send the cursor to a selected screen location. The function then uses an output stream statement to display a label at that spot. (If this doesn't work for you, you might need to call an operating system subroutine rather than use an output stream statement to display text at the current cursor location. Ideally, however, library routines such as gotoxy() should be compatible with C++ streams.)

The class constructor assigns coordinate values to x and y, and copies the label text to memory allocated by new and addressed by char pointer s. Copying text to a block of memory addressed by a class pointer is extremely common, but requires careful memory management. The class destructor, for example, must delete the allocated memory.

Listing 5.4, TLABEL.CPP, tests the Label class.

Note: To compile TLABEL.CPP, if you are not using Borland C++ or Turbo C++, you need to supply a function clrscr() that clears the display and a function gotoxy() that positions the cursor. To compile LABEL.CPP (Listing 5.3) and TLABEL.CPP with Borland C++, enter the commands

```
bcc -c label.cpp
bcc tlabel label.obj
```

Listing 5.4. TLABEL.CPP.

```
#include <iostream.h>
#include <conio.h>       // Borland C++ screen functions
#include "label.h"       // Label class header

// Global array of Label object pointers
Label *form[4];

int main()
{
  int i;       // form[] array index

// Construct Label objects addressed by form array
  form[0] = new Label(8, 4, "Name:          ");
  form[1] = new Label(8, 5, "Address:       ");
  form[2] = new Label(8, 6, "City, St, Zip: ");
  form[3] = new Label(8, 7, "Telephone:     ");
```

```
// Display form using overloaded << operator
  clrscr();  // Clear the screen
  for (i = 0; i < 4; i++)
    cout << *form[i];

// Clean up memory (delete Label objects)
  for (i = 0; i < 4; i++)
    delete form[i];

  gotoxy(1, 24);  // Move cursor to end of screen
  return 0;
}
```

To construct a data-entry form—containing only labels at this stage—the program defines an array named form consisting of four Label object pointers. You might also create a data-entry form as a list of Label objects. Or, you could use a class library container. (Part 2, "Secrets of C++ Data Structures," discusses lists and container classes, so I used a simple array here.)

The main program constructs instances of the Label class. Each instance is given a screen location and string. A for loop then executes this statement to display each label:

```
cout << *form[i];
```

This statement calls the overloaded operator<< function because the compiler recognizes the dereferenced form array pointer as a Label object. Another for loop deletes the memory allocated to each object.

That finishes the first half of the data-entry system. Now let's add som input routines to the mix.

Overloading Input (>>)

The Label class takes care of displaying a data-entry form's labels. To store information entered into a form, we need another class, Field, as declared in Listing 5.5, field.h.

Listing 5.5. field.h.

```
#ifndef __FIELD_H
#define __FIELD_H        // Prevent multiple #includes

class Field {
  Label l;                // Label class object
  int len;                // Input length
  int x;                  // Column coordinate
  static char buffer[];   // Raw input buffer
  char *s;                // Copy of buffer text
  friend ostream & operator<< (ostream &, Field &);
  friend istream & operator>> (istream &, Field &);
public:
  Field(int X, int Y, const char *S, int Len)
    : l(X, Y, S), len(Len), s(0)
    { x = X + strlen(S); }
  ~Field() { delete s; }
  char *gets() { return s; }
};

#endif  // __FIELD_H
```

The Field class's first private data member is Label object. A Field and a Label are loosely related, so it's probably best to have Field *own* a Label rather than have Field be derived *from* the Label class. But there are other design possibilities. I could have created Field independently of Label and used a *third* class to combine Label and Field objects. Or, I could have used multiple inheritance to build this third class. The need to make such choices is ever present, and it's always difficult to know whether you have made the right decision. When faced with many "right" choices, I recall a helpful rhyme: *When in doubt, take the simple way out.* Thus, Field owns a Label. Simple.

Field also declares two integer variables that specify the maximum number of characters to be entered (len) and the cursor's column position (x). The row position is the same as the label's, so Field doesn't need a y data member.

A char pointer s addresses the data entered into the field. For editing purposes, the class declares a static character array named buffer. Because buffer is a static member of the class, only one copy of buffer exists for all class objects. When users enter information into a data-entry field, characters are stored temporarily in buffer, then copied to a string addressed by s. This efficient design neatly avoids wasted memory because all of the form's entries are only as large as necessary to hold the data entered into a form (see Figure 5.5).

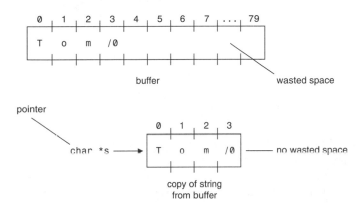

Figure 5.5. Enter text into a static buffer and copy the text to a string allocated just enough memory to hold the characters.

Two friend functions overload the << and >> operators. Because the Label and Field classes are streamable, a program can use output-stream statements to display the form's labels. Likewise, the program can use input-stream statements to prompt users to enter text into the form's fields. To provide these capabilities, Listing 5.6, FIELD.CPP, implements the Field class.

> **Note:** To compile FIELD.CPP, if you are not using Borland C++ or Turbo C++, you need to supply a gotoxy() function as you did for LABEL.CPP. You don't have to compile the module now. You'll do that later when you compile the complete test program, TFIELD.CPP.

Listing 5.6. FIELD.CPP.

```
#include <iostream.h>
#include <iomanip.h>
#include <string.h>
#include <conio.h>      // Borland C++ screen functions
#include "label.h"      // Label class header
#include "field.h"      // Field class header

#define BUFSIZE 80

// Input buffer--static data member of Field class
char Field::buffer[BUFSIZE];

// Overloaded output stream operator
ostream & operator<< (ostream &os, Field &f)
{
  os << f.l;  // Write Label object
  return os;  // Return ostream reference
}

// Overloaded input stream operator
istream & operator>> (istream &is, Field &f)
{
  gotoxy(f.x, f.l.gety());
  is.getline(f.buffer, f.len, '\n');
  delete f.s;
  f.s = new char[strlen(f.buffer) + 1];
  if (f.s) strcpy(f.s, f.buffer);
  return is;
}
```

The Field class's static buffer must be defined as shown near the beginning of FIELD.CPP. Unlike common data members, static declarations in classes are not allocated memory when you construct class objects. Only one static member exists for *all* objects of a class, and you therefore have to define that member's storage externally to the class declaration as shown here. Usually, the best place to define storage for a static object is inside the module that implements the class member functions.

The first two member functions program the overloaded stream operators. The output function, operator<<, simply writes the Field object's Label object to the output stream. The first statement inside operator<< calls the Label class's overloaded << operator function. As explained in the preceding section, this function positions the cursor and writes the label's text.

The overloaded operator>> function is more complex. It positions the cursor, calls the input stream's getline() function to read user input into the static buffer, deletes any existing data addressed by s, then copies the buffer into a newly allocated string.

Listing 5.7, TFIELD.CPP, demonstrates how to use the Field class to create a complete data-entry form.

> **Note:** To compile TFIELD.CPP, if you are not using Borland C++ or Turbo C++, you need to supply a clrscr() function that clears the display. Compile with Borland C++ by entering the commands
>
> ```
> bcc -c label.cpp
> bcc -c field.cpp
> bcc tfield label.obj field.obj
> ```

Listing 5.7. TFIELD.CPP.

```
#include <iostream.h>
#include <iomanip.h>
#include <string.h>
#include <conio.h>       // Borland C++ screen functions
#include "label.h"       // Label class header
#include "field.h"       // Field class header

// Global array of Field object pointers
Field *form[4];
```

continues

Listing 5.7. continued

```
int main()
{
  int i;      // form[] array index

// Construct Field objects addressed by form array
  form[0] = new Field(8, 4, "Name:          ", 40);
  form[1] = new Field(8, 5, "Address:       ", 45);
  form[2] = new Field(8, 6, "City, St. Zip: ", 45);
  form[3] = new Field(8, 7, "Telephone:     ", 12);

// Display and input form using overloaded << and >> operators
  clrscr();
  for (i = 0; i < 4; i++)
    cout << *form[i];
  for (i = 0; i < 4; i++)
    cin >> *form[i];

// Display strings entered into form
  cout << endl << endl;
  cout << "Strings entered into form:" << endl;
  for (i = 0; i < 4; i++)
    cout << form[i]->gets() << endl;

// Clean up memory (delete Field objects)
  for (i = 0; i < 4; i++)
    delete form[i];

  return 0;
}
```

The test program is similar to TLABEL.CPP, but this time defines form as an array of Field class pointers. Each entry in the array addresses one Field object, allocated by new in the main program. Two for loops use input and output stream statements to display the form's labels and to prompt for each field's data.

Run the program and enter sample text into each field, pressing Enter at the end of each line. After you enter the final field, the program displays the strings in the form array before deleting the array's objects.

Note: Depending on your system's editing capabilities, in the sample TFIELD.CPP program, it might be possible to type beyond the end of an input field's maximum length. If that happens, you can repair the problem in the Field class's operator>> function by calling a library function to read a limited-length string into the class's static buffer.

Polymorphic Streams

Overloaded stream operators cannot be virtual functions—the key property of a polymorphic class. C++ programmers frequently forget this fact and attempt to create a class in the following manner:

```
class AClass {
  int a;
  friend ostream & operator<< (ostream &, AClass &);
public:
  AClass(int A): a(A) { }
};
```

The overloaded operator<< function writes the int a data member to an output stream:

```
ostream & operator<< (ostream &os, AClass &ac)
{
  os << "a == " << ac.a << endl;
  return os;
}
```

So far, so good. But trouble brews as soon as you attempt to derive a new class using AClass as a base:

```
class BClass: public AClass {
  int b;
  friend ostream & operator<< (ostream &, BClass &);
public:
  BClass(int A, int B): AClass(A), b(B) { }
};
```

The derived class declares a private data member (b) and a friend function that overloads the << operator. To have output statements write both AClass and BClass data members, you might attempt to implement the overloaded function as

```
ostream & operator<< (ostream &os, BClass &bc)
{
  os << (AClass &)bc;        // ???
  os << "b == " << bc.b << endl;
  return os;
}
```

The first statement calls AClass's output operator function. This works, but the typecast expression is unattractive. Worse, the class doesn't produce the expected results. You might, for example, attempt to construct a BClass object and write its value using statements such as

```
AClass *acp = new BClass(123, 456);
cout << *acp;  // ???
```

Pointer acp can address objects of the base AClass, or of the derived BClass. But writing a BClass object does *not* call that class's operator<< function. Instead, the second statement displays only AClass's value:

```
a == 123
```

We want that statement to display *both* AClass's and BClass's data members by calling the operator<< function in BClass. That would be possible, however, only if operator<< were virtual. Because friend functions cannot be virtual class members, the statement fails to produce the expected results.

The solution is easy, though it remains a secret in many C++ references. To get around this limitation, simply have the overloaded operator call *another* virtual member function in the class. By convention, I always name this function Print(), but you can use another name if you want.

Listing 5.8, POLYSTR.CPP, shows how to use this concept to create virtual output streams.

Listing 5.8. POLYSTR.CPP.

```
#include <iostream.h>
#include <iomanip.h>

class Base {
  int x;
  friend ostream & operator<< (ostream &, Base &);
public:
  Base(int n): x(n) { }
  virtual void Print(ostream &);
};

class Derived: public Base {
public:
  Derived(int n): Base(n) { }
  virtual void Print(ostream &);
};

int main()
{
  Base *bp;  // Pointer to Base or Derived object

  bp = new Base(123);      // Construct a Base object
  cout << *bp << endl;     // Write via overloaded operator
  delete bp;               // Delete object

  bp = new Derived(456);   // Construct a Derived object
  cout << *bp << endl;     // Write via overloaded operator!
  delete bp;               // Delete object
```

continues

Listing 5.8.continued

```
  return 0;
}

// Base class overloaded operator
ostream & operator<< (ostream &os, Base &q)
{
  q.Print(os);   // Call virtual member function
  return os;     // Return ostream reference
}

// Base class virtual member function
void Base::Print(ostream &os)
{
  os << x;       // Write private data member value
}

// Derived class virtual member function
void Derived::Print(ostream &os)
{
  os << "x == ";    // Write label to output stream
  Base::Print(os);  // Call Base class function
}
```

So you can follow the program's logic more easily, I named the two sample classes Base and Derived. The Base class declares a data member x. The overloaded friend operator<< function displays that member's value. Rather than use an output stream statement, however, operator<< calls the class's virtual Print() member function:

```
q.Print(os);   // Call virtual member function
```

This statement passes the stream reference to Print, declared as

```
virtual void Print(ostream &);
```

The Print function carries out the operator's duty, writing the value of x to the output stream:

```
void Base::Print(ostream &os)
{
  os << x;   // Write private data member value
}
```

With that much of the program completed, suppose that you next want to add a label to the output, identifying x's value. You derive a new class Derived from Base, but rather than provide an overloaded operator<< function, you simply redefine Print() to modify the program's output. The replacement function is implemented as

```
void Derived::Print(ostream &os)
{
  os << "x == ";     // Write label to output stream
  Base::Print(os);   // Call Base class function
}
```

After writing the literal label string to the output stream referenced by parameter os, the function calls the Base class's Print() member function to write the value of x.

The main program in POLYSTR.CPP defines a Base class pointer bp. Three statements then allocate a Base object, address it with bp, write its value, and delete the object. Three additional statements allocate a Derived class object, also addressed by bp, write that object, and delete it. On-screen, you see these two lines:

```
123
x == 456
```

Compare the two output statements in function main() that create these lines. *The statements are identical.* Obviously, then, the addressed objects themselves—either of class Base or Derived—select which virtual Print() function to call from inside operator<< in the Base class. Even though stream operator functions cannot be virtual, with the help of a virtual Print() function, the stream behaves polymorphically, reshaping itself according to the types of objects involved.

Final Words

Overloading stream operators makes it possible to construct objects that provide for their own I/O, thus reducing the number of new functions needed in programs. Stream statements look and act pretty much the same for *all* data types.

As the next chapter explains, you can gain similar benefits for your file-handling programs by using *file streams,* an often neglected aspect of C++ streams.

Reading and Writing File Streams

File streams provide an object-oriented way to read and write information in disk files. Trouble is, the file stream library supplied with most C++ compilers is designed to work only with text files. But don't let this limitation turn you off from using streams for file handling. This chapter explains how to use file streams to read and write binary values, text, structures, or any other objects.

File Stream Class

To use file streams, include the fstream.h header file, usually along with iostream.h. Begin your programs like this:

```
#include <iostream.h>
#include <fstream.h>
```

Including the fstream.h header makes available the file-stream classes in Figure 6.1, a pruned branch of the C++ stream tree illustrated in Chapter 2, "Understanding Sinks, Sources, and iostream Classes."

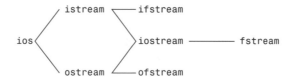

Figure 6.1. Classes in the file stream library.

> **Note:** As with other stream classes, C++ vendors typically rearrange the classes in Figure 6.1. (Is it any wonder that standards are so hard to come by?) Some file stream libraries also include classes not shown in the figure. Borland C++, for example, derives an `fstreambase` class from ios, then partially derives `ifstream`, `ofstream`, and `fstream` from `fstreambase`. Apparently, this reorganization reduces the number of duplicate members in the `ifstream` and `ofstream` classes. These and other minor discrepancies shouldn't affect the use of the classes, however.

Here are some additional points to keep in mind while learning how to use file streams. Also refer back to Table 2.1 in Chapter 2 for descriptions of the classes shown in Figure 6.1.

- All file stream classes except `filebuf` are ultimately derived from class `ios`. Because of their heritage, file streams can use iostream member functions, manipulators, state flags, and other stream-handling techniques explained in the preceding chapters.

- Use the `ifstream` class ("input file stream") for reading data from files. The `ifstream` class is derived from `istream`. It is literally an input-stream expanded to work with files.

- Use the `ofstream` class ("output file stream") for output files. The `ofstream` class is derived from `ostream`. It is literally an output-stream expanded to work with files.

- Use the `fstream` class for reading and writing data in the *same* file. (The current ANSI C++ draft-standard does not have `iostream` and `fstream` classes.)

- The `filebuf` class provides buffered I/O services to the `ifstream`, `ofstream`, and `fstream` classes. You'll rarely, if ever, directly use the `filebuf` class. To keep programs portable, use the file I/O services provided by the `ifstream`, `ofstream`, and `fstream` classes.

Text File Streams

Text file streams are simple and easy to use. They make a great introduction to file streams in general, so let's begin there. There are three main areas to cover:

- Creating text files

- Writing to text files

- Reading from text files

In most cases, you should use the `ifstream` and `ofstream` classes to carry out these tasks. Because text files are usually organized in variable-length lines, it's best not to attempt simultaneous reading and writing to the same text file using the `fstream` class.

Creating and Writing Text Files

To create a new text file, define an object of the `ofstream` class. Pass two arguments to the class constructor: a filename and an `open_mode` enumerated constant:

```
ofstream ofs("NEWFILE.TXT", ios::out);
```

Constructing the `ofstream` object creates the file if it doesn't exist. Notice how different this is from conventional file handling where you might define a file handle, then call a function to create the file. With file streams, you create the file object *and* its associated disk file in one stroke. If the file exists, constructing the `ofstream` object as shown here overwrites the file.

The actual format, number of characters, and other characteristics of the filename string might differ among various operating systems, but a similar statement should work with any up-to-date C++ compiler. The second argument, `ios::out`, selects an access mode for the file. The `ios` class declares out and other modes as open_mode enumerated constants, listed in Table 6.1 in alphabetical order. Specify multiple options by combining constants in logical-OR expressions.

Table 6.1. The `ios` class's `open_mode` constants.

Constant	Standard	Effect
app		The next write operation appends new information to the end of the file. Probably has the same effect as `ate`.
ate	●	Seeks to the end of the file when opened. The word *ate* stands for *at end*. It has nothing to do with "eating" data, as is often supposed.
binary	●	Might be spelled *bin* in some implementations. Opens file in binary (nontext) mode.

Constant	Standard	Effect
in	●	Opens the file for input (reading).
nocreate		If the file does not already exist, does *not* create a new file.
noreplace		If the file already exists, does *not* overwrite the file.
out	●	Opens the file for output (writing).
trunc		Opens and truncates an existing file. New information written to file replaces the file's current contents.

Unfortunately, the constants in Table 6.1 are not the same in all implementations of the ios class. The open_mode type identifier might even be named openmode with no underscore between the two words. The standard names marked with a bullet in the table should be universally available. The others may or may not be defined, and there might be other constants added for special purposes. Also, at least one ANSI C++ draft-standard specification shortens binary to bin.

To help ensure portability, it might be wise to define symbolic constants for use as file mode selectors. For example, you can define a symbolic constant such as OFSMODE:

```
#define OFSMODE ios::out ¦ ios::app
```

Or, even better, define a const value of type open_mode:

```
const ios::open_mode OFSMODE = ios::out ¦ ios::app;
```

Beware, however, that open_mode might be spelled openmode. Whichever method you choose, pass the OFSMODE constant to the ofstream class constructor:

```
ofstream ofs("NEWFILE.TXT", OFSMODE);
```

In this chapter, I'll continue to use ios open_mode constants directly. In a major software project where portability matters, however, I would define constants for this purpose.

After creating or overwriting a file, always check that the ofstream object is ready for use. Perform this check using an if statement like this:

```
ofstream ofs("NEWFILE.TXT", ios::out);
if (!ofs) {
  cerr << "Error: unable to write to NEWFILE.TXT" << endl;
  exit(1);
}
```

The first line constructs an object named ofs of the ofstream class, creating or overwriting a file named NEWFILE.TXT. The parameters passed to the class constructor specify the file name and ios::out open_mode value.

The if statement tests whether the file was properly attached to the ofs object. If not, the program writes an error message to cerr and exits by calling the exit() function, usually declared in stdlib.h.

The form of the if statement bothers a lot of programmers on a first meeting. If ofs is an object of the ofstream class, you might wonder, how can the expression (!ofs) make any sense? After all, the object isn't an int value, so what exactly is being evaluated here?.

The secret is buried in ios class, which overloads the *not* operator (!). The statement

```
if (!ofs) {
...
}
```

calls the operator! function in ios for the ofs file-stream object. That function is probably implemented inline something like this:

```
int operator! () { return fail(); }
```

The operator! function, in other words, simply returns the result of the stream's fail() function. Consequently, the statement

```
if (!ios) { }
```

is exactly equivalent to

```
if (ofs.fail()) { }  // Same as preceding example
```

Create an input file stream using similar techniques, but construct the file object from the `ifstream` class. For example, use these statements to open a file named OLDFILE.TXT:

```
ifstream ifs("OLDFILE.TXT", ios::in);
if (!ifs) {
  cerr << "Error: unable to open OLDFILE.TXT" << endl;
  exit(1);
}
```

Object `ifs` is constructed from the `ifstream` class and initialized with a filename and `open_mode` constant. The `if` statement uses the overloaded `opera-tor!` function on the object to test whether the operation was a success. If so, the object is ready for reading data from the file; otherwise, the program halts with an error message.

That covers the basics of file streams. If you are familiar with conventional methods—opening, creating, and closing files by calling functions—at this stage, you might think some critical factors are missing. Remember, however, that *file streams are object-oriented.* To open a file, simply create an input file stream object then use stream statements to read from the file. To write or create a file, construct an output file stream object and use stream statements to write to the file. When the file stream object goes out of scope or is deleted, the file is automatically closed. Near the end of this chapter, I'll explain how to open and close file stream objects in a more conventional fashion, but for most purposes, you don't have to use file streams that way.

Next, let's examine some sample programs that read and write text files using the techniques outlined so far. There are four important methods to master:

- Reading text a character at a time
- Writing text a character at a time
- Reading text a line at a time
- Writing text a line at a time

Reading Text a Character at a Time

Listing 6.1, RCHAR.CPP, demonstrates how to use a file stream to read a text file one character at a time. Just to keep things interesting, the program also counts the number of characters and lines in the file. Such goals always come with built-in ambiguities—should the definition of a "character," for example, include the newline symbol at the end of a line? I decided not to count end-of-line characters, thus the total character count reported by RCHAR.CPP probably won't match the file's size in the directory.

Listing 6.1. RCHAR.CPP.

```cpp
#include <iostream.h>
#include <fstream.h>
#include <stdlib.h>

int main(int argc, char *argv[])
{
  if (argc <= 1) {
    cerr << "Error: filename missing" << endl;
    exit(1);
  }

  ifstream ifs(argv[1], ios::in);
  if (!ifs) {
    cerr << "Error: unable to open " << argv[1] << endl;
    exit(2);
  }

  char c;
  long nc = 0, nl = 0;
  while (ifs.get(c)) {
    if (c == '\n')
      nl++;  // Count number of lines
    else
      nc++;  // Count number of characters
    cout.put(c);
  }
```

```
    cout << "\n\nTotal characters : " << nc;
    cout << "\nNumber of lines  : " << nl;
    return 0;
}
```

The main() function begins by checking whether you supplied a filename. If not, an error message reminds you to run the program by typing a command such as

```
rchar rchar.cpp
```

That should read and display the program's own source file. The following statement attempts to open the file specified as a command-line argument:

```
ifstream ifs(argv[1], ios::in);
```

If this works, the ifs object is available for use as a source in an input stream statement. A simple while loop, for example, reads all the characters from the file and displays those characters by passing them to cout.put():

```
while (ifs.get(c))
  cout.put(c)
```

Writing Text a Character at a Time

Creating and writing a text file is equally simple, as Listing 6.2, WCHAR.CPP, shows.

Listing 6.2. WCHAR.CPP.

```
#include <iostream.h>
#include <fstream.h>
#include <stdlib.h>

int main(int argc, char *argv[])
{
  if (argc <= 1) {
```

continues

Listing 6.2. continued

```
    cerr << "Error: filename missing" << endl;
    exit(1);
  }

  ifstream ifs(argv[1], ios::in);
  if (ifs) {
    cerr << "Error: " << argv[1] << " already exists" << endl;
    cerr << "         Specify a different filename" << endl;
    exit(2);
  }

  ofstream ofs(argv[1], ios::out);
  if (!ofs) {
    cerr << "Error: unable to write to " << argv[1] << endl;
    exit(3);
  }

  ofs << "1: A string\n";
  ofs.put('2');
  ofs.put(':');
  ofs.put(' ');
  ofs.put('C').put('h').put('a').put('r').put('s');
  ofs << endl;

  return 0;
}
```

Here again, the first job is to display an error message if the filename is missing. Try running the program with a command such as

```
wchar test.txt
```

To prevent WCHAR.CPP from destroying TEST.TXT if that file already exists, the program creates an input stream object for the specified file. If no errors are detected, the program assumes that TEST.TXT exists and halts with an error message.

This part of the program shows how to detect whether a file exists, using an `if` statement such as

```
ifstream ifs("TEST.TXT", ios::in);
if (ifs) {
  // ... File exists
}
```

After constructing the input file stream object, `ifs`, the `if` statement tests whether that operator succeeded. As before, this expression might strike C programmers in the audience as extremely odd. Just what does `if (ifs) { }` accomplish?

Testing the `ifs` stream object in an `if` statement's expression this way is permitted because the `ios` class overloads the `operator void *` function inline as

```
operator void *()
  { return fail() ? 0 : this; }
```

In other words, the *value* of a file-stream object such as `ifs` equals zero (false, or null) if `fail()` is true; otherwise, the value equals a pointer to the object. Thus, with these overloaded operators, the following `if` statement expressions are exact opposites:

```
if (!ifs)...   // Calls overloaded operator! function
if (ifs)...    // Calls overloaded operator void * function
```

Getting back to WCHAR.CPP, if the file does not exist, the program creates the file and constructs an output stream object, `ofs`, ready for use in stream statements:

```
ofstream ofs(argv[1], ios::out);
if (!ofs) {
...
}
```

Again, the result of constructing the object is tested by an `if` statement, using the overloaded `operator!` function in the `ios` class. If no errors occur, you can use the constructed file-stream object as you do any output sink. For example, this writes a line of text to the file:

```
ofs << "Write me to disk" << endl;
```

You can also write individual characters:

```
ofs << 'X';
```

Or, pass characters to the put() member function:

```
ofs.put('X');
```

By the way, because put() returns ostream & (a reference to an object of the ostream class), you can string multiple put() function calls together in an odd-looking construction such as this:

```
ofs.put('A').put('B').put('C');
```

You might see similar *put-put* statements in published listings, but there seems to be little reason to use this cryptic trick. However, perhaps a smart compiler could optimize the compiled code to keep the object references in a register.

Reading Text a Line at a Time

You can usually speed up the show by reading and writing text files a line at a time. On most operating systems, calling a single function to read an entire line of text is faster than executing multiple function calls to read characters one at a time.

Listing 6.3, RLINE.CPP, operates like RCHAR.CPP, but reads a text file a line at a time. Like its counterpart, the program totals the number of characters and lines in a file.

Listing 6.3. RLINE.CPP.

```
#include <iostream.h>
#include <fstream.h>
#include <stdlib.h>
#include <string.h>

#define BUFLEN 128
```

```
int main(int argc, char *argv[])
{
  if (argc <= 1) {
    cerr << "Error: filename missing" << endl;
    exit(1);
  }

  ifstream ifs(argv[1], ios::in);
  if (!ifs) {
    cerr << "Error: unable to open " << argv[1] << endl;
    exit(2);
  }

  char buffer[BUFLEN];
  long nc = 0, nl = 0;
  while (!ifs.eof()) {
    ifs.getline(buffer, sizeof(buffer), '\n');
    if (!(ifs.eof() && strlen(buffer) == 0)) {
      nc += strlen(buffer);
      nl++;
      cout << buffer << endl;
    }
  }
  cout << "\n\nTotal characters : " << nc;
  cout << "\nNumber of lines  : " << nl;
  return 0;
}
```

As when prompting for text interactively, it's best to call the `getline()` member function to read strings from text files. If you simply write

```
ifs >> buffer;   // ???
```

you risk overwriting the end of `buffer` if that array isn't big enough to hold the line at the current file position. Instead of using an input stream statement, read a single line like this:

```
ifs.getline(buffer, sizeof(buffer), '\n');
```

Or, use the setw() manipulator. To read the file one word at a time—words being broken by any white space or the ends of lines—include the iomanip.h header and read strings using this input stream statement:

```
ifs >> setw(BUFLEN) >> buffer;
```

Check if the program has reached the end of the file by calling the eof() member function in reference to the file stream object. The function makes it easy to write a simple while loop that ends after reading the last smidgen of data from the file.

```
while (!ifs.eof()) {
  ifs.getline(buffer, sizeof(buffer), '\n');
  // Process line in buffer
}
```

Writing Text a Line at a Time

The last of the four fundamental text-file techniques writes text files a line at a time. Listing 6.4, WLINE.CPP, demonstrates the method.

Listing 6.4. WLINE.CPP.

```
#include <iostream.h>
#include <fstream.h>
#include <stdlib.h>
#include <string.h>

#define STR "2: Another literal string"

int main(int argc, char *argv[])
{
  if (argc <= 1) {
    cerr << "Error: filename missing" << endl;
    exit(1);
  }
```

```
ifstream ifs(argv[1], ios::in);
if (ifs) {
  cerr << "Error: " << argv[1] << " already exists" << endl;
  cerr << "         Specify a different filename" << endl;
  exit(2);
}

ofstream ofs(argv[1], ios::out);
if (!ofs) {
  cerr << "Error: unable to write to " << argv[1] << endl;
  exit(3);
}

ofs << "1: A literal string" << endl;
ofs.write(STR, strlen(STR));
ofs << endl;
char *c = "String addressed by pointer";
ofs << "3: " << c << endl;

return 0;
}
```

As in WCHAR.CPP, the program begins by checking for a filename and halting if a file by that name already exists. The program then creates the file by constructing an ofstream object, ofs.

To write lines of text to the file, you have two choices. One, you can write a literal string like this:

```
ofs << "Write me to disk!" << endl;
```

Remember to append a new line, either by writing the endl manipulator, or by ending the string with a newline character:

```
ofs << "Write me to disk!\n";
```

Your second option, which might be useful at times, is to call the write() member function, which requires two arguments: a pointer to a string (char *) and the number of characters to write. This writes an entire string addressed by a char pointer s:

```
ofs.write(s, strlen(s));
```

Usually, however, you'll use this kind of statement to write only a specified number of characters from a string. To write the first five characters, for example, use a statement like this:

```
if (strlen(s) >= 5)
  ofs.write(s, 5);
```

Binary File Streams

Don't look for binary file operations in the C++ file stream library. There aren't any. Although you can open a file for binary access—a capability provided by most disk operating systems—reading and writing binary data such as floating point values in their native form is a summit left for programmers to conquer.

The required steps are almost nonexistent in C++ tutorials. To use file streams for reading and writing binary data files, you need to add a few basic capabilities to the stock file stream classes. Extra programming is needed to

- write one or more bytes of any values to a file.

- read one or more bytes of any values from a file.

- translate an object of any size into bytes.

- translate a collection of bytes to any object.

Using Binary File Streams

Construct binary file stream objects in almost the same way as you do text files, but specify the ios::binary (or ios::bin) mode constant. To create a new binary file, construct an ofstream object like this:

```
ofstream ofs("NEWFILE.DAT", ios::out | ios::binary);
if (!ofs) {
  cerr << "Error: unable to create or write to NEWFILE.DAT\n";
  exit(1);
}
```

If that doesn't work, try replacing `binary` with `bin`. To open an existing binary file for reading, construct an `ifstream` object this way:

```
ifstream ifs("OLDFILE.DAT", ios::in | ios::binary);
if (!ifs) {
  cerr << "Error: unable to open OLDFILE.DAT\n";
  exit(2);
}
```

Unfortunately, the `ofs` and `ifs` objects are not yet ready for use with binary data. The next sections explain how to complete the steps needed to read and write binary values using these file objects. First, however, let's take a look at the *wrong* way to proceed—the improper technique reveals the reason file objects can't be used directly with binary values.

The Wrong Solution

Constructing input and output file streams as in the preceding section might seem to work—until, that is, you attempt to use those objects to read and write binary values in files. Consider what happens, for example, if you create a new file like this:

```
ofstream ofs("TEST.DAT", ios::out | ios::binary);
```

You then attempt to write a couple of `double` floating point values to the file using these output stream statements:

```
double d = 3.14159;
ofs << d;       // ???
ofs << d * d;   // ???
```

The program compiles and seems to run correctly. Later, however, you reopen the file by executing:

```
ifstream ifs("TEST.DAT", ios::in | ios::binary);
```

You then attempt to read the file's values with these statements

```
long count = 0;
ifs >> d;  // ???
cout << d << endl;
ifs >> d;  // ???
cout << d << endl;
```

The program's health (and possibly your happiness in the programming profession) are now in serious jeopardy. Instead of the expected two values, 3.14159 and 9.8695877 (pi squared), on-screen the program displays

```
3.141599
0.869588
```

Neither value is correct. Only the first is even close. What's wrong? Examining the first several bytes in the file provides a clue to solving the mystery (see Figure 6.2.).

```
2F54:0100   33 2E 31 34 31 35 39 39-2E 38 36 39 35 38 38 08   3.141599.869588.
2F54:0110   83 C4 06 EB 06 4F 7C 03-E9 7B FF C4 34 00 43 2F   .....O¦..{..4.C/
2F54:0120   1F 26 F7 47 0A 86 00 75-37 83 7E FC 00 74 31 FF   .&.G...u7.~..t1.
```

Figure 6.2. Examining the file's data reveals a bug in the way file streams read and write binary values.

The first several bytes in the file are ASCII characters (see the first line's character representations at far right). Despite the programmer's intentions, the stream wrote the double values in text form, and it didn't even bother to separate one value from the next. Even though the program opened the file using the ios::binary constant, the iostream library *still translates binary data to and from text.* That is, after all, the library's primary job.

This approach for reading and writing binary values in files obviously won't work. Fortunately, the puzzle is not too difficult to solve.

The Right Solution

To read and write binary data *in its native form,* first derive your own binary file-stream classes from ifstream and ofstream. Figure 6.3 illustrates the goals these classes need to achieve. The box in the center of the figure represents an array of char. Because a char in C++ is stored in one byte, the array can be used as a buffer for holding a series of bytes representing any value in binary form. To write a binary `double` value to disk, the program copies the value to the array, which is then written to the file. To read a `double` value, the program reverses these steps. It reads bytes from the file into the character buffer, then it copies those bytes into the memory reserved for the `double` value.

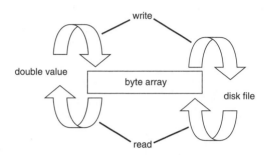

Figure 6.3. To read and write a double value in its native binary form, the value is copied to an array of bytes, which is then written to the file. To read a double value, the steps are reversed.

In practice, you can dispense with the byte array in Figure 6.3 and pretend that a `double` or other value is just an array of bytes. *Any* value of any kind fits that description, so the same technique can be used to read and write data of all types in binary form.

Listing 6.5, WDOUBLE.CPP, demonstrates how to use this method to create a file stream class for writing `double` values in binary to a disk file. Compile the program and run it. You won't see any screen activity (unless an error occurs). Unlike earlier programs in this chapter, the program writes to a predetermined filename, TEST.DAT. You don't have to type a name on the command line.

Listing 6.5. WDOUBLE.CPP.

```
#include <iostream.h>
#include <fstream.h>
#include <stdlib.h>
```

continues

Listing 6.5. continued

```cpp
class bofstream: public ofstream {
public:
  bofstream(const char *fn)
    : ofstream(fn, ios::out | ios::binary) { }
  void writeBytes(const void *, int);
  bofstream & operator<< (double);
};

inline bofstream & bofstream::operator<< (double d)
{
  writeBytes(&d, sizeof(d));
  return *this;
}

int main()
{
  bofstream bofs("TEST.DAT");
  if (!bofs) {
    cerr << "Error: unable to write to TEST.DAT\n";
    exit(1);
  }

  double d = 3.14159;
  bofs << d;
  bofs << d * d;
  bofs << 9.9999999;
  d = 4.7E-8;
  bofs << d;

  return 0;
}

void bofstream::writeBytes(const void *p, int len)
{
  if (!p) return;
  if (len <= 0) return;
  write((char *)p, len);
}
```

To provide a binary output-file class, I derived a new class, bofstream, from ofstream. The class declares three public members:

● bofstream() is the class constructor. For simplicity, it requires only a filename and passes a fixed open_mode expression to the base class constructor.

● writeBytes() writes one or more bytes to the stream from the address specified by void *.

● operator<< overloads the output stream operator so stream statements can be used to write values in binary.

Note: The overloaded stream operator function in bofstream does not have to be a friend of the class because its initial hidden this parameter is of the correct type, bofstream *. This fact might seem to conflict with the requirements of the similar overloaded operator functions described in Chapter 5, "Creating Streamable Classes." Here, bofstream is a file stream object to be used as a sink or source, not as a vessel for the data to be stored in a file—an important distinction to keep in mind. You may overload operators << and >> as member functions in a file stream class, but you must overload those operators as friend functions in classes of objects to be *stored* in files.

An inline function implements the overloaded operator. The function simply calls writeBytes(), passing the address of a double value and its size in bytes. The function returns *this so it can be used in cascaded output stream statements. (Dereferencing this in this case gives a reference to a bofstream object.)

Use bofstream as you do any other file stream class. After opening the file by constructing a bofstream object, this simple statement writes a double value in binary to disk:

```
bofs << d;
```

That statement and the similar ones listed in the program transfer the bytes from d directly to the file (the bytes might be buffered by the file object, however, so a disk write does not necessarily occur immediately).

The binary value is written to disk by member function `writeBytes()`, which calls the inherited `write()` function:

```
write((char *)p, len);
```

Listing 6.6, RDOUBLE.CPP, flips the coin and shows how to read binary double values from TEST.DAT into memory. Running the program displays the values that WDOUBLE.CPP wrote to disk:

```
1: 3.14159
2: 9.86958773
3: 9.9999999
4: 4.7e-08
```

Listing 6.6. RDOUBLE.CPP.

```
#include <iostream.h>
#include <fstream.h>
#include <stdlib.h>

class bifstream: public ifstream {
public:
  bifstream(const char *fn)
    : ifstream(fn, ios::in | ios::binary) { }
  void readBytes(void *, int);
  bifstream & operator>> (double &);
};

inline bifstream & bifstream::operator>> (double &d)
{
  readBytes(&d, sizeof(d));
  return *this;
}
```

```
int main()
{
  bifstream bifs("TEST.DAT");
  if (!bifs) {
    cerr << "Error: unable to open TEST.DAT\n";
    cerr << "         compile and run WDOUBLE first\n";
    exit(1);
  }

  double d;
  long count = 0;

  cout.precision(8);
  bifs >> d;
  while (!bifs.eof()) {
    cout << ++count << ": " << d << endl;
    bifs >> d;
  }

  return 0;
}

void bifstream::readBytes(void *p, int len)
{
  if (!p) return;
  if (len <= 0) return;
  read((char *)p, len);
}
```

To provide a binary input-file stream, I derived class `bifstream` from `ifstream`. To the new class, I added a constructor (similar to `bofstream`'s), a function `readBytes()`, and an overloaded input stream operator.

The inline `operator>>` member function calls `readBytes()` to copy bytes from a binary file stream directly to a `double` object in memory. After opening a file, a simple statement reads a `double` value:

```
bifs >> d;
```

The `readBytes()` member function looks similar to `writeBytes` in WDOUBLE.CPP. This time, however, the function calls the inherited `read()` function to read characters from the stream to the address indicated by `void *p`.

Classes for Binary File I/O

Expanding the concepts in the preceding two sections leads to versatile versions of the `bofstream` and `bifstream` classes that you can use to read and write all native C++ data types in binary form. Listing 6.7, bstream.h, declares the two classes.

Listing 6.7. bstream.h.

```
#ifndef _ _BSTREAM_H
#define _ _BSTREAM_H      // Prevent multiple #includes

#include <iostream.h>
#include <fstream.h>

// Binary output file stream

class bofstream: public ofstream {
public:
  bofstream(const char *fn)
    : ofstream(fn, ios::out | ios::binary) { }
  void writeBytes(const void *, int);
  friend bofstream & operator<< (bofstream &, signed char);
  friend bofstream & operator<< (bofstream &, unsigned char);
  friend bofstream & operator<< (bofstream &, signed short);
  friend bofstream & operator<< (bofstream &, unsigned short);
  friend bofstream & operator<< (bofstream &, signed int);
  friend bofstream & operator<< (bofstream &, unsigned int);
```

```
    friend bofstream & operator<< (bofstream &, signed long);
    friend bofstream & operator<< (bofstream &, unsigned long);
    friend bofstream & operator<< (bofstream &, float);
    friend bofstream & operator<< (bofstream &, double);
    friend bofstream & operator<< (bofstream &, long double);
};

// Binary input file stream

class bifstream: public ifstream {
public:
    bifstream(const char *fn)
        : ifstream(fn, ios::in | ios::binary) { }
    void readBytes(void *, int);
    friend bifstream & operator>> (bifstream &, signed char &);
    friend bifstream & operator>> (bifstream &, unsigned char &);
    friend bifstream & operator>> (bifstream &, signed short &);
    friend bifstream & operator>> (bifstream &, unsigned short &);
    friend bifstream & operator>> (bifstream &, signed int &);
    friend bifstream & operator>> (bifstream &, unsigned int &);
    friend bifstream & operator>> (bifstream &, signed long &);
    friend bifstream & operator>> (bifstream &, unsigned long &);
    friend bifstream & operator>> (bifstream &, float &);
    friend bifstream & operator>> (bifstream &, double &);
    friend bifstream & operator>> (bifstream &, long double &);
};

inline bofstream & operator<< (bofstream &bofs, signed char q)
{
    bofs.writeBytes(&q, sizeof(signed char));
    return bofs;
}

inline bofstream & operator<< (bofstream &bofs, unsigned char q)
{
    bofs.writeBytes(&q, sizeof(unsigned char));
    return bofs;
}
```

continues

Listing 6.7. continued

```cpp
inline bofstream & operator<< (bofstream &bofs, signed short q)
{
  bofs.writeBytes(&q, sizeof(signed short));
  return bofs;
}

inline bofstream & operator<< (bofstream &bofs, unsigned short q)
{
  bofs.writeBytes(&q, sizeof(unsigned short));
  return bofs;
}

inline bofstream & operator<< (bofstream &bofs, signed int q)
{
  bofs.writeBytes(&q, sizeof(signed int));
  return bofs;
}

inline bofstream & operator<< (bofstream &bofs, unsigned int q)
{
  bofs.writeBytes(&q, sizeof(unsigned int));
  return bofs;
}

inline bofstream & operator<< (bofstream &bofs, signed long q)
{
  bofs.writeBytes(&q, sizeof(signed long));
  return bofs;
}

inline bofstream & operator<< (bofstream &bofs, unsigned long q)
{
  bofs.writeBytes(&q, sizeof(unsigned long));
  return bofs;
}
```

```
inline bofstream & operator<< (bofstream &bofs, float q)
{
  bofs.writeBytes(&q, sizeof(float));
  return bofs;
}

inline bofstream & operator<< (bofstream &bofs, double q)
{
  bofs.writeBytes(&q, sizeof(double));
  return bofs;
}

inline bofstream & operator<< (bofstream &bofs, long double q)
{
  bofs.writeBytes(&q, sizeof(long double));
  return bofs;
}

inline bifstream & operator>> (bifstream &bifs, signed char &q)
{
  bifs.readBytes(&q, sizeof(signed char));
  return bifs;
}

inline bifstream & operator>> (bifstream &bifs, unsigned char &q)
{
  bifs.readBytes(&q, sizeof(unsigned char));
  return bifs;
}

inline bifstream & operator>> (bifstream &bifs, signed short &q)
{
  bifs.readBytes(&q, sizeof(signed short));
  return bifs;
}

inline bifstream & operator>> (bifstream &bifs, unsigned short &q)
{
  bifs.readBytes(&q, sizeof(unsigned short));
```

continues

Listing 6.7. continued

```
    return bifs;
}

inline bifstream & operator>> (bifstream &bifs, signed int &q)
{
  bifs.readBytes(&q, sizeof(signed int));
  return bifs;
}

inline bifstream & operator>> (bifstream &bifs, unsigned int &q)
{
  bifs.readBytes(&q, sizeof(unsigned int));
  return bifs;
}

inline bifstream & operator>> (bifstream &bifs, signed long &q)
{
  bifs.readBytes(&q, sizeof(signed long));
  return bifs;
}

inline bifstream & operator>> (bifstream &bifs, unsigned long &q)
{
  bifs.readBytes(&q, sizeof(unsigned long));
  return bifs;
}

inline bifstream & operator>> (bifstream &bifs, float &q)
{
  bifs.readBytes(&q, sizeof(float));
  return bifs;
}

inline bifstream & operator>> (bifstream &bifs, double &q)
{
  bifs.readBytes(&q, sizeof(double));
  return bifs;
}
```

```
inline bifstream & operator>> (bifstream &bifs, long double &q)
{
  bifs.readBytes(&q, sizeof(long double));
  return bifs;
}


#endif  // __BSTREAM_H
```

The new `bofstream` and `bifstream` classes are similar to the ones listed earlier, but they include overloaded input and output operators for all 11 native data types, from `signed char` to `long double`. If the thought of implementing all 22 inline friend functions in both classes horrifies you (as it did me), take heart. In Chapter 7, "Crafting Function Templates," I explain how to reduce the need to enter many similar functions that differ only in the types of data they use. As listed here, however, bstream.h should work with most C++ compilers, even those that don't have templates.

Listing 6.8, BSTREAM.CPP, implements the two other common member functions in the two classes. The `writeBytes()` and `readBytes()` member functions are the same ones you saw earlier, but they are implemented here in a separate module that you can link to programs (examples follow the listing).

Listing 6.8. BSTREAM.CPP.

```
#include "bstream.h"

void bofstream::writeBytes(const void *p, int len)
{
  if (!p) return;
  if (len <= 0) return;
  write((char *)p, len);
}

void bifstream::readBytes(void *p, int len)
{
```

continues

Listing 6.8. continued

```
if (!p) return;
if (len <= 0) return;
read((char *)p, len);
}
```

Writing Binary Files

Include the bstream.h header in your program to read and write binary data of all standard types. On disk, you'll find two test programs, TBDOUBLE.CPP and TBSTREAM.CPP, that show how to use the header file's `bofstream` and `bifstream` classes. With Borland C++, compile the test programs by using the following commands:

```
bcc -c bstream
bcc tbdouble bstream.obj
bcc tbstream bstream.obj
```

Run TBDOUBLE to write and read three floating point values in a file named TBDOUBLE.DAT. Run TBSTREAM to write and read the 11 C++ native data types in a file named TBSTREAM.DAT.

To write values to a data file, construct a `bofstream` object similar to the way you constructed other output files:

```
#define FILENAME "MYINFO.DAT"
bofstream bofs(FILENAME);
if (!bofs) {
  cerr << "Error: unable to write to " << FILENAME << endl;
  exit(1);
}
```

You can then write *any* C++ native object to the file. If v is a `double` value and k is an `int`, write them to `bofs` with stream statements:

```
bofs << v;
bofs << k;
```

Read binary data similarly. Construct a `bifstream` object, then use input stream statements to read values from the file into memory.

```
#define FILENAME "MYINFO.DAT"
bifstream bifs(FILENAME);
if (!bifs) {
  cerr << "Error: unable to open " << FILENAME << endl;
  exit(2);
}
bifs >> v;
bifs >> k;
```

Note: Using the binary file techniques described here, it's your responsibility to read and write values in the correct order. If you write double, char, and long int values in that order, you must read those values back *in the same order.* See Chapter 17, "Preserving Persistent Objects," for a more sophisticated technique that you can use to write class objects of different types in any order, and read those objects back without having to know the file's structure in advance.

Storing Other Objects in Binary Files

By carefully overloading the << and >> operators, you can easily design classes that provide for their own file input and output operations. Suppose you have this class with two integer data members:

```
class TAnyClass {
  int x;  // Data member
  int y;  // Data member
public:
  TAnyClass(): x(0), y(0) { }
  TAnyClass(int X, int Y): x(X), y(Y) { }
};
```

Note: Most of the programming examples in this section are extracted from the disk file TBCLASS.CPP. Compile this program and link to the BSTREAM object code module. Using Borland C++, for example, enter the commands

```
bcc -c bstream
bcc tbclass bstream.obj
```

To make TAnyClass streamable, include the bstream.h header described in the preceding sections, and overload the << and >> operators:

```
#include "bstream.h"
class TAnyClass {
  int x;
  int y;
  friend bofstream & operator<< (bofstream &, TAnyClass &);
  friend bifstream & operator>> (bifstream &, TAnyClass &);
public:
  TAnyClass(): x(0), y(0) { }
  TAnyClass(int X, int Y): x(X), y(Y) { }
};
```

The overloaded operators use file stream statements to read and write the class data members. Here's how you might implement the output operator:

```
inline bofstream & operator<< (bofstream &bofs, TAnyClass &q)
{
  bofs << q.x;  // Write x data member in q to disk
  bofs << q.y;  // Write y data member in q to disk
  return bofs;  // Return stream reference
}
```

The input operator's implementation is similar, but it uses input file stream statements to read values from the stream to data members:

```
inline bifstream & operator>> (bifstream &bifs, TAnyClass &q)
{
  bifs >> q.x;  // Read value into x data member in q
```

```
  bifs >> q.y;   // Read value into y data member in q
  return bifs;   // Return stream reference
}
```

Even better, you can overload the input and output operators *twice each,* once for file streams and again for common ostream and istream references. The complete class then looks like this:

```
class TAnyClass {
  int x;
  int y;
  friend ostream & operator<< (ostream &, TAnyClass &);
  friend istream & operator>> (istream &, TAnyClass &);
  friend bofstream & operator<< (bofstream &, TAnyClass &);
  friend bifstream & operator>> (bifstream &, TAnyClass &);
public:
  TAnyClass(): x(0), y(0) { }
  TAnyClass(int X, int Y): x(X), y(Y) { }
};
```

Because the operator function parameters differ, the compiler can distinguish among the functions based on their uses. Implement the new output stream operator as shown here:

```
ostream & operator<< (ostream &os, TAnyClass &c)
{
  os << "x == " << c.x << endl;
  os << "y == " << c.y << endl;
  return os;
}
```

Implement the output operator to prompt for values interactively:

```
istream & operator>> (istream &is, TAnyClass &c)
{
  cout << "Enter value for X: ";
  is >> c.x;
  cout << "Enter value for Y: ";
  is >> c.y;
  return is;
}
```

You can now prompt for TAnyClass objects from cin, write those objects to cout, and use binary file streams to read and write the objects in disk files. All of these actions use relatively simple stream statements. Define a couple of TAnyClass objects:

```
TAnyClass original, copy;
```

Then, prompt for, read, and confirm object original with these statements:

```
cout << "Enter X and Y values\n";
cin >> original;   // Prompt for and read values
cout << "Your values are:\n";
cout << original;  // Display values entered into object
```

Next, to write the object in binary form to disk, first construct a binary output file stream. I'll call it bofs:

```
#define FILENAME "TBCLASS.DAT"
bofstream bofs(FILENAME);
if (!bofs) {
  cerr << "Error: unable to create " << FILENAME << endl;
  exit(1);
}
bofs << original; // Write class object to disk
bofs.close();     // Close file, flushing data to disk
```

The next-to-last statement writes the original object to the stream, storing its data on disk by virtue of the overloaded << operator-function in the class. The final statement closes the file—necessary only if you need to access the file data while bofs remains in scope.

To reread the object, after closing the output file construct an input file stream and read a copy of the original object like this:

```
bifstream bifs(FILENAME);
if (!bifs ) {
  cerr << "Error: unable to open " << FILENAME << endl;
  exit(2);
}
bifs >> copy;  // Read class object from disk into copy
```

The final statement reads the file, and by calling the overloaded class >> operator-function, loads the object's data from disk into a TAnyClass object named copy. Display copy's value with these statements:

```
cout << "Copy of class object:\n";
cout << copy;
```

Seeking in Streams

For database work, programs need to pick and choose specific records in files. You can do that with input file streams by calling one of two overloaded member functions, inherited from the istream class:

```
istream & seekg(streampos);
istream & seekg(streamoff, ios::seek_dir);
```

The streampos and streamoff data types are typically defined as equivalent to long values:

```
typedef long streampos;
typedef long streamoff;
```

Another compiler, however, might define streampos and streamoff using a different data type, so don't pass long values directly to seekg().

The first overloaded form of seekg() positions an input stream to a specific byte. The second form positions the stream to an offset from one of three positions defined by ios::seek_dir (see Table 6.2).

Table 6.2. The ios::seek_dir **constants.**

Constant	*Value*	*Description*
beg	0	Seek from beginning of file
cur	1	Seek from current file position
end	2	Seek from end of file

Always supply positive offsets for `ios::beg`. Supply positive offsets for `ios::cur` to seek forward toward the end of the file, or use negative offsets to seek backward toward the beginning of the file. Always supply negative offsets for `ios::end`.

To position the internal file pointer for output streams, use the following two overloaded output file stream functions, inherited from the `ostream` class:

```
ostream & seekp(streampos);
ostream & seekp(streamoff, ios::seek_dir);
```

A few examples demonstrate how to use these functions. (I'll use `seekg()` here. The `seekp()` function works identically with output streams.) Using `TAnyClass` from the preceding section, first construct a few objects to store in a disk file:

```
TAnyClass a(0,1), b(2,3), c(4,5), d(6,7), e(8,9);
```

Open a binary output stream, and write the objects to disk:

```
bofstream bofs("ABCDE.DAT");
if (!bofs) {
  cerr << "Error: unable to create ABCDE.DAT\n";
  exit(1);
}
bofs << a << b << c << d << e;
bofs.close();
```

Note: To try the sample programming here, include the bstream.h header and link to the BSTREAM module. Using Borland C++, for example, enter the commands

```
bcc -c bstream
bcc yourfile.cpp bstream.obj
```

To read the objects from disk into memory, first define some additional variables of type `TAnyClass`:

```
TAnyClass aa, bb, cc, dd, ee;
```

Then use a single input file stream statement to read the objects back from disk:

```
bifs >> aa >> bb >> cc >> dd >> ee;
```

Rather than sequentially read all data from the file, however, we want to seek and read *specific* records at random, as you might need to do in a database file of names and addresses. At this point, the file contains the records and values illustrated in Figure 6.4.

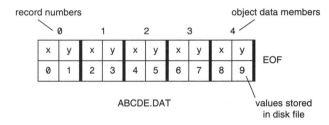

Figure 6.4. The sample ABCDE.DAT file of `TAnyClass` objects.

To seek to record number 3, define a `streampos` variable and call the input file stream object's inherited `seekg()` member function like this:

```
streampos rn = 3;   // Record number
bifs.seekg(sizeof(TAnyClass) * rn);
```

This positions the internal file pointer to the first byte of record number 3. Because record number 0 is the first record in the file, the following statements read and display the *fourth* record:

```
bifs >> aa;
cout << aa;
```

Executing these statements sets object aa's two integer data members to 6 and 7, the values stored in record number 3 (see Figure 6.4). After this step, the internal file pointer is automatically advanced to the *next* record. To seek 2 records backward from that point, pass a negative offset to `seekg()` and specify the `ios::cur` seek direction:

```
rn = 2;   // Number of records to seek backwards
bifs.seekg(-(sizeof(TAnyClass) * rn), ios::cur);
bifs >> bb;
cout << bb;
```

Before executing this code, the file is positioned at record number 4. Seeking 2 records back positions the internal file pointer to record number 2. Reading that record sets object bb to (4,5).

It's sometimes useful to seek backwards from the end of the file. As when seeking backwards from other locations using ios::cur, you must use a negative offset with ios::end:

```
rn = 1;  // Number of records to seek from end of file
bifs.seekg(-(sizeof(TAnyClass) * rn), ios::end);
bifs >> cc;
cout << cc;
```

This loads cc with the last record in the file, regardless of how many records the file holds. Running this fragment sets object cc to (8,9).

The most common operation is to seek forward from the beginning of the file. Because we know the file has five records, seeking to record number 4 positions the internal file pointer to the file's last record. This loads the last record (8,9) into dd:

```
rn = 4;  // Number of records to seek from beginning of file
bifs.seekg((sizeof(TAnyClass) * rn), ios::beg);
bifs >> dd;
cout << dd;
```

To reset the file to its beginning, perhaps to prepare for sequentially rereading data from the first record, seek to record number 0:

```
bifs.seekg(0);
```

Note: I purposely left out error checks in these samples to conserve space. Use the file stream eof() member function to detect whether the internal file pointer is positioned at the end of the file, from which it would be a mistake to read data. You can also use the stream state settings discussed in Chapter 3, "Calling Stream Member Functions," to detect file-statement errors.

Other File Stream Techniques

Here are a few other miscellaneous file stream techniques you won't use every day, but might find handy.

Opening and Closing File Objects

Constructing file stream objects in busy programs that work on multiple files can penalize a program's performance. In such cases, you can construct the objects ahead of time and use them later to open and create files.

To construct an output file stream, but *not* associate that stream with a file, define the object like this:

```
ofstream ofs;
```

The ofs file stream object is not connected to a file, and you can't use the object in an output file stream. To write to or create a file using the object, call its open() member function:

```
ofs.open("NEWFILE.DAT");
if (!ofs) exit(1);  // Exit if any errors are detected
```

Or, you can specify open_mode constants (see Table 6.1). For example, use a statement like this to overwrite and truncate an existing file:

```
ofs.open("NEWFILE.DAT", ios::out | ios::trunc);
```

You can then write to the file and close it:

```
ofs << "First line" << endl;
ofs << "Second line" << endl;
ofs << "Last line" << endl;
ofs.close();
```

Construct unopened input file stream objects in a similar way. First define an ifstream class object, specifying no parameters to the constructor:

```
ifstream ifs;
```

Later in the program, call the object's `open()` member function to open an existing file and read its contents:

```
ifs.open("NEWFILE.DAT");
if (!ifs) exit(1);
while (!ifs.eof()) {
  ifs.getline(buffer, BUFLEN, '\n');
  cout << buffer << endl;
}
ifs.close();
```

After calling the `close()` member function, you can reuse the file stream objects `ofs` and `ifs` to read and write other files.

Getting a File Descriptor

I might be asking for trouble by mentioning this subject, but it's possible to obtain a file stream object's internal file descriptor—sometimes called a *file handle*. After getting this value, you can use it to read and write to the file by calling operating system subroutines. If you decide to use this technique, you probably should abandon all hope of porting your programs to other systems. But the method might be useful at odd times and strange places.

An object of the `filebuf` class provides low-level services to `ifstream` and `ofstream`. Those two file-stream classes declare a member function to return a pointer to their `filebuf` object:

```
filebuf *rdbuf();
```

Use the resulting pointer to call low-level `filebuf` member functions. For example, on my system, member function `fd()` returns a file handle, represented as an integer. To use the function, and to keep the code simple, include the fstream.h header and define a macro to call `fd()`:

```
#include <fstream.h>
#define FD(s) (((s).rdbuf())->fd())
```

You can then construct a file stream object and use the macro to obtain the file's handle:

```
ifstream ifs("ANYFILE.TXT");
cout << "Descriptor == " << FD(ifs) << endl;
```

The second line writes the file handle's value to the standard output—assuming, however, that fd()'s return type can be reduced to a native C++ type.

> **Note:** The ANSI C++ draft-standard does not include the fd() member function in the filebuf class. You might find this member function in your implementation of the fstream library, or you might find a similar function that returns a file descriptor. Or the function might not exist. You're on your own with this one.

Reading and Writing from the Same File

All of the sample listings in this chapter distinguish between input and output files. With many C++ compilers, however, you can construct a single file stream object that you can use for reading and writing to the same file without having to close the file between input and output operations.

Don't expect this technique to work with all compilers. The draft ANSI C++ specification does not include the iostream and fstream classes on which the method depends. (See Figure 6.1.)

One way to perform read and write operations on a single file opened in binary mode is to combine this chapter's bofstream and bifstream classes into a new class, bfstream, derived from the fstream class. Be aware that unless your file stream library implements this class, the technique described here won't work. In that case, you still should be able to use the bofstream and bifstream classes from Listings 6.7 and 6.8.

If your system does provide the fstream class, use the bfstream.h header file and BFSTREAM.CPP module on disk in the PART1 directory. In the header, you'll find a class named bfstream that you can use to read and write records stored in binary files. A test program, BFSTEST.CPP, is also on disk. Compile the test using Borland C++ with the following commands:

```
bcc -c bfstream
bcc bfstest bfstream.obj
```

The bfstream.h header declares class bfstream as follows. (To save space, I deleted all but one of the overloaded operator>> and operator<< functions. See the disk file for the complete class.)

```cpp
class bfstream: public fstream {
  friend bfstream & operator>> (bfstream &, signed char &);
  // ... Other overloaded operator>> functions
  friend bfstream & operator<< (bfstream &, signed char);
  // ... Other overloaded operator<< functions
public:
  bfstream(const char *fn)
    : fstream(fn, ios::in | ios::out | ios::binary) { }
  void writeBytes(const void *, int);
  void readBytes(void *, int);
};
```

The BFSTEST.CPP program demonstrates how to use the bfstream class. The program includes the bfstream.h header and declares a class TAnyClass, which is similar to the class you examined elsewhere in this chapter:

```cpp
#include "bfstream.h"
class TAnyClass {
  int x;
  int y;
  friend ostream & operator<< (ostream &, TAnyClass &);
  friend istream & operator>> (istream &, TAnyClass &);
  friend bfstream & operator<< (bfstream &, TAnyClass &);
  friend bfstream & operator>> (bfstream &, TAnyClass &);
public:
  TAnyClass(): x(0), y(0) { }
  TAnyClass(int X, int Y): x(X), y(Y) { }
};
```

The only difference between this class and the earlier version is the bfstream references in the overloaded operator functions. Use the following statements to construct a few objects of the class, and write them to a file named ABCDE.DAT:

```
#define FILENAME "ABCDE.DAT"
TAnyClass a(0,1), b(2,3), c(4,5), d(6,7), e(8,9);
bfstream bfs(FILENAME);
if (!bfs) {
  cerr << "Error: unable to create " << FILENAME << endl;
  exit(1);
}
bfs << a << b << c << d << e;
```

Define a few more objects to hold data read from the file:

```
TAnyClass aa, bb, cc, dd, ee;
```

Then, using the same bfs file stream object, reset the file to its beginning and read the file's records like this:

```
bfs.seekg(0);
bfs >> aa >> bb >> cc >> dd >> ee;
cout << aa << bb << cc << dd << ee;
```

To rewrite data at random in the file, seek to a specific record by calling the stream's seekp() member function. For example, these four lines change record number 3 (the *fourth* record in the file) to a new TAnyClass object:

```
TAnyClass x(123,456);                // Construct new object
long rn = 3;                         // Define record number
bfs.seekp(sizeof(TAnyClass) * rn);   // Seek to record #3
bfs << x;                            // Write object to file
```

To read a specified record by number, call the stream's seekg() member function, then use an input stream statement to load the data from disk into an object of the appropriate type:

```
TAnyClass y;                         // Construct empty object
bfs.seekg(sizeof(TAnyClass) * rn);   // Seek to record #3
bfs >> y;                            // Read object from file
```

Close the bfstream object in the usual way by calling close():

```
bfs.close();
```

Final Words

File streams are one of the most neglected subjects in C++ tutorials and references. Using file streams brings all of OOP's many benefits to your file-handling chores. Be aware, however, of differences between file stream libraries in various C++ compilers and in the emerging ANSI C++ draft-standard.

This ends Part 1's in-depth look at C++ streams. In Part 2, "Secrets of C++ Data Structures," you'll investigate one of the newest members to be adopted into the ANSI C++ draft-standard family—templates. Chapters in Part 2 introduce templates and show how to use them to build many kinds of class data structures. After you begin using templates in your code, you'll probably wonder why all object-oriented languages don't include a similar tool.

Secrets of
C++ Data Structures

Crafting Function Templates

Programmers who build software using object-oriented techniques soon discover that OOP is far from perfect. Consider container classes. Designed to hold objects of many kinds, containers might seem ideally suited for solving most data storage problems.

In typical container class libraries, however, objects stored in containers *all must be derived from the same base class.* This bump in the road means that, just to store a series of simple integers in a container, you have to encapsulate the values into objects of a class that is derived from another designated base class. What a terrible imposition! Obviously, containers would be a lot more useful if they could store data of any kind, not just objects of classes from a predetermined family.

The secret to cracking this nasty puzzle is a programming tool called a *template.* With templates, you can design functions and classes in blueprint form—similar to an outline for a book. The compiler uses templates to construct actual functions and classes as needed by a program—the way an author might expand an outline into finished chapters. When designed as templates, container classes become highly versatile tools. The compiler can reshape the generic templates to hold whatever kind of data you need to store.

This chapter, the first of Part 2, introduces function templates. Chapter 8 covers class templates. You need to understand the background information in these two chapters before reading most of the other chapters in this part.

> **Note:** Although templates have been adopted into the ANSI C++ draft-standard, not all C++ compilers currently offer templates. Nevertheless, there's little doubt that templates soon will be widely supported by most C++ compilers.

What Are Templates?

A template is a kind of blueprint that describes the characteristics of a function or a class. Templates are particularly useful for creating generic functions— sorting functions, for instance, that can arrange different kinds of objects. You can also use templates to create generic classes that can work with objects of many kinds.

Whether designed as functions or classes, all templates begin with the `template` keyword and a formal parameter list. For example, a single-parameter template might begin like this:

```
template<class T>
```

The angle brackets (< and >) are required after the `template` keyword. The word `class` inside brackets is also required. Literally, `class` in this context means "a user-defined or a native type." The letter `T` identifies this type. The word `class` does *not* refer to a C++ class.

You can use a different identifier for a type parameter if you want. Here's a template with a parameter named `Avocado`:

```
template<class Avocado>
```

Of course, serious programmers don't name their identifiers `Avocado`, but I want to drive home the point that parameter names are for you to pick and choose. `T` is a good choice because it suggests the word *Type*.

A template declaration can list more than one parameter. This template has two parameters, `T1` and `T2`:

```
template<class T1, class T2>
```

Use commas to separate multiple parameters. You must repeat the word `class` for each parameter, but there's no set limit on the number of parameters you can declare. This begins a three-parameter template:

```
template<class T1, class T2, class T3>
```

Parameters like `T1`, `T2`, and `T3` can be reused in other template declarations—the scope of the parameter names extends only to the template. When possible, it's best to use descriptive parameters. I like to begin my identifiers with `T`, reminding me of their template status:

```
template<class TData, class TIndex>
```

That line might begin a container class template that stores objects of type `TData` indexed by values of another type, `TIndex`. Parameters like `TData` and `TIndex` are place holders for real data types to be specified later. `TData` or `TIndex` might be replaced by `int`, `double`, `char`, or other data types. They might also be pointers, or they could refer to classes or structs.

In creating a template, you are stating that you intend to use objects of *unspecified types*. Templates make it possible to design a function or class in a completely general way without having to state in advance the types of every object to be used.

Function Templates

There are two kinds of templates—function templates and class templates. This section introduces function templates and lists example programs. In Chapter 8, I'll explain how to create and use class templates.

Function Template Syntax

Regardless of their nature, function templates all have the same basic form. Figure 7.1 illustrates a single-parameter function template.

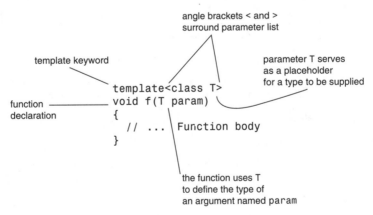

Figure 7.1. Single-parameter function template.

The template keyword in Figure 7.1 begins the template's construction with class T in angle brackets. This designates T as a place holder for a type to be specified when the template is used. The function declaration comes next. It uses T to define param as an argument to be passed to the function.

Every parameter in the template must be used at least once in the function's parameter list. A declaration such as this is not allowed:

```
template<class T1, class T2>
void f(T1 param1)  // ???
{
  // ... Function body
}
```

That function template declares two parameters, T1 and T2, but the function itself uses only T1 to define param1. The correct declaration uses both T1 and T2 at least once in the function's parameter list:

```
template<class T1, class T2>
void f(T1 param1, T2 param2)
{
  // ... Function body
}
```

You can use a template's placeholder parameters such as T or T1 anywhere you could normally use built-in types—to define variables, pointers, casts, and other objects. The parameter list, however, cannot be empty. By their nature, function templates are used to generate *multiple* functions to operate on many types of objects. If the template had no parameters, only one function could be generated, and there would be no reason to write the function as a template.

min and *max* Function Templates

The value of function templates is easier to fathom by examining a few examples. Listing 7.1, minmax.h, declares three classic function templates, min(), max(), and inrange().

Listing 7.1. minmax.h.

```
#ifndef __MINMAX_H
#define __MINMAX_H    // Prevent multiple #includes
```

continues

Listing 7.1. continued

```
template<class T>
T max(T a, T b)
{
  return (a > b) ? a : b;
}

template<class T>
T min(T a, T b)
{
  return (a < b) ? a : b;
}

template<class T>
int inrange(T a, T b, T c)
{
  return (b <= a) && (a <= c);
}

#endif  // __MINMAX_H
```

The header file declares *and implements* the function templates. Each template begins with the required preface:

```
template<class T>
```

In the declaration, T is the type of object on which the function operates. The function header after this line declares a function template named max():

```
template<class T>
T max(T a, T b)
```

The second line declares max() as a function that returns a value of type T. The function requires two arguments, a and b, both also of type T. Remember, T stands for *any* type—its exact nature is unimportant at this stage. Function min() is declared similarly.

The body of the function performs the template's actions:

```
{
  return (a > b) ? a : b;
}
```

If a is greater in value than b, the statement returns a; otherwise it returns b. The variables a and b are of type T (whatever type that happens to be), thus the function, which returns a value of type T, obviously can return a or b. The function template min() is written similarly, but it returns a if a is less than b; otherwise it returns b.

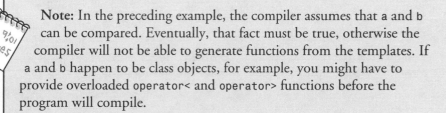

Note: In the preceding example, the compiler assumes that a and b can be compared. Eventually, that fact must be true, otherwise the compiler will not be able to generate functions from the templates. If a and b happen to be class objects, for example, you might have to provide overloaded operator< and operator> functions before the program will compile.

If you are still having trouble grasping function-template syntax, replace T with int in max(), min(), and inrange(), and ignore the template prefaces. The max() function, with the replaced types in bold, now looks like this:

```
int max(int a, int b)
{
  return (a > b) ? a : b;
}
```

Replacing T with int is exactly what the compiler does when it generates an actual function from a template, an action that occurs when a program uses the template. The *use* of a template determines the data types that replace the template's declared parameters. Listing 7.2, MINMAX.CPP, demonstrates a few cases of this concept for min(), max(), and inrange().

Listing 7.2. MINMAX.CPP.

```cpp
#include <iostream.h>
#include "minmax.h"

int main()
{
  int a = 123, b = 456;
  cout << "min(123, 456) == " << min(a, b) << endl;
  cout << "max(123, 456) == " << max(a, b) << endl;

  double c = 3.14159, d = 9.87654;
  cout << "min(3.14159, 9.87654) == " << min(c, d) << endl;
  cout << "max(3.14159, 9.87654) == " << max(c, d) << endl;

  char e = 'q', f = 'a';
  cout << "min('q', 'a') == " << min(e, f) << endl;
  cout << "max('q', 'a') == " << max(e, f) << endl;

  short s1 = 10, low = 5, high = 15;
  cout << "s1 == " << s1 << endl;
  if (inrange(s1, low, high))
    cout << low << " <= s1 <= " << high << endl;
  else
    cout << "s1 is not within range "
      << low << " to " << high << endl;

  return 0;
}
```

Including the minmax.h header file makes the template declarations available to the program. *Calling* a function template causes the compiler to generate actual functions based on the data types of passed arguments. (Taking a function template's address also generates an actual function.)

In MINMAX.CPP, the main program defines two integer values, a and b. Two output stream statements display the result of the two expressions, min(a, b) and max(a, b).

When the compiler encounters these expressions, it hunts for real `min()` and `max()` functions that match the types of arguments a and b. Failing that, the compiler looks for any templates with consistent place-holder parameters. In this case, because a and b are both `int`s, and because the function templates declare and use a single parameter (T), a match is made—if not in heaven, at least in memory—and the compiler generates two functions, exactly as though you had prototyped them as

```
int min(int a, int b);
int max(int a, int b);
```

The next three statements in MINMAX.CPP define two `double` values, c and d. Again, the use of the templates generates actual functions to match the argument types. Replacing the template parameter T with `double`, the compiler generates functions as though you had declared them like this:

```
double min(double a, double b);
double max(double a, double b);
```

The program then defines two `char` variables, e and f. Based on the types of these arguments, the compiler generates two compatible functions:

```
char min(char a, char b);
char max(char a, char b);
```

The program also uses the `inrange()` function to test whether a value is within range of another two values. The expression `inrange(a, b, c)` is true only if b <= a and a <= c.

As you can see, the compiler is writing most of this program, using the templates as guides! Running MINMAX.CPP proves that each function operates independently, producing results that match the argument types. On-screen, you see

```
min(123, 456) == 123
max(123, 456) == 456
min(3.14159, 9.87654) == 3.14159
max(3.14159, 9.87654) == 9.87654
min('q', 'a') == a
max('q', 'a') == q
s1 == 10
5 <= s1 <= 15
```

Forward Function Templates

Templates can be forward declarations, also called incomplete declarations. Declare a forward max() template like this:

```
template<class T> T max(T a, T b);
```

Given this declaration, you can use the template and supply the function template's body elsewhere. Notice that I wrote this declaration all on one line—a format you'll see often. Either format works, but I prefer the clearer two-line model:

```
template<class T>
T max(T a, T b);
```

Explicit Function-Template Prototypes

When a program uses a function template, the *first* argument determines the type of function generated. If you're not careful, this little known but important rule can put your code in hot water.

Suppose, for example, you need a max() function to compare two values of different types. You could design the template this way:

```
template<class T1, class T2>
T1 max(T1 a, T2 b)
{
  return (a > b) ? a : b;
}
```

Function template max() now returns a value of type T1 and requires arguments of two types, T1 and T2. To test this new template, define two variables, one of type int and one of type double:

```
int i = 123;
double d = 1234.5678;
```

We want any generated functions using these two variables to return the same result regardless of argument order. These statements, however, don't have the expected outcome:

```
cout.precision(12);
cout << max(d, i) << endl;
cout << max(i, d) << endl;
```

On-screen, you see this report:

```
1234.5678
1234
```

The first use of max() returns type double—the same type as its first argument. The second use of max() returns an int value, demoted from the double value that the generated int function attempts to return. The answers are correct, but we wish the second value also to be written in floating point. Unfortunately, wishes mean nothing to compilers.

Ambiguities like this crop up frequently in function templates that declare more than one parameter. It's futile to try fixing the problem by writing another function template that returns a value of type T2. For example, this typical repair attempt does not work:

```
template<class T1, class T2>
T2 max(T1 a, T2 b)  // ???
{
  return (a > b) ? a : b;
}
```

Overloaded functions must differ by at least one parameter, and the redeclaration of max(T1 a, T2 b) is not allowed because it duplicates the previous template. Just changing the return type is not enough for the compiler to distinguish between the two templates. Changing or rearranging the parameter names would not help. Each template declares exactly two different parameters, and to the compiler, the templates are therefore identical in form. The order of T1 and T2 is unimportant.

The only way to solve this problem is to declare an *explicit function prototype* that returns type double:

```
double max(double, double);
```

Each of the following statements now writes a `double` value, even though the arguments are passed to `max()` in different orders:

```
cout << max(d, i) << endl;
cout << max(i, d) << endl;
```

The explicit prototype, which the compiler uses to define a conforming function from the template, promotes any `max()` integer arguments to `double` values. If you wanted to demote `double` arguments to `ints`—causing both statements to display integer values—declare this prototype instead:

```
int max(int, int);
```

You must choose between the two prototypes. If you attempted to use them both, the compiler would not be able to determine whether to promote or demote arguments passed to `max()`. The program also would not compile.

Learn this problem and its solution well. It might save you from aggravating debugging sessions. To hammer home the method, I wrapped up the preceding samples into a demonstration program, Listing 7.3, PROTO.CPP.

Listing 7.3. PROTO.CPP.

```
#include <iostream.h>
#include "minmax.h"

// Prototypes (enable one or the other)
double max(double, double);
// int max(int, int);

int main()
{
  int i = 123;
  double d = 1234.5678;

  cout.precision(12);
  cout << max(d, i) << endl;  // #1
  cout << max(i, d) << endl;  // #2
  return 0;
}
```

If you disable both max() function prototypes, the program doesn't compile because the two output statements pass arguments of *different* values to max(). The function templates included from minmax.h are designed to accept and return only values of the same type.

As I mentioned before, one possible solution to this problem would be to declare a new function template with two parameters, perhaps named T1 and T2. But then, we're back at square one—statement #1 would display a double value, whereas statement #2 would display an int.

To force the compiler to generate a double function in both cases, enable the first prototype (it is enabled in the listing printed here). To generate int functions, disable the first prototype and enable the second. If you enable *both* prototypes, the program no longer compiles because the compiler cannot determine whether to promote or demote the arguments passed to max(). Other uses of the templates that do not match the explicit prototypes work normally.

Specific Template Functions

In times of trouble, you might need to override a function template to provide your own version of a specific function, rather than have the compiler generate a function from the template. The replacement function is called a *specific template function*—literally, a specific instance of a function that takes the place of a function that otherwise would be created automatically from a template.

> **Note:** Jot a mental note about the potentially confusing word reversal in these terms. A *function template* is a template declaration. A *template function* is an instance of the template. A *specific template function* overrides a template instance. Just what you need, more terms to memorize, right? The terms are important to know, however, as they appear in many references. There's a movement under way to define less confusing terms than these, but meanwhile, there's little choice but to grin and bear the official terminology.

One subtle, and potentially disasterous, situation can occur if you pass char or other pointers to function templates like min() and max() as declared in minmax.h. For a sample of how these templates can lead you astray, examine Listing 7.4, BADTEMP.CPP. The program is a prime candidate for a specific template function.

Listing 7.4. BADTEMP.CPP.

```
#include <iostream.h>
#include "minmax.h"

int main()
{
  char *c1 = "Philadelphia";
  char *c2 = "Annapolis";
  cout << max(c1, c2) << endl;  // ???
  return 0;
}
```

The program attempts to use max() to compare the strings "Philadelphia" and "Annapolis". The program compiles and runs, but incorrectly reports that "Annapolis" is greater than "Philadelpha". (At least this is the result on my system. You might have to use different strings in different orders to prove that the program is not functioning.)

The bug occurs because the compiler generates the max() function as though it had been written

```
char * max(char *c1, char *c2)
{
  return (c1 > c2) ? c1 : c2;  // ???
}
```

In other words, the generated max() function *compares the character pointers rather than the addressed strings.* To repair the faulty code, rewrite the program as shown in Listing 7.5, GOODTEMP.CPP.

Listing 7.5. GOODTEMP.CPP.

```
#include <iostream.h>
#include <string.h>
#include "minmax.h"

// Override template with specific function
char * max(char *c1, char *c2)
{
  return stricmp(c1, c2) ? c1 : c2;
}


int main()
{
  char *c1 = "Philadelphia";
  char *c2 = "Annapolis";
  cout << max(c1, c2) << endl;
  return 0;
}
```

The specific max() function in the center of the listing prevents the compiler from generating a function from the template. Whenever the compiler can find a real function that matches a statement's use of that function, the compiler uses the real McCoy rather than the template. Use this technique to override a template if the generated version doesn't perform as expected.

 **Note:** Another way to avoid this kind of trouble is to use a string class (see Chapter 10, "Constructing a String Class") rather than a char * pointer.

A Sorting Function Template

How many times have you written and rewritten the same old sorting functions to accommodate new data types, structures, or class objects? If you're like most programmers, the answer is "entirely too often." With templates, you can write a single generic function that can arrange any data of any kind and reduce the need to write new sorters in the future.

Listing 7.6, TEMPSORT.CPP, might not be the ultimate sorter, but it's a running start in the right direction. The program can create, display, and sort an array of objects of most types (but not strings).

Listing 7.6. TEMPSORT.CPP.

```
#include <iostream.h>
#include <iomanip.h>
#include <stdlib.h>
#include <time.h>

// A sample class
class TData {
  int x, y;
public:
  TData(): x(0), y(0) { }
  TData(int n): x(n), y(rand()) { }
  friend ostream & operator<< (ostream &, TData &);
  friend int operator< (TData &, TData &);
};

// Write TData object value to an ostream reference
ostream & operator<< (ostream &os, TData &t)
{
  cout << '(' << t.x << ", " << t.y << ')';
  return os;
}

// Return true if object a is "less than" object b
operator< (TData &a, TData &b)
{
  return (a.x < b.x);
}
```

```cpp
// Fill global array with values taken at random
template<class T>
void FillArray(T *array, int nelem)
{
  srand((unsigned)time(0));         // Randomize
  for (int i = 0; i < nelem; i++)  // Fill array
    array[i] = (T)rand();
}

// Display contents of array before and after sorting
template<class T>
void DisplayArray(T *array, int nelem)
{
  cout << endl;  // Start new display line
  for (int i = 0; i < nelem; i++)
    cout << array[i] << endl;
}

// Quicksort algorithm by C. A. R. Hoare
template<class T>
void Quicksort(T *array, int left, int right)
{
  int i = left;
  int j = right;
  T test = array[(left + right) / 2];
  T swap;

  do {
    while (array[i] < test) i++;
    while (test < array[j]) j--;
    if (i <= j) {
      swap = array[i];
      array[i] = array[j];
      array[j] = swap;
      i++;
      j--;
```

continues

157

Listing 7.6. continued

```
    }
  } while (i <= j);
  if (left < j) Quicksort(array, left, j);
  if (i < right) Quicksort(array, i, right);
}

// Sort n elements in array
template<class T>
void SortArray(T *array, int nelem)
{
  if (nelem > 1) Quicksort(array, 0, nelem - 1);
}

#define ARRAYSIZE 10

main()
{
// Enable one of the following definitions to create
// and sort an array of int, double, char, or TData objects

  int array[ARRAYSIZE];
//   double array[ARRAYSIZE];
//   TData array[ARRAYSIZE];

// Set a few output flags so floating point values
// have decimal points
  cout.setf(ios::showpoint);
  cout.precision(12);

// Use the function templates to fill, display,
// sort, and redisplay the array
  FillArray(array, ARRAYSIZE);
  DisplayArray(array, ARRAYSIZE);
  SortArray(array, ARRAYSIZE);
  DisplayArray(array, ARRAYSIZE);
  return 0;
}
```

Note: To compile TEMPSORT.CPP, you must supply a function `rand()` that returns an `int` value at random, a function `srand()` that "seeds" the random generator, and a `time()` function for providing a seed value. Or, you can replace these functions with a random number generator from your compiler's library. The functions are used in template `FillArray()` and in one of `TData`'s constructors.

Compile and run TEMPSORT.CPP with one of the `main()` function's array definitions enabled. The first definition creates a small array of `int` values. (`ARRAYSIZE` is purposely small so the program can display the before and after results on-screen.) Edit the program to enable the other `array` definitions one at a time.

The first column of numbers you see on-screen are unsorted values. The second are those same values in order. Side by side, the sorted columns look like the samples in Figure 7.2.

```
837        936.0000000      (2166, 7182)
1364       4067.000000      (2446, 26883)
5151       4940.000000      (6254, 5316)
6691       5013.000000      (6942, 18857)
20767      10103.00000      (7563, 26979)
21441      12087.00000      (8557, 19871)
23020      18738.00000      (16345, 2266)
28816      22645.00000      (21331, 14046)
28940      26852.00000      (25081, 11444)
30745      32299.00000      (28645, 14570)
```

Figure 7.2. Sample output from TEMPSORT.CPP.

As this output demonstrates, the program's sorting template can handle integers, floating point values, and even class objects composed of two integers sorted by the first value of each pair. No changes to the program are needed for the template to accommodate these very different types of data.

The program's first function template, `FillArray()`, is declared to accept a pointer to an unspecified type:

```
template<class T>
void FillArray(T *array, int nelem)
```

In addition to its untyped `T *array` pointer, the function also declares an `int` value `nelem`, equal to the number of elements in the array. A statement inside the function demonstrates how to use a template parameter in a cast expression. The statement casts the `rand()` function to an object of type `T`, assigning the result to an array element:

```
array[i] = (T)rand();  // Use T in a cast expression
```

The array's elements are of type `T`, so obviously, you can copy any type `T` object to the array. It might not be appropriate, however, to cast `rand()` this way for every conceivable type that might someday replace `T`, but the results are suitable for this demonstration. (Be cautious about using casts so freely. I used a type-cast expression merely as a quick way to load test values into the array— an acceptable solution here, but not one to be used without careful thought.)

Other functions, `DisplayArray()`, `QuickSort()`, and `SortArray()` have similar designs. Each is a function template, and each declares a parameter, `T *array`. Passing an array of any objects to these function templates causes the compiler to generate compatible functions. In the case of an array of `int` values, when compiled, this statement:

```
FillArray(array, ARRAYSIZE);
```

generates a function with its first parameter of type `int *`, exactly as though you had declared `FillArray()` as

```
void FillArray(int *array, int nelem);
```

Enabling the third array definition in `main()` creates an array of `TData` class objects:

```
TData array[ARRAYSIZE];
```

For this type of array, the compiler generates a `FillArray()` function as though it had been prototyped as

```
void FillArray(TData *array, int nelem);
```

The TData class is perfectly acceptable as a replacement for the template's place holder parameter, T. When passing class objects to function templates, however, those classes must have features that allow the program's statements to compile. In this case, TData requires

● A default constructor (TData()) to initialize an array of objects.

● An overloaded constructor with a single int parameter, so the cast of (T)rand() has a reasonable effect. In this case, the constructor assigns to x the value returned from rand(), and then it randomizes y.

● An operator<< function for writing TData objects using stream statements.

● An operator< function for comparing two TData objects so the array can be sorted.

You can probably ignore other potential requirements. In this case, for example, the program doesn't compare two TData objects for equality, so the class doesn't need an operator= function.

Where to Store Function Templates

Whether to store templates in header files or in modules is a thorny subject. Actual template instances are generated from templates as the compiler encounters the templates in use. In most cases, you have to store template declarations along with their implementations in header files so the compiler "sees" the templates before they are used.

This situation might change as more sophisticated C++ compilers arrive on the scene. Also, check your compiler's references for options you can use with templates. Unless your compiler is light-years ahead of the pack, however, you probably can't store templates in separate modules or in compiled libraries as you can real functions. Because the issue of template compilation is so murky at this point, in this book I store all templates directly in header files. To use the templates, simply include the headers.

Final Words

Function templates turn the compiler into a kind of programming assistant, ready to crank out code on demand, based on the template's guidelines. In the next chapter I explain how *class templates* take this concept even further, giving you a tool for creating data types that can mold themselves to accommodate new information and tasks.

Shaping Class Templates

Programming with class templates is what cooking would be like if you could purchase a generic food stuff, then command the stove to transform one portion into roast beef, convert another into baked trout, and whip any leftovers into chocolate mousse. Even if you're not much of a cook, you're bound to agree that C++ class templates are a special and versatile treat.

Templates in Review

Class templates share some of the same ingredients with function templates. As explained in the preceding chapter, both begin in the identical way with a template declaration such as

```
template<class T>
```

The parameter class T stands for a data type supplied when you use the template. Commas separate multiple parameters between the angle brackets:

```
template<class T1, class T2, class T3>
```

As in function templates, the word class does *not* necessarily refer to a C++ class. It simply means "any built-in or user-defined type." T, T1, T2, and T3 in these examples are placeholders that might be replaced with int, double, char *, or any other type. They might also be structs or classes.

That much of template architecture is identical for function and class templates. What comes after the template declaration, however, radically differs for a class.

Class Templates

To understand class templates, take a moment to reflect on the nature of a nontemplate class, often termed a *data abstraction.* A nontemplate class defines in abstract terms the properties of objects to be constructed from the class. For example, a binary-coded-decimal class defines the characteristics of BCD numbers. *The class is a BCD number in the abstract.*

A class template refines this concept to a further level of abstraction (see Figure 8.1). As you can use a class to define objects, the compiler can use a *class template* to define a class. A class template is a further and more general abstraction of an object's properties. In simple terms, *a template is a class in the abstract.*

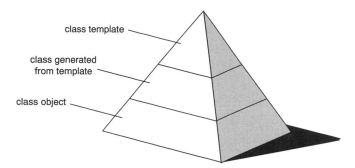

Figure 8.1. The relationship between a class template, a class, and an object.

The three-tier pyramid in Figure 8.1 shows the relationship between a class template, a class generated from the template, and an object constructed from the class. The topmost level represents the template—it defines the general properties of a class. The class comes midway between—there could be many of these real classes generated from a single template, all possessing the template's abstract properties. On the bottom level is the object—the tangible item constructed from one of the generated classes.

Class Template Syntax

To create a class template, follow a template parameter list with a class declaration. Inside the class, use the template's parameters as you do other types like `int` or `double`. You can use template parameters, for example, as data members, as member function return types, or as member function parameters.

> **Note:** The programming in this and the next section is from the file CLTDEMO.CPP (class template demo) stored on disk in the PART2 directory.

Here's a sample class template that stores two values:

```
template<class T>          // Begin template with parameter T
class TAnyTemp {
  T x, y;                  // Private data members of type T
public:
  TAnyTemp(T X, T Y)       // Class constructor
    : x(X), y(Y) { }
  T getx() { return x; }   // Class member function
  T gety() { return y; }   // Class member function
};
```

The first line declares the beginning of a template with a single parameter, T. The class template, TAnyTemp, follows. It declares two private data members, x and y, both of type T. The class template can therefore hold two values of a type that will be specified when the template is used.

Like all good classes, TAnyTemp has a constructor. Carefully examine the constructor's inline definition:

```
TAnyTemp(T X, T Y)
  : x(X), y(Y) { }
```

The constructor requires two arguments, X and Y, both of type T. The private data member x is initialized using the value of X. The private data member y is initialized using the value of Y. The constructor can assign X to x and Y to y because all of these values are of type T. There's nothing else for the constructor to do, so its inline body is empty.

TAnyTemp also declares these two member functions:

```
T getx() { return x; }
T gety() { return y; }
```

Each function returns a value of type T. We still haven't specified what T is, but that doesn't matter. The class member functions obviously can return the values of x and y because these data members are variables also of type T. When performing type checking at the template level, the compiler cares only about compatibility using the most general of syntax rules. At this stage, the compiler doesn't consider the properties of actual data types that eventually will replace T and any other template parameters.

If you are still having trouble grasping the syntax of class templates, load TAnyTemp into your editor and replace T with int. Here's what happened when I did that (replaced parameters are bold):

```
class TAnyTemp {
  int x, y;
public:
  TAnyTemp(int X, int Y)
    : x(X), y(Y) { }
  int getx() { return x; }
  int gety() { return y; }
};
```

Replacing T with int is exactly what the compiler does when a program defines an object of a class template like TAnyTemp. In a way, a class template is similar to a #defined macro. The template is safer to use, however, because the compiler can perform type checking on the generated class's types. You don't actually see a class generated from a template, but you can use the result as though you designed the class exactly as shown here.

Hint: If a class template doesn't behave as expected, load a copy of the source file into your editor, then use a global search and replace command to translate template parameters into specific data types. You can quickly find many syntax errors using this simple trick.

Objects of Class Templates

Class templates are also called *parameterized types*. Feeding the class template a real data type creates a new class, using the specific type in place of the template's parameters.

For reference, here's the TAnyTemp class template again minus its insides:

```
template<class T>
class TAnyTemp {
  ...
};
```

Using this template, you can define an object iObject, replacing parameter T with int:

```
TAnyTemp<int> iObject(123, 456);
```

The expression <int> immediately following TAnyTemp tells the compiler to generate a class from the template and replace all instances of T with int. The name of the generated class becomes TAnyTemp<int>. The name of the defined object is iObject. Two integer values, 123 and 456, are passed to the object's constructor to initialize the object's private data members.

Be sure to understand that the *complete* name of the generated class is TAnyTemp<int>, including the brackets and int data type. To refer to this generated class wherever a common class name is appropriate, simply use the template's complete name, TAnyTemp<int>. Fix this rule firmly in your mind— it will answer many questions you might have about class template syntax.

Objects like iObject constructed from a template-generated class are no different from objects created from a nontemplate class. You can call member functions for the object and use it in expressions. For example, to define iObject and display the values of its x and y private data members, you might use these output stream statements:

```
TAnyTemp<int> iObject(123, 456);
cout << "iObject.x == " << iObject.getx() << endl;
cout << "iObject.y == " << iObject.gety() << endl;
```

Executing these lines displays the *integer* values of x and y. The getx() and gety() functions return integer values because, in defining iObject, the program specifies int as the replacement for the template's T parameter.

To define an object with floating point values and, *using those same member functions,* write those values to the standard output, use statements such as

```
TAnyTemp<double> dObject(3.14159, 9.51413);
cout << "dObject.x == " << dObject.getx() << endl;
cout << "dObject.y == " << dObject.gety() << endl;
```

Object dObject can hold two double values because the TAnyTemp<double> class name generates a class with double in place of the template's T parameter. The getx() and gety() member functions now return double values where before they returned int.

The program now has two instances of the class template, one named `TAnyTemp<int>` and the other named `TAnyTemp<double>`. These are two distinct, unrelated classes with their own member functions and data members. The *only* common ground between the two classes is the fact that both were generated from the same template.

Multiple Template Parameters

Class templates can declare one or more parameters. You can also pass values of specific types to a template. These techniques are especially useful in constructing arrays that shape themselves according to the types of information you need to store.

Listing 8.1, MATRIX.CPP, demonstrates some of these concepts. The program doesn't have all the elements that a real matrix would need, but the code demonstrates several important techniques for using class templates to construct array-like containers.

Listing 8.1. MATRIX.CPP.

```
#include <iostream.h>

template<class TX, class TY, int K = 10>
class Matrix {
  TX x[K];
  TY y[K];
public:
  Matrix() { }
  // ... Other member functions
};

void main()
{
  Matrix<int, char> m1;
  Matrix<double, short, 20> m2;
```

continues

Listing 8.1. continued

```
  Matrix<char *, float, 5> m3;
  Matrix<Matrix<int, int>, Matrix<char, char>, 4> m4;
  Matrix<int, double> *p1;
  p1 = new Matrix<int, double>;
  delete p1;
}
```

The Matrix class template begins in the usual way with a template keyword and a list of parameters. In this case, there are two placeholder parameters, TX and TY, and an int named K. In the generated class, K becomes a constant and, in this case, is given the default value of 10.

Typed parameters don't require default values. I could have written the template preface as

```
template<class TX, class TY, int K>
```

The user of this class would then have to supply data types for TX and TY, and a value for K. To make the class easier to use, however, it's probably best to supply default values for items like K as I did in the listing.

To form a matrix, the class template declares these two private arrays:

```
class Matrix {
  TX x[K];  // An array of K items of type TX
  TY y[K];  // An array of K items of type TY
  ...
};
```

Array x stores K items of type TX. Array y stores K items of type TY. The types and sizes of these arrays are determined when the template is first used to define an object, at which time the compiler generates a real class from the template. The template is a completely general representation of an object containing two arrays of unknown size and type. The two arrays could store the same type of data, or they could have objects of different types.

The test program, MATRIX.CPP, defines several objects using the `Matrix` class template. Examine these objects with your system's debugger—the results may surprise you. Object `m1` is defined as

```
Matrix<int, char> m1;
```

Given this definition, the compiler generates a class from the template, replacing the first parameter, `TX`, with `int` and the second, `TY`, with `char`. Because no literal value is given for `K`, the generated class uses the default value of 10. Given these arguments, the generated class acquires two private ten-element arrays as though you had declared them as

```
int x[10];
char y[10];
```

The next definition in the sample program constructs a different sort of object, this time with `double` and `short` arrays:

```
Matrix<double, short, 20> m2;
```

In object `m2`, array `x` can hold 20 `double` values. Array `y` can have 20 `short` values. The explicit value 20 overrides `K`'s default value of 10. These versions of the class's private arrays are generated as though they had been declared like this:

```
double x[20];
short y[20];
```

The program next defines object `m3`, specifying an array of five `char` pointers and `five` floats:

```
Matrix<char *, float, 5> m3;
```

Again, the private `x` and `y` arrays take on the types of the arguments, `char *` and `float`. Each array can hold five elements of its declared type.

Complex Templates

Even more complex constructions are possible. In any definition but the simplest, however, the syntax can quickly build to mind-fogging density. Avoid confusion by remembering that a class generated as

```
Matrix<int, int>
```

represents the *complete* class name. This means you can use Matrix<int, int> at any place where a common class name is appropriate. Matrix alone is not a class name.

These rules become especially important when defining a class from a template using other class templates. Here's an extreme case:

```
Matrix<Matrix<int, int>, Matrix<char, char>, 4> m4;
```

That line might win a prize in one of those C obfuscation contests that programming clubs hold, but it's simpler than it looks. A couple of macros help clean up the mess:

```
#define IntIntClass Matrix<int, int>
#define CharCharClass Matrix<char, char>
```

Replace the inner Matrix<TX, TY> class names with the IntIntClass and CharCharClass macros to see how object m4 is actually formed:

```
Matrix<IntIntClass, CharCharClass, 4> m4;
```

Now the syntax is clearer. Object m4 has two arrays, each element of which is *another* Matrix<TX, TY> object with two more arrays. If an int takes two bytes, m4 occupies 240 bytes. With a single stroke, you have created a matrix of matrices—a difficult data structure to create and use with conventional programming.

Finally in the test MATRIX.CPP program is a pointer to an object constructed of a Matrix class template. This defines the pointer:

```
Matrix<int, double> *p1;
```

The pointer p1 can address an object of type Matrix<int, double>. To use this pointer, construct an object and assign its address to p1 by using new:

```
p1 = new Matrix<int, double>;
```

Here's where many newcomers to templates become confused. The statement does *not* pass int and double values anywhere as it may appear to do. Matrix<int, double> *is the full name of the class.* The compiler has already generated a class of this type—you are just referring to it again by its name as you would refer to any other class name.

It's especially important to realize that you can't construct an object like this:

```
p1 = new Matrix;  //???
```

That doesn't work because Matrix is not a class name. The complete name is Matrix<int, double>, including the types like int and double that replace the template's parameters.

Class Templates in Practice

That wraps up the theory of class templates. Following are several examples that will help answer questions you might have about how to use and implement class templates of various kinds.

Member Functions in Class Templates

Implement member functions for class templates just as you do member functions for nontemplate classes. The syntax rules, however, might seem unusual until you have walked through the steps a few times.

As usual, an example is the best way to explain the proper techniques. On disk, locate files members.h and the test program MEMBERS.CPP in the PART2 directory. The program declares this class template:

```
template<class T>
class TCoord {
  friend ostream & operator<< (ostream &, TCoord<T> &);
  friend istream & operator>> (istream &, TCoord<T> &);
public:
  TCoord();              // Default constructor
  TCoord(T X, T Y);      // Constructor
  virtual ~TCoord();     // Destructor
  virtual T getx();      // Member function
  virtual T gety();      // Member function
private:
  T x, y;                // Data members
};
```

The class template TCoord<T> declares a single parameter, T. Overloaded iostream operators << and >> provide input and output services for class objects. The class has two constructors, a virtual destructor, and two virtual member functions. The class also declares two private data members of type T. In short, TCoord has many of the elements found in a typical C++ class.

The class template's default constructor shows the basic form required to implement member functions:

```
template<class T>
TCoord<T>::TCoord()
{
  x = 0;  // Initialize both data members to 0
  y = 0;  // Note: Implies that T is numeric!
}
```

Each and every implemented member function, including any constructors, must begin with the template keyword and a parameter list, the same preface used in declaring the class. The second line (it's often written to the right of the first instead of on a separate line as I've done here) states that the default constructor named TCoord() is a member of the class TCoord<T>.

When implementing constructors, don't make this common error:

```
TCoord<T>::TCoord<T>() // ???
```

The correct declaration is

```
TCoord<T>::TCoord()
```

The *class* name is TCoord<T>. The *constructor's* name is TCoord(). Like all constructor implementations, the constructor name is preceded by the class name and a scope resolution operator (::).

Inside the constructor's implementation, assigning literal zero values to x and y implies that, in any class generated from the template, these data members are numeric. If that's not the case, the program might not compile. You could attempt to head off this potential problem with a cast, but you might be ambushing your code if you initialize the members like this:

```
x = (T)0;  // ???
y = (T)0;  // ???
```

Whether these casts work depends on T's eventual type. If that type's objects can't be cast to an integer zero, a serious problem will occur, or the program might not compile. Watch that similar assignments of literal values don't lock your class into assumptions about T's eventual type.

Implement other member functions similarly:

```
template<class T>
T TCoord<T>::getx()
{
  return x;
}
```

Again, `template<class T>` begins the implementation of the member function. Each member function must begin in this same way. The function, `getx()`, returns a value of type T. The function's class name is `TCoord<T>`. You must specify the full parameterized class name (including `<T>`) before the scope resolution operator (`::`), identifying the function as a member of the class. The function's return type (`T`) comes first, as return types always do.

Admittedly, the syntax looks obscure until you get used to the style. Figure 8.2 labels the parts and pieces of the preceding function.

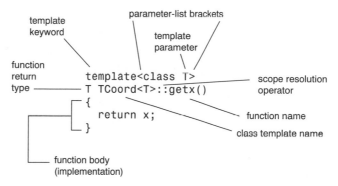

Figure 8.2. Parts of a class template member function.

The overloaded friend functions for operators `<<` and `>>` also look complex, but they follow the same general rules for all class template function implementations:

```
template<class T>
ostream & operator<< (ostream &os, TCoord<T> &t)
{
  cout << '(' << t.getx() << ", " << t.gety() << ')';
  return os;
}
```

The template header on the first line is the same as before. The function, operator<<, is implemented as it might be for a nontemplate class. A significant difference, however, is the reference parameter TCoord<T> &t, literally a reference named t to an object of a class named TCoord<T>. The full parameterized name of the class identifies this argument's type in a completely general way.

Derived Classes and Class Templates

You can use class templates and nontemplate classes to derive new classes. These three combinations are possible:

● A class template derived from a class template

● A nontemplate class derived from a class template

● A class template derived from a nontemplate class

All three techniques are vital to learn. You might use the first method to build a hierarchy of class templates. The second is useful for creating specific classes from templates, rather than permitting the compiler to generate those classes automatically in cases where the results from the compiler don't meet your expectations. The third technique makes it possible to create a generalized template from any existing class. You could use this method to create class templates based on a nontemplate class library.

Note: The programming in the next three sections is extracted from the disk file DERIVED.CPP stored in the PART2 directory.

A Class Template Derived from a Class Template

One class template can be a base class for another class template. The syntax is easily understood by remembering that TBaseClass<T> is the full class name. Keeping that fact in mind, examine class TDerivedA, derived from the TCoord<T> base class in the disk file, members.h:

```
template<class T>
class TDerivedA : public TCoord<T> {
public:
  TDerivedA(T X, T Y, T Z)
    : z(Z), TCoord<T>(X, Y) { }
private:
  T z;
};
```

TDerivedA publicly inherits the base class by its full name, TCoord<T>. The class constructor requires three arguments of type T. Argument Z is used to initialize TDerivedA's private data member, z, of type T, declared at the bottom of the class. The other two arguments are passed to the base class constructor, referred to by the class name, TCoord<T>.

When a program uses TDerivedA, the compiler generates two distinct classes—a base class TCoord<T> (with T replaced by an appropriate type), and a TDerivedA<T> class. You might construct an object of this class with the statement

```
TDerivedA<int> objectA(1, 2, 3);
```

Note: Examine objectA in your debugger to see its contents, and if your debugger allows, to view the hierarchy of classes from which the object is constructed. Figure 8.3 shows how my debugger (Borland's Turbo Debugger) depicts TDerivedA and other classes in the next two sections. (The templates show real data types such as int and double because the diagram was generated by viewing objects of the class types. The unusal ellipses and trailing angle brackets (...>) apparently are just the debugger's way of designating parameterized types.)

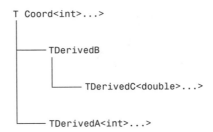

Figure 8.3. Classes and templates derived from `TCoord`.

A Nontemplate Class Derived from a Class Template

You can derive a nontemplate class from any class template. Use this technique when you have a template but you need to override the compiler's automatic generation of a class. You might do this, for example, to add specific elements to a derived class that the compiler could not provide automatically.

Here's a sample of a nontemplate-derived class, `TDerivedB`, that inherits a class template, `TCoord<T>`:

```
class TDerivedB : public TCoord<int> {
public:
  TDerivedB(int X, int Y, int Z)
    : z(Z), TCoord<int>(X, Y) { }
private:
  int z;
};
```

As in any class inheritance, you can replace `public` in the first line with `protected` or `private`. You can also use multiple inheritance to derive a class from two or more base classes. Notice that the inherited class, `TCoord<int>`, is given an explicit data type. The derived class is no longer a template, so you must specify real data types for any inherited template parameters. In other words, you cannot derive a nontemplate class such as `TDerivedB` from the template `TCoord<T>`. You must replace `T` with a data type like `int` as shown in the example.

See Figure 8.3 for the position of `TDerivedB` in the class hierarchy. You might construct an object of the class like this:

```
TDerivedB objectB(4, 5, 6);
```

A Class Template Derived from a Nontemplate Class

Finally, it's possible to create a new class template from a nontemplate class. This method is especially useful for translating existing class libraries into generalized template versions.

Using the nontemplate TDerivedB class from the preceding section, here's a new class template, TDerivedC<T>, that inherits TDerivedB:

```
template<class T>
class TDerivedC : public TDerivedB {
public:
  TDerivedC(int X, int Y, int Z, T Q)
    : q(Q), TDerivedB(X, Y, Z) { }
private:
  T q;
};
```

Figure 8.3 shows where TDerivedC<T> fits into the class hierarchy. This branch of the class family tree begins with the class template TCoord<int>, extends to the nontemplate derived class TDerivedB, and continues to another class template TDerivedC<T>.

The important observation here is that templates do not have to be at the root of a class hierarchy, although that's often the case. Using inheritance, *any* class can become a template, and any template can become a class.

Hint: Designing class templates from scratch can be extremely difficult. Usually, it's best not to attempt that approach. Instead, create a sample class with the properties you would want the compiler to generate *if* a template were available. After debugging this sample class, try to identify characteristics suitable for the class template, but be prepared to fail—not all abstractions lead to useful templates. You'd be hard pressed, for example, to generalize the concept of a null-terminated string without getting trapped in specifics. You might, however, be able to generalize the properties of an array, and then use *that* abstraction to generate a family of string classes. In practice, though, even this approach rarely pays big dividends. Creating perfectly general, useful templates isn't easy!

Final Words

Templates are fast becoming one of the most talked about subjects in C++ programming. They are certainly among the most versatile tools in the language. In the next chapter, you'll use function and class templates to build a *container class*—a data structure that can store values and objects of many differents sizes and types.

Vectoring
In On Arrays

There are few data structures more basic than arrays. In fact, maybe they're *too* basic. Arrays are so fundamental, so low-level in nature, they practically beg for abuse. What programmer hasn't crashed a program by using an out-of-range array index? Who hasn't pondered array statements that obviously *have* to work—but don't?

Distilling the essence of an array into a class is an excellent way to add an extra shot of safety to array-handling code. Of course, array classes come with their own problems—they aren't idiot-proof. As class templates, however, arrays become versatile tools for creating safe and reliable data structures.

Single Index Vectors

To distinguish between common arrays and classes, from now on, I use the term *vector* to refer to array classes and objects. The word *array* refers to the run-of-the-mill C and C++ array.

> **Note:** In graphics programming, the term *vector* is sometimes used to define a coordinate in space, but we are interested here in vectors used for data storage.

As all beginning C and C++ programmers learn, given an array named simply a, programs can use index expressions such as a[2] to access objects in the array (see Figure 9.1).

```
array                         array
in program                    in memory

a[0]  ———————————  object_0
a[1]  ———————————  object_1
a[2]  ———————————  object_2
a[...]———————————  ...
a[n-1]———————————  object_{n-1}
```

Figure 9.1. Common array expressions access objects in the array a[ ].

Our goal is to produce a vector class that can be used in most of the same ways as a common array, but is safer and more versatile without sacrificing performance.

To start on the right foot, the first step is to identify the abstract properties shared by all arrays—a job that's often more difficult than it sounds. One of the most important properties is the capability of using index expressions to access an array's contents *at random*. As Figure 9.2 illustrates, the goal is to use vector expressions, identical in look and feel to array expressions, to access elements in the structure stored in memory one after the other (probably).

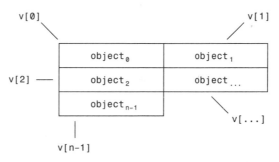

Figure 9.2. A vector class accesses objects in v[ ] much as an array does.

The vector class might also store pointers to objects, possibly of different sizes, resulting in a structure known as an *indirect vector*. Complex structures like the one illustrated by Figure 9.3 are best handled by a vector class, especially when the arrayed objects have their own pointers to other objects, character strings, or even other vectors. Careful memory management is essential to ensure proper allocations and deletions of these intertwined objects.

Quick and Dirty Vector Class

It doesn't take much effort to list some basic requirements for a Vector class. The class needs a default constructor (in case you want to construct an array of Vector objects, for example), another constructor to build a vector capable of holding a specified number of objects, a destructor, and an access method. For simplicity, the early version ignores errors and can store only values of type double. We'll lift those limitations in a later version.

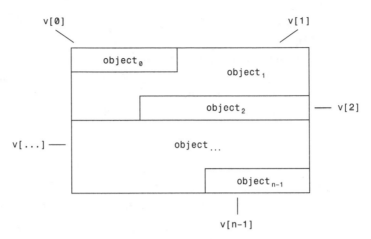

Figure 9.3. Indirect vector `iv[ ]` to variable size objects.

> **Note:** The programming in this section is extracted from the disk file, VECT1.CPP, located in the PART2 directory.

So far, the `Vector` class looks like this:

```
class Vector {
public:
  Vector(): size(0), pdata(0) { }
  Vector(int Size): pdata(0) { Init(Size); }
  ~Vector() { delete[] pdata; }
  void Init(int Size);
  double & operator[] (int i);
private:
  int size;    // Number of objects in array
  double *pdata;  // Pointer to first object
};
```

The `Init()` member function provides a means to construct a vector object of a certain size. If you define a vector object as

```
Vector avect;
```

the default constructor sets the private `size` data member to zero and also sets `pdata` to null. You might then initialize the vector by calling `Init()`:

```
avect.Init(100);
```

The alternate constructor also calls `Init()`, providing a more convenient way to build vector objects. This statement constructs a vector of 10 `double` values:

```
Vector v(10);
```

After constructing a vector object, you can use it as an array, filling it with values:

```
int i;
for (i = 0; i < 10; ++i)
  v[i] = 3.14159 * (i + 1);
```

You can then write those values using an output stream statement:

```
for (i = 0; i < 10; ++i)
  cout << "v[" << i << "] == " << v[i] << endl;
```

Expressions such as `v[i]` are possible because the `Vector` class overloads `operator[]` (the indexing operator):

```
double & Vector::operator[] (int i)
{
  return pdata[i];
}
```

The `operator[]` function returns a reference to a `double` value, using a common array expression `pdata[i]`. If `v` is a `Vector` object, the expression `v[i]` resolves to the type `double &`, permitting statements to assign new values to vectors:

```
v[i] = 3.14159;
```

and to retrieve existing values:

```
cout << "Value == " << v[i] << endl;
```

So far, all that `Vector` has achieved is to encapsulate a common array inside a class. The primitive class offers no extra safety and, because it can store only `double` values, it is no more versatile than a common array. The version in the next section expands `Vector` into a more practical data structure.

Improved Vector Class

One of the obvious improvements we can make to Vector is to prevent the use of out-of-range index values. Checking for this error is easy; what to do about detected problems is another matter. One solution simply displays a message and halts:

```
void Error(const char *message)
{
  cout << endl << "Error: " << message << endl;
  exit(-1);
}
```

> **Note:** The programming in this section is extracted from the disk file, VECT2.CPP. The program has intentional mistakes that demonstrate error handling. Read the comments in the listing for directions on fixing these errors.

Using the Error() function, operator[] can halt the program on detecting an out-of-range index value:

```
double & Vector::operator[] (int i)
{
  if (i < 0 || i >= size)
    Error("Index out of range");
  return pdata[i];
}
```

In this version, if index i is less than zero or greater than or equal to size, the operator calls Error() to halt the program with an error message. The function is not completely safe, however, because pdata might be null. The obvious solution, checking pdata for validity, is unattractive:

```
if (!pdata) Error("Attempt to use null pointer");
```

This works, but it costs too much in efficiency by requiring *every* indexing operation to test pdata. It's probably just as well to test the pointer once during the object's construction. This is similar to the common technique for testing memory allocated by new:

```
anyPointer = new AnyObject;
if (!anyPointer) Error("Out of memory");
```

A similar technique is possible for Vector objects by overloading operator!—the *not,* or *negation,* operator. The overloaded operator is easily written as an inline function:

```
int operator! () { return !pdata; }
```

The operator returns the negation of pdata—the Vector class's internal pointer. If the pointer is null, the operator returns true (non-null). If the pointer is non-null, the operator returns false. With the overloaded operator in place, you can construct Vector objects and test them for validity similar to the way you test the result returned by new:

```
Vector v1(10);
if (!v1) Error("Can't construct vector v1");
```

The if statement expression (!v1) calls the overloaded operator! function to determine whether v1 is valid. (Because the function is coded inline, however, there's no actual subroutine call.) The statement operates as though you had written it like this:

```
if (v1.pdata == 0) Error(...);  // ???
```

You can't actually do that, however, because pdata is private to the Vector class. Instead, an overloaded operator! provides a clean method to test whether the object was constructed properly without requiring direct access to protected and private members.

Don't confuse this technique with a test of a pointer's validity. If you construct a pointer to a Vector object, you'd have to test it twice:

```
Vector *pv = new Vector(10);
if (!pv) Error("Null pointer returned by new");
if (!*pv) Error("Vector object construction failed");
```

The first if statement tests whether the *pointer* returned by new is null, in which case the program is probably out of memory. The second if statement tests whether the *object* addressed by the pointer has been properly constructed.

In order for the second `if` statement to work, the `Vector`'s `Init()` member function also needs to be revised:

```cpp
void Vector::Init(int Size)
{
  size = Size;
  delete[] pdata;
  if (size <= 0)
    pdata = 0;
  else
    pdata = new double[size];
}
```

The function sets `pdata` to 0 (null) if `size` is less than or equal to zero. The pointer is set to null also if `new` fails to allocate the requested amount of memory. No matter what causes `pdata` to become null, the user of the class can test the pointer's validity by using `operator!`, without having to access the pointer directly. This technique for testing object construction is much easier than more complicated schemes that call for aborting a constructor in case of memory allocation problems or other troubles.

With its new additions, the improved `Vector` class catches two of the most common array mistakes. The overloaded `operator!` function traps object construction errors:

```cpp
Vector v2(-10);   // ???
if (!v2) Error("Can't construct vector v2");
```

The class also guards against index range errors. The expression `i <= 10` should be `i < 10` (or `i <= 9`) in this faulty code:

```cpp
for (i = 0; i <= 10; ++i) // ???
  cout << "v2[" << i << "] == " << v2[i] << endl;
```

Error Handling

The `Vector` class is safer to use than a common array, but you might object to halting the program on detecting an error. A better solution is possible; a perfect one might not be. In the overloaded `operator[]` indexing function, for example, there are at least four ways to handle index range errors:

- Halt the program.

- Return a dummy value that represents an erroneous value, similar to the way a null pointer signifies an invalid pointer.

- Change an invalid index to a valid value.

- Handle the fault with an exception.

The first solution is simple and effective, but highly unfriendly. The second makes good sense—if, that is, you can easily define the nature of an *erroneous value*. This might be difficult to do in a perfectly general way, and the class probably would need a virtual function to supply this value for every type of object to be stored in a vector. The resulting `Vector` class would be dependent on the objects to be stored, restricting its versatility.

The fourth solution is the best, but unfortunately, few C++ compilers implement exceptions as proposed in the ANSI C++ draft-standard. Until C++ compilers catch up with the current specifications, solution number three might be the best compromise—forcing invalid indexes to a valid value. In the `operator[]` function, for example, you could check and modify `i`'s value like this:

```
if ((i < min) || (i > max))
  i = min;  // Range error
```

Any range errors cause the index to refer to the vector's first value, `min`. This simple solution also permits the operator to return an erroneous value if you store that value in the vector's first position. It's now up to the user of the class to decide whether to ignore range errors or halt the program:

```
Vector v(10);  // Construct vector object
v[0] = -1;     // Set erroneous value
int i = 100;   // ???
cout << v[i];  // Ignore error; write v[0]
if (v[i] == -1) Error("Range error");
```

The Finished Vector Class Template

The `Vector` class introduced in the preceding sections is well on its way to becoming a useful data structure. To make the class more versatile, it should be able to store values of any types, not only floating point `doubles`. There are two ways to accomplish this goal:

- Require all objects to be stored in a vector to be derived from the same base class.

- Convert `Vector` into a class template.

I prefer the second approach, but don't discount the first too quickly. Templates tend to take extra time to compile, and not all C++ compilers support them. If you are developing a class library for general distribution, templates might not be the best choice until this new feature becomes widely supported.

Classes to Templates

When designing a template, the best course usually is to write a finished version of the class, and only then, after debugging, convert the product to a general-purpose template. This is the approach I took in writing the code for this chapter. Rather than develop `Vector` as a template from the start, I wrote the class to store `double` values, making it easy to test the class before using it to store values of other kinds.

After debugging, it's relatively easy to translate `Vector` into a template. Just add a `template` preface and then follow with the class, replacing all instances of `double` with `T` (changes are in bold to make them stand out here):

```
template<class T>
class Vector {
public:
  Vector(): size(0), pdata(0) { }
  Vector(int Size): pdata(0) { Init(Size); }
  ~Vector() { delete[] pdata; }
```

```
  void Init(int Size);
  T & operator[] (int i);
  int operator! () { return !pdata; }
private:
  int size;   // Number of objects in array
  T *pdata;   // Pointer to first object
};
```

Note: The programming in this section is extracted from the disk file, VECT3.CPP, stored in the PART2 directory.

You also need to revise any member functions not written inline. Here's the operator[] function rewritten for the template:

```
template<class T>
T & Vector<T>::operator[] (int i)
{
  if (i < 0 || i >= size)
    Error("Index out of range");
  return pdata[i];
}
```

Compare this version with the original (see disk file VECT2.CPP). The only differences are the template preface, T in place of double, and Vector<T> as the class name. Similar changes are needed by member function Init:

```
template<class T>
void Vector<T>::Init(int Size)
{
  size = Size;
  delete[] pdata;
  if (size <= 0)
    pdata = 0;
  else
    pdata = new T[size];
}
```

With these modifications, the Vector class template is completely generalized, and it can be used to construct actual classes for storing objects of different kinds. Here's how to create a vector of ten integers:

```
Vector<int> v1(10);
if (!v1) Error("Can't construct vector v1");
```

Or, to store double values, use these lines:

```
Vector<double> v2(10);
if (!v2) Error("Can't construct vector v2");
```

You can store values in v1 and v2:

```
v1[0] = 123;
v2[0] = 3.14159;
```

And you can get values out using simple statements:

```
cout << v1[0];
cout << v2[0];
```

In every case, the compiler generates an appropriate class based on the template's design.

The vector.h Header

The finished Vector class template listed next is similar to the test versions listed so far, but satisfies these additional requirements:

- Indexes do not need to begin with zero.

- Inline functions return minimum and maximum index values as well as the number of elements in a vector.

- An assignment operator (=) permits a vector object to be assigned to another existing vector object.

- A copy constructor permits a vector object to be used to construct a new vector.

I could go on, adding features to the class, but in that direction lies the danger of overburdening the class with member functions that will rarely be used. For Vector to qualify as a useful fundamental data structure, it should have only the minimum number of elements required to do its job. Listing 9.1, vector.h, shows the final Vector class template. Because it's a template, from now on, I refer to the class by its full name, Vector<T>.

Note: The following listing is stored on disk in the LIB\CLASSLIB subdirectory.

Listing 9.1. vector.h.

```
#ifndef __VECTOR_H
#define __VECTOR_H    // Prevent multiple #includes

#include <stddef.h>

template<class T>
class Vector {
public:
  Vector();
  Vector(int Min, int Max);
  Vector(Vector &);
  ~Vector();
  void Init(int Min, int Max);
  int GetMin() const { return min; }
  int GetMax() const { return max; }
  int GetNElem() const { return nelem; }
  int operator! () { return !pdata; }
  void operator= (const Vector<T> &);
  T & operator[] (int i) const;
protected:
  int min;              // Minimum (base) index
  int max;              // Maximum index
  T *pdata;             // Pointer to first element
  int nelem;            // Number of elements
  size_t vectorSize;    // Size of structure in bytes
};
```

continues

Listing 9.1. continued

```cpp
// Vector default constructor
template<class T>
Vector<T>::Vector()
  : min(0), max(0), pdata(0), nelem(0), vectorSize(0)
{
}

// Vector constructor
template<class T>
void Vector<T>::Vector(int Min, int Max)
  : pdata(0) // Because Init() deletes pdata
{
  Init(Min, Max);
}

template<class T>
void Vector<T>::Init(int Min, int Max)
{
  min = Min;
  max = Max;
  nelem = max - min + 1;
  vectorSize = sizeof(T) * nelem;
  delete[] pdata;  // Delete any current array
  if ((min > max) || (nelem <= 0) || (vectorSize <= 0))
    pdata = 0;  // Object construction failed!
  else
    pdata = new T[nelem];  // Allocate memory to vector
}

// Vector copy constructor
template<class T>
Vector<T>::Vector(Vector<T> &copy)
{
  pdata = 0;      // Prevent deletion of random pdata
  *this = copy;   // Calls operator=() to perform copy
}
```

```
// Vector destructor
template<class T>
Vector<T>::~Vector()
{
  delete[] pdata;   // Note special form of delete[]
}


// Vector assignment operator (=)
template<class T>
void Vector<T>::operator= (const Vector<T> &copy)
{
  if (this == &copy) return;    // Can't copy self to self
  delete[] pdata;
  min = copy.min;
  max = copy.max;
  nelem = copy.nelem;
  vectorSize = copy.vectorSize;
  pdata = new T[nelem];
  if (pdata)
    for (int i = 0; i <= max - min; ++i)
      pdata[i] = copy.pdata[i];
}


// Vector index operator ([])
template<class T>
T & Vector<T>::operator[] (int i) const
{
  if ((i < min) || (i > max))
    i = min;  // Range error causes index to equal base
  return pdata[i - min];
}


#endif  // __VECTOR_H
```

Because the finished `Vector<T>` class template is stored completely in a header file, you must write a host program before you can compile the listing. This fact is true of most class templates.

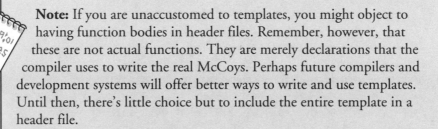

> **Note:** If you are unaccustomed to templates, you might object to having function bodies in header files. Remember, however, that these are not actual functions. They are merely declarations that the compiler uses to write the real McCoys. Perhaps future compilers and development systems will offer better ways to write and use templates. Until then, there's little choice but to include the entire template in a header file.

Another improvement to `Vector<T>` is the use of `const` member functions such as `GetMin()` and `GetMax()`. These functions do not modify any data members in `Vector<T>` objects, and making them `const` permits other statements to call the functions for `const` vector objects. A good example of this technique is a function that declares a `const` reference parameter:

```
template<class T>
void f(const Vector<T> &r)  // const reference parameter
{
  cout << "min == " << r.GetMin() << endl;
  cout << "max == " << r.GetMax() << endl;
}
```

Elsewhere in the program, statements efficiently pass `Vector<T>` objects by address to `f()`, but statements inside the function are permitted to call *only* `const` member functions for those objects. Defining a vector object and passing it to `f()` cannot modify that object:

```
Vector<int> v(1, 10);
f(v);  // Guaranteed not to modify v
```

Generally, `const` reference parameters improve performance, reduce stack use, and prevent accidental changes to objects that must not change. Using this technique can add an extra helping of reliability to most C++ programs.

> **Note:** On disk in the LIB\CLASSLIB subdirectory is a sample program, TVECTOR.CPP, that tests the Vector<T> class template. (Many sample statements in this chapter are extracted from, or are similar to, statements in the disk file.) Compile the test program with Borland C++ using these commands:
>
> ```
> bcc -c -ml tclass
> bcc -ml tvector tclass.obj secrets.lib
> ```
>
> The -c option in the first instruction compiles a module, TCLASS.CPP, for linking to the finished program. (The module, listed later in this chapter, provides a sample class for storing objects in a vector.) The -ml option selects the large memory model. You might also need to supply a directory pathname for SECRETS.LIB. (Any easier way to compile the listing is to run the automated MAKE utility as described in Appendix A.) Of course, these instructions will differ for other compilers. To run the program under MS-DOS, direct its output to a file:
>
> ```
> tvector >results.txt
> ```
>
> View the file while you read the TVECTOR.CPP test program listing on disk. The program shows many different ways to use the Vector<T> class template.

Vector Protected Data Members

Unlike common arrays, the Vector<T> class permits vectors to have nonzero base indexes. You can even use negative indexes. For example, to construct a vector of TClass objects indexed from −4 to 5, you can write

```
int low = -4, high = 5;
Vector<TClass> oVector(low, high);
```

The expression `Vector<TClass>` declares a `Vector<T>` class capable of storing `TClass` objects. As usual, follow the definition of the vector object, `oVector`, with a test of its validity:

```
if (!oVector) Error("Can't create oVector");
```

You can use the vector to store objects of the designated type, in this case, `TClass`:

```
oVector[-4] = TClass(123, 456, "A string");
oVector[ 2] = TClass(789, 012, "Another string");
```

As in the sample `Vector` classes listed earlier in this chapter, the `Vector<T>` template (see Listing 9.1) declares a pointer, `pdata`, to the type of objects to be stored:

```
T *pdata;
```

In addition to this pointer, three `int` values record the number of elements in the array and the minimum and maximum index values. Another data member, `vectorSize`, holds the size of the array in bytes. The data members are protected so that a derived class can use them, although they are not accessible from outside of the class. You could therefore change the data types of these members without affecting the use of the class.

> **Note:** An even more general template might provide a type parameter for index values rather than use `int` values for `min` and `max`. In other words, I could have written a class named `Vector<T1, T2>`, where `T1` is the type of data to be stored in the array and `T2` is the type of the indexes to be used. The resulting class is called an *associative array,* because the index values of type `T2` can be used to refer to associated objects of type `T1`. In a dictionary, for example, `T2` might be a word; `T1` a definition. A statement `definitions[word]` could return a reference to the definition of a word. This more complex class would no longer be practical, however, for use as a plain vector because it would no longer be possible to assume that index values of type `T2` are integers.

Vector Constructors and Destructor

Vector<T> has three constructors. A default constructor initializes all protected data members to default values. A second constructor requires minimum and maximum index values. You might use this constructor to create a vector of ten long integers, indexed from 10 to 19:

```
Vector<long> v1(10, 19);
if (!v1) Error("Can't create v1 vector");
```

Next is a *copy constructor,* which enables a vector object to be used to construct another vector. To copy the v1 vector to a new vector named v2, you can write

```
Vector<long> v2(v1);
```

In this statement, object v1 is used to initialize a new vector v2. The new vector starts out in life as an exact replica of v1. To copy the existing object v1 to the new object v2, the copy constructor executes these two statements:

```
pdata = 0;
*this = copy;
```

I use this technique often in copy constructors. The first line sets pdata to 0 (null). To understand why this step is necessary, you first have to study the effect of the second line, which copies an existing object (v1 in this example) to the new object being constructed (v2). The copy parameter to the left of the equals sign refers to v1. The this pointer refers to v2. A simple assignment is therefore all that's needed to copy v1 to v2.

When using this technique, however, it's vital to consider the effect on any copied pointers. In this case, copying pdata to the new object would result in two vector objects addressing the same internal array, a dangerous situation that is likely to lead to serious problems if both objects are deleted (see Figure 9.4).

The problem with double pdata pointers is easily prevented by overloading the assignment operator for the class. The operator= function (described in detail in a moment) deletes any existing array addressed by pdata, allocates a new array, then copies the arrayed elements to that memory. The resulting vectors address distinct internal arrays, and either or both vectors can be deleted safely (see Figure 9.5).

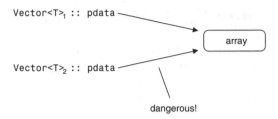

Figure 9.4. Copying one Vector<T> object to another could result in two copies of pdata addressing the same array, a dangerous condition.

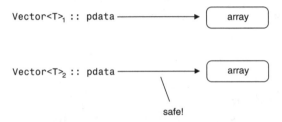

Figure 9.5. The overloaded operator= function safely copies a vector's internal array.

In many of the classes I write, I commonly include three constructors—a default constructor, one with parameters, and a copy constructor. In Vector<T>, the simple-looking default constructor makes it possible to construct arrays of vectors—in other words, a matrix with rows and columns. First, define some constants and variables:

```
const int rows = 10;
const int cols = 5;
int i, j;
```

Then, construct an array va of Vector<double> objects:

```
Vector<double> va[rows];
```

The vectors must next be initialized to hold a specified number of elements. A for loop does the trick:

```
for (i = 0; i < rows; ++i)
  va[i].Init(1, cols);
```

You now have ten Vector<double> objects stored in the va array. These are the rows. Each vector object can store five double values (the columns). Assign values to individual matrix elements using two index operators:

```
for (i = 0; i < rows; ++i)
  for (j = 1; j <= cols; ++j)
    va[i][j] = 3.14159 * (i + j);
```

Display the matrix in a table using these nested for loops:

```
for (i = 0; i < rows; ++i) {
  cout << endl;
  for (j = 1; j <= cols; ++j)
    cout << setprecision(12) << setw(14) << va[i][j];
}
```

Even better, you can construct a *vector* of vectors. Start with a typedef alias for a class named Vector<double>:

```
typedef Vector<double> Columns;
```

Then, construct the matrix va as a Vector<Columns> class:

```
Vector<Columns> va(0, rows - 1);
```

My compiler needs the Columns alias for Vector<double>, but you might also be able to construct the matrix directly. The following does not compile on my system, though it should be equivalent to the preceding statements:

```
Vector<Vector<double>> va(0, rows - 1);  // ???
```

Vector Initialization

The Vector<T> class's Init() member function is straightforward. Because a vector might be reinitialized after construction, Init() deletes any array addressed by pdata. Note the special form of delete[] used in the statement

```
delete[] pdata;
```

The brackets ensure that a destructor is called if the addressed items are class objects. As in earlier Vector class samples in this chapter, Init() performs no checks on memory allocations, leaving that job to users of the class. Always call the overloaded operator! function to test whether vectors are properly constructed.

Vector Inline Member Functions

Vector<T> has several inline member functions and no virtual members (see Listing 9.1). These are key elements of a well written fundamental data structure. Because of its low-level nature, Vector<T> objects might be responsible for more than a fair share of a program's performance, and it is important not to burden users of the class with having to make function calls for simple operations.

Inline member functions in Vector<T> return the values of the protected min, max, and nelem data members. The vectorSize member has no similar inline function because this value holds the number of bytes in the memory block addressed by pdata, a fact that users of the class do not need to know. (If they had this information, it might be possible to write code that depends too heavily on a Vector<T>'s internal workings, thus making future modifications more difficult.)

Listing 9.2 shows the WriteAll() function template from the disk file TVECTOR.CPP, located in the LIB\CLASSLIB subdirectory.

Listing 9.2. (from TVECTOR.CPP).

```
template<class T>
void WriteAll(const Vector<T> &a)
{
  int i;
  cout << "Vector contents (" << a.GetNElem() << " items):\n";
  for (i = a.GetMin(); i <= a.GetMax(); ++i)
    cout
      << " vector["
      << setfill(' ')
      << setw(2)
      << setiosflags(ios::showpos)
      << i
      << resetiosflags(ios::showpos)
      << "] == "
      << a[i]
      << endl;
}
```

The function requires a reference to a Vector<T> object—in other words, any object of a class constructed from the Vector<T> template. Inside the function, a for loop uses the GetMin() and GetMax() inline functions to access all elements in the vector passed to WriteAll(). Because this is a function template, the compiler creates an actual WriteAll() function for every Vector<T> object passed as an argument.

To use WriteAll(), first construct a vector:

```
Vector<double> dVector(low, high);
if (!dVector) Error("Can't create dVector");
```

Then, pass the object to WriteAll() to display the vector's contents:

```
for (i = low; i <= high; ++i)
  dVector[i] = i * 3.14159;
WriteAll(dVector);
```

Vector Overloaded Operators

Two of Vector<T>'s three overloaded operators should be familiar. The class provides operator! for validating constructed objects. Of course, operator[] provides indexing capabilities. Because this is the *only* method provided for accessing a vector's contents, other unsafe access paths—using pointer arithmetic, for example—are prohibited.

The overloaded assignment operator is new. It provides a clean way to copy one Vector<T> object to another *existing* vector. For example, create a vector of four floats, and fill it with values:

```
Vector<float> original(1, 4);
if (!original) Error("Can't create original vector");
for (int i = 1; i <= 4; ++i)
  original[i] = i * 3.14159;
```

Next, create another float vector of any size:

```
Vector<float> copy(10, 20);
if (!copy) Error("Can't create copy vector");
```

To copy the `original` vector to the `copy`, use an assignment statement:

```
copy = original;
if (!copy) Error("Assignment failed");
```

Don't try this with common arrays! The overloaded `operator=` makes this statement possible for type-compatible `Vector<T>` objects. Any original data stored in `copy` is destroyed, and the new `copy` vector is the same size as the `original`.

As I mentioned before, `Vector<T>`'s copy constructor uses the overloaded `operator=` function. In the constructor, this statement:

```
*this = copy;
```

calls `operator=` to copy the vector referenced by the `copy` parameter to `*this`.

Vector Storage Requirements

One of my goals in designing `Vector<T>` was to create a general class that can store any kind of objects and then access those objects at random. Despite the generality of templates, however, class objects and pointers to be stored in vectors still require special handling—a fact that tends to be true of most templates designed as general-purpose containers.

Vectors of Class Objects

Listing 9.3, tclass.h, is a sample class that you can use as a starting place to design your own classes for storing objects in data structures like `Vector<T>`. The class details the basic requirements of objects that can be stored in vectors.

Note: The tclass.h file is located on disk in the LIB\CLASSLIB directory.

Listing 9.3. tclass.h.

```
#ifndef _ _TCLASS_H
#define _ _TCLASS_H    // Prevent multiple #includes

class TClass {
  friend ostream & operator<< (ostream &, TClass &);
  friend int operator< (TClass &, TClass &);
  friend int operator==(const TClass &, const TClass &);
  friend int operator!=(const TClass &, const TClass &);
public:
  TClass();
  TClass(int X, int Y, const char *S);
  TClass(const TClass &);
  ~TClass();
  TClass & operator= (const TClass &);
private:
  int x, y;  // Represents common data
  char *s;   // Represents pointer-addressed data
};

#endif  // _ _TCLASS_H
```

The class implementation is stored on disk in file TCLASS.CPP. Most of the programming is simplistic, so I won't list all of it here.

Three private data members represent values that might be stored by a typical class. There are two integers and one pointer, which requires careful handling, as pointers typically do. I overloaded the output stream operator, but I did not provide for input. The overloaded operator< function permits vectors of TClass objects to be sorted. For demonstration purposes, the operator compares only the x integer values in two TClass objects to determine which object is less.

The class's public section declares a default constructor, a constructor with parameters, and a copy constructor. A destructor deletes any string addressed by the char pointer, s. The overloaded operator= function permits a TClass object to be assigned to a compatible object and also carries out the copy constructor's duties.

Create a vector of `TClass` objects like this:

```
Vector<TClass> objects(1, 3);
if (!objects) Error("Can't create objects");
```

Then, assign newly constructed objects to the vector, using index expressions:

```
objects[1] = TClass(1, 2, "aaa");
objects[2] = TClass(3, 4, "bbb");
objects[3] = TClass(5, 6, "ccc");
```

When `objects` goes out of scope, C++ calls the `TClass` destructor for every object in the vector, properly disposing of any strings or other allocated memory.

Indirect Storage

`Vector<T>` can handle pointers, but some of the ground rules are a bit different. To construct a vector of pointers, for example, name the class `Vector<T *>`. Here's how to construct a vector of pointers to `double` values:

```
Vector<double *> pVector(1, 10);
if (!pVector) Error("Can't create pVector");
```

The pointers in the vector are uninitialized, so the next step is to call `new` for each one:

```
for (i = low; i <= high; ++i)
  pVector[i] = new double;
```

You can then store a value in the vector using an index expression:

```
*pVector[1] = 3.14159;
```

That stores the value 3.14159 in the `double` object addressed by the pointer stored in `pVector[1]`. You must dereference this pointer, or the compiler won't permit the assignment—type checking is in full force, helping to prevent disasterous errors. You also must dereference pointers in any output statements:

```
cout << "value == " << *pVector[1];
```

If you don't dereference pVector, the output statement displays the *address* of the first element in the vector:

```
cout << "address == " << pVector[1];
```

Unlike common arrays, with Vector<T> objects, it's always clear whether a statement is working with an address value or with the object stored at that address.

Before the vector goes out of scope, be sure to delete its addressed objects:

```
for (i = low; i <= high; ++i)
  delete pVector[i];
```

> **Note:** To have the vector delete its objects automatically, you could create an indirect vector class template, perhaps named IVector<T *>. This brings up the subject of object ownership. Which object should delete owned objects: The vector that contains them, or the program that constructed the objects? In Vector<T>, any pointers are your responsibility to delete, but there's no single correct answer to this question.

You can also define a pointer to a Vector<T> object:

```
Vector<double> *pa;
```

Pointer pa can address a Vector<T> object that can store double values. Construct the vector with new, and assign the object's address to pa.

```
pa = new Vector<double>(1, 10);
```

Of course, you can perform the preceding two steps with one statement:

```
Vector<double> *pa = new Vector<double>(1, 10);
```

Two tests are now required to check whether the vector has been properly constructed. First, test whether new returned null:

```
if (!pa) Error("Memory allocation failed");
```

Then, check that the addressed vector is ready for use:

```
if (!*pa) Error("Object construction failed");
```

That statement calls the overloaded operator! function in the Vector<double> class. The prior statement tests the value of pointer pa directly.

Because pa is a pointer to a vector, you can't use it as an array. This won't compile:

```
pa[5] = 3.14159;  // ???
```

Instead, you must dereference the pointer:

```
(*pa)[5] = 3.14159;
```

Parentheses are required because the index operator has a higher precedence than the pointer dereference operator (*). Vectors and pointers do not share the same direct relationship as do common arrays and pointers.

If dereferencing pointers turns you off, define an alias as a reference to the Vector<double> object addressed by pa:

```
Vector<double> &ref = *pa;
```

Now, you can use the reference in familiar indexing expressions:

```
ref[5] = 3.14159;
```

That's exactly equivalent to

```
(*pa)[5] = 3.14159;
```

Don't forget to delete the vector object when finished:

```
delete pa;
```

Sorted Vector Template

Sorting arrays of values is one of the most common chores that programmers do. To provide sortable vectors, Listing 9.4, svector.h, derives a new class template from Vector<T>, demonstrating how one template can be derived from another. As in the vector.h file, the entire template is stored in the header file.

Note: The svector.h file is located on disk in the LIB\CLASSLIB directory.

Listing 9.4. svector.h.

```
#ifndef __SVECTOR_H
#define __SVECTOR_H    // Prevent multiple #includes

#include "vector.h"

template<class T>
class SVector: public Vector<T> {
public:
  SVector(int Min, int Max)
    : Vector<T>(Min, Max) { }
  SVector(SVector<T> &v)
    : Vector<T>(v) { }
  ~SVector() { }
  void Sort();
private:
  void QuickSort(int left, int right);
};

// Sort items in array using QuickSort algorithm
// Note: array is zero based at this level!
template<class T>
void SVector<T>::QuickSort(int left, int right)
{
  int i = left;
  int j = right;
  T test = pdata[(left + right) / 2];
  T swap;

  do {
    while (pdata[i] < test) i++;
    while (test < pdata[j]) j--;
```

continues

Listing 9.4. continued

```
    if (i <= j) {
       swap = pdata[i];
       pdata[i] = pdata[j];
       pdata[j] = swap;
       i++;
       j--;
     }
   } while (i <= j);
   if (left < j) QuickSort(left, j);
   if (i < right) QuickSort(i, right);
}

// Call QuickSort recursive function
// Note: array is zero based at this level!
template<class T>
void SVector<T>::Sort()
{
   if (nelem > 1) QuickSort(0, nelem - 1);
}

#endif  // __SVECTOR_H
```

The derived SVector<T> class template adds a public sort() member function and a private QuickSort() function that performs the actual sorting. The public function calls the private one, permitting the sorting algorithm to be changed easily without affecting programs that use the class—always a praiseworthy goal, but not always attainable. In this case, I used a recursive QuickSort algorithm. You might want to replace the private function with an optimized version if it is supplied with your development system.

Listing 9.5, SVECTOR.CPP, demonstrates how to use the SVector<T> class template.

Note: SVECTOR.CPP uses a module, MEMUSE, listed and explained in the next chapter. The module displays memory-use information. To compile SVECTOR.CPP with Borland C++, enter the following commands (see Appendix A for detailed compilation instructions):

```
bcc -c -ml tclass
bcc -ml svector tclass.obj secrets.lib
```

Listing 9.5. SVECTOR.CPP.

```cpp
#include <iostream.h>
#include <iomanip.h>
#include <stdlib.h>
#include <stddef.h>
#include <memuse.h>
#include "tclass.h"
#include "svector.h"

void SortVector();

int main()
{
  HeapReport("Initial memory use");
  SortVector();
  HeapReport("Final memory use");
  return 0;
}

// Display error message and halt program
void Error(const char *message)
{
  cout << "\nError: " << message << endl;
  exit(1);
}
```

continues

Listing 9.5. continued

```cpp
// Display vector contents
template<class T>
void WriteAll(SVector<T> &a)
{
  int i;
  cout << "Vector contents (" << a.GetNElem() << " items):\n";
  for (i = a.GetMin(); i <= a.GetMax(); ++i)
    cout
      << " vector["
      << setfill(' ')
      << setw(2)
      << setiosflags(ios::showpos)
      << i
      << resetiosflags(ios::showpos)
      << "] == "
      << a[i]
      << endl;
}

// Test function
void SortVector()
{
  int low = 1, high = 8;
  SVector<double> dVector(low, high);
  if (!dVector) Error("Can't create dVector");
  dVector[1] = 12.56636;
  dVector[2] = 18.84954;
  dVector[3] = 28.27431;
  dVector[4] = 6.28318;
  dVector[5] = 9.42477;
  dVector[6] = 21.99113;
  dVector[7] = 25.13272;
  dVector[8] = 3.14159;
  cout << "Before sorting:";
  WriteAll(dVector);
  dVector.Sort();
  cout << "After sorting:";
  WriteAll(dVector);
}
```

The sample program shows how to use the SVector<T> class template. To sort a vector of double values, construct the object as usual:

```
SVector<double> dVector(1, 8);
if (!dVector) Error("Can't create dVector");
```

Then, fill it with values:

```
dVector[1] = 12.56636;
dVector[2] = 18.84954;
// ... etc.
```

To sort, call the Sort() member function:

```
dVector.Sort();
```

Final Words

I saved the subject of string vectors for these parting words. If you attempt to store char * strings in a Vector<T> object, you'll discover no problems—until that is, you attempt to sort the strings.

Sorting strings is complicated by the fact that plain, null-terminated, C-style character strings can't be compared using greater-than and less-than operators. If c1 and c2 are pointers of type char *, this expression:

```
(c1 < c2)   // ???
```

is true if the *pointer value* of c1 is less than c2—in other words, if the string located at c1 is at a lower address than the string at c2. Despite appearances, the statement does not compare the strings addressed by the pointers.

There are two possible solutions to this common dilemma. One, you can write another version of the Vector<T> class template that can compare strings (perhaps by calling a library function). Or, you can create a String class that overloads the comparison operators. Among other benefits, a String class permits objects of the class to be compared easily, and it exercises good control over the memory that a string occupies. As the next chapter illustrates, however, writing the ideal String class is no simple job.

Constructing a String Class

M ost C++ development systems come with a String class ready to go. Should you use the one that's supplied with your compiler? Should you write your own class? Or, should you continue to use char pointers to null-terminated strings—also called *C-style strings*—until the ANSI C++ draft-standard committee publishes a standard String class?

These are perplexing questions to which there are few clear answers. You probably should be wary of using existing String classes, as their interfaces might change when ANSI C++ becomes a reality sometime in the mid 1990s. Until then, however, it would be a shame not to take advantage of the benefits that a String class can provide. But even if you have no desire to write your own String class, it's worth examining the techniques that have emerged from the industry-wide crusade to define the ultimate String.

In this chapter, you follow the step-by-step construction of a String class. Along the way, you meet several methods and C++ programming tips that apply generally to the development of many useful classes.

Strings as Vectors

Templates are well-suited for creating general-purpose data structures, but not all classes make good templates. String classes, for example, are probably too specific in nature to be easily distilled into template form. Likewise, it's difficult to design a String class using another template for a base.

For instance, because character strings are just arrays of char values, it might seem logical to base a String class on the Vector<T> class template from Chapter 9, "Vectoring in on Arrays." In practice, however, this doesn't turn out to be the best solution. To see the problem, try to build a vector-based string class, declared as

```
class String: public Vector<char> {
  ...
};
```

The String class inherits a base class, Vector<char>, generated from the Vector<T> template. Of course, the new class needs one or two constructors, and perhaps, an output stream function. Adding these elements, the class now looks like this:

```
class String: public Vector<char> {
  friend ostream & operator<< (ostream &os, String &s);
public:
```

```
String()
  : Vector<char>() { }
String(int Max)
  : Vector<char>(0, Max) { }
};
```

The default constructor simply defaults to the base class constructor. The alternate constructor creates a zero-based vector of char, indexed from 0 to Max. The friend operator<< function writes a String object to an output stream. You might implement the operator using code such as this:

```
ostream & operator<< (ostream &os, String &s)
{
  for (int i = 0; s[i]; ++i)
    cout << s[i];
  return os;
}
```

If there was a smoke detector for bad programming, that for loop should cause the buzzer to scream its fool head off. Using a for loop to write each character of a string isn't going to win any performance awards. Worse, the loop expects the string to be terminated with a null, a requirement the class apparently does nothing to ensure. But let's ignore these problems for now and complete the example. You can construct a String object of a specified length:

```
String s(80);
```

But you now face the problem of how to get characters into the object. One solution is to insert them individually using index expressions:

```
s[0] = 'C';
s[1] = '+';
s[2] - '+';
s[3] = '\0';
```

That's mighty inconvenient, and if you forget to add the null terminator, the results are unpredictable. A good String class would permit objects to be constructed more safely from literal strings:

```
String s("A literal string");
```

The class also should provide for assignment statements:

```
s = "Another string";
```

And it should be possible to compare strings using common logical expressions:

```
String s1, s2;
...
if (s1 == s2) cout << "Strings are equal";
else if (s1 < s2) cout << "String s1 is less than s2";
else if (s1 > s2) cout << "String s1 is greater than s2";
```

It would be possible to expand the vector-string class to perform these operations, but like the overloaded output stream operator, each low-level operation would need to use indexing expressions to access string characters one at a time. The end result would be highly inefficient and probably unusable. Basing a String class on a fundamental data structure such as Vector<T> seems like a clean idea, but comes out dirty in the wash.

One reason this is so is because C++ already "knows" how to work with literal strings. C++ also comes stocked with a rich library of string functions, inherited from C and designed to operate on char pointers to null-terminated strings. Basing the String class on Vector<char> creates a new data type that can't easily take advantage of these existing capabilities. Rather than create a totally new String, we need a better solution, one that wraps existing string features into the class.

A String Wrapper Class

Some of the world's best known discoveries are not new at all. They're just old objects in new wrappers. An automobile, for instance, is just a carriage with an internal combustion engine in place of a horse. A compact disc is just a phonograph record played with a needle of light.

A String class might be reinvented in a similar way by wrapping existing C-style string capabilities into the class. The resulting old-but-new class offers all the usual advantages of data hiding, memory management, automatic construction and destruction, and so on. Inside the class, however, strings are addressed by char pointers to familiar, C-style, null-terminated, arrays of char (see Figure 10.1). If you please, you can even use standard string functions on String objects.

```
class String {
public:
    // Constructors, destructor
    // and other class members
private:
    char *sp; ──────────────────▶  "Null-terminated string"
};
```

Figure 10.1. Internally, a string class might address a familiar C-style string.

This isn't the only workable design for a `String` class, but it's one of the easiest to implement, and it permits the class to use standard string functions for its internal operations. In most development systems, these functions are highly optimized, so it makes sense to use them.

Data Members

Our `String` class needs at least one data member—a `char` pointer to address the string's characters. It might also include a value representing the string's length. These members can be private to the class:

```
class String {
  ...
private:
  int len;    // Number of characters in string
  char *sp;   // Pointer to null-terminated string
};
```

Note: The programming in this and the next several sections is extracted from the disk file, STRING.CPP, located in the PART2 directory.

Most `String` classes have at least these two data members. The `char` pointer `sp` is either null or it addresses a memory block of at least one byte. The integer `len` indicates the number of significant characters in the string. If `sp` is null, `len` is undefined. The `len` value can be initialized by calling the standard `strlen()` library function, which counts characters up to the string's terminating null.

Subsequent references to len do not require repeating this operation, thus improving performance if a string's length is needed often. Maintaining the length value, however, takes careful programming.

To this basic design, you might want to add two more data members—a value representing the string's original size in bytes, and another value to hold an error code. Now the class looks like this:

```
class String {
  ...
private:
  int err;    // Current error code
  int size;   // Size of memory block in bytes
  int len;    // Number of characters in string
  char *sp;   // Pointer to null-terminated string
};
```

The size data member adds safety to the class by giving member functions the information they need to prevent access beyond the string's allotted memory. A concatenation operator that joins two strings, for example, might use this value to prevent overwriting a string's end. (Or, the operator could reallocate a new string if the string is in danger of growing too large.)

Error Control

Rather than use an int value to hold the current error code, it's a good idea to provide a public enumerated type in the class that defines symbols for each possible error condition. Making that change, the class now appears as

```
class String {
public:
  enum StringErr {
    no_error = 0,    // No error detected
    out_of_memory,   // Not enough memory for operation
    out_of_range     // String index out of range
  };
private:
  StringErr err;    // Current error code
  ...
};
```

You can use a similar technique with any class. You might also assign literal values to the out_of_memory and _out_of_range symbols, and you might consider packing multiple error codes into a bit field, but these options are excessively complicated to handle only a small number of error conditions.

Even one missed error is a bee in the program's bonnet, so we also need a function to deal with problems. My preferred solution is to use a virtual member function:

```
class String {
public:
  virtual StringErr Error(StringErr e = no_error);
  ...
};
```

The function, Error(), returns a StringErr value. It also requires a like argument, which if unspecified, is given the default value no_error. Here's a possible implementation for Error():

```
String::StringErr String::Error(StringErr e)
{
  StringErr copy = err;   // Copy current error code
  err = e;                // Assign e to error code
  return copy;            // Return previous error code
}
```

The function's declaration line might seem confusing. The first part, String::StringErr is the function's return type—it must be qualified with the class name and scope resolution operator (String::) because StringErr is defined inside the String class. The function's qualified name, String::Error, comes next, followed by the StringErr e parameter. This reference to StringErr does not require qualification because, by this time, the compiler is aware that it is compiling a String function.

The Error() function returns the current error code, and it has the intentional side effect of resetting the class's internal err data member to no_error. Because of these actions, this statement:

```
String::StringErr myErrCode = s.Error();
```

sets myErrCode to the current error value in a String object, s, and also resets that internal code to no_error. This statement passes out_of_memory to Error():

```
s.Error(String::out_of_memory);
```

Error() is made virtual for easy trapping of error conditions—an especially useful debugging technique. To use the class this way, first define a symbol named DEBUG:

```
#define DEBUG
```

Or, you can use a compiler switch to define the symbol. Derive a new class from String, replacing the inherited Error() function:

```
class DerivedString: public String {
public:
  virtual StringErr Error(StringErr e = no_error);
  ...
};
```

Implement the replaced function to halt the program if any errors are received, but to call the base class function if DEBUG is not defined:

```
String::StringErr DerivedString::Error(StringErr e)
{
#ifdef DEBUG
  if (e != String::no_error) {
    cout << "Error code #" << e << endl;
    cout << "Previous error #" << String::Error() << endl;
    exit(-1);  // Halt program
  }
#endif
  return String::Error(e);  // Call base-class function
}
```

Because Error() is virtual, simply replacing it in a derived class redirects *all* errors to the new function, even those that occur inside the original String class. After debugging, simply undefine or delete the DEBUG symbol.

Constructors and Destructors

Constructors define the methods that programs can use to construct objects of a class. Destructors, of course, define how objects are destroyed.

Because our developing String class has data members such as len and size, and also a pointer, sp, the class makes a good "typical case" for examining object construction and destruction. In general terms, most classes with any meat on their bones require at least three constructors:

- A *default constructor* to handle initializations of objects in arrays or for creating objects in advance of their use.

- An *alternate constructor* with parameters that shape the object according to various needs.

- A *copy constructor* to initialize new objects from existing ones.

This is not a comprehensive list. Other constructors might also be needed, but let's start with these common ones. The choices you have to make when implementing these basic kinds of constructors largely determine how programs use objects of the class, so it's important to consider their effects carefully.

Default Constructor

A default constructor's official duty is to assign default values to data members of class objects. This process, however, is often a precursor for other initializations that follow. A default constructor often creates an embryonic object that is just barely viable, but without the faculties that bring it fully to life:

```
String s1;  // Construct embryonic string
```

A default constructor is, of course, just the class name with no parameters. Here's String with a default constructor:

```
class String {
public:
  String();  // Default constructor
  ...
}
```

If needed, C++ can generate default public constructors, but only if the class has no other constructors. Most classes have more than one constructor, so most need a default model as shown here. This rule is vital especially when the class has pointer members, which you must set to known values *for all possible objects*. Neglecting this rule might lead to the deletion of an uninitialized pointer—a disastrous situation that is sure to cause serious malfunctions.

Default constructors are typically easy to write. Here's the implementation for `String`'s default constructor:

```
String::String()
  : err(no_error), size(0), len(0), sp(0)
{
}
```

The constructor assigns default values to all data members, usually zero for numeric values and pointers. The body of the constructor has no actions to perform and is typically blank. (You might also define an inline constructor this way directly in the class.)

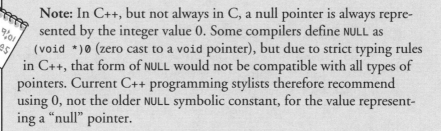

> **Note:** In C++, but not always in C, a null pointer is always represented by the integer value 0. Some compilers define NULL as `(void *)0` (zero cast to a void pointer), but due to strict typing rules in C++, that form of NULL would not be compatible with all types of pointers. Current C++ programming stylists therefore recommend using 0, not the older NULL symbolic constant, for the value representing a "null" pointer.

Given these values, all class member functions must do something reasonable for the embryonic object. For example, before using the `sp` pointer, a member function should test its value:

```
if (sp) cout << sp;
```

This rightly brings up the question of efficiency, and some programmers prefer to write classes that guarantee the validity of all internal pointers. You might, for example, rewrite the default `String` constructor to allocate a null string (a zero-length string) of a preset size:

```
String::String()
{
  len = 80;
  size = 81;
  sp = new char[size];
```

```
if (sp) {
  *sp = '\0';  // Set string's first byte to null character
  Error(no_error);
} else
  Error(out_of_memory);
}
```

With this approach, every construction of a String object either succeeds, or the object is considered unusable. It is still necessary, however, to consider what happens if memory can't be allocated to the object—during a later concatenation of two strings, for example. Personally, I prefer the simpler default construction tactic of setting all pointers to null (0).

Destructor

To destroy most objects sensibly, simply delete any memory assigned to pointer members. Declare String's destructor as

```
class String {
public:
  ~String();
  ...
}
```

Then, implement the destructor like this:

```
String::~String()
{
  delete sp;
}
```

Or, it's probably just as well in this case to declare and implement the destructor inline:

```
class String {
public:
  ~String() { delete sp; }
  ...
}
```

C++ permits deleting null pointers, so it's not necessary to test the value of sp before deleting any memory allocated to the pointer. The following statement works, but the if statement isn't required:

```
if (sp) delete sp;  // Okay, but not required
```

That might, however, eliminate a function call if your version of `delete` is not defined inline.

In complex classes with many pointers, it's often useful to have a destructor call a member function, perhaps named `Destroy()`:

```
String::~String()
{
  Destroy();
}
```

Note: The `String` class on disk in file `STRING.CPP` does not include the `Destroy()` function suggested here as an optional technique.

The `Destroy()` function takes care of deleting objects sensibly, but it also should set any pointers to null:

```
void String::Destroy()
{
  delete sp;      // Delete any memory addressed by sp
  sp = 0;         // Set sp to null
}
```

`Destroy()` is useful for destroying an object's contents without having to throw the entire object away:

```
String *s;      // Define a String object pointer
s = new String; // Allocate object
...             // Use the object
s->Destroy();   // Destroy object; s is still valid
```

Calling `Destroy()` causes the object addressed by s to return to its default, embryonic state. In other words, destroying the object should be the same as constructing one with a default constructor—the object can still be used to hold new information. The same is not true if you delete the pointer:

```
delete s;       // Destroy object; s is no longer valid!
```

After this, s no longer addresses a valid object. Before reusing s, you must reconstruct a String object with new and assign its address to s. Never, ever, use a pointer after it has been deleted.

Another important consideration when designing destructors is whether to make them virtual. Programmers who do that automatically might declare String like this:

```
class String {
public:
  virtual ~String();  // ???
  ...
}
```

The virtual destructor might be unnecessary. In deciding whether to make a destructor virtual, ask yourself these questions:

- Will you derive new classes from the class?
- Will those derived classes add new data members that require deletion?
- Will you use base-class pointers to address derived-class objects?

Answering these questions correctly may require the foresight of a financial wizard, but strictly speaking, destructors must be virtual only if all three conditions are affirmative. When in doubt, hedge your bet and make the destructor virtual, but at least consider the alternatives.

Don't attempt, however, to make the destructor inline and virtual at the same time:

```
class String {
public:
  virtual ~String() { delete sp; }  // ???
  ...
}
```

The compiler accepts *virtual inline definitions,* but like the oxymoron "thunderous silence," the term contradicts itself. Virtual functions can't be inline because, by definition, calls to any virtual method, whether to a member function or destructor, are made indirectly. The compiler must therefore convert a virtual inline function into a subroutine that has an address. Even so, it is occasionally convenient to define simple virtual inline functions rather than implement them separately. Just be aware that you gain no performance benefits—the only advantages are a little less typing and a slightly more compact source code file.

Alternate Constructor

If a default constructor is a hammer, an alternate constructor is a crescent wrench—a refined tool for constructing objects initialized using values of specific data types. Classes might have one or more alternate constructors, but beware of the common tendency to declare too many alternate constructors in an attempt to cover every possible angle.

To decide what sorts of alternate constructors a class needs, consider the ways in which programs will use the class. In other words, apply top-down programming to the design. Sometimes the choices are obvious. It should be possible, for example, to construct String objects from literal strings:

```
String literalString("To be or not to be");
```

To handle the construction of literalString, the String class needs a constructor that can accept a const char pointer:

```
class String {
public:
  String(const char *cs);  // Alternate constructor
  ...
}
```

The constructor also permits objects to be constructed using char pointer variables.

```
const char *lyricalString = "We all live in a Yellow Submarine";
String line(lyricalString);
```

The pointer argument can be const as it is here, but it doesn't have to be. You can always assign a non-const pointer to a const pointer parameter of the same base type. It would be a mistake, however, to declare the constructor using a non-const parameter:

```
class String {
public:
  String(char *cs);  // ???
  ...
}
```

That constructor is, in effect, stating its right to alter a string passed as an argument—a bad idea, tantamount to assigning an integer to a variable and having the original value incremented. Besides, if the constructor parameter is not const, then only variable strings—not literals or const char pointers—could be used to construct String objects.

Listing 10.1 shows the implementation for the String class alternate constructor.

Listing 10.1. STRING.CPP (alternate constructor).

```
// Construct string object from a C-style string
String::String(const char *cs)
  : err(no_error)
{
  if (cs == 0) {
    sp = 0;
    size = len = 0;
  } else {
    len = strlen(cs);
    size = len + 1;
    sp = new char[size];
    if (sp)
      strcpy(sp, cs);
    else
      Error(out_of_memory);
  }
}
```

The constructor zeros all data members if parameter cs is null; otherwise, it sets len to the length of the string addressed by cs. It then sets size to len + 1, allowing one byte for the string's null terminator. If new can allocate a memory block of this size, the constructor calls strcpy() to copy the characters to the object. Any allocation errors set the internal err value to out_of_memory.

Because the constructor calls the string functions `strlen()` and `strcpy()`, the class module must include the standard string.h header. This is the first example of how the `String` class uses some of the functions from the standard library.

The listing also demonstrates an important principle in object construction. The constructor *copies* the information received in parameter `cs`. It would be a grievous error to assign the pointer directly to `sp`:

```
sp = cp;  // ???
```

In fact, the compiler won't permit this statement because `cp` is `const`, and `sp` is not. This is another good reason always to declare unchanging parameters `const`. By doing that, the compiler helps detect dangerous pointer assignments that in this case would cause `sp` and `cp` to address the same memory block—a bug that will cause serious harm if that memory is deleted twice or used in other careless ways.

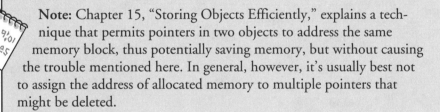

> **Note:** Chapter 15, "Storing Objects Efficiently," explains a technique that permits pointers in two objects to address the same memory block, thus potentially saving memory, but without causing the trouble mentioned here. In general, however, it's usually best not to assign the address of allocated memory to multiple pointers that might be deleted.

Copy Constructor

The third most common constructor is a *copy constructor,* declared in the `String` class as

```
class String {
public:
  String(const String &copy);
  ...
}
```

The parameter should be const to prevent the constructor from modifying an object that is used to initialize a new String instance. To implement String's copy constructor, use the technique explained in Chapter 9:

```
String::String(const String &copy)
  : err(no_error), sp(0)
{
  *this = copy;  // Dangerous unless assignment operator defined!
}
```

When using this technique, never fail to initialize any pointers to null as done here for sp. The assignment statement transfers the contents of the referenced parameter (copy) to the new String object under construction. In the presence of pointers, however, this is dangerous if the assignment operator is not overloaded. In that case, C++ copies object data fields en masse, thus duplicating any pointers in the objects. The aliased pointers might cause allocated memory to be deleted multiple times, and they can lead to other troubles as well. (See "Operators" later in this chapter for String's assignment operator.)

Naming the constructor's reference parameter copy makes it clear which is the new object being constructed and which is the copy (that is, the source object). The constructor initializes pointer sp to null so the overloaded assignment operator can safely delete any memory allocated to sp.

These observations lead to three general rules that you can use in writing any copy constructor:

- Set any pointer members to null.

- Assign the constructor's referenced parameter to *this.

- If the class declares any pointers, overload the assignment operator to prevent copied pointers from addressing the same memory block.

Other Constructors

When designing general-purpose classes, it's easy to imagine all sorts of ways to construct class objects. We might, for example, want to create strings of a certain length, fill strings with designated characters, create string representations of integer and floating point values, form multibyte-character strings, and so on.

At such times, it's usually wise to put on the brakes and take a hard look at the original goals for the class. In the case of the String class, the aim is to wrap null-terminated strings into a class so we can take advantage of object-oriented programming techniques but use time-tested string library functions. It's probably a good idea to have constructors for creating strings of a certain length, and perhaps, to fill strings with designated characters. Other constructors would just be extra trimming.

Here are the final two constructors:

```
class String {
public:
  String(int n);
  String(char c, int n = 1);
  ...
}
```

The first constructor creates a zero-length string capable of holding n characters. The second constructor creates a string of n characters equal to c. This constructor's length defaults to 1.

Using these constructors, you can define a blank 80-character string by specifying an integer value in parentheses:

```
String s(80);
```

This is *not* the same as the following incorrect definition:

```
String s[80];   // ???
```

That creates an array of 80 String objects. The former statement creates a zero-length string capable of holding 80 characters.

To fill a String object with designated characters, construct the object by using the second alternate constructor:

```
String s1('@');        // String of one @ character
String s2('-', 40);    // String of 40 dashes
String s3(' ', 80);    // String of 80 blanks
```

Listing 10.2 shows the implementations for the two constructors that handle these kinds of objects. The programming is similar in both cases, but a close examination reveals subtle differences. For example, the first constructor creates a null string of a specified length, so it always sets len to zero. The second constructor sets len to the number of characters in a filled string of a specified length.

Listing 10.2. STRING.CPP (alternate constructors).

```cpp
// Construct null string of n characters
String::String(int n)
{
  len = 0;
  if (n < 0) {
    size = 0;
    sp = 0;
    Error(out_of_range);
  } else {
    size = n + 1;
    sp = new char[size];
    if (sp) {
      *sp = '\0';   // Insert null terminator
      Error(no_error);
    } else
      Error(out_of_memory);
  }
}


// Construct filled string of n characters
String::String(char c, int n)
{
  if (n < 0) {
    size = len = 0;
    sp = 0;
    Error(out_of_range);
  } else {
    len = n;
    size = len + 1;
    sp = new char[size];
    if (sp)  {
```

continues

Listing 10.2. continued

```
        if (len > 0)
          memset(sp, c, len);   // Fill string
        sp[len] = '\0';         // Insert null terminator
        Error(no_error);
      } else
        Error(out_of_memory);
    }
}
```

Despite their differences, the two constructors in Listing 10.2 seem to share many of the same statements. Look back a few pages to the constructor in Listing 10.1. That constructor also duplicates many of the statements listed here.

These observations raise a difficult question. To rid the constructors of their duplicated statements, would it be better to have the constructors call a general-purpose initializing function? You might declare the function like this:

```
class String {
protected:
  void Init(int n);
  ...
}
```

The idea is to have Init() allocate n bytes of memory and to prepare other class data members accordingly. Rather than initialize class objects directly, constructors would call Init() to perform most of the required initializations. Init() is potentially dangerous to use, so it's probably best to make the function a protected class member. That way, only other class members in String or in a derived class (or a friend) can call Init(). You could also make Init() private to the class, but then, *only* String's member functions and friends would be able to call the function.

I bring up the subject of a general-purpose initializing function only as food for thought. Such functions are occasionally useful, but a small amount of duplication among class constructors is not necessarily bad. An Init() member function might reduce this duplication, but not without cost in extra time spent programming and debugging the initializer.

If you're looking for an afternoon project, try to implement Init() to rid the String class constructors of as much duplication as possible. Beware, however, that the added complexity to the program might not be worth shaving a tiny amount of duplication among multiple constructors.

Class Debugging

Writing a complex class like String takes lots of testing and debugging. The old programming rule *test as you go* applies as well to object-oriented programming as it does to conventional techniques. This is a good place, then, to pause in the design of String to conduct a few tests.

I tend to use two main test methods. When constructing a new class, a function, or a module, I build a prototype design directly into a test program such as STRING.CPP (included on disk and listed piece by piece in this chapter). I also use a debugger, not only to locate errors, but to verify that the test program is operating as expected.

I sometimes also build test code directly into a class. One especially useful technique is to use a friend function (I call it Dump()) that writes all of a class's private data to the standard output. Declare the function in the class's private section like this:

```
class String {
#ifdef DEBUG
   friend void Dump(const char *msg, String &s);
#endif
   ...
}
```

Dump() is a friend so it has direct access to private data members in String. The function needs direct access also because it must avoid calling class member functions under test. In other words, Dump() should use the class's len value directly; it should *not* call a Length() function that returns len because that function might be the one being tested. To use the function, first define a DEBUG symbol:

```
#define DEBUG
```

Also include the assert.h header:

```
#ifdef DEBUG
  #include <assert.h>
#endif
```

Listing 10.3 shows the completed function. Notice that the function, its declaration, and the assert.h header are easily removed by simply undefining the DEBUG symbol (or by not defining it in the first place). This means you can leave the debugging code in place for reactivating if a future problem occurs.

Listing 10.3. STRING.CPP (Dump function).

```
#ifdef DEBUG
// Display string and various values
void Dump(const char *msg, String &s)
{
  cout << "\n----------\n" << msg << endl
    << " err:    " << s.err << endl
    << " size:   " << s.size << endl
    << " len:    " << s.len << endl
    << " strlen: " << strlen(s.sp) << endl
    << " sp:     " << (void *)s.sp << endl
    << " *sp:    ";
  if (s.sp)
    cout << "\"" << s.sp << "\"" << endl;
  else
    cout << "[null]\n";
  assert(s.len == strlen(s.sp));
}
#endif  // DEBUG
```

To use Dump(), pass it a literal-string label and a String object. For example, these statements define a string and dump its contents:

```
String sample("Test string");
Dump("String sample", sample);
```

Running that fragment writes the following report to the standard output file:

```
String sample
 err:    0
 size:   12
 len:    11
 strlen: 11
 sp:     0x30e30004
 *sp:    "Test string"
```

The report shows the values of the err, size, len, strlen, and sp members. It also displays the string (if any) addressed by sp. To display sp's address value (the hexadecimal integer 0x30e30004 in the sample report), Dump() casts sp to void *. The cast is necessary because output streams are programmed to write char pointers as strings.

As a safety check, Dump() displays the value returned by the standard function strlen(). Something is seriously amiss if this value and the len data member don't agree, in which case Dump() halts the test with the assertion

```
assert(s.len == strlen(s.sp));
```

You can insert any expression inside assert()'s parentheses as long as the expression reduces to a true or false value. Take care, however, not to introduce side effects in using assert()—calling a function, for example, that reads from a file or modifies a global variable. The assert() macro executes the expression as a statement in the program. If the expression evaluates to a true result, the program continues normally. If the expression is false, assert() halts the program and writes the expression in text form to the standard error output file along with the module name and line number where the problem originated.

Here's what happened when I forced an error by setting len incorrectly in the String constructor from Listing 10.1 (notice that the len and strlen values do not match):

```
String sample
 err:    0
 size:   13
 len:    12
```

```
strlen: 11
sp:     0x302c0004
*sp:    "Test string"
Assertion failed: s.len == strlen(s.sp), file string.cpp, line 133
Abnormal program termination
```

In the rush to complete programs, it's easy to neglect testing and debugging. But these are not dirty chores to be left for the end of a programming project. Integrate test code directly into your programs, and you are likely to discover that the time you spend testing your code will help you to complete more work overall.

Operators

For convenience, the String class should have several overloaded operators. I stress the word *convenience*. Operations like joining two strings, indexing a character, and so on can be handled by member functions. Overloaded operators, however, can sometimes make using class objects natural and intuitive. For example, to join strings s1 and s2, and construct a new string s3 from the "concatenated" result, it would be convenient to use a simple statement such as

```
String s3 = s1 + s2;
```

There's no mistaking that statement's purpose. It obviously joins s2 to the end of s1 and assigns the result to s3. *A good overloaded operator should produce expected results.* Compare the statement to the less meaningful alternative that calls a member function to perform the same job:

```
String s3;
s3.Concat(s1, s2);
```

Using the Concat() member functions requires you to look up the syntax to be certain that something like this isn't expected:

```
s1.Concat(s3, s2);  // ???
```

The arithmetic-like addition shows clearly that s1 and s2 are joined and assigned to s3. The Concat() statements don't make clear which objects are being joined to which others, or in what order.

Overloaded operators require careful programming. The two most important operators to overload for the String class, and for most nontrivial classes, are assignment and arithmetic operators. Others are stream, comparison, and index operators.

Following are some possible operator implementations for the String class. Listing 10.4, a partial listing of String, shows the class's operator declarations.

Listing 10.4. STRING.CPP (overloaded operators only).

```
class String {
    ...

    // I/O stream operators
    friend ostream & operator<< (ostream &os, String &s);
    friend istream & operator>> (istream &is, String &s);

    // Operator friend functions
    friend int Compare(const String &s1, const String &s2);
    friend String operator+(const String &s1, const String &s2);
    friend int operator==(const String &s1, const String &s2);
    friend int operator!=(const String &s1, const String &s2);
    friend int operator<(const String &s1, const String &s2);
    friend int operator>(const String &s1, const String &s2);
    friend int operator<=(const String &s1, const String &s2);
    friend int operator>=(const String &s1, const String &s2);

public:
    ...
    // Operator member functions
    int operator! () { return !sp; }
    String & operator=(const String &copy);
    String & operator=(const char *copy);
    String & operator+=(const String &s);
    const char & operator[](int index);
    ...
};
```

Assignment operator (=)

Of course it should be possible to assign one string to another. Given two String objects, a simple statement assigns s2 to s1:

```
s1 = s2;
```

The overloaded assignment operator copies the contents of s2 to s1, replacing s1's original information. Listing 10.5 implements the operator.

Listing 10.5. STRING.CPP (operator=).

```
String & String::operator=(const String &copy)
{
  if (this != &copy) {     // Can't copy self to self
    delete sp;
    size = copy.size;
    len = copy.len;
    err = copy.err;
    if (copy.sp) {
      sp = new char[size];
      if (sp)
        strcpy(sp, copy.sp);
      else
        Error(out_of_memory);
    } else
      sp = 0;
  }
  return *this;
}
```

The first if statement prevents assigning an object to itself. Always do this, or perform a similar action, by comparing this (the object to be assigned to) with &copy (the address of the object being assigned). You should compare the object addresses, not their values, to detect if the objects are one and the same.

If the objects are different, the operator= function directly copies data members like size and len from the copy to the current object. The function also makes a fresh copy of any string addressed by sp.

One important issue in all assignment operator functions is what to return as the function result. You can declare the operator to return `void`:

```
void operator=(const String &copy);
```

Or, you can declare it to return a reference to a class object:

```
String & operator=(const String &copy);
```

Returning `void` is easiest but prevents cascaded assignments that assign more than one value at once:

```
s1 = s2 = s3 = s4;
```

If the `operator=` function returns `void`, those assignments would have to be written the long way:

```
s3 = s4;
s2 = s3;
s1 = s2;
```

Notice how the `String` class `operator=` function returns the value `*this`. That's the proper response in any member function that is to return a reference to the object for which the function was called.

At times, you might want to *prevent* assignments of objects. For example, an object with a huge buffer might cause severe memory problems if programmers start assigning them to other objects. To perform this trick, declare—*but do not implement*—a copy constructor and an assignment operator. Here's a sample:

```
class AnyClass {
  int x, y;
public:
  AnyClass(): x(0), y(0) { }
  AnyClass(int X, int Y): x(X), y(Y) { }
  AnyClass(AnyClass &);  // Copy constructor
  AnyClass & operator=(const AnyClass &);  // Assignment
};
```

`AnyClass` declares, but does not implement, a copy constructor and an overloaded assignment operator. It's perfectly okay to define `AnyClass` objects like this:

```
AnyClass x(123, 456);
AnyClass y;
```

By *not* implementing the copy constructor and assignment operator, however, these statements compile but do not link:

```
AnyClass z(x);   // ???
y = x;           // ???
```

The first requires a copy constructor. The second requires an overloaded assignment operator. Note that in the absence of an overloaded operator, C++ permits the assignment, performing a direct byte-by-byte copy of the data elements in x to y. The only way to prevent this from happening is to declare but not implement the operator—a trick that is used extensively in class libraries.

In addition to the overloaded operator in Listing 10.5, String provides a second, similar operator. Here are both overloaded operators as declared in the class:

```
String & operator=(const String &copy);
String & operator=(const char *copy);
```

The first operator function requires a reference to a String object. The function is used in assignments such as

```
String s1 = s2;
```

The second operator function requires a const char pointer to a null terminated string. This function is used in assignments such as

```
String s1 = "My dog has fleas.";
```

Actually, the second operator= form is not required because String already defines a class constructor that can accept a literal string (see Listing 10.1). But if you do not implement the alternate operator, C++ has to create a *temporary* object to perform the assignment. In other words, the preceding line would be implemented as though the operator= function had been programmed like this:

```
String & String::operator=(const char *copy)
{
  return *this = String(copy);
}
```

This works but isn't necessary because C++ does that anyway. The String(copy) expression creates a temporary copy of the null-terminated string passed as an argument. Then, this temporary object is assigned to *this, an action that calls the *other* overloaded operator= function.

Hint: A temporary object is undesirable. It takes time to form, it occupies memory, and it is just going to go out of scope soon after its use. It is not incorrect or dangerous. If, however, you receive a compiler error or warning that a "temporary" was used in an assignment, watch out! This generally means that the address of (or a reference to) a temporary object has been retained. Because the object is temporary, its use beyond its scope could destroy the program's sanity. The object might be stored on the stack, for example, and addressing it outside of its defining block could lead to disaster if that stack space is overwritten. Temporary objects are not always bad, but warnings about the use of temporary objects frequently indicate serious trouble and should never be ignored.

Listing 10.6 implements the second form of `operator=` to eliminate the construction of temporary `String` objects in assignment statements.

Listing 10.6. STRING.CPP (overloaded `operator=`**).**

```
// Overloaded assignment operator (optional)
String & String::operator=(const char *copy)
{
  if (copy == 0) {
    size = len = 0;
    delete sp;
    sp = 0;
    Error(no_error);
  } else {
    int newLen = strlen(copy);
    char *newString = new char[newLen + 1];
    if (newString) {
      len = newLen;
      size = len + 1;
      delete sp;
```

continues

Listing 10.6. continued

```
        sp = newString;
        strcpy(sp, copy);
        Error(no_error);
      } else
        Error(out_of_memory);
    }
  return *this;
}
```

Arithmetic operators (+, +=)

Some nonnumeric class objects are naturally used in arithmetic-like expressions. As I mentioned, to join two strings, nothing is clearer than the simple statement

```
String s3 = s1 + s2;
```

We should also be able to join two strings using the common shorthand:

```
s3 += s2;
```

Unfortunately, other operators don't produce equally clear code. It is difficult, for instance, to think of any intuitive application for the multiplication operator on strings. Subtraction might be used for string deletions, but the result is not exactly obvious. What do you suppose the following line should do?

```
String s3 = s1 - s2;   // ???
```

Maybe such a statement could search for s2 in s1, delete the substring if found, and assign the result to s3, but somehow, the effect doesn't seem as clear as addition used for joining strings. For these reasons, I decided to limit String's operators to operator+ and operator+= functions, because their meanings are crystal clear—always a good plan when overloading mathematical operators for nonmathematical purposes. Listing 10.7 shows the implementations for both functions.

Listing 10.7. STRING.CPP (operator+ **and** operator+=).

```cpp
// Return concatenation of two String objects
String operator+(const String &s1, const String &s2)
{
  String result(s1.len + s2.len);
  if (!result) return String::ErrorString;
  if (s1.sp) strcpy(result.sp, s1.sp);
  if (s2.sp) strcat(result.sp, s2.sp);
  result.len = strlen(result.sp);
  return result;
}


// Concatenation operator (shorthand version)
String & String::operator+=(const String &s)
{
  *this = *this + s;
  return *this;
}
```

The operator+ friend function can be used as shown earlier, and also in multipart statements such as

```cpp
String s4 = s3 + s2 + s1;
```

The second function, operator+=, is a class member, and is always used in a simpler fashion:

```cpp
s3 += s1;
```

This is, of course, equivalent to

```cpp
s3 = s3 + s1;
```

Study the operator+= implementation and you'll discover that this is exactly what the overloaded operator is programmed to do.

By the way, you must implement both functions. If you include only the operator+ function, C++ cannot infer operator+= even if you also overload the assignment operator. Programs use the += operator as shorthand, but to C++, it's just another symbol, completely independent of operator+.

Stream operators (<<, >>)

Part 1 covered stream operators, so I'll touch briefly on their use in String. Listing 10.8 shows the implementations for operator<< and operator>> in the String class. Notice how the input stream operator sets the maximum width using the setw() manipulator.

Listing 10.8. STRING.CPP (stream operators).

```
// Output stream operator
ostream & operator<< (ostream &os, String &s)
{
  if (s.sp) os << s.sp;
  return os;
}


// Input stream operator
istream & operator>> (istream &is, String &s)
{
  if (s.sp) is >> setw(s.size) >> s.sp;
  return is;
}
```

Comparison operators (==, !=, <, <=, >, >=)

Comparison operators are among the most important in a class like String. Very likely, programs will need to compare strings for equality, determine if one string is alphabetically less than another, sort arrays of strings, and so on. Listing 10.9 implements comparison operators for the String class.

Listing 10.9. STRING.CPP (comparison operators).

```
// Return result of comparing s1 and s2
// 0 == (s1 == s2); < 0 == (s1 < s2); > 0 == (s1 > s2)
int Compare(const String &s1, const String &s2)
{
  const char *sp1 = s1.sp, *sp2 = s2.sp;
```

```
    if (!sp1) sp1 = String::NullString;
    if (!sp2) sp2 = String::NullString;
    return strcmp(sp1, sp2);
}

// True if s1 equals s2
int operator==(const String &s1, const String &s2)
{
    return Compare(s1, s2) == 0;
}

// True if s1 is not equal to s2
int operator!-(const String &s1, const String &s2)
{
    return Compare(s1, s2) != 0;
}

// True if s1 is less than s2
int operator<(const String &s1, const String &s2)
{
    return Compare(s1, s2) < 0;
}

// True if s1 is greater than s2
int operator>(const String &s1, const String &s2)
{
    return Compare(s1, s2) > 0;
}

// True if s1 is less than or equal to s2
int operator<=(const String &s1, const String &s2)
{
    return Compare(s1, s2) <= 0;
}

// True if s1 is greater than or equal to s2
int operator>=(const String &s1, const String &s2)
{
    return Compare(s1, s2) >= 0;
}
```

In most classes, I find that I either implement all six comparison operators, or none at all. So, in this case, it makes good sense to cut out as much duplication as possible by writing a Compare() member function for each operator to call.

In Compare (see the beginning of Listing 10.9), if either of the two strings to be compared is null, I assign to it a static NullString variable declared as one of three static class members:

```
class String {
  static String ErrorString;
  static char ErrorChar;
  static char *NullString;
  ...
};
```

These members must be defined (given storage) at some place in the program. STRING.CPP satisfies this requirement with these definitions:

```
String String::ErrorString("!Error");
char String::ErrorChar = '!';
char *String::NullString = "";
```

Rather than signal an error in Compare() if a statement attempts to use a null string in an expression, I simply use the static NullString pointer. In other words, for the purpose of comparison, I define a null *pointer* to be equivalent to a null *string*—a small trick that saves much aggravation in tracking down null pointers used in comparisons. (String tables and similar structures, for example, might use null pointers to indicate blank lines, and in that case, comparing the pointers with other strings such as when sorting the table should not produce fatal errors.)

Given the Compare() function and operators in Listing 10.9, we can now compare strings easily. Here are a few samples:

```
String s1("Philadelphia");
String s2("Los Angeles");
...
if (s1 == s2) doSomething();
if (s1  < s2) doSomething();
if (s2 >= s1) doSomething();
```

The logical expressions are natural and easy to use—much more so than calling standard string functions to perform comparisons. You can compare literal strings with String objects:

```
if (s1 == "New York") doSomething();
```

You can also place the literal string first:

```
if ("Philadelphia" <= s2) doSomething();
```

Here again, however, temporary objects are constructed for the literal strings. To prevent that from happening, you would have to overload *each* operator to use all possible combinations of operands, a tremendous load of work. The operator== function, for instance, could alone have three variations:

```
friend int operator==(const String &s1, const String &s2);
friend int operator==(const String &s, const char *cs);
friend int operator==(const char *cs, const String &s);
```

The first operator is the only one strictly required, but the other two prevent the creation of temporary String objects. If you want to make this change, you will need similar multiple declarations for all comparison operators.

Index operator ([])

Finally in String is an overloaded index operator. I implemented the function as in Listing 10.10, but this is not the only possible variation.

Listing 10.10. STRING.CPP (index operator).

```
// Index operator
const char & String::operator[](int index)
{
  if (!sp || index < 0 || index > len)
    return ErrorChar;
  return *(sp + index);
}
```

Use the operator to return a character at a specified index. This statement, for example, sets c to 'y':

```
String s("Any string");
char c = s[2];
```

In some classes, it's more common to return a reference or a pointer than to return a *constant* reference as I've done here. Suppose you declare the indexing operator as

```
char *operator[](int index);   // ???
```

This works, but you have just given users of the class an arrow that they can shoot directly into the heart of the object's private data! A simple assignment:

```
char *p = s[2];
```

provides a pointer p that looks *inside* the very data that the class is designed to keep private. Generally, it's best to avoid this kind of dangerous programming, although that ideal goal is not always easy to achieve.

Member Functions

Like most classes, String also has several member functions for performing a variety of actions. Listing 10.11 shows the miscellaneous members declared for the class.

Listing 10.11. STRING.CPP (other member functions).

```
class String {
  ...
  virtual StringErr Error(StringErr e = no_error);
  int Length() { return len; }
  const char *Get() { return sp; }
  int Pos(const String &pattern);
  int Pos(const char *cs);
  int Delete(int index, int count);
  String Copy(int index, int count);
  String Extract(int index, int count);
  int Truncate(int index);
  ...
};
```

This is by no means all the members that a complete String class would need, but these seem to be the most important. Their implementations are on disk in the STRING.CPP file—I won't list every function here, because their internal statements are fairly simple to understand.

Here's a brief synopsis of each member and how to use it.

- Length() returns a string's length in characters. This is an inline member function.

- Get() returns a constant pointer to a String object's null-terminated string. The result is const to prevent attempts to modify this string; consider Get() to be a "read only" function. This is an inline member function.

- Pos() Returns the index where a substring pattern is found in a String object. If s1 equals "file.txt" and s2 equals ".txt", the expression s1.Pos(s2) equals 4. An overloaded form of this function permits you to use literal string patterns. The expression s1.Pos(".txt") also equals 4. The function returns –1 if the search pattern is not found.

- Delete() removes and closes up count characters from a specified index position. Returns the number of deleted characters, which might be zero, or –1 if any errors are detected.

- Copy() returns a new String object containing count characters starting from a specified index. Returns NullString for senseless operations— specifying a zero count, for example. Also returns NullString for errors.

- Extract() is equivalent to calling Copy() then Delete() with the identical parameters. Same return values as Copy().

- Truncate() chops a string at the specified index. Returns the length of the resulting string or –1 if any errors are detected.

In designing String, other possible member functions came to mind. String could have functions to convert strings between upper- and lowercase. Perhaps I could have added a comparison method that is not case-sensitive, and I thought long and hard about devising several types of search functions. Reason and this book's deadline prevailed over ambition, however, and besides, my aim in presenting a String class in this chapter is not to cover every angle, but rather to show the techniques required in writing a complex class such as String. The following section lists the completed class declaration.

The Finished String Class

On disk in the PART2 directory, you can find the complete STRING.CPP listing, printed piecemeal throughout this chapter. Compile the program with Borland C++ by following directions in Appendix A, or enter command such as

```
bcc -ml string secrets.lib
string >results.txt
```

Run the STRING.EXE program by directing its output to a file such as RESULTS.TXT, then use a text editor to view the file. The program has many test procedures that exercise the String class and serve as additional examples of how to use it.

If you receive errors, make sure the compiler can find SECRETS.LIB, which contains a module you can use with Borland C++ to calculate the amount of memory available on the heap. Listings 10.12, memuse.h, and 10.13, MEMUSE.CPP, list this module, located on disk in the LIB\MEMUSE directory.

Listing 10.12. memuse.h.

```
#ifndef __MEMUSE_H
#define __MEMUSE_H    // Prevent multiple #includes

void HeapReport(const char *s);
long HeapSize();

#endif  // __MEMUSE_H
```

Listing 10.13. MEMUSE.CPP.

```cpp
#include <stdlib.h>
#include <iostream.h>
#include <alloc.h>
#include "memuse.h"

// Display memory use
void HeapReport(const char *s)
{
  long result;

  cout << s << endl;
  result = HeapSize();
  if (result < 0) {
    cout << "- No near heap or error!" << endl;
    exit(1);
  } else
    cout << "- Heap size == " << result << endl;
}

// Return size of near heap free space or -1 for error
long HeapSize()
{
  unsigned long count;
  struct heapinfo info;

  info.ptr = 0;
  if (heapcheck() != _HEAPOK)
    return -1L;
  count = coreleft();
  while (heapwalk(&info) == _HEAPOK)
    if (info.in_use == 0)
      count += info.size;
  return count;
}
```

To make it easy for other programs in future chapters to use the String class, the finished programming is stored in modular form on disk in directory LIB\STRING. The compiled module is also stored in SECRETS.LIB for easy linking to programs. To avoid conflicts with the standard string.h header, String's header is named str.h, printed here in Listing 10.14 for reference. A copy of str.h is also stored in the INCLUDE directory.

Listing 10.14. str.h (final String class declaration).

```
#ifndef __STR_H
#define __STR_H    // Prevent multiple #includes

#include <iostream.h>
#include <iomanip.h>
#include <string.h>

class String {

#ifdef DEBUG
  friend void Dump(const char *msg, String &s);
#endif

  // Static class members (strstats.cpp)
  static String ErrorString;
  static char ErrorChar;
  static char *NullString;

  // I/O stream operators (strio.cpp)
  friend ostream & operator<< (ostream &os, String &s);
  friend istream & operator>> (istream &is, String &s);

  // Operator friend functions (strfrnds.cpp)
  friend int Compare(const String &s1, const String &s2);
  friend String operator+(const String &s1, const String &s2);
  friend int operator==(const String &s1, const String &s2);
  friend int operator!=(const String &s1, const String &s2);
  friend int operator<(const String &s1, const String &s2);
```

```
        friend int operator>(const String &s1, const String &s2);
        friend int operator<=(const String &s1, const String &s2);
        friend int operator>=(const String &s1, const String &s2);

public:

    enum StringErr {
      no_error = 0,    // No error detected
      out_of_memory,   // Not enough memory for operation
      out_of_range     // String index out of range
    };

    // Constructors (strctor.cpp)
    String();
    String(const char *cs);
    String(const String &copy);
    String(int n);
    String(char c, int n = 1);

    // Destructor
    ~String() { delete sp; }

    // Operator member functions (strops.cpp)
    int operator! () { return !sp; }
    String & operator=(const String &copy);
    String & operator=(const char *copy);
    String & operator+=(const String &s);
    const char & operator[](int index);

    // Other member functions (strmfs.cpp)
    virtual StringErr Error(StringErr e = no_error);
    int Length() { return len; }
    const char *Get() { return sp; }
    int Pos(const String &pattern);
    int Pos(const char *cs);
    int Delete(int index, int count);
```

continues

Listing 10.14. continued

```
   String Copy(int index, int count);
   String Extract(int index, int count);
   int Truncate(int index);

private:
   StringErr err;   // Current error code
   int size;        // Size of memory block in bytes
   int len;         // Number of characters in string
   char *sp;        // Pointer to null-terminated string
};


#endif  // __STR_H
```

To use the modular String class in directory LIB\STRING (and also stored in SECRETS.LIB), include the str.h header file:

```
#include <str.h>
```

You can then define String objects as explained in this chapter. To compile your program with Borland C++, specify the large memory model and link to SECRETS.LIB:

```
bcc -ml myprog secrets.lib
```

Any errors probably mean the compiler can't find the compiled library or the str.h header file. See Appendix A for help if you have trouble compiling programs.

Strings and Templates

Although Part 2 of this book uses templates extensively, my String class doesn't. As I mentioned near the beginning of this chapter, a String class is far too specific to make a good general-purpose template. It's also awkward to build String from another template such as Vector<T>. These facts don't mean, however, that classes such as String can't be used *with* templates.

Consider, for example, the problem of comparing strings alphabetically. Using the min() and max() function templates from Chapter 7, if s1 and s2 are pointers of type char *, this statement fails to work correctly:

```
char *s3 = Max(s1 < s2);  // ???
```

Because s1 and s2 are pointers, the template assigns to s3 the lesser of the two *addresses* in s1 and s2. But we don't want to compare addresses; we want to compare the strings the pointers address. The String class neatly solves that problem by giving the min() and max() templates a data type that can be compared using logical operators > and <. Listing 10.15 demonstrates the solution. The program is located in the PART2 directory.

Listing 10.15. STRMAX.CPP.

```
#include <iostream.h>
#include <str.h>
#include "minmax.h"

int main()
{
  String s1("Earth");
  String s2("Venus");

  cout << "s1 == " << s1 << endl;
  cout << "s2 == " << s2 << endl;
  cout << "min(s1, s2) == " << min(s1, s2) << endl;
  cout << "max(s1, s2) == " << max(s1, s2) << endl;

  return 0;
}
```

The program includes the str.h and minmax.h headers. Function main() constructs two String objects, s1 and s2, each assigned a different string. Simply using the min() and max() templates generates conforming functions that can handle String objects. When you run the program, you might be surprised to see the final two output statements display character strings. This works because the compiler reshapes the templates to return String objects. Well-written templates should be able to accommodate just about any data type, even highly specific types like String.

Final Words

Writing a class as extensive as String is a lot of work, but the payoffs can be significant. Even if you already have a String class in your system's library, investigating the implementation of a class of this complexity is a great way to learn many useful programming techniques.

The next chapter returns to templates, using them to explore fundamental data structures—the first step in this part's final goal of creating a *container class library,* one of the most useful components in any C++ development system.

Implementing Fundamental Data Structures

All first-year computer science students learn about vectors, lists, double-linked lists, and other *fundamental data structures*. These rock-solid building blocks form the foundations of many software applications, and for most programmers, it's a real eye opener to discover the amazing versatility of a linked list or the high potential of an array.

Basing software on fundamental data structures, however, can lead programmers into a powerful trap. For example, in a program that stores objects in lists, it's common to find dozens of list-traversal statements strewn throughout the program's text. When the program's specifications change, programmers are astonished to discover how difficult it is—if not downright impossible—to replace lists with vectors or hash tables, which might boost performance, save memory, or conserve disk space.

C++ class templates offer at least a partial solution to this problem by providing tools for constructing fundamental data structures that are easily adapted to new tasks. Based on templates, fundamental data structures become key components in a versatile container class library—a set of related classes that you'll create in this chapter and the next.

Introduction to Fundamental Data Structures

Think of a *fundamental data structure,* or FDS, as a kind of brick from which you can construct higher-order structures. On the construction site, a brick is a basic building material. If you smash a brick, it crumbles into sand, fiber, and clay—or whatever bricks are made of, but anyway, once crushed, it is no longer a brick. In programs, FDS classes such as lists and vectors are similarly basic and indivisible.

Contrast this notion with another kind of structure called an *abstract data type,* or ADT. An ADT might be compared to a house built from bricks. If you wreck the house, you no longer have a dwelling, but you still have a pile of bricks that you can use to build another structure. (See Figure 11.1.) You could also rebuild the house using a *different* raw material—wood, for example, or cement. A house is a house, regardless of its construction materials. A brick, however, is a brick *because* it is made of certain elements.

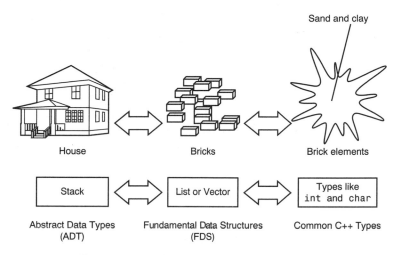

Figure 11.1. If an abstract data type is a house, fundamental data structures are like bricks—raw materials composed of relatively common elements.

In programming, examples of fundamental data structures include vectors and lists—the "bricks" on which higher-order structures depend. Abstract types such as sets and stacks are typically based on fundamental structures. A stack, for instance, is a high-order structure that can be implemented using a vector or a list. Lists are fundamental; they are defined by their structures. Stacks are abstract; they can be constructed using different kinds of raw materials.

Vector Revisited

Chapter 9, "Vectoring in on Arrays," introduced vectors and the class template, Vector<T>. A vector is a fundamental data structure. It provides only the minimum services needed to store and retrieve objects at random.

Note: A fundamental data structure like Vector<T> is also sometimes called a *concrete data type,* or CDT. In general, the terms FDS and CDT are interchangeable, but I'll continue to use FDS here.

One of the advantages of using class templates like Vector<T> is the way they can be reshaped to accommodate objects of different types. This characteristic, however, is imperfect. In Chapter 9, for instance, I mentioned that Vector<T> was able to store most kinds of objects, but not strings addressed by pointers of type char *.

There are two possible ways around this limitation. You could write a new Vector nontemplate class to handle char * strings, or you can wrap strings into a String class like the one in Chapter 10, "Constructing a String Class," then store String objects in a class generated from the template.

Listing 11.1 demonstrates this concept by combining the Vector<T> class template from Chapter 9 with the String class from Chapter 10. The result is an object-oriented vector of strings.

Note: The following listing uses the String class stored in the LIB\STRING directory and declared in file str.h, a copy of which is also stored in the INCLUDE directory. Using Borland C++, you must link the following program to the String class module, stored in SECRETS.LIB. If you have trouble compiling the program, see Appendix A. On disk, file STRVECT.CPP is located in the PART2 directory.

Listing 11.1. STRVECT.CPP.

```
#include <iostream.h>
#include <vector.h>
#include <str.h>

#define MAX 4
#define BUFSIZE 80

char buffer[BUFSIZE];
```

```
int main()
{
  int i;
  Vector<String> sv(1, MAX);

  cout << "Enter " << MAX << " strings:\n";
  for (i = 1; i <= MAX; ++i) {
    cout << "sv[" << i << "]? ";
    cin >> setw(BUFSIZE) >> buffer;
    sv[i] = buffer;
  }
  cout << "\nHere are your strings:\n";
  for (i = 1; i <= MAX; ++i)
    cout << "sv[" << i << "] == " << sv[i] << endl;
  return 0;
}
```

This listing demonstrates an important principle in using fundamental data structures as general purpose containers. Despite compiler vendor claims to the contrary, it's not always possible or desirable to have container classes that can hold any type of data object under the sun. But it usually *is* possible to store objects of a class type in a container. To store String objects, I constructed a container named sv with the statement

```
Vector<String> sv(1, MAX);
```

The notation Vector<String> causes the compiler to generate a class of that name using the Vector<T> template. The vector, sv, can then store objects of type String, indexed from 1 to MAX.

Most of the sample program is straightforward. Expressions like sv[i] refer to String objects at a specified index, but hide the true complexity of the vector operators and String methods inside.

Inheritance as a Problem Solver

One bottleneck in Listing 11.1 is the way the first for loop reads new strings into vector slots. After prompting you to enter a string into a global buffer, that buffer is assigned to a String object with the statement

```
sv[i] = buffer;
```

It would be more convenient just to read strings *directly* into String objects. But doing that would require initializing the String objects to be a certain size, a capability the Vector<String> class does not provide. That's why I was forced to use a global buffer to hold raw input.

Commonplace problems such as this are usually easy to solve by using inheritance. Rather than ponder how to cause Vector to initialize String objects of a preset size, simply design a derived String class of the size you need and use it to generate a new class from the Vector<T> template. Listing 11.2, STRVECT2.CPP, shows how.

Listing 11.2. STRVECT2.CPP.

```cpp
#include <iostream.h>
#include <vector.h>
#include <str.h>

#define MAX 4

class String80: public String {
public:
  String80(): String(80) { }
};

int main()
{
  int i;
  Vector<String80> sv(1, MAX);

  cout << "Enter " << MAX << " strings:\n";
  for (i = 1; i <= MAX; ++i) {
    cout << "sv[" << i << "]? ";
    cin >> sv[i];
  }
  cout << "\nHere are your strings:\n";
  for (i = 1; i <= MAX; ++i)
    cout << "sv[" << i << "] == " << sv[i] << endl;
  return 0;
}
```

Class String80 makes it possible to construct a string object that can hold up to 80 characters. By generating a Vector<String80> class for the string vector, the program now can use simple statements to read text directly into String objects:

```
cin >> sv[i];
```

List Class

The perfect complement to a vector is a list. Unlike a vector in which objects are physically stored one after the other, a list's objects might be stored anywhere in memory. To chain list nodes, one or more pointer fields in objects address other objects, forming links that programs can follow to access the list's information (see Figure 11.2).

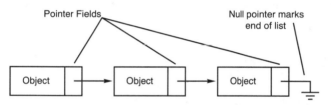

Figure 11.2. A list uses pointers to chain multiple objects.

A more sophisticated list might use two pointers in each object, creating a *doubly-linked* list. With this design (see Figure 11.3), a pointer p that addresses any object can easily locate the previous or next object in the list just by referencing the address held by a pointer (labeled *P* for *previous* or *N* for *next* in the figure).

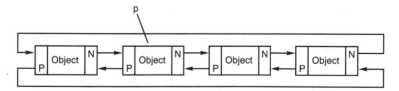

Figure 11.3. Two pointers in each object create a doubly-linked list.

The list in Figure 11.3 is circular—in other words, all objects are joined by their next and previous pointers. A similar noncircular, doubly linked list, has two ends (see Figure 11.4), making it possible to identify the list's head and tail.

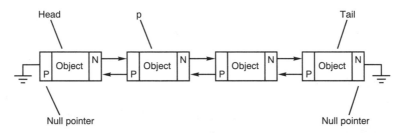

Figure 11.4. A noncircular, doubly linked list has two ends.

We'll develop a List class to implement the list as illustrated in Figure 11.4. First, however, we need to examine a few problems posed by these common list structures.

Direct Lists

The lists in Figures 11.2, 11.3, and 11.4 are direct lists—that is, they directly store their objects. Because of their designs, the lists require the objects themselves to include pointer fields. To store an object of a class in a list, you must declare the class with pointers to next and previous objects:

```
class Item {
public:
  Item(): next(0), prev(0) { }
private:
  Item *prev;  // Points to previous Item object
  Item *next;  // Points to next Item object
};
```

The Item class shown here includes two private Item pointers, which address any objects attached to this one. The class constructor sets each pointer to null. Objects of the Item class approximate the objects in Figures 11.3 and 11.4.

Although this approach to list management is typical—and makes a good example of list processing for beginning programmers—several problems arise from the design in more advanced uses. For one, you can't store simple values of type `double` or `int` in lists. Instead, you must construct a class like `Item` to hold values of these types, which don't come with built-in `next` and `previous` pointers.

Another problem concerns the list class. In order to join objects into a list and to perform other list-management duties, the class must be written to accept objects of type `Item`. Objects of other classes like `String` can't easily be stored in lists without modification because they, too, lack the necesssary pointers.

Indirect Lists

Divorcing a list from the listed objects neatly solves the dilemmas posed in the preceding section. Rather than store objects directly, each listed item includes a third pointer that addresses the listed data (see Figure 11.5). The list nodes now serve as *carriers* that can be used to list any objects of any type. In the figure, each carrier includes a pointer, `ip`, that addresses the list's items.

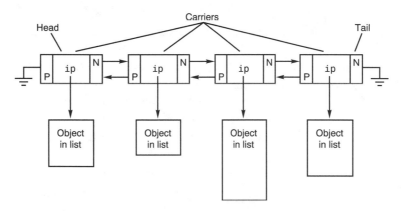

Figure 11.5. Using carriers, a list can store any type of object.

Using carriers for list nodes also permits listed items to be different sizes. Even more important, the listed objects are not connected directly, implying that any item can be listed without requiring pointer fields to be added to the item classes. Generalizing this design into a template class makes it possible to create lists that are easily molded to store simple values, structures, class objects, strings—or any objects that can be stored in memory and addressed by pointers. The next sections develop this template.

List Class Declarations

Listing 11.3, misc.h, is used by the next listing and others in this chapter. The file simply defines two symbols, TRUE and FALSE, which help clarify statements in various functions that return true or false values.

Listing 11.3. misc.h.

```
#ifndef __MISC_H
#define __MISC_H    // Prevent multiple #includes

#ifndef FALSE
  #define FALSE 0
#endif
#ifndef TRUE
  #define TRUE 1
#endif

#endif  // __MISC_H
```

Listing 11.4, list.h, declares two class templates. Carrier<T> stores a list's internal mechanisms, creating objects equivalent to those shown at the top of Figure 11.5. List<T> manages the list, keeping track of the list's head and tail, and providing member functions to insert and delete items. Because this listing is fairly long, I'll describe it in relatively small chunks.

Note: Because the Carrier<T> and List<T> classes are templates, they are completely declared and implemented in the list.h header file. On disk, the misc.h and list.h files are located in the LIB\CLASSLIB subdirectory. Copies of these files are also stored in the INCLUDE directory.

Listing 11.4. list.h.

```
#ifndef __LIST_H
#define __LIST_H    // Prevent multiple #includes

#include "misc.h"

template<class T>
class Carrier {
public:
  Carrier(T *item);
  ~Carrier();
public:
  Carrier<T> *next;  // Points to next carrier object
  Carrier<T> *prev;  // Points to previous carrier object
  T *ip;             // Points to carried item
};

template<class T>
class List {
public:
  List();
  List(const List<T> &copy);
  ~List();
  T * LinkHead(T *item);
  T * LinkHead(T item);
  T * LinkTail(T *item);
  T * LinkTail(T item);
  T * UnlinkHead();
  T * UnlinkTail();
  T * UnlinkItem(T *item);
  T * UnlinkItem(T item);
  void DeleteAll();
  void operator= (const List<T> &copy);
  int operator! ();
  int ItemCount() const { return count; }
  Carrier<T> *GetHead() const { return head; }
  Carrier<T> *GetTail() const { return tail; }
```

continues

269

Listing 11.4. continued

```
private:
  Carrier<T> *head;   // Points to first carrier in list
  Carrier<T> *tail;   // Points to last carrier in list
  int count;          // Number of carriers in list
};
```

The Carrier<T> class is a simple affair, having only a constructor and destructor as member functions. The constructor requires a Carrier<T> object to be constructed using a pointer to an item of type T. Remember, this is a template, making T an unspecified type—a placeholder to be supplied when the template is used. T might eventually be a simple double type, or it could be replaced by a class like String.

Three public data members in Carrier<T> form the pointers illustrated in Figure 11.5. These members are public to make them easily accessible. Carrier<T>'s design is so basic, it probably won't require modification, so the public data members, while unusual, are not likely to cause trouble. Good classes don't require *every* data member to be private to the class.

Notice that the next and prev pointers are of type Carrier<T> *. In other words, these pointers address Carrier<T> objects as illustrated in the top of Figure 11.5. Pointer ip is of type T *, a pointer to an item of type T.

The List<T> class template has several member functions, most of which have obvious purposes. LinkHead(), for example, links an item of type T to the head of the list. Some of these functions are overloaded so programs can pass pointers or item values as arguments. I'll describe many of these functions more fully along with their implementations.

List<T> demonstrates another subject that confuses many C++ programmers. Look closely at the declaration of ItemCount(), repeated here for reference:

```
int ItemCount() const { return count; }
```

In earlier chapters, you saw examples of functions that returned const values—values that cannot be changed, at least without resorting to trickery. In this case, however, ItemCount() is declared as a *const member function*. The function's value isn't constant; *the function's use is.* In other words, declaring a member function const prohibits the function from changing or assigning values to any of the class's data members. ItemCount(), for instance, is not allowed to assign a value to the count data member or to modify the head or tail pointers.

Using `const` member functions helps produce solidly reliable code, but this requires careful attention to detail. Functions like `ItemCount()` may be called for `List<T>` objects *and for const `List<T>` objects*. If `ItemCount()` were not declared `const`, the compiler would not allow you call `ItemCount()` for a `const` object.

Get in the habit of using `const` objects, particularly as function arguments (especially references) to which you want to prevent modifications. Declaring `const` member functions in classes ensures that a statement cannot call a non-`const` function for the constant object—an important safeguard that can go a long way toward making code more robust. The general rule is this: If a function doesn't modify any data member, it should be `const`.

Carrier<T> Implementation

The implementation of the `Carrier<T>`, in the continuation of Listing 11.4, seems surprisingly simple. Even so, this simple class template plays a key role in the formation of every list.

Listing 11.4. list.h (continued).

```
// ------------------------------------------------------------
// class Carrier
// ------------------------------------------------------------

// Constructor
template<class T>
Carrier<T>::Carrier(T *item)
  : next(0), prev(0)
{
  ip = new T(*item);  // Construct T object from *item
}


// Destructor
template<class T>
Carrier<T>::~Carrier()
{
  delete ip;    // Delete item in carrier
  delete next;  // Delete carrier list recursively
}
```

The Carrier<T> constructor sets the next and prev pointers to null (0). In the constructor's body, a single statement uses the new operator to construct a copy of the item passed by address to the constructor. The resulting copy's address is assigned to the Carrier<T> pointer, ip.

The Carrier<T> destructor might seem flawed on a first reading, but actually, it is capable of deleting an entire list along with all addressed items. Consider how the destructor works when a list is deleted or goes out of scope. First, the statement delete ip deletes the item addressed by this carrier (see Figure 11.5). Next, the statement delete next; *deletes the next carrier.* That statement recursively calls the Carrier<T> destructor, which again deletes the item and next carrier. This process continues until the next pointer becomes null, at which time the recursion unwinds. The memory occupied by the list carriers is then reclaimed for future use by the C++ delete operator.

In list classes, a recursive destructor makes list deletion a simple matter of deleting one pointer. If head addresses the first carrier object, this statement deletes the entire list:

```
delete head;
```

You won't have many opportunities to use recursive destructors, but it's useful to keep in mind that these and other member functions in classes can be called recursively, even though the program might not make that fact perfectly clear.

List Ownership

Ownership is an important factor in the design of fundamental structures and container classes. Should the list illustrated in Figure 11.5 own the addressed items, or should the program assume ownership over the data? Or, should both situations be permitted, perhaps selecting ownership rules at runtime by calling a member function?

These are difficult questions to which there are no absolutely right answers. To make my classes as easy to use as possible, I decided to have the List<T> and other classes assume ownership over their objects. This means that, when you insert an item into a list, the list makes a *copy* of the object. The list can then delete that copy automatically. If you unlink an object from the list, it becomes your responsibility to delete it.

As later sample programs show, these rules lead to classes that are easy to use, but they also impose restrictions on items to be stored in lists. If the item is a class object, for instance, it must have a copy constructor, perhaps declared as

```
class Item {
public:
  Item(const Item &copy);  // Copy constructor
  void operator= (const Item &copy);  // Assignment operator
...
};
```

For most classes, you'll provide an assignment operator to carry out the copy constructor's duties, as explained in Chapters 9 and 10, so these requirements are not too imposing. Class objects that can be safely copied byte-for-byte (that is, they have no pointer members) do *not* require copy constructors or assignment operators. Also, simple types such as int and double can already be copied without special programming; thus objects of simple types can be stored on List<T> lists without having to embed the objects in classes.

List<T> Implementation

One of my primary goals in designing the List<T> class was to avoid direct references to carrier objects. In other words, it should be possible to use a list as though it were constructed as in Figure 11.4, when in fact, it actually is created as in Figure 11.5. The fewer pointers a program has to manipulate directly, the better. Programs should be oblivious to the Carrier<T> objects that actually link the list's nodes.

As a consequence of these goals, my List<T> class does not have member functions to scan a list's elements. This might seem wrong-headed, but we'll deal with the apparent deficiency later by providing another class called an *iterator*. At this stage, as in the Vector<T> class, I intended to distill the raw essence of a list into a class. I therefore chose only the minimum number of services that create lists, insert objects, delete objects, and delete entire lists.

Listing 11.4 continues with the implementation of the List<T> class template.

Listing 11.4. list.h (continued).

```cpp
// ----------------------------------------------------------------
// class List
// ----------------------------------------------------------------

// Default constructor
template<class T>
List<T>::List()
  : head(0), tail(0), count(0)
{
}

// Copy constructor
template<class T>
List<T>::List(const List<T> &copy)
{
  head = tail = 0;   // Prepare for operator=()
  *this = copy;       // Calls operator=()
}

// Destructor
template<class T>
List<T>::~List()
{
  DeleteAll();  // Delete carriers and items
}

// Adds item to head of list
// Null entries not allowed
// Returns item or null for errors
template<class T>
T * List<T>::LinkHead(T *item)
{
  if (!item) return 0;      // Can't add a null item
  Carrier<T> *p =
    new Carrier<T>(item);   // Create Carrier object
  if (!p) return 0;         // Return null if new fails
  if (count == 0)           // If list is empty,
    head = tail = p;        // start a new list.
```

```
  else {
    head->prev = p;         // Attach Carrier to head
    p->next = head;         // Address next carrier
    head = p;               // Assign new head pointer
  }
  count++;                  // Increment items in list
  return item;              // Return item pointer
}


// Same as preceding but links item passed by value
// Note: Do not declare inline!
template<class T>
T * List<T>::LinkHead(T item)
{
  return LinkHead(&item);
}


// Adds item to tail of list
// Null entries not allowed
// Returns item or null for errors
template<class T>
T * List<T>::LinkTail(T *item)
{
  if (!item) return 0;      // Can't add a null item
  Carrier<T> *p =
    new Carrier<T>(item);   // Create Carrier object
  if (!p) return 0;         // Return null if new fails
  if (count == 0)           // If list is empty,
    head = tail = p;        // start a new list.
  else {
    tail->next = p;         // Attach Carrier to tail
    p->prev = tail;         // Address previous carrier
    tail = p;               // Assign new tail pointer
  }
  count++;                  // Increment items in list
  return item;              // Return item pointer
}


// Same as preceding but links item passed by value
// Note: Do not declare inline!
```

continues

Listing 11.4. continued

```cpp
template<class T>
T * List<T>::LinkTail(T item)
{
  return LinkTail(&item);
}


// Deletes carrier object from head of list
// Sets new head and deletes carrier
// Adjusts list count and returns item pointer
template<class T>
T * List<T>::UnlinkHead()
{
  if (!head) return 0;        // List is empty; return null
  Carrier<T> *p = head;       // Address head of list with p
  head = head->next;          // Assign new list head pointer
  if (head)                   // If head pointer not null,
    head->prev = 0;           // null Carrier's prev pointer.
  else                        // Else if head pointer is null,
    tail = 0;                 // set tail (list is empty).
  T *ip = p->ip;              // Assign pointer to item
  p->next = 0;                // Null Carrier's next pointer
  p->prev = 0;                // Null Carrier's prev pointer
  p->ip = 0;                  // Null Carrier's item pointer
  delete p;                   // Delete Carrier object
  count--;                    // Decrement items in list
  return ip;                  // Return item pointer
}


// Deletes carrier object from tail of list
// Sets new tail and deletes carrier
// Adjusts list count and returns item pointer
template<class T>
T * List<T>::UnlinkTail()
{
  if (!tail) return 0;        // List is empty; return null
  Carrier<T> *p = tail;       // Address tail of list with p
  tail = tail->prev;          // Assign new list tail pointer
  if (tail)                   // If tail pointer not null,
    tail->next = 0;           // null Carrier's next pointer.
```

```
    else                      // Else if head pointer is null,
      head = 0;               // set tail (list is empty).
    T *ip = p->ip;            // Assign pointer to item
    p->next = 0;              // Null Carrier's next pointer
    p->prev = 0;              // Null Carrier's prev pointer
    p->ip = 0;                // Null Carrier's item pointer
    delete p;                 // Delete Carrier object
    count--;                  // Decrement items in list
    return ip;                // Return item pointer
}

// Unlink specified item if found
// Returns null if item is not found
template<class T>
T * List<T>::UnlinkItem(T *item)
{
  if (!head) return 0;        // List is empty; return null
  Carrier<T> *p = head;       // Address head of list with p
  while (p && *p->ip != *item) // Search for item in list,
    p = p->next;              // stopping if p becomes null.
  if (!p) return 0;           // Return null if item not found
  if (p == head)              // If Carrier is at head of list,
    return UnlinkHead();      // default to UnlinkHead().
  if (p == tail)              // If Carrier is at tail of list,
    return UnlinkTail();      // default to UnlinkTail().
  T *ip = p->ip;              // Copy pointer in Carrier
  p->next->prev = p->prev;    // Unlink from next Carrier
  p->prev->next = p->next;    // Unlink from previous Carrier
  p->next = 0;                // Null Carrier's next pointer
  p->prev = 0;                // Null Carrier's prev pointer
  p->ip = 0;                  // Null Carrier's item pointer
  delete p;                   // Delete Carrier object
  count--;                    // Decrement items in list
  return ip;                  // Return item pointer
}

// Same as preceding but unlinks item passed by value
// Note: Do not declare inline!
template<class T>
T * List<T>::UnlinkItem(T item)
{
```

continues

Listing 11.4. continued

```cpp
    return UnlinkItem(&item);
}

// Delete all items recursively
template<class T>
void List<T>::DeleteAll()
{
  delete head;
  head = tail = 0;
  count = 0;
}

// Assign list to list, copying listed items
template<class T>
void List<T>::operator= (const List<T> &copy)
{
  if (this == &copy) return;    // Can't copy self to self
  DeleteAll();                  // Delete any current list
  Carrier<T> *cp = copy.head;   // Address head of list
  while (cp) {                  // While not at end of list
    LinkTail(cp->ip);           // Link copy of item to this list
    cp = cp->next;             // Do next carrier object
  }
}

// Always returns false, meaning list is valid,
// because an empty list is not an error.
template<class T>
inline int List<T>::operator! ()
{
  return FALSE;
}

#endif  // __LIST_H
```

Most of the programming in List<T>'s implementation is commented. I'll describe only a few of the less obvious sections. Two member functions link objects to the head of a list. These are

```
T * LinkHead(T *item);
T * LinkHead(T item);
```

I overloaded these two member functions to permit listing items passed by address (T *item) or by value (T item). Each function returns a pointer to the item as an error control device. If the function returns null, something went wrong (probably due to a memory shortage). An important principle that I have tried to follow is that errors not produce fatal conditions. A list might refuse to accept a new item, but that refusal should not cause any damage to items already on the list.

Two similar functions link items to the tail of a list:

```
T * LinkTail(T *item);
T * LinkTail(T item);
```

There are no functions for linking items into the middle of a list. Such operations would imply an ordering capability that is too sophisticated for this fundamental type.

Four functions unlink items, at the head and tail, and of a specific value:

```
T * UnlinkHead();
T * UnlinkTail();
T * UnlinkItem(T *item);
T * UnlinkItem(T item);
```

Each function returns a pointer to the unlinked item, which must be deleted by the program. Once you unlink an item from the list, that item becomes your responsibility. If the item remains in the list, the list takes care of its deletion. Other designs are possible, and you'll run into many variations of this theme in different class libraries. My scheme works, however, and it is simple to manage.

Iterator Classes

As you scan the List<T> member functions, the class might seem incomplete. There are no functions, for instance, to scan listed items. Is something missing?

Yes and no. The List<T> class is only partially usable. It's complete in its ability to link, unlink, and delete objects, but the class obviously lacks many needed features such as those to search a list for an object or to perform actions on an entire list. Too often, faced with similar apparently missing elements, C++ programmers stuff every possible nut and banana into their classes, overloading them like desserts in an ice cream eating contest. I prefer a slimmer class design, using multiple classes rather than scooping feature after feature onto one plate.

The problem of sifting through a list of objects makes a good demonstration of this approach to designing useful classes. Rather than add search functions to List<T>, I developed an *iterator class* that can scan any list of objects. The resulting two classes are smaller, and therefore, easier to maintain. Also, multiple iterators can hunt for objects in the *same* list—a task that would be difficult if the list itself handled the search.

List Iterator

The iterator class in this section provides access to a list. (Later in this chapter are iterators for other containers.) Because the iterator is separate from the list, a program can use multiple iterators to search listed objects in various ways. One iterator, for example, might scan a list for a specified object, then halt while another iterator performs a search for a different value. If the list provided its own iteration functions, only one such operation could be performed at a time.

You might imagine an iterator to be a kind of robot that walks through a list of objects (see Figure 11.6). Because the iterator "robots" operate independently, two or more of them can hunt through a list, possibly "walking" in opposite directions.

Before digging into the techniques of writing an iterator class, it helps to examine a program that uses an iterator object to scan a list of other objects. Listing 11.5, TLIST.CPP, also demonstrates how to use the List<T> class template.

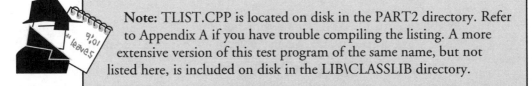

Note: TLIST.CPP is located on disk in the PART2 directory. Refer to Appendix A if you have trouble compiling the listing. A more extensive version of this test program of the same name, but not listed here, is included on disk in the LIB\CLASSLIB directory.

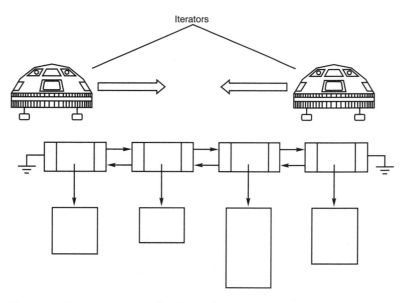

Figure 11.6. An iterator works like a robot that can scan a list of objects.

Listing 11.5. TLIST.CPP.

```
#include <iostream.h>
#include <iomanip.h>
#include <str.h>
#include <list.h>
#include <listiter.h>
#include <memuse.h>

void ShowString(String *sp);
void IntList();
void DoubleList();
void StringList();

int main()
{
  HeapReport("Initial memory use");
  IntList();
```

continues

Listing 11.5.continued

```cpp
    DoubleList();
    StringList();
    HeapReport("\nFinal memory use");
    return 0;
}

// List of int values
void IntList()
{
  cout << "----------\n";
  cout << "List of int values\n";

  // Construct and fill list of int values
  List<int> ilist;
  for (int i = 1; i <= 6; ++i)
    ilist.LinkTail(i);

  // Extract and delete items the "hard way"
  while (ilist.ItemCount() > 0) {
    int *ip = ilist.UnlinkHead();
    cout << setw(8) << *ip;
    delete ip;
  }
  cout << endl;
}

// List of double values
void DoubleList()
{
  cout << "----------\n";
  cout << "List of double values\n";

  // Construct and fill list of double values
  List<double> dlist;
  for (int i = 1; i <= 6; ++i)
    dlist.LinkHead(i * 3.14159);
```

```
  // Access items using an iterator
  ListIterator<double> iter(&dlist);
  if (iter.GetFirst())
  do {
    cout << *iter.CurrentItem() << endl;
  } while (iter.GetNext());
}

// Display String object addressed by sp
// Called by list iterator
void ShowString(String *sp)
{
  cout << '"' << *sp << '"' << endl;
}

// List of Strings
void StringList()
{
  cout << "----------\n";
  cout << "List of String objects\n";

  // Construct list of String objects
  List<String> strlist;

  // Insert a literal String
  strlist.LinkTail("Literal string");

  // Insert a constructed String object directly
  strlist.LinkTail(String("Direct string"));

  // Insert a constructed String object indirectly
  String s("Indirect string");
  strlist.LinkTail(s);

  // Insert a pointer to a String object
  String *sp;
  sp = new String("Pointer to string");
  strlist.LinkTail(sp);
  delete sp;  // Okay because list copies object
```

continues

Listing 11.5. continued

```
// Display list using an iterator object
ListIterator<String> iter(&strlist);
iter.Iterate(ShowString);
}
```

Using the List<T> template, test-function IntList() constructs a list of integer values with the statement

```
List<int> ilist;
```

When the compiler reads the expression List<int>, it creates a class from the List<T> template to hold int values. To link an integer i at the tail of the list, the program calls the LinkTail() member function:

```
ilist.LinkTail(i);
```

Because of the class's design, you can also link literal values into a list:

```
ilist.LinkTail(10);
```

Or, you can pass a pointer to an int variable:

```
ilist.LinkTail(&i);
```

Replace LinkTail() with LinkHead() to insert items into the head of a list. To delete objects the "hard way," use a while or other loop something like this:

```
while (ilist.ItemCount() > 0) {
  int *ip = ilist.UnlinkHead();
  cout << setw(8) << *ip;
  delete ip;
}
```

Simply stated, the loop cycles while the list's ItemCount() function indicates the list is not empty. Each int object is unlinked by calling UnlinkHead(), assigning the resulting pointer to ip. (You could also call UnlinkTail().) Each item is displayed, then deleted.

Notice that you must delete each item this way regardless of how items were inserted into a list. The simple rule is this: After unlinking an item, that object becomes your responsibility. (Other class libraries define ownership differently, so don't assume that all list classes work the same as mine.)

The `while` loop works but is inconvenient to use. A better, and more versatile, way to scan a list is to use a `ListIterator<T>` object. Construct the object like this:

```
ListIterator<double> iter(&dlist);
```

The iterator class is a template named `ListIterator<T>`. Replacing `T` with `double` creates an iterator object that can scan through a list of type `List<double>`. Notice how the address of a list object is passed to the iterator's constructor as `&dlist`.

After constructing the iterator, you can use it in several different ways. For example, you can call `GetFirst()` and `GetNext()` iterator functions to scan listed items:

```
if (iter.GetFirst())
do {
  cout << *iter.CurrentItem() << endl;
} while (iter.GetNext());
```

These two functions return true if they can find the designated item. `GetFirst()` starts a scan from the head of the list. `GetNext()` returns true if it can advance to another object. `CurrentItem()`, another iterator function, returns a pointer to the current listed object.

The iterator class also has an `Iterate()` member function that can call *another* function for all listed objects. This is a handy device—one that you might implement similarly in other classes. To use this feature, construct a list and insert some objects. For demonstration, you might use the `String` class from Chapter 10:

```
List<String> strlist;
```

Next, link one or more literal strings into the list:

```
strlist.LinkTail("Literal string");
```

Or, you can construct and insert a `String` object and insert it:

```
String s("Indirect string");
strlist.LinkTail(s);
```

Function `StringList()` in Listing 11.5 demonstrates other ways to insert `String` objects into a list. To display all listed strings, the program uses an iterator:

```
ListIterator<String> iter(&strlist);
iter.Iterate(ShowString);
```

The Iterate() member function is declared as

```
void Iterate(void (* f)(T *ip));
```

In English, the Iterate() function's parameter f is a pointer to a function that returns void and requires an argument ip of type T *. Function ShowString() fits that bill perfectly:

```
void ShowString(String *sp)
{
  cout << '"' << *sp << '"' << endl;
}
```

Simply calling the iterator's Iterate() member function passes the address of each String object in the list to ShowString(). Listing 11.6, listiter.h, declares and implements the iterator class template, ListIterator<T>.

Note: The listiter.h file is located on disk in the LIB\CLASSLIB directory. A copy of the file is also in the INCLUDE directory.

Listing 11.6. listiter.h.

```
#ifndef __LISTITER_H
#define __LISTITER_H    // Prevent multiple #includes

#include "list.h"
#include "misc.h"

template<class T>
class ListIterator {
public:
  ListIterator(const List<T> *lptr);
  ListIterator(const List<T> &lref);
  int GetFirst();
```

```
  int GetNext();
  int FindFirst(const T &item);
  int FindNext(const T &item);
  T *CurrentItem();
  void Iterate(void (* f)(T *ip));
private:
  const List<T> *lp;      // Points to list to be iterated
  Carrier<T> *current;  // Points to current object in iteration
};


// ---------------------------------------------------------------
// class ListIterator
// ---------------------------------------------------------------

// Constructor (List pointer argument)
template<class T>
ListIterator<T>::ListIterator(const List<T> *lptr)
  : lp(lptr)
{
  GetFirst();  // Sets current to head of list
}


// Constructor (List reference argument)
template<class T>
ListIterator<T>::ListIterator(const List<T> &lref)
  : lp(&lref), current(lref.GetHead())
{
}


// Sets current to head of list
// Returns true for success; false for errors
template<class T>
int ListIterator<T>::GetFirst()
{
  current = lp ? lp->GetHead() : 0;
  return current != 0;
}


// Sets current to next object in list
// Returns true for success; false for errors
```

continues

287

Listing 11.6. continued

```cpp
template<class T>
int ListIterator<T>::GetNext()
{
  current = current ? current->next : 0;
  return current != 0;
}

// Sets current to first object equal to item
// Returns true for success; false for errors
template<class T>
int ListIterator<T>::FindFirst(const T &item)
{
  if (!GetFirst()) return FALSE;
  do {
    if (current->ip && *current->ip == item)
      return TRUE;
  } while (GetNext());
  return FALSE;
}

// Sets current to next object equal to item
// Returns true for success; false for errors
template<class T>
int ListIterator<T>::FindNext(const T &item)
{
  if (!GetNext()) return FALSE;
  do {
    if (current->ip && *current->ip == item)
      return TRUE;
  } while (GetNext());
  return FALSE;
}

// Returns address of current item (inside Carrier object)
// Returns null for errors
template<class T>
T * ListIterator<T>::CurrentItem()
```

```
{
  return current ? current->ip : 0;
}

// Calls user function for all items in list
template<class T>
void ListIterator<T>::Iterate(void (* f)(T *ip))
{
  if (!GetFirst()) return;
  do {
    f(CurrentItem());
  } while (GetNext());
}

#endif  // __LISTITER_H
```

The ListIterator<T> class template is only a sample of one kind of many possible iterators you might invent. You could expand this class (or write others) to scan a list in reverse, to replace listed items, or to provide other services. The importance of the technique is the separation of the list data structure from iteration operations that perform work on the list's objects.

To simplify construction of iterator objects, I added two constructors to the ListIterator<T> class template. These are declared as

```
ListIterator(const List<T> *lptr);
ListIterator(const List<T> &lref);
```

The first constructor requires a pointer to a List<T> object. The second requires a reference to an object of that class. Given the List<String> list-object slist, either of these two statements constructs a proper iterator:

```
ListIterator<String> iter1(&slist);  // By pointer
ListIterator<String> iter2(slist);   // By reference
```

Both statements perform the identical job of constructing an iterator for the String list, slist. Having both forms available simply means you don't have to look up the syntax in a reference. You might use a similar trick in other classes initialized or associated with class objects.

In addition to `GetFirst()` and `GetNext()` member functions, I also added `FindFirst()` and `FindNext()`. These two functions search for items, returning true if found. The four functions mix easily. Suppose you construct a list of integers:

```
List<int> list;
```

Next, you insert some values into the list:

```
for (int i = 1; i < 10; ++i)
  list.LinkTail(i);
```

Construct an iterator for the list like this:

```
ListIterator<int> iter(list);
```

Then, to find the first instance of the value 5, call the iterator's `FindFirst()` function. If true, continue the search by calling `GetNext()`:

```
if (iter.FindFirst(5))
do {
  cout << *iter.CurrentItem() << endl;
} while (iter.GetNext());
```

Given the preceding statements, this `if` statement displays the values 5 through 10. To search for all fives in the list, replace `GetNext()` with `FindNext(5)`.

As you read through the implementation for `ListIterator<T>` in Listing 11.6, refer to Figure 11.5. The programming is straightforward. The iterator merely keeps a pointer to a `Carrier<T>` object, and follows the pointers (*P* and *N* in the figure) to scan listed objects. The iterator encapsulates these pointer operations, eliminating the need to manipulate pointers in programs—a common cause of bugs in conventional code.

Vector Iterator

Vectors can also have iterators. We'll need one in the next chapter, so I'll list it here. Listing 11.7, vectiter.h, provides a `VectorIterator<T>` class template for scanning `Vector<T>` objects. The member functions in the iterator are similar to those in `ListIterator<T>`, giving programs a consistent means to scan vectors and lists—two very different fundamental data structures.

Note: The vectiter.h file is located on disk in the LIB\CLASSLIB directory. A copy of the file is also in the INCLUDE directory.

Listing 11.7. vectiter.h.

```
#ifndef __VECTITER_H
#define __VECTITER_H    // Prevent multiple #includes

#include "vector.h"
#include "minmax.h"
#include "misc.h"

template<class T>
class VectorIterator {
public:
  VectorIterator(const Vector<T> *vptr);
  VectorIterator(const Vector<T> &vref);
  int GetFirst();
  int GetNext();
  int FindFirst(const T &item);
  int FindNext(const T &item);
  T *CurrentItem();
  void Iterate(void (* f)(T *ip));
private:
  const Vector<T> *vp;   // Points to vector to be iterated
  int current;           // Index of current object in iteration
};

// ----------------------------------------------------------------
// class VectorIterator
// ----------------------------------------------------------------

// Constructor (Vector pointer argument)
template<class T>
VectorIterator<T>::VectorIterator(const Vector<T> *vptr)
```

continues

Listing 11.7. continued

```cpp
  : vp(vptr)
{
  GetFirst();
}

// Constructor (Vector reference argument)
template<class T>
VectorIterator<T>::VectorIterator(const Vector<T> &vref)
  : vp(&vref), current(vref.GetMin())
{
}

// Sets current to first index in vector
// Returns true for success; false for errors
template<class T>
int VectorIterator<T>::GetFirst()
{
  if (!vp) return FALSE;
  current = vp->GetMin();
  return TRUE;
}

// Sets current to next index in vector
// Returns true for success; false for errors
template<class T>
int VectorIterator<T>::GetNext()
{
  if (!vp) return FALSE;
  if (current < vp->GetMax()) {
    ++current;
    return TRUE;
  } else
    return FALSE;
}

// Sets current index to first object equal to item
// Returns true for success; false for errors
template<class T>
```

```
int VectorIterator<T>::FindFirst(const T &item)
{
  if (!GetFirst()) return FALSE;
  do {
    if ((*vp)[current] == item)
      return TRUE;
  } while (GetNext());
  return FALSE;
}

// Sets current index to next object equal to item
// Returns true for success; false for errors
template<class T>
int VectorIterator<T>::FindNext(const T &item)
{
  if (!GetNext()) return FALSE;
  do {
    if ((*vp)[current] == item)
      return TRUE;
  } while (GetNext());
  return FALSE;
}

// Returns address of current item
// Returns null for errors
template<class T>
T * VectorIterator<T>::CurrentItem()
{
  if (!vp) return 0;
  if (!inrange(current, vp->GetMin(), vp->GetMax()))
    return 0;
  return &(*vp)[current];
}

// Calls user function for all items in vector
template<class T>
void VectorIterator<T>::Iterate(void (* f)(T *ip))
```

continues

Listing 11.7. continued

```
{
  if (!vp) return;
  for (int i = vp->GetMin(); i <= vp->GetMax(); ++i)
    f(&(*vp)[i]);
}

#endif  // __VECTITER_H
```

Use a VectorIterator<T> object similar to the way you use an object of type ListIterator<T>. For example, you might construct a vector of four Strings, indexed from 1 to 4:

```
Vector<String> vs(1, 4);
```

Then, assign String objects to each vector position:

```
vs[1] = String("Abcdefg");
vs[2] = String("Hijklmn");
vs[3] = String("Opqrstu");
vs[4] = String("Vwxyz");
```

To display the vector's Strings, use a VectorIterator<T> object. Construct the iterator by passing the vector vs to the constructor:

```
VectorIterator<String> iter(vs);
```

Then use the iterators GetFirst() and GetNext() member functions to scan the Strings in low to high order:

```
if (iter.GetFirst())
do {
  cout << *iter.CurrentItem() << endl;
} while (iter.GetNext());
```

This isn't the only way to access objects in a Vector<T> container (see Chapter 9). Interestingly, however, the code is identical to that used to scan lists (see TLIST.CPP, Listing 11.5).

Tree Class

There are a number of fundamental data structures that would make useful classes. My aim in this chapter, however, is not to present all possible data structures in the galaxy, but to investigate techniques for designing your own class libraries.

One structure that poses a sizable challenge is a *binary tree*. Tree classes seem to be rare, perhaps because they are more difficult to write than lists and vectors. As you probably know, a tree can be implemented as an ordered linked list in disguise. Pointers in tree nodes address left and right branches of the tree. Accessing nodes by using those pointers accesses objects in specific orders (see Figure 11.7).

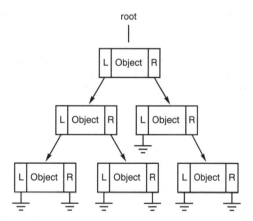

Figure 11.7. A binary tree might be implemented as an ordered linked list.

Compare Figures 11.7 and 11.5. If the nodes in the tree are made to point to other items, the tree can be generalized as a template much as List<T> was programmed. Also, using an iterator, complex tree operations are relatively easy to write.

Listing 11.8, tree.h, declares and implements a Tree<T> class template and an associated IteratorTree<T> class. These templates demonstrate how an iterator can become an integral part of the class for which it is designed. Because this listing is lengthy, I'll describe it in sections.

Note: On disk, file tree.h is located in the LIB\CLASSLIB directory. A copy of the file is also stored in the INCLUDE directory.

Listing 11.8. tree.h.

```
#ifndef __TREE_H
#define __TREE_H   // Prevent multiple #includes

template<class T>
class Node {
public:
  Node(T *item);
  ~Node();
public:
  Node *left;   // Points to node at left
  Node *right;  // Points to node at right
  T *ip;        // Addresses item in node
};

template<class T>
class Tree {
  friend class TreeIterator<T>;
public:
  Tree();
  ~Tree();
  void Insert(T *item);
  void Insert(T item);
  void DeleteAll();
private:
  Node<T> *root;  // Points to root of tree
};
```

The Node<T> class is similar to Carrier<T> in Listing 11.4, list.h. It might be possible to remove this small amount of duplication, but because of the way trees are structured, deleting nodes requires special care, so I decided to create a different "carrier" class for tree objects; more on this later.

The Tree<T> class template is short and sweet. It contains a bare minimum of declarations, having only the capabilities of constructing trees, inserting items by address or value, and deleting tree nodes.

Listing 11.8 continues with the TreeIterator<T> class template declaration. Notice that this class is declared in Tree<T> as a friend, thus giving the iterator access to Tree<T>'s private members.

Listing 11.8. tree.h (continued).

```
template<class T>
class TreeIterator {
public:
  TreeIterator(Tree<T> *t);
  TreeIterator(Tree<T> &t);
  void PreOrder(void (* f)(T *ip));
  void InOrder(void (* f)(T *ip));
  void PostOrder(void (* f)(T *ip));
  void Search(T *ip, void (* f)(T *ip) = 0);
protected:
  void XPreOrder(Node<T> *node);
  void XInOrder(Node<T> *node);
  void XPostOrder(Node<T> *node);
  void XSearch(Node<T> *&node);
private:
  void (* fn)(T *ip);   // Points to user function
  T *key;               // Item to insert or find in tree
  Tree<T> *tree;        // Tree associated with iterator
};
```

The two constructors in TreeIterator<T> are similar to those in ListIterator<T> and VectorIterator<T>. The four public member functions are different, however. Functions PreOrder(), InOrder(), and PostOrder() perform recursive scans of tree nodes—classic binary tree operations. These functions call a user function for each node, similar to the way the Iterate() function works in ListIterator<T>.

Function Search() locates items in trees. If the item addressed by parameter ip is found, the function calls the user-supplied function (if non-null). If the item is not found, Search() inserts a new node in the tree for this item. These operations compare objects, so when inserting class objects into trees, the class must provide operator<(), operator>(), and operator==() functions.

I'll get back to the TreeIterator<T> class in a moment. First, let's examine the Node<T> template in Listing 11.8's continuation.

Listing 11.8. tree.h (continued).

```
// -----------------------------------------------------------
// class Node
// -----------------------------------------------------------

// Constructor
template<class T>
Node<T>::Node(T *item)
  : left(0), right(0)
{
  ip = new T(*item);  // Insert copy of item into node
}

// Destructor
template<class T>
Node<T>::~Node()
{
  delete ip;      // Delete item in node
  delete left;    // Delete left tree branches recursively
  delete right;   // Delete right tree branches recursively
}
```

The constructor operates identically to Carrier<T>'s constructor, copying the passed item and assigning its address to ip.

The destructor is different. After deleting the addressed item, the left and right branches of the tree are deleted in turn. If either or both left and right are non-null, these statements recursively call the destructor, continuing to delete items and nodes one by one until the entire tree is snuffed out of RAM.

Now, let's examine how the `TreeIterator<T>` class works. Its operation is crucial to the `Tree<T>` class.

Listing 11.8. tree.h (continued).

```
// -------------------------------------------------------------
// class TreeIterator
// -------------------------------------------------------------


// Constructor (Tree pointer argument)
template<class T>
TreeIterator<T>::TreeIterator(Tree<T> *t)
  : tree(t), fn(0), key(0)
{
}


// Constructor (Tree reference argument)
template<class T>
TreeIterator<T>::TreeIterator(Tree<T> &t)
  : tree(&t), fn(0), key(0)
{
}


// Performs pre order scan of tree nodes
// Calls user function f for each node
template<class T>
void TreeIterator<T>::PreOrder(void (* f)(T *ip))
{
  fn = f;                   // Save user function address
  XPreOrder(tree->root);    // Start recursive scan
}


// Performs in order scan of tree nodes
// Calls user function f for each node
template<class T>
void TreeIterator<T>::InOrder(void (* f)(T *ip))
{
  fn = f;                   // Save user function address
  XInOrder(tree->root);     // Start recursive scan
}
```

continues

Listing 11.8. tree.h (continued).

```cpp
// Performs post order scan of tree nodes
// Calls user function f for each node
template<class T>
void TreeIterator<T>::PostOrder(void (* f)(T *ip))
{
  fn = f;                     // Save user function address
  XPostOrder(tree->root);  // Start recursive scan
}


// Search for item at ip
// If item is found, call user function f (unless null)
// If item is not found, insert item into tree
template<class T>
void TreeIterator<T>::Search(T *ip, void (* f)(T *ip))
{
  fn = f;                  // Save user function address
  key = ip;                // Save search argument
  XSearch(tree->root);  // Start recursive search / insert
}


// Recursive pre order scan
template<class T>
void TreeIterator<T>::XPreOrder(Node<T> *node)
{
  if (node) {
    fn(node->ip);
    XPreOrder(node->left);
    XPreOrder(node->right);
  }
}


// Recursive in order scan
template<class T>
void TreeIterator<T>::XInOrder(Node<T> *node)
{
  if (node) {
    XInOrder(node->left);
    fn(node->ip);
```

```
    XInOrder(node->right);
  }
}


// Recursive post order scan
template<class T>
void TreeIterator<T>::XPostOrder(Node<T> *node)
{
  if (node) {
    XPostOrder(node->left);
    XPostOrder(node->right);
    fn(node->ip);
  }
}


// Search, update, and insert nodes into tree
template<class T>
void TreeIterator<T>::XSearch(Node<T> *&node)
{
  if (!node) node = new Node<T>(key);
  else if (*key < *node->ip) XSearch(node->left);
  else if (*key > *node->ip) XSearch(node->right);
  else if (fn) fn(node->ip);  // Update node via user function
}
```

Each of the public member functions in TreeIterator<T> has a corresponding protected member, beginning with X. The public PreOrder() function's protected partner, for example, is XPreOrder().

I designed the class this way to hide the construction and design of Node<T> objects from tree users, and in the process, simplifying these naturally recursive operations. Similar techniques come in handy in the design of many other classes. In PreOrder(), for instance, it takes only two statements to start a recursive search rolling:

```
fn = f;                // Save user function address
XPreOrder(tree->root); // Start recursive scan
```

The user-function address in f is saved in the class's private fn data member. This way, XPreOrder(), which calls itself recursively, can call f() without having to pass that function's address to every level of the recursion. Skip down to XPreOrder() to see how this works. The protected function implements the classic binary-tree pre-order search:

```
if (node) {
  fn(node->ip);
  XPreOrder(node->left);
  XPreOrder(node->right);
}
```

If the node at this level is non-null, the program calls the user function fn(), passing the item pointer ip as an argument. Then, XPreOrder() continues the search of the left and right tree branches. Saving the function address in the class's fn data member makes that function available to other members.

The InOrder, XInOrder, PostOrder(), and XPostOrder() member functions are implemented similarly, but perform the classic binary-tree maneuvers that their names suggest. The only difference between the functions is the place during the search that user function f() is called.

One other function, Search(), hunts for and inserts objects into a tree. Examine this function closely. It executes three statements:

```
fn = f;                // Save user function address
key = ip;              // Save search argument
XSearch(tree->root);   // Start recursive search / insert
```

Again, the user function f() address is saved in fn. In this case, the search key ip is also saved in the data member key. Following these two steps, Search() calls XSearch(), the protected function that performs the actual recursive search of tree nodes, also inserting a new node if necessary. Assigning the user function address to fn and the search argument to key avoids passing these values to each level of the recursion, which might otherwise consume too much stack space. In this case, fn and key become globally available to all class member functions—a useful technique for passing values to functions without using function parameters.

The protected member function XSearch() carries out the recursive search of tree nodes and also inserts new nodes. The function declares a single parameter of type Node<T>:

```
Node<T> *&node
```

Literally, node is a pointer to a reference of type Node<T>, in other words, a double indirection—one of the more difficult concepts in C and C++ programming to master. When XSearch() is called, node addresses *another address,* at which the real item (a Node<T> object) is found. Figure 11.8 illustrates node's double indirection.

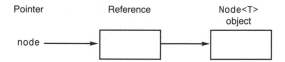

Figure 11.8. Parameter node's double indirection.

When Search() calls XSearch(), it passes the tree's root pointer with the statement

```
XSearch(tree->root);
```

Inside XSearch(), node initially addresses the root pointer. If the root is null, XSearch() creates a new Node<T> object, saving the search key inside the node:

```
if (!node) node = new Node<T>(key);
```

If node is not null, then it addresses a branch of the tree. Two if statements inside XSearch() compare the search key with the items in the current node, calling XSearch() recursively. If the key is less than the node's item, the search continues along the branch addressed by node->left. If the key is greater, the search goes to node->right.

Upon entry to each of these recursions, node again addresses a Node<T> reference. Except for the initial search at the tree's root, *these pointers refer to the* left *and* right *data members inside each node.* Simply stated, the tree grows by attaching new nodes to itself—an action that might be easier to see by executing sample code in a debugger.

During the search, if an item is located in the tree, XSearch() calls a user function addressed by fn, unless that member is null, in which case the search merely ends with no action.

You might want to add additional search functions to TreeIterator<T> similar to Search() and XSearch(). Another function, for example, might locate objects in trees without making an insertion if the object isn't found.

Finally in Listing 11.8 is the Tree<T> class template's implementation. Because the TreeIterator<T> template performs so much of the tree's functions, the actual Tree<T> class has surprisingly little to do.

Listing 11.8. tree.h (continued).

```
// ---------------------------------------------------------------
// class Tree
// ---------------------------------------------------------------

// Default constructor
template<class T>
Tree<T>::Tree()
  : root(0)
{
}

// Destructor
template<class T>
Tree<T>::~Tree()
{
  DeleteAll();  // Deletes nodes and items in nodes
}

// Insert item into tree
template<class T>
void Tree<T>::Insert(T *item)
{
  if (!item) return;          // Can't insert null items
  TreeIterator<T> iter(this); // Construct iterator object
  iter.Search(item);          // Let iterator perform insertion
}

// Same as preceding but inserts item passed by value
// Note: Do not declare inline!
template<class T>
void Tree<T>::Insert(T item)
{
  Insert(&item);
```

```
}

// Delete all nodes and items in tree
template<class T>
void Tree<T>::DeleteAll()
{
  delete root;   // Causes recursive deletion of entire tree
  root = 0;      // Reset tree to empty
}

#endif  // __TREE_H
```

Tree<T>'s member functions are short and sweet. The constructor and destructor have obvious purposes. Member function Insert() simply constructs a TreeIterator<T> object, and calls its Search() function to insert items into the tree. Insert() is overloaded so you can pass arguments by address or by value. DeleteAll() disposes of an entire tree by deleting its root—the recursive Node<T> destructors ensure a proper cleanup.

Listing 11.9, TTREE.CPP, demonstrates how to use the Tree<T> class.

Note: The TTREE.CPP file is located on disk in the PART2 directory. A similar test program of the same name is also stored in the LIB\CLASSLIB directory. Consult Appendix A if you have trouble compiling the program.

Listing 11.9. TTREE.CPP.

```
#include <iostream.h>
#include <str.h>
#include <memuse.h>
#include <tree.h>
```

continues

Listing 11.9. continued

```cpp
void PerformTest();

int main()
{
  HeapReport("Initial memory use");
  PerformTest();
  HeapReport("\nFinal memory use");
  return 0;
}

void ShowString(String *sp)
{
  cout << " ¦ " << *sp;
}

void PerformTest()
{
  Tree<String> t;

  t.Insert("Red");
  t.Insert("Orange");
  t.Insert("Yellow");
  t.Insert("Green");
  t.Insert("Blue");
  t.Insert("Indigo");
  t.Insert("Violet");

  TreeIterator<String> iter(t);
  cout << "Pre order\n";
  iter.PreOrder(ShowString);
  cout << "\nIn order\n";
  iter.InOrder(ShowString);
  cout << "\nPost order\n";
  iter.PostOrder(ShowString);
}
```

Use `Tree<T>` much the same as `List<T>` and `Vector<T>`. To construct a tree of `double` values, use a statement such as

```
Tree<double> tree;
```

To construct trees of other types, insert the type names inside the template brackets. For example, here's how to construct a tree of `String` objects:

```
Tree<String> t;
```

Insert `String` objects or literal strings by calling the tree's `Insert()` member function:

```
t.Insert("Red");
t.Insert("Orange");
...
t.Insert("Violet");
```

You could also construct a `String` object and insert it into the tree:

```
String s1("White");
t.Insert(s1);
```

Or, to reduce stack usage, and prevent constructing a copy of s1 on the system stack, pass the string to `Insert()` by address:

```
String s2("Black");
t.Insert(&s2);
```

Whatever method you use to insert `String` objects into the tree, the next step is to perform an operation for them in a defined order. This is where an iterator object is invaluable. Construct one for the `Tree<String>` object t like this:

```
TreeIterator<String> iter(t);
```

You can then call the `iter` object's member functions to scan tree nodes. Provide a function for the members to call:

```
void ShowString(String *sp)
{
  cout << " ¦ " << *sp;
}
```

Then, pass the function name (that is, its address) to the `PreOrder()`, `InOrder()`, and `PostOrder()` member functions in `TreeIterator<T>`:

```
cout << "Pre order\n";
iter.PreOrder(ShowString);
cout << "\nIn order\n";
iter.InOrder(ShowString);
cout << "\nPost order\n";
iter.PostOrder(ShowString);
```

Final Words

A common misconception with commercial class libraries is that fundamental data types like vectors, lists, and trees are for the library's private consumption. Some libraries provide abstract data types—sets, arrays, stacks, and so on—that are implemented using other fundamental structures. It's often not clear, however, which of these classes are proper to use. For example, should you build your code using an abstract stack, or is it okay to go straight to the heart of the matter and employ a fundamental vector?

The question is important because your decision might have far reaching consequences. If you elect to use a vector class, you might find switching to a list difficult if that becomes necessary in the future. Fundamental class templates like List<T> and Tree<T> in this chapter provide general purpose structures that can store objects of many kinds, but they don't prevent you from binding your code to a particular kind of structure. Converting list class objects into vector class objects might not be any easier than changing conventionally written lists into arrays.

In the next chapter, you'll develop *abstract data types* that help to reduce this kind of dependency, resulting in container classes that can be used identically regardless of their implementation. With this technique, a single new statement can completely reconfigure a program that bases its data structures on vectors into a program that uses lists—a high level of versatility that's hard to beat.

Developing Abstract Container Classes

I t takes a great deal of faith to write a successful computer program—not necessarily religious faith, but faith that functions and commands will produce the expected results. Too often, however, our trust in these and other programming tools is rewarded with bugs that arise kicking and squirming from tested code that used to work perfectly until it was adapted to new tasks.

Container classes, primarily used for storing objects of various kinds, can help prevent revised code from becoming infested with new bugs. A container class embodies a fundamental data structure such as a list or a vector, hiding the complexity of these low-level types from higher-level uses. With container classes, you can construct *abstract data types*—arrays, sets, stacks, queues, deques, and others—that serve as simple but faithful data-storage engines.

Introduction to Container Classes

A container class is like a magician's hat that can store one or more objects, then give back those objects on demand (see Figure 12.1). You might not be able to pull a rabbit out of a hat, but if you could program a hare, you could store one in a container class object.

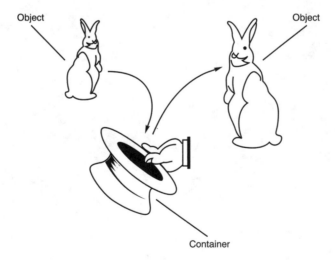

Figure 12.1. A container class is like a magician's hat that can store and retrieve any kind of object (but maybe not a rabbit).

You can use containers to store objects without even considering how the containers are constructed. Or, you might select from among several different containers to gauge their relative benefits in performance or memory savings. Containers exhibit several common properties, and are therefore ideally suited as base classes for other abstract data types.

Most C++ class libraries provide one or more container classes. It's useful to construct your own, however, both as an exercise in programming and to lessen the dependency of your code on one vendor's specifications. There's more than one way to design a container class library, but in general terms, most containers probably need to...

- count the number of objects contained
- optionally limit the maximum number of objects
- add new objects
- delete existing objects
- retrieve objects
- find objects by value

Before looking at some code, it will help your understanding of this chapter's listings to know where we are heading. I used top-down programming to write the containers and abstract classes that I'll describe here, but I'll present the classes from the bottom up to show how they fit together. Figure 12.2 illustrates the class hierarchy, using the FDS (fundamental data structure) classes from Chapters 9 and 11.

Figure 12.2. Container class hierarchy.

Not all container class libraries are structured this way. In fact, every vendor seems to follow a unique path in class design (and of course every vendor will tell you that its implementations are the best that money can buy.) In some libraries, containers are used as base classes for fundamental types. In others, fundamental lists and vectors serve the purposes of containers as I am defining them here. Also, a commercial library might provide many more classes than the limited collection I selected for this chapter.

Though there's little agreement on how to write a class library, at least most C++ vendors seem to agree on the usefulness of general-purpose container classes. Let's see how you might construct a container or two using the fundamental class templates from Chapter 11.

List and Vector Containers

From Figure 12.2, it might seem unnecessary to interpose the *vectorContainer* and *listContainer* classes between the fundamental data structures (FDS) and abstract data types (ADT) at top and bottom. In this library's design, however, FDS classes are extremely low on the totem pole. They provide only bare minimum services, making them less than ideal as general-purpose containers. As I constructed my library's container classes, I kept several objectives in mind:

- *Safety.* Container classes can provide safe access to potentially dangerous low-level fundamental structures.

- *Data and complexity hiding.* The container classes in Figure 12.2 inherit their fundamental data structures privately, hiding the complexity of the underlying fundamental types. Abstract classes such as *sets* and *queues* are permitted to call *only* container class functions. A *stack* class, for example, is not allowed to call a *list* class member function directly.

- *Portability.* As a consequence of the preceding point, the entire class library can be ported to a new compiler simply by rewriting the mid-level containers. For example, the library could be revised to use other fundamental types simply by providing new *vectorContainer* and *listContainer* classes.

- *Object ownership.* Containers can reduce concerns over object ownership. On the abstract level (bottom of Figure 12.2), we want the containers to own the objects passed to them, but to relinquish ownership when those objects are retrieved. For instance, it should be possible to push an item onto a *stack,* giving the stack ownership of the object. Popping the item from the stack should return ownership of the removed object to the program.

- *Error handling.* Container classes can provide consistent error handling. Ideally, proposed ANSI C++ draft-standard *exceptions* would be used to respond to error conditions. Because exceptions are not yet widely available, however, I implemented a rudimentary error class for the library in this chapter.

- *Iterations.* Containers can provide iterator objects (see Chapter 11) for safely accessing fundamental data structures. Rather than call member functions to scan a container, for example, you can ask the container to provide an iterator for that purpose. The key advantage of using iterators is the ability to perform multiple search operations on the same container.

List and Vector Containers

Listing 12.1 declares and implements the two mid-level container classes illustrated in Figure 12.2. The classes are written as templates, using the class templates declared in list.h, vector.h, listiter.h, and vectiter.h as explained in Chapters 9 and 11. Because the listing is lengthy, I'll describe it in relatively small sections.

Note: On disk, file contain.h is stored in the LIB\CLASSLIB directory. A copy of the file is also stored in the INCLUDE directory.

Listing 12.1. contain.h.

```
#ifndef __CONTAIN_H
#define __CONTAIN_H    // Prevent multiple #includes

#include <limits.h>
#include "list.h"
#include "vector.h"
#include "listiter.h"
#include "vectiter.h"

class ContainerError {
public:
  enum err {
    err_noerror = 0,    // No error detected
    err_underflow,      // Too few items in container
    err_overflow        // Too many items in container
  };
  virtual int Error(err e);
        };
```

First in contain.h is the ContainerError class, inherited by each container template. The class provides a simple error mechanism. Errors inside containers and abstract classes derived from containers call the class's Error() member function passing an enum err symbol. The Error() function is virtual, so you can override it in a derived class to trap faulty conditions—a stack overflow, for example.

Error() returns *true* if no errors are detected, which might seem backwards at first. If Error()'s result is *false,* then err e was either err_underflow or err_overflow. These facts mean you can't use Error() in an if statement as might seem logical:

```
if (Error()) { ... } // ???
```

That doesn't work because, in C and C++, zero represents "no error." Because zero also means *false,* Error()'s result is intended to be returned by *another* true/false function such as

```
int TrueFalse()
{
  if (!operation())
    return Error(ContainerError::err_overflow);
  return TRUE;
}
```

You could use this `TrueFalse()` function in an `if` statement to test whether an operation succeeded or failed:

```
if (!TrueFalse()) yourErrorHandler();
```

Listing 12.1 continues with the declaration for the `ListContainer<T>` class template.

Listing 12.1. contain.h (continued).

```
template<class T>
class ListContainer
  : public ContainerError,
    private List<T>
{
public:
  ListContainer();
  ListContainer(int maxItems);
  int IsFull() const;
  int IsEmpty() const;
  int ContainerMax() const;
  int PutAtHead(T &item);
  int PutAtTail(T &item);
  int RemoveAtHead(T &item);
  int RemoveAtTail(T &item);
  int RemoveItem(T &item);
  void RemoveAll();
  ListIterator<T> MakeIterator() const;
  List<T>::operator!;  // Selectively qualify as public
private:
  int max;  // Maximum items permitted in list
      };
```

I won't dwell on the member functions in ListContainer<T>—most have obvious purposes. The key feature here is the private inheritance of the List<T> class. Because the base class is private to its derived class, the details of list management are hidden at the container level. Any new classes derived from ListContainer<T> can use only the container's member functions.

Judging from published source code, C++ programmers do not use the private keyword often enough. This important tool can help produce more reliable code by limiting access to base class members.

In some cases, however, it's necessary to provide *selective* access to privately inherited base classes. Here, for example, it seems pointless to rewrite the operator! function for the container. To make that function available to classes derived from ListContainer<T>, I selectively qualified it in the class's public section using the line:

```
List<T>::operator!;  // Selectively qualify as public
```

In effect, this line says "bump the privately inherited operator! function to public status." Notice the absence of function parentheses in the declaration. Strictly speaking, it is the *symbol* operator! that is affected. The function is not redeclared; only its status is upgraded from private to public.

Notice also the class's use of the const keyword—another C++ tool not employed as much as it probably should be. The IsFull() and IsEmpty() member functions do not change any data members in ListContainer<T> or in its base classes, so I declared them as const. These member functions can therefore be called for any const objects of type ListContainer<T>, a good way to prevent bugs in functions such as this hypothetical example:

```
void f(const ListContainer<int> &c)
{
  if (c.IsEmpty()) YourErrorFunction();  // Okay
  int i = c.RemoveAtHead();  // ???
}
```

Here, function f() declares a const reference parameter of type ListContainer<int>. With this design, arguments are passed to f() by address (that is, by reference), but the function is not permitted to call member functions that would alter the container's contents. The first statement in the sample function is okay—it calls the const function IsEmpty(), which does not alter any data members in the class, and thus can be safely called for the const object c. The second statement does not compile because it attempts to call the non-const function RemoveAtHead() for a const object.

> **Note:** The compiler detects any misuse of const objects at compile time, not at runtime. Use const as shown here to help the compiler reject calls to member functions that might alter an object's contents.

The ListContainer<T> class provides a function MakeIterator(), which returns an object of type ListIterator<T>. The iterator provides a controlled method for accessing list elements, while still permitting the container to hide the list's internal structures in the private base class.

The VectorContainer<T> class template is next in Listing 12.1.

Listing 12.1. contain.h (continued).

```
template<class T>
class VectorContainer
  : public ContainerError,
    private Vector<T>
{
public:
  VectorContainer();
  VectorContainer(int maxItems);
  VectorContainer(int min, int max);
  int ContainerMax() const;
  void PutAt(int i, const T &item);
  void GetAt(int i, T &item);
  VectorIterator<T> MakeIterator() const;
  Vector<T>::operator!;    // Selectively qualify as public
  Vector<T>::operator[];   // Selectively qualify as public
};
```

Like `ListContainer<T>`, the `VectorContainer<T>` class provides safe access to fundamental `Vector<T>` objects. Here again, I used the const keyword for member functions `ContainerMax()` and `MakeIterator()`, thus designating these as the only members that can be called for const objects of type `VectorContainer()`.

I also selectively bumped the status of the two inherited operator functions from private to public. There was no good reason to rewrite these functions in the derived container.

Listing 12.1 continues with the implementation of `ListContainer<T>`.

Listing 12.1. contain.h (continued).

```
// --------------------------------------------------------------
// class ListContainer
// --------------------------------------------------------------

// Default constructor
template<class T>
ListContainer<T>::ListContainer()
  : List<T>()
{
  max = INT_MAX - 1;
}

// Alternate constructor
template<class T>
ListContainer<T>::ListContainer(int maxItems)
  : List<T>()
{
  if (maxItems <= 0)
    max = INT_MAX - 1;
  else
    max = maxItems;
  if (maxItems == INT_MAX)
    maxItems = INT_MAX - 1;
}
```

```
// Returns true if container is full, else returns false
template<class T>
int ListContainer<T>::IsFull() const
{
  return ItemCount() >= max;
}

// Returns true if container is empty, else returns false
template<class T>
int ListContainer<T>::IsEmpty() const
{
  return ItemCount() <= 0;
}

// Returns maximum number of items container can hold
template<class T>
int ListContainer<T>::ContainerMax() const
{
  return max;
}

// Inserts item of type T at head of list container
// Returns true for success; false for errors
template<class T>
int ListContainer<T>::PutAtHead(T &item)
{
  return LinkHead(&item) != 0;
}

// Inserts item of type T at tail of list container
// Returns true for success; false for errors
template<class T>
int ListContainer<T>::PutAtTail(T &item)
{
  return LinkTail(&item) != 0;
}
```

continues

Listing 12.1. continued

```cpp
// Removes item of type T from head of list
// Assigns item to referenced argument
// Deletes item in list's container
// Returns true for success; false for errors
// If false, item is unchanged
template<class T>
int ListContainer<T>::RemoveAtHead(T &item)
{
  T *p = UnlinkHead();
  if (p) {
    item = *p;
    delete p;
  }
  return p != 0;
}

// Removes item of type T from tail of list
// Same result as RemoveAtHead()
template<class T>
int ListContainer<T>::RemoveAtTail(T &item)
{
  T *p = UnlinkTail();
  if (p) {
    item = *p;
    delete p;
  }
  return p != 0;
}

// Removes item equal to argument item
// Copies removed item to item
// Returns true for success; false for errors
template<class T>
int ListContainer<T>::RemoveItem(T &item)
{
  T *p = UnlinkItem(&item);
  if (p) {
```

```
    item = *p;
    delete p;
  }
  return p != 0;
}

// Removes all items in container
template<class T>
void ListContainer<T>::RemoveAll()
{
  DeleteAll();
}

// Returns an iterator object for this container
template<class T>
ListIterator<T> ListContainer<T>::MakeIterator() const
{
  return ListIterator<T>(this);
}
```

As you study this listing, you'll notice that ListContainer<T> is merely a thin disguise for a List<T> class. The container adds some error handling, controls object ownership (by deleting items in Remove...() functions), and creates iterator objects (MakeIterator()).

Some of the container's programming could be redeclared inline, thus removing the layers of function calls added on top of the List<T> class. I used inline member functions sparingly in order to make debugging easier. (The debugger I use, Turbo Debugger, is easily confused by inline members in template classes.) You might want to revise some of the smaller functions to be inline.

In fact, for the best efficiency, you could declare *all* ListContainer<T> (and VectorContainer<T>) member functions inline. That way, the class would still fulfill its role as a buffer between the abstract and fundamental classes in the library, but would not cost you a penny in performance.

Finally in Listing 12.1 is the implementation of the `VectorContainer<T>` class template.

Listing 12.1. contain.h (continued).

```
// --------------------------------------------------------------
// class VectorContainer
// --------------------------------------------------------------

// Default constructor
template<class T>
VectorContainer<T>::VectorContainer()
  : Vector<T>()
{
}

// Construct vector of specified number of items
template<class T>
VectorContainer<T>::VectorContainer(int maxItems)
  : Vector<T>(0, maxItems - 1)
{
}

// Construct vector indexed from min to max
template<class T>
VectorContainer<T>::VectorContainer(int min, int max)
  : Vector<T>(min, max)
{
}

// Return maximum number of items vector can store
template<class T>
int VectorContainer<T>::ContainerMax() const
{
  return GetNElem();
}
```

```
// Put item at vector index i
template<class T>
void VectorContainer<T>::PutAt(int i, const T &item)
{
  (*this)[i] = item;
}

// Get item from vector at index i
// Item remains in vector
template<class T>
void VectorContainer<T>::GetAt(int i, T &item)
{
  item = (*this)[i];
}

template<class T>
VectorIterator<T> VectorContainer<T>::MakeIterator() const
{
  return VectorIterator<T>(this);
}

#endif  //  __CONTAIN_H
```

Here again, the container serves mostly as an interface for Vector<T> objects. It doesn't add much of anything new, except for a function MakeIterator() to return an iterator object. Even so, the VectorContainer<T> class effectively serves as a buffer between higher-level classes and fundamental Vector<T> objects. For best results, you might want to rewrite the class to use all inline member functions.

Error Handling

Because nearly all of the fundamental data structures, container classes, and abstract types in this part are implemented as templates, their programming is completely contained in their header files. There are no corresponding .CPP modules, as there would be in a nontemplate library.

The one exception is the ContainerError() class, which does not need to be in template form. Listing 12.2 implements the class's single Error() member function.

Listing 12.2. CONTAIN.CPP.

```
#include "contain.h"

// Return true if error equals err_noerror, else return false
// Declared virtual so you can override to trap errors
int ContainerError::Error(err e)
{
  return e == err_noerror;
}
```

Introduction to Abstract Data Types

Using container classes, it's relatively easy to create abstract data types (ADT) such as the five in this section: arrays, stacks, queues, deques, and sets. These classes are completely separated from their implementations, and are therefore safer to use and easier to maintain or port to other compilers. A queue, for example, might be implemented as a list or a vector. Regardless of how it is implemented, a program uses the queue in exactly the same way.

Array Type

First on the list is a simple array class. As a convention, I named the class ArrayAsVector<T>, indicating its category (array) and its implementation (vector). I named other abstract classes similarly. Thus StackAsList<T> is an abstract stack class implemented using a List<T> fundamental data structure.

Actually, an array *is* a vector, and in this case, the resulting `ArrayAsVector<T>` class template is merely a shell. Even so, the shell provides a simplified interface to a twisted path that leads from the abstract class, to the container, and finally down to the lowest level of the `Vector<T>` template from Chapter 9. You could use a `Vector<T>` class directly, but an `ArrayAsVector<T>` abstract container is simpler and probably safer.

Listing 12.3 declares and implements the `ArrayAsVector<T>` template. The listing also serves as an example of more complex ADT classes that follow.

Note: On disk, file array.h is stored in the LIB\CLASSLIB directory. A copy of the file is also stored in the INCLUDE directory.

Listing 12.3. array.h.

```
#ifndef __ARRAY_H
#define __ARRAY_H    // Prevent multiple #includes

#include "contain.h"

template<class T>
class ArrayAsVector
  : public VectorContainer<T>
{
public:
  ArrayAsVector();
  ArrayAsVector(int maxItems);
  ArrayAsVector(int min, int max);
};


// ----------------------------------------------------------------
// class ArrayAsVector
// ----------------------------------------------------------------
```

continues

Listing 12.3. continued

```
// Default constructor
template<class T>
ArrayAsVector<T>::ArrayAsVector()
  : VectorContainer<T>()
{
}

// Construct array to hold specified number of items
// Allowable indexes are 0 to maxitems - 1
template<class T>
ArrayAsVector<T>::ArrayAsVector(int maxItems)
  : VectorContainer<T>(maxItems)
{
}

// Construct array to hold items indexed from min to max
template<class T>
ArrayAsVector<T>::ArrayAsVector(int min, int max)
  : VectorContainer<T>(min, max)
{
}

#endif  // __ARRAY_H
```

As you can see, the ArrayAsVector<T> class merely provides an interface to its VectorContainer<T> base class. That container hides the Vector<T> fundamental structure used to implement the abstract array.

ArrayAsVector<T> in Use

As a simple example, here's how to construct an array of ten integer values, indexed from 0 to 9:

```
ArrayAsVector<int> iarray(10);
```

Note: The programming in this section is extracted from the file ADTDEMO1.CPP, located on disk in the PART2 directory. To compile this and similar demonstrations in this chapter, using Borland C++, enter a command such as

```
bcc -ml adtdemo1 secrets.lib
```

You might have to specify a path to SECRETS.LIB, located on disk in the LIB directory. See Appendix A for additional help with compiling programs.

The `iarray` object is roughly equivalent to a common `int` array. To fill the array with values, use the object's index operator, inherited from the `Vector<T>` class template:

```
for (int i = 0; i < 10; ++i)
  iarray[i] = i;
```

You can use similar expressions to access objects stored in `iarray`. A simple `for` loop displays the values in the array:

```
for (i = 0; i < 10; ++i)
  cout << iarray[i] << endl;
```

To avoid having to write many such loops for a program's various array objects, you might create a function template to which you can pass an `ArrayAsVector<T>` reference. Here's one possible way to write the function:

```
template<class T>
void ShowArray(ArrayAsVector<T> &a)
{
  VectorIterator<T> iter = a.MakeIterator();
  if (iter.GetFirst())
  do {
    cout << " " << *iter.CurrentItem() << endl;
  } while (iter.GetNext());
}
```

Notice how the first statement calls the container's `MakeIterator()` member function, then uses the iteration techniques in Chapter 11 to access items in the array.

You might also use `ArrayAsVector<T>` to define and fill an array of `double` values:

```
ArrayAsVector<double> darray(1, 5);
for (int i = 1; i <= 5; ++i)
  darray[i] = 3.14159 * i;
```

Here again, I used a simple `for` loop and an index expression to assign values to `double` objects in the array. Display this array by calling the function template:

```
ShowArray(darray);
```

This use of `ShowArray()` causes the compiler to construct a new function capable of using an `ArrayAsVector<double>` object.

You can also copy one `ArrayAsVector<T>` array to another of the same type. Construct the copy (with or without a size parameter), then assign a compatible array like this:

```
ArrayAsVector<double> copy;
copy = darray;
```

The two arrays must be of type `ArrayAsVector<double>`, but they don't have to be of the same size. You can also use one array to construct another. This has the same effect as the preceding two statements, but is a tad more efficient:

```
ArrayAsVector<double> copy(darray);
```

Either way, `copy` is a replica of `darray`. Display the copy by again calling the `ShowArray()` function template:

```
ShowArray(copy);
```

You are not limited to storing values of simple types like `int` and `double`. You can also store complex class objects in `ArrayAsVector<T>` containers. Include the `String` class from Chapter 10 (declared in header file str.h), then construct a `String` array container like this:

```
ArrayAsVector<String> sarray(-15, -1);
```

Just for fun, I used negative index values. ArrayAsVector<T> indexes do not have to be positive, and unlike common arrays, they do not have to begin with zero. Assign literal strings or String class objects to the array:

```
sarray[-15] = "France";
sarray[-14] = "Germany";
sarray[-13] = "Australia";
...
sarray[ -2] = "Russia";
sarray[ -1] = "Italy";
```

Then, as you might have guessed, call the function template to display the array's contents:

```
ShowArray(sarray);
```

Sorted Arrays

Sooner or later, when using container class libraries, the topic of "sorting" bubbles up. Sorting methods, and their use in container classes, are as varied as the colors in a box of crayons. Some class libraries provide base classes with sorting capabilities, others provide sortable objects that can be inserted into containers. Still others handle sorting in different ways, and it's difficult to select a winner from all the possible candidates.

Rather than take the standard OOP approach of providing containers that have sorting capabilities built in, I decided to follow a different course that uses a function template and a class template to sort an array of objects.

My sorting solution also shows how a class template can be used to call standard library functions like qsort() declared in stdlib.h. This task is complicated by qsort()'s requirement of a comparison function that, if the template is to be successful, *must itself be a part of the template design.* In other words, the goal is to construct a comparison function that the compiler can shape into the necessary code to sort any kind of object. Using the template, you don't have to write individual qsort() comparison functions for every kind of object your programs need to sort. Unfortunately, achieving this goal is not as simple as it may seem.

First, let's declare the function template that will sort an object of type `ArrayAsVector<T>`. Just to be fancy, I'll include parameters to permit the entire array or any portion to be sorted—a refinement not often found in sorting subroutines, but occasionally useful. You might, for example, construct an array to be sorted in chunks, perhaps representing categories of some kind.

Here's how I declare the `Sort()` function template in the sample program on disk:

```
template<class T>
void Sort(ArrayAsVector<T> &array, int low, int high);
```

The first parameter, `array`, is a reference to the `ArrayAsVector<T>` object to be sorted. This parameter satisfies the requirement that function templates refer to each type placeholder (the only such placeholder here is `T`). The `int` values `low` and `high` define the range of index values for the objects to be sorted in `array`.

`Sort()` seems simple enough, but attempting to call `qsort()` from inside `Sort()` isn't possible without further programming. To understand the problem—a typical one when attempting to mix standard functions with classes and templates—take a look at `qsort()`'s requirements. The function is declared as

```
void qsort(void *base, size_t nelem, size_t width,
  int (*fcmp)(const void * const void *));
```

The first three parameters are straightforward. The `void` pointer `base` addresses the first object in the array to be sorted. The two parameters `nelem` and `width` specify the number of objects to be sorted and the size of each object in bytes.

The final parameter, on the second line here, poses a difficult challenge. Literally, `fcmp` is declared as a "pointer to a function that returns an `int` value and requires two `const void *` pointer arguments." A suitable comparison function might be written like this:

```
int compare(const void *a, const void *b)
{
}
```

The function returns −1 if the object addressed by pointer a is less than the object addressed by pointer b, 0 if the objects are equal, or +1 if the object at a is greater than the object at b. To sort a 100-element array defined as double *data, you could call qsort() as follows, passing the necessary arguments and the address of the compare() function:

```
qsort(data, 100, sizeof(double), compare);
```

The compare() function would use type cast expressions to tell the compiler the type of objects the void pointers a and b address. You could implement compare() something like this:

```
int compare(const void *a, const void *b)
{
  if (*(double *)a < *(double *)b) return -1;
  if (*(double *)a > *(double *)b) return +1;
  return 0;
}
```

All of this is straightforward C programming, but here comes the kink in the tail. To sort an ArrayAsVector<T> object passed to our Sort() function, we are faced with the problem of passing to compare() the *type* of objects to be sorted. Unfortunately, however, a data type is not something that can be passed as an argument. You can't solve the puzzle by converting compare() to a function template because the function's parameters must be void pointers. This won't work:

```
template<class T>
int compare(const T *a, const T *b);  // ???
```

The linker won't be able to find this function if you attempt to pass it to qsort() because the parameters are not of type void *. Using the correct parameters in the template is no help either:

```
template<class T>
int compare(const void *a, const void *b);  // ???
```

This function is in the correct form, but it breaks the rule that function template parameters refer at least once to every type placeholder. Before, the program wouldn't link. Now it won't compile.

The best way to escape this and similar mazes is to encase the `compare()` function in another class template. The function cannot be a member (because it can't have a hidden `this` pointer). But it *can* be a static member, and thus participate in the template. Here's how to design the class:

```
template<class T>
class Sorter {
public:
  static int cmp(const void *a, const void *b);
};
```

Implement the static `cmp()` function as you would any other class template member:

```
template<class T>
int Sorter<T>::cmp(const void *a, const void *b)
{
  if (*(T *)a < *(T *)b) return -1;
  if (*(T *)a > *(T *)b) return +1;
  return 0;
}
```

Compare the `cmp()` function with the earlier `compare()`. They are similar, but the static member is now completely generalized, and is able to use the placeholder type `T` rather than the explicit `double`. The `Sorter<T>` class template merely serves as a convenient shell that provides this placeholder type name to the function—the `Sorter<T>` class is never instantiated as an object. You can use a similar technique to encapsulate any common function inside a template.

Armed with these devices, we can now conquer the `Sort()` function template. Here's the final code:

```
template<class T>
void Sort(ArrayAsVector<T> &array, int low, int high)
{
  void *base = &array[low];    // Address of first object
  int width = sizeof(T);       // Size of one object in bytes
```

```
    int nelem = high - low + 1;   // Number of objects to sort
    if (nelem > 1)
      qsort(base, nelem, width, Sorter<T>::cmp);
}
```

For clarity, I assigned individual parameters to local variables base, width, and nelem. Notice how width is assigned the size of an object of the unspecified type T. Especially important is the technique used to pass qsort() the address of the static cmp() function. The expression

```
Sorter<T>::cmp
```

"takes the address of" cmp(), an action that causes the compiler to generate a new comparison function from the Sorter<T> template (unless a function of the correct type is already available). Merely taking the address of the static function in the class template, in other words, causes the compiler to construct the necessary code to compare objects of type T.

Finally, we can sort our ArrayAsVector<String> object simply by passing it to Sort() along with appropriate index values:

```
ArrayAsVector<String> sarray(-15, -1);
...   // Fill array with strings
Sort(sarray, -15, -1);
```

Stack Type

A stack is one of the best examples of an abstract data type that can be implemented using different fundamental structures. The classic stack uses a linked list, where items are "pushed" onto the head of the stack, then "popped" off at the top (see Figure 12.3). Stacks are also called *last in, first out* or *LIFO* structures because the last (in other words, most recent) item pushed onto the stack is the first available.

An important principle of a stack is the restriction on access to objects beneath the stack's top. According to classic stack rules, programs may perform only two stack operations: pushing new items onto the top of a stack, and popping existing items off the top. Items in the middle are in never-never land— they are strictly "hands off."

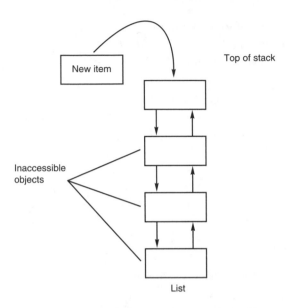

Figure 12.3. The classic stack implemented using a linked list.

Of course, you can always cheat. But dipping into a stack and rearranging its objects—to name one of several possible "illegal" maneuvers—invites trouble with other code that might expect stacks to behave normally.

You might also implement a stack using a vector as the fundamental data structure (see Figure 12.4). In this design, an integer *stack pointer* addresses the top of the stack. To "push" an object onto the stack, the program adds 1 to the pointer and stores an object in the vector using the stack pointer as an index. To "pop" an object from the stack, the program copies the object at the stack pointer to another location, then subtracts 1 from the pointer.

Of course, we also need to be concerned about what happens if an object is pushed onto a full stack, or if the program attempts to pop an object from a stack that is empty. In a low-level system stack of subroutine addresses, these kinds of errors are serious and might bring the entire system down. On the application level, the problems are more easily dealt with using the error mechanism introduced earlier.

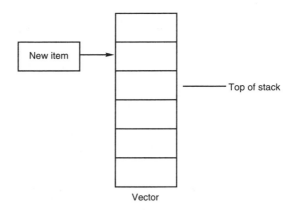

Figure 12.4. A stack implemented as a vector.

Most important is the notion that operations such as pushing objects onto stacks and popping objects off are independent of the fundamental structures used to implement the stack. Designing a stack class template in a completely general way makes it possible to change the stack's storage device without affecting the stack's use.

The code that follows in Listing 12.4, stack.h, demonstrates this important concept by implementing two stack class templates. The first class, StackAsList<T>, is derived from ListContainer<T>. The second class, StackAsVector<T>, is derived from VectorContainer<T>. Except for their inheritance, the public members of the two abstract data types are identical.

Note: On disk, file stack.h is stored in the LIB\CLASSLIB directory. A copy of the file is also stored in the INCLUDE directory.

Listing 12.4. stack.h.

```
#ifndef __STACK_H
#define __STACK_H    // Prevent multiple #includes
```

continues

Listing 12.4. continued

```cpp
#include "contain.h"
#include "misc.h"

template<class T>
class StackAsList
  : public ListContainer<T>
{
public:
  StackAsList();
  StackAsList(int maxItems);
  int Push(T item);
  T Pop();
};

template<class T>
class StackAsVector
  : public VectorContainer<T>
{
public:
  StackAsVector();
  StackAsVector(int maxItems);
  int Push(T item);
  T Pop();
  int IsEmpty() const { return sp < 0; }
private:
  int sp;  // Stack pointer
};

// ----------------------------------------------------------------
// class StackAsList
// ----------------------------------------------------------------

// Default constructor
template<class T>
StackAsList<T>::StackAsList()
  : ListContainer<T>()
{
}
```

```
// Construct stack to hold specified number of items
template<class T>
StackAsList<T>::StackAsList(int maxItems)
  : ListContainer<T>(maxItems)
{
}

// Push an item onto the stack
// Returns true for success; false for errors
template<class T>
int StackAsList<T>::Push(T item)
{
  if (IsFull())
    return Error(err_overflow);
  return PutAtTail(item);
}

// Pop an item from the stack
// Function result is undefined for stack underflow
template<class T>
T StackAsList<T>::Pop()
{
  T item;
  if (IsEmpty())
    Error(err_underflow);
  else
    RemoveAtTail(item);
  return item;
}

// ---------------------------------------------------------------
// class StackAsVector
// ---------------------------------------------------------------

// Default constructor
template<class T>
StackAsVector<T>::StackAsVector()
```

continues

337

Listing 12.4. continued

```cpp
  : sp(-1), VectorContainer<T>()
{
}


// Construct stack to hold specified number of items
template<class T>
StackAsVector<T>::StackAsVector(int maxItems)
  : sp(-1), VectorContainer<T>(maxItems)
{
}


// Push an item onto the stack
// Returns true for success; false for errors
template<class T>
int StackAsVector<T>::Push(T item)
{
  if (sp == ContainerMax())
    return Error(err_overflow);
  PutAt(++sp, item);
  return TRUE;
}


// Pop an item from the stack
// Function result is undefined for stack underflow
template<class T>
T StackAsVector<T>::Pop()
{
  T item;
  if (sp < 0)
    Error(err_underflow);
  else
    GetAt(sp--, item);
  return item;
}

#endif  // __STACK_H
```

In StackAsList<T>, the Push() member function first tests whether the stack is full. Even though the stack is implemented using a list, the ListContainer<T> class permits placing an upper limit on the container's size, a feature that might be important in preventing a runaway stack or other structure from eating all available memory. If the stack is not full, Push() calls the container's PutAtTail() function to link a new item onto the top of the stack. (I implemented the stack with its "top" at the tail—you could implement it the other way around, but the direction in which the stack grows isn't important.)

The Pop() member function works similarly. If the stack is empty, the function calls Error(); otherwise, it calls the container's RemoveAtTail() function to "pop" an object from the top of the stack.

StackAsVector<T> uses an integer stack pointer to a vector, but otherwise implements the identical Push() and Pop() functions. The functions are not particularly difficult to write. What's important is the way the two classes implement the same functions using different data structures. I added the const function IsEmpty() because the base class has no way to detect an empty vector. (A stack can be empty, but a vector is always filled with data. A list, however, can be empty by definition. The list-based class inherits IsEmpty(); the vector-based class must provide this function.)

The StackAsList<T> class is easy to use. Replace T with a data type name and define a stack object like this:

```
StackAsList<double> stack(10);
```

Note: The programming in this section is taken from the disk file ADTDEMO2.CPP, located in the PART2 directory.

To push values onto the stack, call the object's Push() member function:

```
for (i = 1; i <= 10; ++i)
  stack.Push(i * 3.14159);
```

To pop items from the stack, call Pop():

```
for (i = 1; i <= 10; ++i)
  cout << stack.Pop() << endl;
```

You can replace StackAsList<double> with StackAsVector<double> without having to make any other changes. Ideally, abstract data types should operate the same regardless of how they are implemented.

One side issue in the design of the stack classes is the value returned by Pop(), which is declared as

```
T Pop();
```

You might ask whether Pop() should instead return a pointer or a reference to avoid passing an object of type T on the system stack. Pop()'s value will be copied to another object, however, so this isn't much of a problem. The copying of object to and from the stack, however, might lead to performance problems—issues tackled in Part 3's discussion of memory management.

An even more important question is this: What happens if Pop() fails? Suppose the stack is empty, and the program calls Pop(). What object should the function return?

There are several possible answers. The error could halt the program—a drastic action that's hardly acceptable. Pop() might be written to return a "dummy" object of type T—a common solution, but one that requires defining the dummy somewhere, thus wasting space.

In stack.h, I took the easy way out by calling the Error() function inherited by the class if the stack is empty. If not, I remove an item from the list or vector, storing the item in a local variable of type T. Here's the list version from stack.h with the local variable highlighted:

```
template<class T>
T StackAsList<T>::Pop()
{
  T item;
  if (IsEmpty())
    Error(err_underflow);
  else
    RemoveAtTail(item);
  return item;
}
```

The return statement returns item, which remains uninitialized if an error occurs. In other words, the function result is undefined in the event of an error.

If T is a simple type such as int or double, the return value is whatever happens to be on the system stack when space is allocated to item. If T is a class, however, *the return value is an object built using the class's default constructor.*

It won't do, however, to ignore errors completely. To trap stack errors, create a new class derived from one of the stack templates. Here's an example:

```
class StringStack: public StackAsList<String> {
public:
  StringStack(int maxItems)
    : StackAsList<String>(maxItems) { }
  virtual int Error(err e);
};
```

The StringStack class is derived from StackAsList<String>. The result is no longer a template. Instead, it uses the StackAsList<T> template to build a basic class for storing String objects on a stack. The only reason for declaring a derived class is to override the virtual Error() member function. Any errors in stacks of the StringStack class are now directed to the new Error() handler.

It's up to you to decide what the Error() function should do. To display a message and halt the program for stack overflows and underflows, you could implement Error() like this:

```
int StringStack::Error(err e)
{
  if (e == ContainerError::err_noerror)
    return 0;
  else if (e == ContainerError::err_underflow)
    cout << "stack underflow";
  else if (e == ContainerError::err_overflow)
    cout << "stack overflow";
  else
    cout << "unspecified stack error";
  exit(e);
}
```

Construct and push a few strings onto a stack of type StringStack:

```
StringStack stack(3);
stack.Push("Blue");
stack.Push("White");
stack.Push("Red");
```

If you then attempt to pop too many items from the stack, the overridden `Error()` function halts the program:

```
for (int i = 1; i <= 4; ++i)    // ???
  cout << stack.Pop() << endl;
```

Queue Type

A queue operates just like a stack, except that objects pushed onto one end are popped from the other side. A good analogy of a queue is a line of cars at a fuel pump (see Figure 12.5). Cars are pushed into the queue from the end farthest from the pump. After filling with fuel, cars leave the queue from the head.

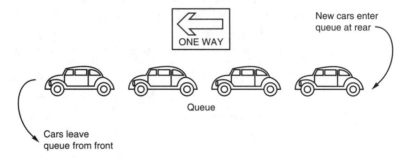

Figure 12.5. A queue operates like a line of cars at a fuel pump.

As with stacks, queues can be implemented as lists or vectors. Queues as lists are relatively simple to construct—you just attach new objects at one end of the list and take them off from the other. As vectors, however, queues require careful management of two pointers or index values, one at the head of the queue and the other at the tail.

Listing 12.5, queue.h, shows one way to write `QueueAsList<T>` and `QueueAsVector<T>` class templates.

 **Note:** On disk, file queue.h is stored in the LIB\CLASSLIB directory. A copy of the file is also stored in the INCLUDE directory.

Listing 12.5. queue.h.

```
#ifndef __QUEUE_H
#define __QUEUE_H    // Prevent multiple #includes

#include "contain.h"
#include "misc.h"

template<class T>
class QueueAsList
  : public ListContainer<T>
{
public:
  QueueAsList();
  QueueAsList(int maxItems);
  int InsertAtHead(T item);
  T RemoveFromTail();
};

template<class T>
class QueueAsVector
  : public VectorContainer<T>
{
public:
  QueueAsVector();
  QueueAsVector(int maxItems);
  int InsertAtHead(T item);
  T RemoveFromTail();
  int IsEmpty() const { return hp == tp; }
protected:
```

continues

Listing 12.5. continued

```cpp
  int hp, tp;   // Head and tail pointers
};

// ----------------------------------------------------------------
// class QueueAsList
// ----------------------------------------------------------------

// Default constructor
template<class T>
QueueAsList<T>::QueueAsList()
  : ListContainer<T>()
{
}

// Construct queue to hold specified number of items
template<class T>
QueueAsList<T>::QueueAsList(int maxItems)
  : ListContainer<T>(maxItems)
{
}

// Insert item at head of queue
// Returns true for success; false for errors
template<class T>
int QueueAsList<T>::InsertAtHead(T item)
{
  if (IsFull())
    return Error(err_overflow);
  return PutAtHead(item);
}

// Remove item from tail of queue
// If queue is empty, return value is undefined
template<class T>
T QueueAsList<T>::RemoveFromTail()
{
```

```
  T item;
  if (IsEmpty())
    Error(err_underflow);
  else
    RemoveAtTail(item);
  return item;
}


// ---------------------------------------------------------------
// class QueueAsVector
// ---------------------------------------------------------------


// Default constructor
template<class T>
QueueAsVector<T>::QueueAsVector()
  : hp(0), tp(0), VectorContainer<T>()
{
}


// Construct queue to hold specified number of items
template<class T>
QueueAsVector<T>::QueueAsVector(int maxItems)
  : hp(0), tp(0), VectorContainer<T>(0, maxItems)
{
}


// Insert item at head of queue
// Returns true for success; false for errors
template<class T>
int QueueAsVector<T>::InsertAtHead(T item)
{
  int k = hp;
  (hp == 0) ? hp = ContainerMax() - 1 : --hp;
  if (hp == tp) {
    hp = k;
    return Error(err_overflow);
```

continues

Listing 12.5. continued

```
  }
  PutAt(k, item);
  return TRUE;
}


// Remove item from tail of queue
// If queue is empty, return value is undefined
template<class T>
T QueueAsVector<T>::RemoveFromTail()
{
  T item;
  if (tp == hp)
    Error(err_underflow);
  else {
    GetAt(tp, item);
    (tp == 0) ? tp = ContainerMax() - 1 : --tp;
  }
  return item;
}

#endif  // __QUEUE_H
```

As with `StackAsList<T>` and `StackAsVector<T>`, the two queue class templates are interchangeable. You can construct a queue of `Strings`, capable of holding 10 objects:

```
QueueAsList<String> queue(10);
```

Note: The sample programming in this section is extracted from the disk file ADTDEMO3.CPP, located in the PART2 directory.

Then, insert strings into the queue by calling the template's `InsertAtHead()` member function:

```
queue.InsertAtHead("Red");
queue.InsertAtHead("White");
queue.InsertAtHead("Blue");
```

Extract objects from the queue by calling `RemoveFromTail()`. The objects come out in the order they went in (just like the line of cars at the fuel pump). This `for` loop prints the strings *Red, White,* and *Blue* in that order:

```
for (int i = 1; i <= 3; ++i)
  cout << queue.RemoveFromTail() << endl;
```

Try changing `QueueAsList<String>` to `QueueAsVector<String>`. Now the program stores the queue as a vector rather than a list. No other changes are necessary. As in the stack classes, `QueueAsVector<T>` provides the `const` function `IsEmpty()`. The list-based queue inherits this function from its base class; the vector-based queue has to provide it directly because low-level vectors can't distinguish between empty and nonempty states.

Deque Type

A *deque* is an abbreviation for "double-ended queue." In simple terms, a deque is a queue in which objects can enter and leave at both ends. A good analogy of a deque is a train of boxcars (see Figure 12.6.) Cars can be attached and detached at either end—in fact, those are the only ways to insert new cars and remove existing ones. Like queues, deques are often used in algorithms for scheduling, where the oldest objects in the system are the first to leave.

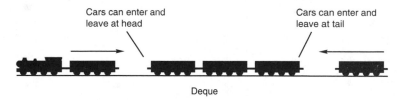

Figure 12.6. A deque, or double-ended queue, resembles a train of boxcars.

Because a deque is a queue with two ends, it makes sense to derive the deque classes from queues. Listing 12.6, deque.h, takes this approach, implementing two class templates, DequeAsList<T> and DequeAsVector<T>.

Note: On disk, file deque.h is stored in the LIB\CLASSLIB directory. A copy of the file is also stored in the INCLUDE directory.

Listing 12.6. deque.h.

```
#ifndef __DEQUE_H
#define __DEQUE_H    // Prevent multiple #includes

#include "queue.h"
#include "misc.h"

template<class T>
class DequeAsList
  : public QueueAsList<T>
{
public:
  DequeAsList();
  DequeAsList(int maxItems);
  int InsertAtTail(T item);
  T RemoveFromHead();
};

template<class T>
class DequeAsVector
  : public QueueAsVector<T>
{
public:
  DequeAsVector();
  DequeAsVector(int maxItems);
  int InsertAtTail(T item);
  T RemoveFromHead();
};
```

```
// -------------------------------------------------------------
// class DequeAsList
// -------------------------------------------------------------


// Default constructor
template<class T>
DequeAsList<T>::DequeAsList()
  : QueueAsList<T>()
{
}


// Construct deque to hold specified number of items
template<class T>
DequeAsList<T>::DequeAsList(int maxItems)
  : QueueAsList<T>(maxItems)
{
}


// Insert item at tail of deque
// Returns true for success; false for errors
template<class T>
int DequeAsList<T>::InsertAtTail(T item)
{
  if (IsFull())
    return Error(err_overflow);
  return PutAtTail(item);
}


// Remove item from head of deque
// If deque is empty, return value is undefined
template<class T>
T DequeAsList<T>::RemoveFromHead()
{
  T item;
  if (IsEmpty())
    Error(err_underflow);
```

continues

Listing 12.6. continued

```
  else
    RemoveAtHead(item);
  return item;
}


// -----------------------------------------------------------------
// class DequeAsVector
// -----------------------------------------------------------------


// Default constructor
template<class T>
DequeAsVector<T>::DequeAsVector()
  : QueueAsVector<T>()
{
}


// Construct deque to hold specified number of items
template<class T>
DequeAsVector<T>::DequeAsVector(int maxItems)
  : QueueAsVector<T>(maxItems)
{
}


// Insert item at tail of deque
// Returns true for success; false for errors
template<class T>
int DequeAsVector<T>::InsertAtTail(T item)
{
  int k = tp;
  (tp == ContainerMax() - 1) ? tp = 0 : ++tp;
  if (tp == hp) {
    tp = k;
    return Error(err_overflow);
  }
  PutAt(tp, item);
  return TRUE;
}
```

```
// Remove item from head of deque
// If deque is empty, return value is undefined
template<class T>
T DequeAsVector<T>::RemoveFromHead()
{
  T item;
  if (hp == tp)
    Error(err_underflow);
  else {
    (hp == ContainerMax() - 1) ? hp = 0 : ++hp;
    GetAt(hp, item);
  }
  return item;
}


#endif  // __DEQUE_H
```

The programming is similar to that in queue.h, but adds `InsertAtTail()` and `RemoveFromHead()` member functions to the inherited queue classes. Construct and use deques as in these sample statements:

```
DequeAsList<int> d1(100);      // Deque of int values
DequeAsList<double> d2(10);    // Deque of double values
DequeAsList<String> d3;        // Deque of String objects
DequeAsVector<int> d4(100);    // Vector based deque of int values
DequeAsVector<int> d5;         // Deque of int values
d5 = d4;                       // Assign deque d4 to d5
```

Note: The programming in this section is extracted from the file ADTDEMO4.CPP, located on disk in the PART2 directory.

Use the `InsertAtHead()` and `InsertAtTail()` member functions to insert objects into a deque. Use `RemoveFromHead()` and `RemoveFromTail()` to extract objects. These functions are similar to those in the queue class templates.

> **Note:** A deque implemented as a list can store one more item than a deque implemented as a vector. A vector-based deque always wastes one item because the deque's head and tail pointers, when equal, indicate an empty structure. If the vector-based deque were allowed to become completely full, the head and tail pointers would again become equal, causing the same condition (head equals tail) to indicate an empty *and* a full structure.

Set Type

Finally in this chapter is an abstract type that many programmers believe should have been native to C from the beginning. Sets are so useful, it's amazing that so much good software has been written without them.

The set in this section is not the same as a *bit* set in which single bits represent the presence (1) or absence (0) of items. Instead, I implemented the SetAsList<T> class template to store sets of any kind of objects in lists. This design takes more space than bit sets, of course, but is more versatile, and there is no practical restriction on the kinds of objects my set can hold. (Bit sets can typically hold only integer values). With my template, you can store sets of integers, floating point numbers, or even strings.

Listing 12.7, set.h, declares and implements the class template SetAsList<T>. There is no corresponding SetAsVector<T> because representing sets as vectors is difficult (particularly in operations that insert and delete objects) and wastes space.

> **Note:** On disk, file set.h is stored in the LIB\CLASSLIB directory. A copy of the file is also stored in the INCLUDE directory.

Listing 12.7. set.h.

```
#ifndef __SET_H
#define __SET_H   // Prevent multiple #includes

#include "contain.h"
#include "misc.h"

template<class T>
class SetAsList
  : public ListContainer<T>
{
  friend SetAsList<T> operator+
    (const SetAsList<T> &s1, const SetAsList<T> &s2);   // Union
  friend SetAsList<T> operator*
    (const SetAsList<T> &s1, const SetAsList<T> &s2);   // Intersection
  friend SetAsList<T> operator-
    (const SetAsList<T> &s1, const SetAsList<T> &s2);   // Difference
public:
  SetAsList();
  SetAsList(int maxItems);
  int AddToSet(T item);
  int RemoveFromSet(const T item);
  void RemoveAllFromSet();
  int InSet(T item) const;
  int IsEmpty() const;
  SetAsList<T> & operator+=(const SetAsList<T> &s);   // Union
  SetAsList<T> & operator*=(const SetAsList<T> &s);   // Intersection
  SetAsList<T> & operator-=(const SetAsList<T> &s);   // Difference
};


// -------------------------------------------------------------
// class SetAsList
// -------------------------------------------------------------

// Default constructor
template<class T>
```

continues

Listing 12.7. continued

```cpp
SetAsList<T>::SetAsList()
  : ListContainer<T>()
{
}

// Construct set to hold a specified number of items
template<class T>
SetAsList<T>::SetAsList(int maxItems)
  : ListContainer<T>(maxItems)
{
}

// Add item to set
// Does nothing if item already in set
// Returns true for success; false for errors
template<class T>
int SetAsList<T>::AddToSet(T item)
{
  if (IsFull())
    return Error(err_overflow);
  if (!InSet(item))
    return PutAtTail(item);
  else
    return FALSE;
}

// Remove item from set
// Does nothing if item not in set
// Returns true for success; false for errors
template<class T>
int SetAsList<T>::RemoveFromSet(const T item)
{
  T tempItem(item);
  return RemoveItem(tempItem);
}
```

```
// Remove all items from set
// Result is called the "null set"
template<class T>
void SetAsList<T>::RemoveAllFromSet()
{
  RemoveAll();
}


// Returns true if specified item is a set member
template<class T>
int SetAsList<T>::InSet(T item) const
{
  ListIterator<T> iter = MakeIterator();
  return iter.FindFirst(item);
}


// Returns true if set is empty (is the null set)
template<class T>
int SetAsList<T>::IsEmpty() const
{
  return ListContainer<T>::IsEmpty();
}


// Performs set "union" operation
// Ex. result = s1 + s2;
template<class T>
SetAsList<T> operator+(const SetAsList<T> &s1, const SetAsList<T> &s2)
{
  T item;
  SetAsList<T> result(s1);
  if (!result) {
    result.Error(ContainerError::err_overflow);
    return result;
  }
  ListIterator<T> iter = s2.MakeIterator();
  do {
```

continues

Listing 12.7. continued

```
      if (iter.CurrentItem())
        result.AddToSet(*iter.CurrentItem());
  } while (iter.GetNext());
  return result;
}

// Performs set "intersection"
// Ex. result = s1 * s2;
template<class T>
SetAsList<T> operator*(const SetAsList<T> &s1, const SetAsList<T> &s2)
{
  T item;
  int count = max(s1.ContainerMax(), s2.ContainerMax());
  SetAsList<T> result(count);
  if (!result) {
    result.Error(ContainerError::err_overflow);
    return result;
  }
  ListIterator<T> iter = s2.MakeIterator();
  do {
    if (s1.InSet(*iter.CurrentItem()))
      result.AddToSet(*iter.CurrentItem());
  } while (iter.GetNext());
  return result;
}

// Performs set "difference"
// Ex. result = s1 - s2;
template<class T>
SetAsList<T> operator-(const SetAsList<T> &s1, const SetAsList<T> &s2)
{
  T item;
  SetAsList<T> result(s1);
  if (!result) {
    result.Error(ContainerError::err_overflow);
    return result;
  }
```

```
  ListIterator<T> iter = s2.MakeIterator();
  do {
    if (iter.CurrentItem())
      result.RemoveItem(*iter.CurrentItem());
  } while (iter.GetNext());
  return result;
}


// Shorthand set "union"
// Ex. result += s;
template<class T>
SetAsList<T> & SetAsList<T>::operator+=(const SetAsList<T> &s)
{
  *this = *this + s;
  return *this;
}


// Shorthand set "intersection"
// Ex. result *= s;
template<class T>
SetAsList<T> & SetAsList<T>::operator*=(const SetAsList<T> &s)
{
  *this = *this * s;
  return *this;
}


// Shorthand set "difference"
// Ex. result -= s;
template<class T>
SetAsList<T> & SetAsList<T>::operator-=(const SetAsList<T> &s)
{
  *this = *this - s;
  return *this;
}


#endif  // __SET_H
```

The `SetAsList<T>` class template is more complex than other abstract data types in this chapter. Most of the added complexity is in the overloaded operator functions. Table 12.1 lists these operators and their related set operations.

Table 12.1. `SetAsList<T>` **operators.**

Operator	Set operation	Example
+	Union	s1 = s2 + s3;
*	Intersection	s1 = s2 * s3;
–	Difference	s1 = s2 – s3;
+=	Shorthand union	s1 += s2;
*=	Shorthand intersection	s1 *= s2;
–=	Shorthand difference	s1 –= s2;

Implementing overloaded operators for sets makes good sense. As the *Example* column in Table 12.1 shows, set arithmetic is natural and intuitive. Of course, I could have used member functions for union, intersection, and difference. But in this case, it seemed best to use operators for these common set operations.

To construct a set, specify a data type such as `int` or `double` for `T` in the `SetAsList<T>` template. Here's how to create a set of `String` objects:

```
SetAsList<String> set;
```

Or, to limit a set to a specific number of items, specify a maximum value in parentheses:

```
SetAsList<String> set(10);
```

On disk, file ADTDEMO5.CPP in the PART2 directory shows examples of various set operations. To make it easy to view a set of `String` objects, the program defines a nonmember function, `ShowItemInSet()`:

```
void ShowItemInSet(String *sp)
{
  cout << *sp << ':';
}
```

Another function uses an iterator to call `ShowItemInSet()` for each object in a set passed by reference to the function:

```
void ShowSet(const char *msg, SetAsList<String> &s)
{
  cout << ' ' << msg << " == ";
  ListIterator<String> iter = s.MakeIterator();
  iter.Iterate(ShowItemInSet);
  cout << endl;
}
```

Notice that in this case I specified the parameter's data type as `SetAsList<String>`. The `ShowSet()` function is *not* a template: it's a plain function that can accept only sets of the specified type. When you know in advance the types of classes you will generate from templates, you can write other functions to use objects of those classes. You don't have to write every function as a template just because it happens to use classes based on template designs.

Final Words

All too often, C++ programmers construct abstract types seemingly in one sitting, designing a `Set` class, for instance, from scratch with all the members that a set needs. This approach is almost always wasteful, and it fails to make intermediate classes such as containers available for other uses. As I've tried to show in this and the preceding chapters, a modular library of fundamental data structures, container classes, and abstract data types leads to simple-to-use data types that are easily molded to meet new demands.

I've also tried to show many examples of templates, which seem likely to become key tools in C++ programming, especially in the design of general-purpose class libraries. Templates are just now being used in software development—their real power has yet to be realized.

This brings Part 2 to a close. In the next part, we'll turn our sights inward, and look closely at how objects are stored in memory and on disk. There's a lot you can do to control object construction, and in the process, gain benefits in efficiency and storage that might make or break a program's success.

3

Secrets of
C++ Memory and
Data Management

Managing
Dynamic Memory

D ynamic memory has more aliases than a crime boss in the roaring twenties.
Some of the colorful names applied to this memory zone—which some
programmers might view as a *war* zone—include *free store, core, heap,* or just
plain *storage area.*

I prefer *heap,* but the exact name doesn't matter. Whatever you call it, a heap typically encompasses memory not used by the program's stack, code, and global data. On simple computer systems, the heap might be all memory left after a program and its data are loaded and after space is reserved for a stack. On more complex hardware, an operating system might provide each new program with one or more blocks of RAM further subdivided into heap, stack, code, and data areas. In still other multitasking systems, many programs might share the same heap, making the most possible memory available to each program, but greatly increasing the damaging effects of memory management errors.

This chapter reviews memory management techniques for storing C++ class objects and other data on the heap. I'll also point out several tips for making good use of the C++ heap operators, `new` and `delete`.

Dynamic Objects

It's important to understand the key differences between dynamic objects stored on the heap and other objects that a program might use. By *dynamic object,* I mean any object constructed by the `new` operator and stored on the heap.

Dynamic objects are unique for several reasons:

● The scope of dynamic objects is always global.

● It is your responsibility to create and delete dynamic objects. They are never created or deleted automatically.

● The creation of dynamic objects can fail if enough free heap space is not available. Programs must guard against this possibility.

● Dynamic objects are usually accessed with pointers. It's also possible, though potentially dangerous, to use references to access dynamic objects as explained later in this chapter.

Due to these points, using dynamic objects requires more care than using global or automatic objects defined in functions. Dynamic objects offer several benefits, however, that make them especially attractive.

Addressed by pointers, dynamic objects can contain pointer members that address other objects, forming lists. You saw several examples of this technique in Part 2. Another advantage is that heaps tend to have more free space available than global data areas and stacks. Large objects that won't fit elsewhere can often be stored on the heap. It's also possible to construct variable-size objects that take different amounts of memory depending on how much heap space is available. These and other advantages are difficult to achieve with objects stored in global data areas and created automatically as function variables.

Operators *new* and *delete*

Using new and delete is one of the early skills that C++ programmers learn. There are, however, several important facts about the use of these operators that are easy to neglect, and deserve repeating here. Memorize these facts and review them often.

Constructors

The new operator allocates space for objects *before* C++ calls the object's class constructor (if it has one). Operator new, therefore, never operates directly on objects because object construction always follows new's operation.

You might think of new as a kind of saw that cuts a chunk of memory onto which a constructor inserts an object (see Figure 13.1).

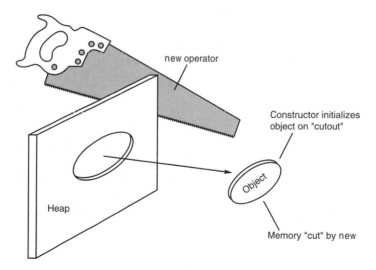

new operator

Constructor initializes
object on "cutout"

Object

Heap

Memory "cut" by new

Figure 13.1. The new operator cuts out a chunk of memory into which a constructor inserts an object.

Destructors

C++ calls the object's class destructor (if it has one) *before* calling `delete` to return to the heap the memory occupied by the object. When you delete a pointer to a class object, C++ calls the class destructor, then calls the `delete` operator function to recover the object's memory. Operator `delete` can therefore never use an object being deleted because the object has already been destroyed by the time `delete` receives the object's address.

You might think of `delete` as a reverse saw that uses a destructor to extract an object inserted onto a chunk of memory, then returns that chunk to the hole previously cut by `new` (see Figure 13.2).

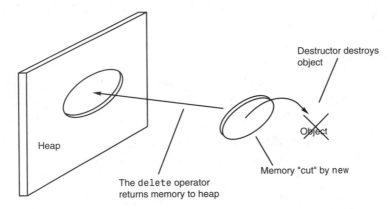

Figure 13.2. A destructor erases (destroys) an object from a chunk of memory, then `delete` returns the chunk to the hole cut earlier by `new`.

Null Pointers

Operator `new` returns null (zero) if enough space is not available to construct an object on the heap. Operator `delete` ignores null pointers, a convenience that eliminates the need to test whether pointers are null before deleting them.

Value of Null

C++ defines null as being equivalent to 0. Because some compilers define the symbol `NULL` as a `void * ` pointer, C++ programs should use 0, not `NULL`, to represent null pointers.

Deleted Pointers

Deleting a pointer does not change that pointer's value, inviting a common mistake—using a deleted object. This is *always* a grievous error because the deleted memory has been returned to the heap's pool of available RAM.

Some C++ memory managers erase deleted memory blocks; others merely link the blocks into a chain of available bytes to be used by subsequent calls to new. Regardless of the particular method used by the system to reclaim deleted memory, you should consider the use of a deleted object to be strictly taboo.

Overloading

A class may overload new and delete (as a class may overload other operators) to provide custom memory management for objects of the class. Derived classes inherit new and delete operators overloaded in a base class. It's also possible to overload the global new and delete operators to take over all heap allocations, although this technique isn't usually recommended.

Standard Functions

Most C++ experts recommend never mixing standard heap functions such as malloc() and free() with new and delete. Only use delete on memory allocated by new. Only call free() for memory allocated by malloc() (or calloc(), realloc(), or other similar memory functions provided with your compiler).

Practically speaking, however, it's common for new and delete to be defined in terms of malloc() and free(). You also can customize the default new and delete operators (as I'll explain in the next chapter). For these reasons, you might be able to mix standard C and C++ memory management techniques with no harmful effects. Never do that, however, unless you are prepared to take total command over all aspects of the program, its libraries, and the hardware. (For instance, a ROM-based embedded controller—just to pick an example out of thin air—might provide some kind of exotic memory management functions that cooperate with custom versions of new and delete.) For best results, never mix C and C++ memory management techniques.

Responsible Object Construction

Following a few simple rules, it's easy to stay out of memory management trouble. These rules are broken more often than a politician's promises, so even though some of the following is familiar to you (at least it should be), each point in *italic type* bears repeating like a religious mantra.

Test Pointers

Always test pointers allocated by new. Given a class TClass, construct a dynamic object of the class like this:

```
TClass *p;          // Define pointer
p = new TClass;  // Construct object
if (!p) Error("Unable to construct object");
```

If new fails, it returns zero, causing p to become null. The if statement tests for this condition. For demonstration purposes, I assume that Error() halts the program after printing a message.

> **Note:** Later in this chapter and in the next, I'll introduce techniques that reduce the need to test pointers every single time you call new.

Empty Parentheses

The middle line in the preceding code fragment calls the TClass default constructor. Alternatively, you may use empty parentheses after the class name:

```
p = new TClass();  // Construct object
```

The parentheses are optional; they have no practical significance. Some programmers add the extra parentheses to indicate the fact that a constructor is called. You can also combine the definition of a pointer with the use of new, joining the two steps into one statement:

```
TClass *p = new TClass;  // Define pointer and construct object
```

Delete Objects

Never fail to delete objects addressed by pointers, especially those that are scheduled to go out of scope. Usually, this rule means that any objects addressed by pointers defined inside a function must be deleted before the function ends. Consider a sample:

```
void f()
{
  TClass *p = new TClass;
  ...
  delete p;  // Last opportunity to delete object!
}
```

If the program permitted function f() to end without deleting the object addressed by p, the address held by the pointer would be permanently lost when p goes out of scope. Because dynamic objects are always global in scope and are never deleted automatically, the object addressed by p would remain on the heap until the program ends. Worse, in multitasking systems with a shared heap, it's possible for undeleted objects to remain in memory beyond the program's shutdown, perhaps until the entire system is switched off.

In programs that run correctly for a while, then slowly become lethargic, the likely cause is a function that fails to delete memory allocated to a local pointer. The obvious cure is to delete that memory before the function ends. Another possibility is to return the pointer as the function result:

```
TClass *football()  // Returns an object by address
{
  TClass *p = new TClass;  // Construct object
  ...
  return p;  // Return object address
}
```

Local pointer p still goes out of scope, but the function preserves the object's address by returning that value as the function result. Now it's the responsibility of a receiver to "catch" the returned pointer. To do that, the program might call football() like this:

```
TClass *p = football();
if (!p) Error("Function football() returned null");
```

If p is not null, the program can use the object addressed by p. Eventually, the receiver is expected to delete that object:

```
delete p;  // Game is over, at least for this object!
```

Figure 13.3 shows how these steps construct an object on the heap. The object has global scope—it persists after function football() ends. The program can therefore use the object created in the function, which returns the object's address as a pointer.

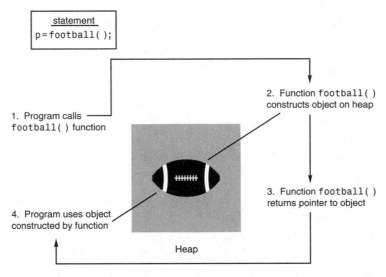

Figure 13.3. Objects in the heap persist until deleted. A function can therefore construct a dynamic object and return its address for other parts of the program to use.

Return by Value

Never permit functions to return dynamic objects by value. A common error is to write the football() function to return an object by value. To distinguish this poor practice from the preceding correct function, I'll rename the function fumble():

```
TClass fumble()   // Returns an object by value
{
  TClass *p = new TClass;
  ...
  return *p;   // ???  DON'T DO THIS!!!
}
```

Consider what happens when the program uses this function:

```
TClass oof;        // Define object oof
oof = fumble();   // ???
```

The object constructed by fumble() is returned by value directly to oof, but the address of the original object constructed by the function is lost. The oof object is not a pointer, and there is no longer any way to delete the dynamic object. If oof goes out of scope, the class's destructor will be called, but the object's memory will remain allocated on the heap.

Dynamic Arrays

Always delete dynamic arrays using the special form of delete[] *followed by empty square brackets.* Define an array of objects by using new and specifying the number of objects in brackets. Delete that array using delete[]:

```
TClass *array;             // Define pointer
array = new TClass[100];   // Construct array of 100 objects
...
delete[] array;            // Delete array using delete[]
```

This critical technique has two important consequences. To construct the array, C++ calls the default constructor for TClass once for each object in the array. The class TClass is required to have a default constructor. Every object in the array is therefore initialized to the value of k as though that object were defined as

```
TClass k;   // Construct k using default TClass constructor
```

The second key effect concerns the array's deletion. Consider what happens if you delete an array using delete without brackets:

```
delete array;   // ???
```

Many C++ programmers mistakenly assume that this statement deletes only a single object addressed by array. That is not what happens. Operator new saves the sizes of all allocated memory blocks so that `delete` always disposes of the proper number of bytes.

> **Note:** C++ doesn't specify how or where new saves the sizes of allocated memory blocks, only that new must do this. Typically, new (or a memory-allocator function called by new) inserts the size of a reserved block into a couple of bytes hidden somewhere in the block.

The danger in deleting arrays without brackets is that `new` does not differentiate between common dynamic objects and objects in arrays. In other words, `new` inserts no information into an allocated block to indicate the type of objects in the array. Using `delete` without brackets deletes the entire array but calls the destructor only for the *first* object in the array. In order to call the class destructor for every arrayed object, you must add brackets to `delete[]`:

```
delete[] array;  // Calls destructor for array's objects
```

This form of `delete[]` destroys each object in the array and then deletes the entire memory block occupied by the array. You do not have to tell `delete[]` the size of the array or the number of objects it contains. Because `new` saves the size of the memory block allocated to `array`, the `delete[]` operator can easily calculate the number of objects as `size / sizeof(TClass)`.

If you construct an array of common values that do not have destructors, then *you may use either form of* `delete`. Arrays constructed like this:

```
double *darray;           // Define pointer
darray = new double[100]; // Construct array of 100 double values
```

may be deleted using either of the following two statements:

```
delete darray;    // Okay
delete[] darray;  // Also okay, but probably better
```

The second form is usually recommended for consistency and because if a later change causes `darray` to contain objects of a class with a destructor, the first form would no longer be correct.

Bad References

Ordinarily, you should use pointers to address dynamic objects stored on the heap. It's also possible, but usually unwise, to refer to dynamic objects with a reference. The technique shows up here and there, and you should be aware of it, if only to recognize a trouble spot that is probably best avoided.

To use a reference to address a dynamic object, you might attempt to construct the object like this:

```
TClass &ref = *new TClass;  // ???
```

That's never a good idea because you have no way of knowing if the operation succeeded. If new returns null, the reference is invalid, a fact that is impossible to verify. References *must* address valid objects—no ifs, ands, or buts.

The three-step solution is to use a pointer to address the object, test the pointer, and then create the reference:

```
TClass *p = new TClass;
if (!p) Error("Cannot construct TClass object");
TClass &ref = *p;
```

Assuming that Error() halts the program, ref is now guaranteed to refer to a valid object—the one also addressed by p. The reference might be easier to use than a pointer in some circumstances. Suppose TClass has a member named Print(). You can call that member in one of three ways:

```
ref.Print();
p->Print();
(*p).Print();
```

All three statements are functionally equivalent, but programmers with limited experience (or those who simply dislike using pointers) might find the first statement easier to understand. Unfortunately, if the pointer p goes out of scope, the only way to delete the object is to use the statement

```
delete &ref;
```

This is acceptable, but if you forget to delete the object, it might be left on the heap, causing a loss of memory. (This error is easy to make because ref is not obviously a pointer.)

In practice, it's rare to use references as just described. More commonly, a function returns a reference to an object constructed on the heap:

```
TClass &f()
{
  TClass *p = new TClass;
  if (!p) Error("Cannot create TClass object");
  return *p;  // ???
}
```

The danger here is that calling f() does not obviously construct a dynamic object. For example, a statement can call f() to construct a TClass object, assigning the resulting address to a reference:

```
TClass &ref = f();
```

Again, you must remember to delete the referenced object with a statement such as

```
delete &ref;
```

All of this works, but there's little advantage in using the technique. A reference might, however, address a dynamic object that should never be deleted (until the program ends, that is). In that case, a reference might simplify the source code by eliminating the need to use pointer dereference operations. Naive programmers who use your code might also be less likely to delete a critical dynamic object by accident.

In most instances, you should use pointers to address dynamic objects. By all means, learn how to use references to dynamic objects, but keep this technique locked in its cage. Let it out only when you feel like playing rough.

Good References

You might wonder, are there any practical uses for references to dynamic objects? Yes. As function parameters, references are invaluable. Here's a sample function prototype that declares a reference to an object of type TClass:

```
void f(TClass &ref);
```

Inside the function, the reference `ref` can be used as though it were a common variable. For example, to call the `Print()` member function, you can implement function `f()` as

```
void f(TClass &ref)
{
  ref.Print();
}
```

Elsewhere, a statement can construct a dynamic object and pass it to the function:

```
TClass *p = new TClass;
if (!p) Error("Cannot construct TClass object");
f(*p);
```

Because `f()` requires a *reference* to an object, p must be dereferenced to pass the object that p addresses. You can also pass to `f()` an object created globally or automatically inside another function:

```
void g()
{
  TClass object;
  f(object);
}
```

Function `f()` receives a reference to (that is, the address of) the `object` constructed automatically in function `g()`. The advantage here is that `f()` does not have to use pointer dereference operations to access the object.

Note: As a rule, a function should never assume anything about the location of an object passed to a reference parameter. The object addressed by the reference could be in a global data area, on the stack, or on the heap.

Safe Object Construction

Earlier, I mentioned that new's result should always be tested. That's true, but it's often possible to delay the time *when* that test needs to be performed. For example, consider this class:

```
class TClass {
public:
  TClass();  // Constructor
  ~TClass() { delete c1; delete c2; }
  int AOK() { return c1 != 0 && c2 != 0; }
private:
  AnotherClass *c1;  // Pointer to object of AnotherClass
  AnotherClass *c2;  // Pointer to object of AnotherClass
};
```

TClass represents a typical class that uses a couple of private pointers to objects of another class, c1 and c2. Because deleting a null pointer is harmless, the class destructor can be written simply as shown. Member function AOK() returns true if both pointers are non-null; otherwise, the object is considered unsafe to use.

Using a function like AOK() to verify an object's state simplifies memory management for objects of the class. A program can call AOK() to determine whether an object was successfully constructed. Examine how this code fragment uses the technique:

```
TClass *p = new TClass;
if (!p ¦¦ !p->AOK()) {
  delete p;  // Okay even if p is null!
  Error("TClass object improperly formed");
}
```

First, the program constructs an object of type TClass and assigns the address of that object to p. If p is null or if AOK() returns false, the program deletes the object and Error() halts the program. The delete statement works perfectly well even if p is null. The statement works also if either or both of the object's pointer members c1 and c2 are null. *It is always okay to delete a null pointer.*

This important memory management technique allows the constructor to be simply written as

```
TClass::TClass()
{
  c1 = new AnotherClass;
  c2 = new AnotherClass;
}
```

No checks or calls to error functions are required after each use of new. Any memory shortages simply set one or both pointers to null. Users of the class are expected to call AOK() to determine whether the object was properly constructed. For better readability, instead of using a member function like AOK(), you can overload operator!() to perform object verification. In the TClass declaration, for example, you can replace AOK() with

```
int operator!()
  { return c1 != 0 && c2 != 0; }
```

Of course, you don't have to implement the operator inline—you can code it in a separate module. The operator could also test other conditions to verify an object's construction. Using the operator, an if statement with two logically ORed expressions thoroughly tests whether an object is safe to use:

```
TClass *p = new TClass;
if (!p || !(*p)) {
  delete p;  // Okay even if p is null!
  Error("Cannot construct TClass object");
}
// Object addressed by p is safe to use
```

In the if statement, the first subexpression (!p) tests whether p is null. If so, new was unable to allocate space for a TClass object. If p is not null, the second subexpression (!(*p)) tests whether the object addressed by p was constructed properly. If either condition fails, the object is deleted and Error() is called to halt the program.

Another useful technique is to roll the methods described here into a function that returns a pointer to a dynamic object or null if anything goes wrong during the object's construction:

```
TClass *makeObject()
{
  TClass *p = new TClass;   // Construct object on heap
  if (!p || !(*p)) {        // If anything goes wrong,
    delete p;               // : delete the object (if any)
    p = 0;                  // : set p to null
  }
  return p;  // Return object address or null
}
```

You can now call makeObject() to construct an object on the heap. A simple if statement tests whether the construction succeeded:

```
TClass *p = makeObject();
if (!p) Error("Out of memory");
```

This method is especially useful in complex classes that have many pointers. Even if just one of those pointers is null (or if any other problem develops during the object's construction), makeObject() returns null, giving the program a simple and safe way to verify that objects are correctly formed.

Final Words

Managing dynamic objects on the heap requires careful programming and a good understanding of how new and delete work. In the next chapter, you'll explore techniques for customizing these important C++ operators.

Overloading *new* and *delete*

S ome memory managers are as easy to penetrate as an armored tank. C++ is different. Unlike many programming languages, C++ doesn't keep its heap manager under heavy guard. By overloading the new and delete operators, you can gain total control over how dynamic objects are constructed and destroyed.

This chapter reviews the basics of overloading new and delete—globally and on a class-by-class basis. I'll also point out related memory-management techniques that aren't usually found in C++ tutorials, such as how to create a mark-and-release heap and how to use a reserved memory pool.

Running in Overload

There are two ways to overload the new and delete operators. You can customize the global default operators, affecting all memory allocations and deletions. Or, you can overload the operators for a specific class, customizing dynamic object construction for that class without affecting other uses of new and delete.

Global *new* and *delete* operators

You can completely replace the C++ memory manager simply by overloading the global new and delete operators. The main secret in doing this is to include the new.h header, which declares the operators. *After* including new.h, you can redefine the operators in any way you wish. Listing 14.1, GLOBAL.CPP, shows how.

Note: On disk, GLOBAL.CPP is located in the PART3 directory. See Appendix A if you have trouble compiling this or other sample programs in this chapter.

Listing 14.1. GLOBAL.CPP.

```
#include <iostream.h>
#include <iomanip.h>
#include <malloc.h>      // Declare malloc() and free()
#include <new.h>         // Required to overload global operators
```

```
// Prototypes for overloaded global operators
void * operator new(size_t size);
void operator delete(void *p);

int main()
{
  cout << "Constructing object of type double\n";
  double *dp = new double;  // Uses overloaded new
  cout << "Deleting object of type double\n";
  delete dp;  // Uses overloaded delete

  cout << "Constructing object of type int\n";
  int *ip = ::new int;  // Uses overloaded new
  cout << "Deleting object of type int\n";
  ::delete ip;  // Uses overloaded delete
  return 0;
}

// Overloaded new operator
void * operator new(size_t size)
{
  return malloc(size);
}

// Overloaded delete operator
void operator delete(void *p)
{
  if (p) free(p);
}
```

Prototypes for overloaded new and `delete` operator functions appear in the lines preceding `main()`. You must use these exact declarations or the program will not compile. Operator new must return `void *`, and it must specify a single parameter of type `size_t`. This unsigned value indicates the number of bytes that new should reserve. If new cannot fulfill a memory allocation request, it should return null (zero); otherwise, new should return a pointer to the first byte of the reserved memory.

In this sample program, the overloaded `new` operator simply calls `malloc()`, the standard C-library memory allocator. Change `malloc()` to `calloc()` to fill reserved memory with all zero bytes—a handy tool for debugging or just to ensure a clean slate for all dynamic objects (at the expense of a little time spent performing the fill). Or, you could fill reserved memory with another value— `0xff` for example—making allocated memory blocks easy to find in a memory dump.

The sample overloaded `delete` operator calls the standard `free()` function to return a memory block to the heap. The sample does not call `free()` if `p` is null, satisfying the rule that `delete` ignores null pointers.

The `main()` function demonstrates two uses of the overloaded `new` and `delete` operators. In the second section of `main()` after the blank line, the scope resolution operator prefaces the operators' use:

```
int *ip = ::new int;   // ???
::delete ip;           // ???
```

Contrary to popular belief, these statements do *not* access the original C++ operators. Overloading the global, default `new` and `delete` as shown here completely overrides the C++ memory manager. As the next section explains, however, when used with overloaded operators in classes, the scope resolution operator has a different effect when it prefaces `new` and `delete`.

Note: C++ requires `new` to save the size of an allocated memory block so that `delete` can properly return that memory to the heap. The standard `malloc()` function does this automatically, but if your version of `new` does not call `malloc()`, it is your responsibility to save the sizes of reserved blocks. The easiest technique is to store a block's size along with the reserved memory, perhaps just ahead of the address returned by `new`. You might also store reserved memory block sizes in a linked list or an array.

Class *new* and *delete* operators

Overloading the global default new and delete operators is a drastic measure that is best avoided except when absolutely necessary. The technique is sometimes useful for debugging, but writing your own heap manager is not a simple task to while away a rainy Sunday afternoon.

An easier and safer technique provides custom memory management for individual classes. By overloading new and delete as static members of a class, you take over dynamic allocations of memory for objects of the class. Other uses of new and delete are unaffected.

To overload new and delete in a class, declare the operators inside the class like this:

```
class Overload {
public:
  ...
  void * operator new(size_t size);
  void operator delete(void *p);
};
```

Declare new as you do when overloading the default global operator. The function must return void *, and it must specify a single parameter of type size_t, indicating the number of bytes to reserve.

Operator delete is normally declared as shown—again, this is the same declaration used when overloading the global default operator. The function must return void, and it specifies a parameter to hold the address of a memory block to be deleted.

You may also add a second parameter to delete:

```
void operator delete(void *p, size_t size);
```

In this case, C++ sets size to the number of bytes occupied by the object to be deleted. Unlike the global default delete operator—which cannot have this same parameter—the size of deleted class objects is always known because this form of delete can only be used with objects of the class. In other words, size simply equals the number of bytes that an object of the class occupies. When using this form of delete, then, an overloaded new for a specific class is not required to save the size of an allocated memory block.

Listing 14.2, MYMEM.CPP, overloads the new and delete operators for a class named Base. (The reason for this class name will become clear when we look at new and delete in derived classes.) The program also demonstrates the difference between the two possible forms of delete.

> **Note:** On disk, MYMEM.CPP is located in the PART3 directory. Depending on your compiler, you might have to change header malloc.h to stdlib.h, or to another header that declares the malloc() and free() functions.

Listing 14.2. MYMEM.CPP.

```
#include <iostream.h>
#include <iomanip.h>
#include <malloc.h>

class Base {
public:
  Base(int X): x(X) { }
  void * operator new(size_t size);
  void operator delete(void *p);
private:
  int x;  // Data in object
};

int main()
{
  Base *p = new Base(10);  // Construct dynamic object
  delete p;                // Delete object
  return 0;
}

// Overloaded new operator for class
void * Base::operator new(size_t size)
{
```

```
  cout << "new: size == " << size << endl;
  return (void *)malloc(size);
}

// Overloaded delete operator for class
void Base::operator delete(void *p)
{
  cout << "delete: void p == " << p << endl;
  if (p) free(p);
}
```

Just to give Base something to store, I gave the class a private data member of type int. The main program constructs a dynamic object of the Base class, then immediately deletes the object. Those statements call the overloaded new and delete operators for the class, which take precedence over the global default operators. Usually, you will overload both operators, but you may overload either one separately if that makes sense for your application.

The global default forms of new and delete are still available. To use them, precede their names with a scope resolution operator. In other words, to bypass the overloaded operators, change the sample program's two statements in main() to

```
Base *p = ::new Base(10);
::delete p;
```

Note: This trick works only for overloaded operators in a class. As I mentioned, applying the scope resolution operator to overloaded global new and delete operators does not gain access to the original memory manager functions.

The implementations for the overloaded operators in class Base follow main(). For the demonstration, the sample operators simply call malloc() and free() to handle memory allocations and deletions. In addition, the overloaded operators display a message, indicating in new the size of an object being allocated and, in delete, the address of an object being destroyed. With these statements, running the program displays

```
new: size == 2
delete: void p == 0x2d670004
```

Of course, the address value might not be the same on your computer. Notice that size equals 2, the number of bytes that an int takes on my system.

To use the alternate form of delete, which receives the address and size of an object to be deleted, replace the class declaration of delete with

```
void operator delete(void *p, size_t size);
```

Then, replace delete's implementation with the following code:

```
void Base::operator delete(void *p, size_t size)
{
  cout << "delete: void p == " << p
    << "; size == " << size << endl;
  if (p) free(p);
}
```

Declared and implemented like that, delete receives the size of the object being deleted. When you run the modified program, it displays a report similar to

```
new: size == 2
delete: void p == 0x2d670d12; size == 2
```

Note: In any given class, you can use only one form of delete, never both. Either form is used identically, however, so you can switch back and forth between the two forms without affecting statements outside of the class.

Inheritance

Overloaded new and delete operators in a class are inherited by derived classes. If you provide custom memory management for a base class, C++ uses that code for objects of the base and for objects of classes derived from the base.

To demonstrate the effect of inheritance on overloaded new and delete operators, derive a new class from Base:

```
class Derived: public Base {
public:
  Derived(): Base(123) { }
};
```

Next, construct and delete an object of the class. The overloaded new and delete operators in Base handle the memory management chores:

```
Derived *dp = new Derived;
delete dp;
```

When using these techniques, keep in mind that new and delete are static members, even though you don't declare them as such. This fact means the operators do not receive a this pointer, and most important, they do not have access to objects being constructed or deleted. The operators are strictly limited to allocating and deleting memory *for* objects; they do not operate directly *on* objects.

Virtual Destructors

In complex class hierarchies with overloaded new and delete operators, you should normally provide virtual destructors to ensure that the proper delete operator is called. Declare a destructor in the base class, then redeclare it in derived classes as needed.

For example, using MYMEM.CPP (Listing 14.2), add a virtual destructor:

```
class Base {
public:
  ...
  virtual ~Base() { }  // destructor
  ...
};
```

Virtual member functions cannot actually be inline, but it's sometimes convenient to write them that way. In this sample, C++ creates a normal, callable function for the apparently inline ~Base().

Next, derive a new class from Base, similar to the one in the preceding section:

```
class Derived: public Base {
public:
  Derived(): Base(123), y(0) { }
  virtual ~Derived() { }  // destructor
  void operator delete(void *p, size_t size);
private:
  int y;
};
```

The class provides a destructor and redefines the inherited delete operator. The derived class continues to use the base class new. (It could also redefine new if necessary.) Implement the redefined delete operator like this:

```
void Derived::operator delete(void *p, size_t size)
{
  cout << "Inside Derived delete\n";
  cout << "delete: void p == " << p
    << "; size == " << size << endl;
  if (p) free(p);
}
```

Next, modify the main program to construct an object of the Derived class, *but assign the address to a base class pointer:*

```
Base *dp = new Derived;
delete dp;
```

Despite the fact that dp is of type Base *, it may address an object of type Derived. Because of the virtual destructors in the classes, deleting the object addressed by dp calls the correct delete operator, whether that object is of type Base or Derived. To see this more clearly, change the first of the two preceding statements to

```
Base *dp = new Base(10);
```

Now, the delete statement calls the base class delete operator because dp addresses an object of that class. Virtual destructors ensure that all deleted objects of a class hierarchy clean up after themselves and put away their toys.

Public or Private?

Normally, you should overload new and delete operators in a class's public section. If the operators are private, only their declaring class members and friends can use them. If the operators are protected, base class, derived class members, and friends can call the operators. Only if the operators are public are they available to statements outside of their class.

It might seem ridiculous to overload new and delete privately, thus preventing any outside statements from constructing objects of the class. Surprisingly, however, the technique has practical value. To demonstrate, convert new and delete to private members in MYMEM.CPP (Listing 14.2), changing class Base to

```
class Base {
public:
  Base(int X): x(X) { }
private:
  void * operator new(size_t size);  // Private!
  void operator delete(void *p);     // Private!
  int x;  // Data in object
};
```

You can no longer compile the program. Statements that used to work in main() now produce errors complaining that new and delete are "inaccessible" (or an equally unfriendly message):

```
Base *p = new Base(10);  // ???
delete p;                // ???
```

In some cases, you can use this method to *prevent* programs from constructing dynamic objects of a class. It's still possible to use ::new or ::delete to construct objects dynamically, but normal uses of the heap operators are barred access to the class.

A related but more powerful technique is to declare *constructors* private or protected. Because new is followed by a call to a constructor, you can privatize all of a class's constructors to limit the use of new to class members or friends. Making constructors protected does the same, but extends access to derived classes.

The benefits of private constructors are easier to see from an example. Listing 14.3, RESTRICT.CPP, demonstrates the pros and cons of the technique.

Listing 14.3. RESTRICT.CPP.

```
#include <iostream.h>
#include <malloc.h>

// Class with private constructor
class Restrict {
private:
  Restrict(int X): x(X) { }  // Private constructor
public:
  void *operator new(size_t size);
  void operator delete(void *p);
  friend Restrict *Create(int X);
private:
  int x;
};

// Restrict rglobal;  // ???

int main()
{
//  Restrict r1;  // ???
//  Restrict *rp = new Restrict;  // ???

  Restrict *okay = Create(123);
  delete okay;

  return 0;
}
```

```
// Overloaded new operator for class
void * Restrict::operator new(size_t size)
{
  return malloc(size);
}

// Overloaded delete operator for class
void Restrict::operator delete(void *p)
{
  if (p) free(p);
}

// Must call Create() to construct objects of class
Restrict *Create(int X)
{
  return new Restrict(X);
}
```

To restrict construction of class objects, all of the class's constructors must be private or protected. In this example, class Restrict has only one constructor in its private section. The class also declares public new and delete operators, plus a friend function named Create(). (More on this function later.)

Because the class constructor is private, it is not possible to define objects of the class globally. This does not compile:

```
Restrict rglobal;  // ???
```

That same statement inside a function also fails to compile. Because Restrict's constructor is private, statements outside of the class are prevented from calling Restrict's constructor, so it is not possible for a program to construct Restrict objects globally or automatically in a function.

Despite the fact that the class declares a public new operator, it is also not possible for program statements to construct dynamic Restrict objects using new. The following statement does not compile:

```
Restrict *rp = new Restrict;  // ???
```

The use of operator new implies the use of a constructor. Because the constructor is private to the class, the compiler rejects the statement even though new is public.

Is there any way to construct an object of the Restrict class? Yes, but only one: call another function such as Create(), declared here as friend of Restrict. Friends of a class have access to the class's private and protected members, *including any private constructors.* In the sample program, Create() returns a pointer to a dynamic Restrict object constructed on the heap:

```
Restrict *Create(int X)
{
  return new Restrict(X);
}
```

This use of new is permitted because the friend function has access to Restrict's private constructor. In fact, this is the *only* way an object of Restrict can be constructed.

All of these restrictions might seem overly harsh, but there are two important effects demonstrated by the sample Restrict class:

● All objects must be constructed using the Create() function, giving the class total control over object construction.

● Because of the prior point, all objects in this example are guaranteed to be allocated space on the heap. It is not possible (except by cheating) to construct a Restrict object globally or automatically in a function.

That second observation might be critical in the design of class libraries where certain classes occupy large amounts of memory. Restricting object construction of class objects to the heap may help programmers to use the classes correctly.

Arrays and Overloaded *new* and *delete*

If you overload new and delete for a class, C++ does not use those operators to construct arrays of class objects. The following sample code always uses the global default new operator, even if TClass overloads new:

```
TClass *array = new TClass[100];  // Calls C++ default new
```

This restriction on overloading new makes more sense when you consider that an array of objects is not the same type as a single object of the class. An overloaded new operator is used *only* for class objects, so (the reasoning goes), arrays of objects do not qualify for construction using an overloaded new.

Be especially aware of this restriction in cases where the class overloads delete. If TClass does that, this statement calls the global default delete operator:

```
delete[] array;  // Calls C++ default delete[]
```

If you forget to add the brackets, you might introduce a serious bug into the code:

```
delete array;  // ??? Calls overloaded operator
```

The array was constructed by the global default new, but is now deleted by the overloaded delete operator in TClass. The compiler does not warn you of any problem, but this poor practice might produce a dragon of a bug depending on how the custom delete is programmed. Always use delete[] with brackets to delete arrays of class objects, and you'll probably never have to fight this monster.

Debugging with *new* and *delete*

Overloading new and delete is frequently useful for investigating a program's use of memory and for debugging dynamic objects. Earlier in this chapter, I suggested filling allocated memory with a known value—or, you could overload new and call the standard calloc() function to allocate blocks initialized to all zero bytes.

A related maneuver is to force new to return null, perhaps on demand or after a certain amount of time passes. This trick simulates an out-of-memory condition, testing how the program responds to a shortage of space. On multitasking systems with large amounts of memory shared by many tasks, the technique is less drastic than the traditional way of allocating memory blocks until the heap fills to overflowing.

Try this. Declare a class with an overloaded new operator (you could also overload delete):

```
class TClass {
public:
  TClass(): x(0) { }
  void * operator new(size_t size);
private:
  int x;
};
```

Implement new something like this:

```
void * TClass::operator new(size_t size)
{
  static int count = 0;
  if (count >= 10) return 0;
  count++;
  return malloc(size);
}
```

Every time the program calls new, the operator increases the static count value. When that value reaches a predetermined maximum, new returns null, simulating an out-of-memory condition without actually bringing your development system to its knees.

Many other debugging techniques are possible by overloading new and delete. You might, for example, create a linked list of all memory blocks allocated by new. It would then be possible to walk that list, using utility functions to investigate memory allocations. You could also have new save information about how much memory is allocated during the course of a program's runtime existence. This information might be useful for determining a program's memory usage, for specifying minimum stack and heap sizes, and so on.

Caution: When you overload the global new and delete operators, be aware that startup and shutdown code in your C++ implementation might call *your* operators. For that reason, it might be unsafe to insert I/O statements into global operator functions or to call other functions that depend on system-dependent settings—an interrupt vector, for example, initialized by your system's startup routines. You can use I/O statements to trace operators overloaded inside classes (as examples in this chapter demonstrate), but doing the same for the global new and delete operators may cause problems.

Mark-and-Release Memory Management

An obscure but highly useful memory management technique treats the heap as a kind of stack. New objects are pushed onto the heap-stack, and old objects are deleted simply by adjusting a heap pointer that works much like a stack pointer (see Figure 14.1).

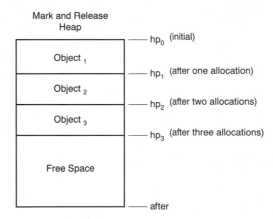

Figure 14.1. The mark-and-release memory management technique treats the heap as a kind of stack.

In Figure 14.1, the mark-and-release heap is represented as a large rectangle. Symbol hp_0 represents the initial position of the heap pointer, which could be an integer index or an address value. To allocate space on the heap, an overloaded new operator returns the current location of the heap pointer and advances the pointer by the number of bytes requested. The class constructor can then stuff an object into the reserved space. Heap pointers hp_1, hp_2, and hp_3 show the effects of using new to allocate space for constructing three objects, $Object_1$, $Object_2$, and $Object_3$.

Deleting objects reverses the parade—in effect sending objects marching out of memory from back to front—and it's here that the technique's benefits become evident. To delete $Object_3$ in Figure 14.1, for example, the delete operator simply resets hp_3 to hp_2. The memory occupied by that object is then available for storing another object.

Even better, to delete *all* objects in a mark-and-release heap, the program simply resets the heap pointer to hp_0! In cases where a program manages hundreds or thousands of objects, it's possible to delete them all rapidly with a single statement. Typically, a mark-and-release heap will have multiple "marks" to which the program releases the heap pointer, thus deleting all objects above that high-water mark.

Listing 14.4, MARK.CPP, implements a mark-and-release heap for a specific class. Only that class uses the method for storage; other classes and objects could be created dynamically in the usual way.

Listing 14.4. MARK.CPP.

```
#include <iostream.h>
#include <iomanip.h>
#include <string.h>

#define HEAPSIZE 2048           // Size of heap in bytes
char heap[HEAPSIZE];            // Heap in data segment
char *hp = heap;                // Heap pointer
char *after = &heap[HEAPSIZE];  // Points to end of heap + 1

// Mark and release class
class MRClass {
  friend ostream & operator<< (ostream &, MRClass &);
public:
  MRClass(int X): x(X) { }
```

```cpp
  void * operator new(size_t size);
  void operator delete(void *p);
private:
  int x;   // Data in object
};

void SubFunction();
void Report();

int main()
{
  Report();
  MRClass *mark = new MRClass(1);
  cout << "*mark == " << *mark;
  Report();
  SubFunction();
  delete mark;
  cout << "At end\n";
  Report();
  return 0;
}

// Construct objects and throw away their addresses
// Note: Don't usually do this!
void SubFunction()
{
  for (int i = 0; i < 3; ++i) {
    MRClass *p = new MRClass(2 + i);
    cout << "*p" << (i + 1) << "   == " << *p;
    Report();
  }
}

// Report on heap
void Report()
{
  cout << "hp == " << (void *)hp << endl;
```

continues

Listing 14.4. continued

```cpp
  cout << "heap contents [0] ... [10]:\n";
  for (int i = 0; i < 10; ++i)
    cout << " " << (int)heap[i];
  cout << endl;
}

// Output data in object c to output stream os
// Appends new line
ostream & operator<< (ostream &os, MRClass &c)
{
  os << '[' << c.x << ']' << endl;
  return os;
}

// Overloaded new operator for MRClass class
// Add object to top of heap (MARK)
void * MRClass::operator new(size_t size)
{
  if (size == 0) return 0;   // Ignore zero size
  char *p = hp;              // Initialize function result
  while (size--) {           // Loop on size
    if (hp == after) {       // Test for overflow
      hp = p;                // : reset hp
      return 0;              // : return null for overflow
    }
    hp++;                    // Advance heap pointer
  }
  return p;   // Return address of reserved block on heap
}

// Overloaded delete operator for MRClass class
// Reduce heap to p (RELEASE)
void MRClass::operator delete(void *p)
{
  hp = (char *)p;   // Deletes all objects above p!
}
```

Figure 14.2 shows the program's output. The heap pointer (hp) address is printed in hexadecimal. (These addresses will probably be different on your display.) Simple objects containing integer values (1, 2, 3, and 4) are placed onto the heap, shown as a row of digits, initially all zeros. Notice how the heap pointer's address increases as new objects are pushed onto the heap. Then, at the end of the program, hp returns to its original value, deleting all objects on the heap (but not altering integer values stored in memory).

```
hp == 0x2b9a046a
heap contents [0] ... [10]:
 0 0 0 0 0 0 0 0
*mark == [1]
hp == 0x2b9a046c
heap contents [0] ... [10]:
 1 0 0 0 0 0 0 0
*p1   == [2]
hp == 0x2b9a046e
heap contents [0] ... [10]:
 1 0 2 0 0 0 0 0
*p2   == [3]
hp == 0x2b9a0470
heap contents [0] ... [10]:
 1 0 2 0 3 0 0 0
*p3   == [4]
hp == 0x2b9a0472
heap contents [0] ... [10]:
 1 0 2 0 3 0 4 0 0
At end
hp == 0x2b9a046a
heap contents [0] ... [10]:
 1 0 2 0 3 0 4 0 0
```

Figure 14.2. Sample output from MARK.CPP (Listing 14.4).

To create a mark-and-release heap, the program defines an array named heap containing space for 2048 bytes. Pointer hp is set to address the first byte of the heap. Another pointer named `after` addresses the byte just after the heap's end. If `hp` is ever greater or equal than `after`, the heap has overflowed (see Figure 14.1).

Note: You don't have to use a global array. You could allocate space for a mark-and-release heap on the regular heap using another `new` statement. In that way, the mark-and-release heap could be sized at runtime.

For constructing objects on the heap, class `MRClass` has a constructor and overloaded versions of `new` and `delete`. The main program calls `new` to construct an `MRClass` object, passing the initializing value 1 to the constructor. A `Report()` function displays the first several bytes of the heap plus other information shown in Figure 14.2.

Function `SubFunction()` breaks the rule that you should never construct objects in functions without deleting those objects or otherwise saving their addresses for later deletion. If this were a test of normal C++ memory management, `SubFunction()` would receive a failing grade. Using a mark-and-release stack, however, the "lost" memory is easily recovered when the main program executes the statement

```
delete mark;
```

This action resets `hp` to the beginning of the heap, thus returning the heap to its startup condition and deleting all objects stored there. The space occupied by the objects constructed in `SubFunction()` is not lost after all, and is again available for use. A mark-and-release heap can reclaim memory even if individual object addresses are not available.

Mark-and-release `new` and `delete` operators are not difficult to write. The versions shown here demonstrate the technique and explain how to prevent heap overflows. If the requested `size` is zero, operator `new` returns null (an unlikely event but a wise safeguard); otherwise, a temporary pointer `p` is set equal to `hp`'s current value.

Next, a `while` loop decrements `size` and increments `hp` to reserve the number of bytes specified by `size`. If `hp` becomes equal to `after`, the heap does not have enough room to fulfill the allocation request. Rather than halt with an error, new sets hp back to its original value and returns null. That way, overflow errors do not destroy the heap or prevent its further use.

> **Note:** You might be able to improve the inner while loop if your system allows pointer arithmetic. Be careful, though, as this change might make your code unportable. In a segmented memory architecture such as used in PCs, adding size to hp and then testing whether the final pointer is greater or equal to after might fail to work correctly depending on the program's memory model.

If no errors occur, new returns the temporary pointer p. A constructor would next deposit an object into the reserved memory at the location addressed by p.

The overloaded delete operator has little to do, merely setting hp to the address of the object being deleted. This action also deletes any objects "above" that one. (I quote "above" in part because your computer is probably under your desk, but more importantly because the direction of up and down in RAM is not strictly defined.)

Mark-and-release memory management lacks the sophistication of modern linked-list memory managers typically provided with a C++ development system, but it is still a useful method to learn. It's especially adept at deleting many objects all at once, an operation that can reduce performance in linked-list allocation schemes. A mark-and-release heap can also reduce fragmentation by storing multiple objects in one large buffer. Depending on how you implement the operators, however, deleting single objects buried inside a mark-and-release heap might be difficult or even impossible.

Setting the *new* Handler

Programmers face a constant battle in writing code to deal with errors. Screaming at errors never helps. They only disappear with careful programming and good debugging practices.

In managing dynamic memory, good error handling becomes even more critical. There's no telling how much memory your customers' computers will have, and your code probably will have to compete for space with other tasks. Today, even simple desktop computers run sophisticated multitasking operating systems, placing extra demands on programmers—and prompting extra screaming at things that go bump in RAM.

Out of Memory

Overloading new and delete along with good memory management practices can help prevent a *heap* of disasters. But these measures still don't reach the root of the problem—what to do when a program runs out of room. Usually, when that happens, recovery is difficult. Despite your best efforts to write robust code, even a slick error-recovery system might become RAM starved and therefore subject to failure.

Careful programmers go to great lengths to detect low memory conditions and take appropriate actions at the first sign of trouble—always testing if new returns null, for instance. That's a good idea, but it's not the final solution. In fact, the test statements *waste the very commodity you are attempting to conserve!* All those if statements take up valuable space, and their execution wastes time. But don't give up. There's one way to have reliable objects *without* testing them too.

The Low Memory Pool

Here's one way to manage memory efficiently and trap most errors without following every use of new with an if statement. The technique centers around a function, LowMemory(), that returns true if allocated memory reaches a specified low level.

The goal is to eliminate the need to write code like this:

```
TClass *p1 = new TClass;   // Construct object
if (!p1) Error();          // Test object
TClass *p2 = new TClass;   // Construct object
```

```
if (!p2) Error();        // Test object
TClass *p3 = new TClass; // Construct object
if (!p3) Error();        // I'm tired of this. How about you?
```

Instead of repeating `if` statements like a broken record, we want to allocate several objects and then test whether available memory has sunk to an all-time low. If so, a fast recovery deletes the objects most recently constructed and calls an error function:

```
TClass *p1 = new TClass; // Construct objects
TClass *p2 = new TClass;
TClass *p3 = new TClass;
if (LowMemory()) {       // Check if memory is low.
  delete p1;             // Zounds! Time to bail out
  delete p2;
  delete p3;
  Error();               // Tell user to delete something
}
```

The three `delete` statements might be wrapped into a function that could be used in other circumstances, so there's little waste in the technique. We don't care whether one, two, or all three pointers are null—if we are out of memory, we are out of memory, and it's time to take action. Most of the time, `LowMemory()` will report false, and performance will improve due to the lack of `if` statements after each use of `new`.

Having decided on the solution, the question remains: How is it possible to write `LowMemory()` in a completely portable way? Operating systems and C++ compilers have different methods for determining how much memory is lying around—and few if any of those methods are compatible from one system to the next.

One solution is to reserve a pool of memory when the program begins. Another function called `_new_handler()` (you can use another name) dips into this pool if `new` reports a shortage of RAM. If the pool is sufficiently large, low-memory conditions are detectable *before* the problem becomes too severe. The program recovers gracefully from a partial memory vacuum rather than choking to death by running completely out of air.

The secret to implementing this memory management technique is to call set_new_handler() to engage a little-used feature of the global, default new operator. Passing the address of a *new-handler* function to set_new_handler() tells new to call the function repeatedly if a memory request fails. The new-handler must be written in this form:

```
void myhandler();
{
  // Take action for out-of-memory condition
}
```

To engage the function, pass its name to set_new_handler() at the beginning of your program (or whenever you want the function to take effect):

```
set_new_handler(myhandler);  // Pass address of myhandler
```

After this step, if new runs out of room, the operator calls myhandler() repeatedly. Pay special attention to the word *repeatedly*. The error-handler function must either

1. Release memory for new to use, or

2. Report a fatal out-of-memory error.

If the new-handler function simply returns, new will again attempt to allocate memory, and if that fails, new will again call the new-handler function. To prevent an endless loop (and endless telephone calls from angry customers) the new-handler must take whatever action is necessary to change the conditions that caused the low-memory condition to occur. Only if no alternatives exist should the new-handler function take the drastic step of shutting down the program. You can prevent that unhappy situation by always checking LowMemory() before you allocate a *total* amount of space greater than the size of the reserved pool. If LowMemory() returns true, objects already constructed are safe to use, but no new objects should be created until the low-memory danger has passed.

Listing 14.5, HANDLER.CPP, demonstrates how to use set_new_handler() with a reserved memory pool. The program allocates objects until a low memory condition occurs, then continues allocating objects beyond that point until halting with a fatal out-of-memory error.

Listing 14.5. HANDLER.CPP.

```cpp
#include <iostream.h>
#include <stdlib.h>
#include <new.h>

void Initialize();
void Recover();

void main()
{
  Initialize();
  for (;;) {
    cout << "Allocating 1024 bytes at";
    void *p = new[1024];
    cout << p << endl;
  }
}

static void *reserve;   // Addresses reserve pool of memory

// Set new memory-error handler
// and initialize reserve pool
void Initialize()
{
  set_new_handler(Recover);  // Set out-of-memory handler
  reserve = new[4096];        // Reserve a "pool" of memory
}

// Attempt to recover from out-of-memory error
// by deleting the reserved pool
void Recover()
{
  cout << "\nMEMORY ERROR: ";
  if (!reserve) {
    cout << "Really out of memory! Halting program.\n";
    exit(-1);
  }
```

continues

405

Listing 14.5. continued

```
    cout << "Low memory! Deleting reserve.\n";
    delete reserve;  // Delete reserved memory pool
    reserve = 0;     // Mark pool empty
}


/* Sample "low memory" function (not used by program)
int LowMemory()
{
  return reserve = 0;  // If true, memory is dangerously low
}
*/
```

When you compile and run the program, it begins constructing objects of 1024 bytes each, reporting their addresses one by one. Eventually, the program runs out of space, ending with lines on-screen that look something like these:

```
Allocating 1024 bytes at0x9ec90004
Allocating 1024 bytes at0x9f4a0004
Allocating 1024 bytes at
MEMORY ERROR: Low memory! Deleting reserve.
0x2eeb0004
Allocating 1024 bytes at0x2e6a0004
Allocating 1024 bytes at0x2de90004
Allocating 1024 bytes at
MEMORY ERROR: Really out of memory! Halting program.
```

To blow up the heap until it bursts, main() calls new over and over to reserve 1024-byte blocks of space:

```
void *p = new[1024];
```

Note: By the way, this is the proper way to allocate memory blocks that have no specific data type. The memory block must be addressed by a void * pointer.

To reserve a block of memory, the program defines a static void pointer named reserve:

```
static void *reserve;   // Addresses reserve pool of memory
```

Function Initialize() assigns a value to the pointer, and also calls set_new_handler(). To that function, Initialize() passes the address of the program's new handler, Recover(). After that, Initialize() uses new to reserve a 4096-byte pool of memory to be used when new runs low.

Recover() releases the reserved memory pool unless the reserve pointer is null, indicating that the pool was already released and is no longer available. When new runs out of space the first time, it calls Recover(), which releases the pool, allowing the program to call new a few more times. The next time new runs out of space, however, the operator again calls Recover, but this time the reserved pool is bone dry and the program halts.

Here are some refinements to the technique that you might want to try:

● Write a function LowMemory() to return true if the reserve pointer is null. A sample function is commented out in Listing 14.5.

● Design an Error() function to be called after detecting a low-memory condition. Error() should not return until reestablishing the reserved memory pool and reclaiming as much other room as possible. (To gain space, Error() might discard or transfer I/O buffers to disk, for example, or the function could ask users to close a file.)

● To prevent new from repeatedly calling the new-handler function, you must call set_new_handler() *and* override the global default new operator. In that case, it's your responsibility to call the new handler.

● Use the other techniques in this chapter to account for a program's use of dynamic memory. Analyze this information to select the best size for the reserved pool.

Final Words

Overloading new and delete gives you global or class-by-class control over C++ memory management. You can even construct your own heaps (using the mark-and-release method, for example), or you can write other code to improve your program's use of RAM.

The next chapter continues this theme, developing several techniques that you can use to store objects efficiently in memory.

Storing Objects
Efficiently

E fficient class objects conserve RAM and help programs run fast. Well-
designed classes might even make the difference between a program that
operates smoothly and one that never gets up to full steam.

Designing efficient classes isn't limited to making class objects as small as
possible—though size and efficiency are closely related. Storing objects

efficiently also means taking advantage of C++ techniques that help you fine-tune exactly how, when, and where your programs construct class objects in memory.

This chapter covers five techniques that you can use in the design of classes to improve object storage efficiency:

- *Objects and Pointers*—How to decide whether an object should store data directly or use pointers to address data stored separately.

- *Object Clones*—How to design a class object that can clone itself.

- *Objects and Placement-Syntax*—How to pass arguments to new, and how to place a class object at a specific address.

- *Variable-Size Objects*—How to construct an object that expands to occupy only as much space as needed, leaving no waste.

- *Duplicate Object References*—How to make two or more objects refer safely to multiple copies of data (identical strings, for example).

Objects and Pointers

One of the first tricks that C++ programmers learn is how to design a class that has pointers to other objects. Constructing an object of the class results in a spider's web of pointers, with each "strand" leading to one of several pieces of information (see Figure 15.1).

It's a mistake to assume that using pointers in objects automatically improves efficiency. As a spider traps a fly, several factors can trap your code in a sticky mess:

- Pointers occupy memory, though only a small amount.

- Dereferencing pointers takes time.

- Deleting many small objects can fragment the heap.

- Object destruction is more time consuming because each distinct piece of data must be deleted separately.

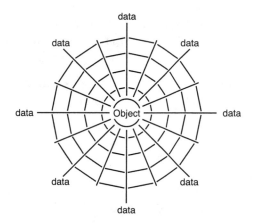

Figure 15.1. A class object might have a web of pointers leading to other data.

I'm not suggesting that using pointers in classes is wrong, but doing so without considering the alternatives can be foolish and might lead to wasteful, inefficient object storage—exactly the opposite of the results that most programmers expect from using pointers. Consider the following struct, representing some data you need to store in memory:

```
struct Object {
  char data[128];
};
```

In a class, you could use pointers to address multiple Object instances, designing the class something like this:

```
class Indirect {
public:
  Indirect(): p1(0), p2(0), p3(0) {}
  ~Indirect() { delete p1; delete p2; delete p3; }
private:
  Object *p1;  // Pointer to Object
  Object *p2;  //    "    "    "    "
  Object *p3;  //    "    "    "    "
};
```

Of course, this sample `Indirect` class would need other members, but the design is typical. Pointers `p1`, `p2`, and `p3` address `Object` instances, constructed by `new` and possibly stored at nonadjacent locations in memory.

There's nothing wrong with this common and useful approach to class design. But it's also possible to store `Object` members directly in a class. Compare the preceding class with this one:

```
class Direct {
public:
  Direct() { }
private:
  Object d1;    // Direct Object
  Object d2;    //    "    "    "
  Object d3;    //    "    "    "
};
```

Class `Direct` is simpler, and it does not require a destructor. Instead of using pointers to address dynamic `Object` instances, the class defines three `Objects` directly, `d1`, `d2`, and `d3`. (Not shown, however, are any methods for initializing these objects.)

None of these samples reveals any earth-shaking news, but consider what happens when a program defines `Indirect` and `Direct` objects. Global or local variables have very different effects on object storage. Let's consider all possible cases—the process you should go through in designing classes. First, here's an `Indirect` object (the one with pointer members) defined globally or locally in a function:

```
Indirect object1;
```

Only the pointer members inside `object1` are defined in global or local storage. Pointers `p1`, `p2`, and `p3` inside the object address data stored on the heap. In other words, although simply defined, this object's storage is divided between two *different* memory regions (unless, that is, your heap and stack are combined somehow). Some of the object is in global or local storage (perhaps on the stack); other data is in the heap (see Figure 15.2).

Figure 15.2 illustrates the near ideal use of memory for class objects with multiple pointers. Relatively small portions of the object are stored globally or locally; larger pieces are stored on the heap and addressed by pointers. The heap is typically larger than the program's global data area or stack, so this arrangement tends to use memory well. Also, the objects on the heap do not need to be stored consecutively.

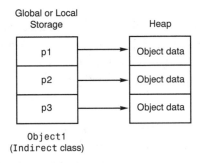

Figure 15.2. An object of the Indirect class.

However, compare object1 with another object of type Direct, again defined globally or locally to a function:

```
Direct object2;
```

Because the Direct class stores its data directly, all of object2's information is placed at the object's location—in a global data area, perhaps, or on a stack. Figure 15.3 shows how this object appears in memory.

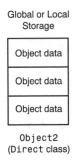

Figure 15.3. An object of the Direct class.

Figure 15.3 often, but not always, represents the worst possible use of available memory. Because global and local storage is usually limited, many such objects might easily cause problems. It's probably best to define only small objects this way.

The obvious solution is to construct a dynamic object of the Direct class and store it on the heap, but this is where programmers often make the wrong choice in the class design. Consider what happens when you construct a dynamic instance of the Indirect class:

```
Indirect *pointer1 = new Indirect;
```

Figure 15.4 shows how this new object is stored. Only pointer1 is stored globally or locally. The entire Indirect object is stored on the heap, including that object's pointer members. The three pointers p1, p2, and p3 are stored on the heap along with the Object structures those pointers address. Is this the best design?

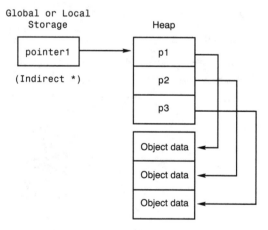

Figure 15.4. A pointer to a dynamic object of the Indirect class.

The arrangement of pointers and objects in Figure 15.4 works well in many cases, but unless you are aware of how your objects are organized in memory, you might end up using pointers needlessly. You can, for example, eliminate the pointers and reduce the object's complexity simply by defining a dynamic instance of the Direct class:

```
Direct *pointer2 = new Direct;
```

Figure 15.5 shows the result. Now, the entire object is stored on the heap, with all Object structures in adjacent positions.

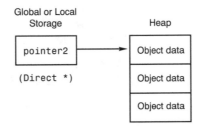

Figure 15.5. A pointer to a dynamic object of the Direct class.

The important observation is that none of the preceding four examples is necessarily more efficient than the other three. You can decide which method is best only by considering how your program uses the classes and how the program's class objects compete for space. Too often, programmers blindly use pointers, assuming that the results will be more efficient. This isn't always the case, however, and you should carefully consider the alternatives described here before selecting a final design. If the Direct object in Figure 15.5 is small, for example, it might be best to store it in one memory block rather than divide the object with pointers as in Figure 15.4 and risk fragmenting the heap.

Listing 15.1, HEAP.CPP, demonstrates some of the preceding concepts. Compile and run the sample program, preferably in a debugger, and read the comments in the listing while you consider where objects and addressed data are stored.

Listing 15.1. HEAP.CPP.

```cpp
#include <iostream.h>

// Represents data to be stored in a class
struct Object {
  char data[128];
};

// Example of class that addresses data via a pointer
class ClassOne {
public:
  ClassOne() { op = new Object; }
  ~ClassOne() { delete op; }
private:
  Object *op;  // Always stored on the heap
};

// Example of class that contains data as a member
class ClassTwo {
public:
  ClassTwo() { }
private:
  Object ob;   // Not always stored on the heap
};

int main()
{
  cout << "Storing objects on heap\n";

  // ClassOne "Object" is always stored on the heap
  ClassOne k1;  // Object is on heap
  ClassOne *p1 = new ClassOne;  // Object is on heap

  // ClassTwo "Object" is not always stored on the heap
  ClassTwo k2;  // Object is *not* on heap
  ClassTwo *p2 = new ClassTwo;  // Object is on heap
```

```
// Destroy objects addressed by pointers
delete p1;  // Requires destructor call
delete p2;  // Does not require destructor call

return 0;
}
```

Object Clones

It's often necessary to make an exact replica of an object—in other words, a *clone.* Perhaps you need to save an object's state, or you might need to pass a temporary copy of an object to a function, protecting the original from harm.

Whatever the reason, cloning objects is not always as simple as the job may seem. This fact is especially true when using base-class pointers to objects of derived classes. In fact, if the program can't determine in advance what kind of object a pointer addresses (a typical situation in C++ programs), it might not be possible to clone an object safely without taking the measures described in this section.

The Wrong Way to Clone

Understanding the *wrong* way to clone objects is the first step in mastering the proper technique. Consider a base class declared as

```
class Base {
public:
  Base(int K): k(K) { }
  virtual void Print();
private:
  int k;
};
```

Class `Base` has a single `int` data member `k` and a virtual `Print()` function that displays `k`'s value. Next, derive a class from `Base`:

```
class Derived: public Base {
public:
  Derived(int K, int M): Base(K), m(M) { }
  virtual void Print();
private:
  int m;
};
```

Class `Derived` adds a second `int` data member `m`, and overrides `Print()` to display both values. You might implement the two `Print()` functions as

```
void Base::Print()
{
  cout << "k == " << k << endl;
}


void Derived::Print()
{
  Base::Print();
  cout << "m == " << m << endl;
}
```

So far, so good. You can define a pointer and call `new` to construct an object of the `Base` class:

```
Base *p = new Base(123);
```

You can then call the virtual `Print()` member function to display the object's value, and call `delete` to reclaim the object's space:

```
cout << "p->Print():\n";
p->Print();
delete p;
```

All of that is straightforward C++ programming. Now, let's repeat the same steps, but this time construct an object of the Derived class using the same Base class pointer p:

```
p = new Derived(456, 789);
cout << "p->Print():\n";
p->Print();
```

The p->Print() statement finds the correct class function because Print() is virtual. Even though p is declared as a Base class pointer, the program calls the Derived class's Print().

That too is straightforward C++, but here comes the problem. What is the proper way to clone the object that p addresses? Suppose you define a Base class pointer named clone:

```
Base *clone;
```

The goal is for clone to address an exact replica of the object addressed by p. You can't simply assign p to clone. That would cause both pointers to address the *same* object:

```
clone = p;  // ???
```

If subsequent statements delete both clone and p, the heap is almost certain to become corrupted. To keep the heap squeaky clean, you might attempt to clone the object like this:

```
Derived temp = *p; // ???  Doesn't compile!
```

That will not compile. The compiler knows only that p is a Base class pointer. Although p may address an object of class Base or Derived, the statement assumes that p *always* addresses a Derived object. The compiler views this situation as an unresolvable conflict, and it refuses to budge until you identify exactly what you intend to do.

There is a partial solution to this mess, but it is not a very good one. A cast expression satisfies the compiler and clones the object addressed by p:

```
Derived temp = *(Derived *)p;  // ???
```

That copies the `Derived` object addressed by p into `temp`. Unfortunately, however, the statement's worth is questionable because the program still assumes that p *always* addresses a `Derived` object. If p addresses a `Base` class object, the program will develop a serious bug.

We have reached the dead end of the alley. Fortunately, there's another path that leads to safe clones.

The Right Way to Clone

Now that you've seen the wrong way to clone, here's the right way to go about the job. The secret is to add two elements to each of the classes: a copy constructor and a virtual `Clone()` member function. Together, the constructor and function make it possible to clone objects safely, even when using base class pointers to address objects of the base or of derived class types.

Listing 15.2, CLONE.CPP, demonstrates how to write and use a virtual `Clone()` member function along with a copy constructor for safe object cloning.

Note: On disk, CLONE.CPP is located in the PART3 directory. To compile CLONE.CPP and remaining programs in this chapter, enter this Borland C++ command (see Appendix A for additional instructions):

```
bcc -ml clone secrets.lib
```

Listing 15.2. CLONE.CPP.

```
#include <iostream.h>
#include <memuse.h>
#include <string.h>

// Base class with cloning capability
class Base {
```

```
  friend ostream & operator<< (ostream &os, Base &c);
public:
  Base(): s(0) { }
  Base(const char * S);
  Base(const Base &copy);
  virtual ~Base() { delete s; }
  virtual Base * Clone() const;
private:
  char * s;
};

// Derived class with overridden Clone()
class Derived: public Base {
  friend ostream & operator<< (ostream &os, Derived &d);
public:
  Derived(): Base(), value(0) { }
  Derived(const char * S, double v): Base(S), value(v) { }
  Derived(const Derived &copy);
  virtual Base * Clone() const;
private:
  double value;
};

// Function prototype
void PerformTest();

int main()
{
  HeapReport("Initial memory use");
  PerformTest();
  HeapReport("\nFinal memory use");
  return 0;
}

// Clone objects
void PerformTest()
```

continues

Listing 15.2. continued

```
{
  Base * bp;      // Base or Derived object pointer
  Base * clone;   // Pointer to object clone

  // Clone a Base class object
  bp = new Base("Base class object");
  cout << "\n*bp == " << *bp << endl;
  clone = bp->Clone();
  cout << "*clone == " << *clone << endl;
  delete clone;
  delete bp;

  // Clone a Derived class object
  bp = new Derived("Derived class object", 3.14159);
  cout << "\n*bp == " << *bp << endl;
  clone = bp->Clone();
  cout << "*clone == " << *clone << endl;
  delete clone;
  delete bp;
}

// Output stream operator for Base objects
ostream & operator<< (ostream &os, Base &c)
{
  os << c.s;
  return os;
}

// Output stream operator for Derived objects
ostream & operator<< (ostream &os, Derived &d)
{
  os << (Base &)d << ", " << d.value;
  return os;
}

// Construct Base class object from string pointer
Base::Base(const char * S)
```

```
{
  s = new char[strlen(S) + 1];
  if (s) strcpy(s, S);
}

// Base class copy constructor
Base::Base(const Base &copy)
  : s(0)
{
  if (copy.s) {
    s = new char[strlen(copy.s) + 1];
    if (s) strcpy(s, copy.s);
  }
}

// Base class clone member function
// Returns Base class pointer
Base * Base::Clone() const
{
  return new Base(*this);  // Calls copy constructor
}

// Derived class copy constructor
Derived::Derived(const Derived &copy)
  : Base(copy)
{
  value = copy.value;
}

// Implement Derived Clone member function
// Still returns base class pointer!
Base * Derived::Clone() const
{
  return new Derived(*this);  // Calls copy constructor
}
```

When you run the sample program, it displays several lines as it constructs and clones two objects, one of a base class and one of a class derived from the base. (For clarity, I named these classes Base and Derived.) The program also uses the MEMUSE module from Chapter 10 to display before and after heap sizes, verifying that the objects and clones are properly deleted before the program ends. Here's what the program displayed on my screen:

```
Initial memory use
- Heap size == 447552
*bp == Base class object
*clone == Base class object
*bp == Derived class object
*clone == Derived class object
Final memory use
- Heap size == 447552
```

In the program, pointer bp is first assigned the address of a Base class object. That object is cloned and addressed by another pointer named clone of type Base *. Using these same pointers, the program constructs and clones a Derived class object—the task that in the preceding section caused so much trouble.

Closely examine the statements that perform these actions. First, the program constructs and clones the Base class object:

```
bp = new Base("Base class object");
cout << "\n*bp == " << *bp << endl;
clone = bp->Clone();
cout << "*clone == " << *clone << endl;
delete clone;
delete bp;
```

The third statement calls the virtual Clone() function, which returns the address of a cloned object. Clone() returns Base * (see the listing), so its result obviously can be assigned to the type-compatible clone.

After deleting clone and bp—reclaiming the space occupied by the original object and its clone—the program next constructs and clones a Derived class object. Here's the code:

```
bp = new Derived("Derived class object", 3.14159);
cout << "\n*bp == " << *bp << endl;
clone = bp->Clone();
cout << "*clone == " << *clone << endl;
delete clone;
delete bp;
```

Compare these statements with the preceding ones. *Only the first statement is different!* Again, the Base class pointer bp is assigned the address of a new object, but this time, of the Derived class. The third statement clones that object, assigning its address to clone. This is the *identical* statement that cloned the Base class object—positive proof that the program can clone objects with no prior knowledge of those objects' types. The objects can be of type Base or of a derived class such as Derived.

> **Note:** I duplicated the statements in the preceding examples just to drive home the point that the program can clone objects without having direct information about the objects' types. The duplicated statements could be wrapped into a function, creating a kind of object factory that produces "knockoff" object copies.

To perform safe cloning, the Base class uses a copy constructor and a virtual Clone() member function, declared as

```
Base(const Base &copy);       // Copy constructor
virtual Base * Clone() const; // Member function
```

Similar declarations appear in the Derived class:

```
Derived(const Derived &copy); // Copy constructor
virtual Base * Clone() const; // Member function
```

Notice that the inherited Clone() function is declared identically in both classes—a requirement of inherited virtual member functions. The function in Derived returns type Base *, *not* Derived *.

The listing shows the copy constructor implementations. These are similar to other copy constructors you have seen throughout this book (in Chapter 10's `String` class, for example). The `Base` class copy constructor allocates space for a character string, then calls the standard `strcpy()` function to transfer the string from the source object (identified by `copy`) to the new object the constructor is building. The `Derived` class copy constructor calls the `Base` constructor, then transfers the `double` member from `copy` to the object under construction.

The secret to implementing the virtual `Clone()` member functions in both classes is to call the class copy constructors to build object replicas. The `Base` class `Clone()` is implemented as

```
Base * Base::Clone() const
{
  return new Base(*this);  // Calls copy constructor
}
```

Literally stated, the function returns "a pointer to a newly constructed object of type `Base` initialized with the object addressed by `this`." In this constructor, the `this` pointer is of type `Base *`. When dereferenced, `*this` refers to a `Base` class object—the one that is being cloned. Notice that this statement automatically returns null if there isn't enough heap space to construct the clone—there's no need to add any additional error tests.

Next, compare the `Base` class version of `Clone()` with that function in `Derived`. The two functions are almost twins:

```
Base * Derived::Clone() const
{
  return new Derived(*this);  // Calls copy constructor
}
```

The replacement function must *not* call its inherited ancestor function—a vital rule in this technique. Instead, the function returns a newly constructed object of the `Derived` class, using that class's copy constructor. That constructor *does* call the `Base` class constructor to initialize the inherited portion of the object.

You can continue to provide `Clone()` functions in further derivations. For example, to derive another class from `Derived`, give it a copy constructor and a virtual `Clone()` member function. If the class is named `MyClass`, the `Clone()` function would execute the statement

```
return new MyClass(*this);
```

If `p` and `clone` are `Base`-class pointers, a single statement is guaranteed to construct a safe clone:

```
clone = p->Clone();
```

If `clone` is null after this step, the object could not be cloned; otherwise, `clone` addresses an exact replica of the object addressed by `p` without requiring the program to specify the object's type.

> **Note:** You might have noticed that I declared `Clone()` as a `const` function. This designation is not required, but it permits `const` objects of `Base` and `Derived` classes to be cloned. Because the `Clone()` function doesn't modify the object being cloned, the function probably should be `const`.

Objects and Placement Syntax

Placement syntax is a relatively obscure C++ feature that can provide a higher level of control over dynamic object construction. You can use placement syntax to pass values of any types to an overloaded `new` operator, but the most common use is to place objects at specific addresses. I'll cover both uses of the syntax here.

Passing a Flag to *new*

By attaching additional parameters to an overloaded `new` operator, you can pass flags and other values to `new` during an object's construction. Operator `new` is always called *before* an object is constructed, so the technique might be used to prepare memory in one of several possible ways before the object's class constructor has the chance to use that memory.

To demonstrate the method, define some flag values, perhaps as enumerated constants:

```
enum Flag { flag_one, flag_two, flag_three };
```

Note: The programming in this section is extracted from the disk file FLAG.CPP located in the PART3 directory.

Next, design a class with an overloaded new operator. Let's say you want to pass a Flag value and a string to new. Here's how you might design the class:

```
class Placer {
public:
  Placer(int N): n(N) { }
  void * operator new(size_t size, const char *s, Flag f);
  int GetN() { return n; }
private:
  int n;
};
```

Operator new's parameter list must begin with the usual size_t parameter, but in this example, it also has two extra parameters (highlighted in bold)—a char pointer s and a Flag value f. Examine how this unusual form of the new operator might be implemented:

```
void * Placer::operator new(size_t size, const char *s, Flag f)
{
  cout << "\nInside new: s == " << s << ", f == " << f << endl;
  return ::operator new(size);
}
```

An output statement displays the values of the string and Flag arguments passed to new. You might use the flag value f to select memory control options—perhaps choosing between one of several heaps or other reserved memory locations. In this sample, the function merely returns the value of the global new, called using its full function name. You could not write that return statement as

```
return new(size);  // ???
```

That doesn't work because C++ treats new specially, always passing the requested size as the first argument. In other words, that statement causes C++ to hunt for an operator in the form new(int, int). To defeat that default action, you can use new's full-dress name, *including* the operator keyword:

```
return ::operator new(size);
```

Now C++ recognizes new(int) as it normally does. It might also be possible to call new with no parameters, but this may or may not work on all compilers, so try the following with a large grain of salt:

```
return ::new;  // ??? (but maybe okay)
```

Rather than pass a flag value to new as shown here, you can also select a buffer or perform some action that alters how memory is allocated, perhaps based on the passed Flag value. You could even reserve a fixed amount of space for the object. For example, although the sample class here requires only two bytes, you could reserve 128 bytes for objects of the class by using this return statement:

```
return new char[128];  // Reserve too much space for object
```

In some cases, storing objects in fixed-sized chunks (128, 256, 1024 bytes, and so on) might help reduce heap fragmentation. In that case, you can use this technique to force objects to grow to sizes larger than absolutely needed. Even if the object needs only 32 bytes, it still gets 128.

Using placement syntax might seem highly unusual until you get used to the form. Here's how the sample program can use new to construct an object of type Placer:

```
Placer *p = new("String", flag_three) Placer(123);
```

Notice the two parameters passed in parentheses to new (highlighted in bold)—a literal string and the constant flag_three. The class constructor is called in the usual way by specifying the class name (Placer) and any required values (123).

Placing Objects at Specific Addresses

Placement syntax is particularly useful for placing objects at specific addresses. To use new this way generally requires three steps:

1. Overload new and specify two parameters, the first of type `size_t` and the second of type `void *`.

2. Implement new to return the *same* `void *` address value passed as an argument. You can ignore the `size_t` parameter.

3. To use the overloaded new, pass it the address where you want an object to be stored. The overloaded new simply returns this same address.

Listing 15.3, PLACE.CPP, puts these steps into action, storing an object in a global buffer. You can use the same technique to store objects in other fixed locations.

Listing 15.3. PLACE.CPP.

```cpp
#include <iostream.h>
#include <string.h>

#define STRINGSIZE 21

// Example of class that stores a char array directly
class HardWired {
  friend ostream & operator<< (ostream &os, HardWired &t);
public:
  HardWired() { s[0] = 0; }  // Constructor nulls string
  HardWired(const char *S);  // Constructor copies string
  void * operator new(size_t, void * bp);
  void operator delete(void *);
private:
  char s[STRINGSIZE];  // Character array
};

// Objects constructed via new are placed in buffer
int objectInBuffer = 0;  // If nonzero (true), buffer is full
char buffer[sizeof(HardWired)];

// Construct a HardWired object globally
HardWired global("Global object");
```

```
int main()
{
  // Construct a HardWired object automatically in function
  HardWired local("Automatic object");

  // Construct a HardWired object with new
  HardWired *p = new(buffer) HardWired("Object in buffer");

  // Display objects
  cout << "The three objects are:\n";
  cout << "global == " << global << endl;
  cout << "local == " << local << endl;
  cout << "*p == " << *p << endl;

  // Force error by attempting to reuse buffer
  cout << "\nAttempting to add second object to buffer\n";
  HardWired *bad = new(buffer) HardWired("Bad object");
  if (!bad) cout << "Error (expected): Buffer is full!\n";

  // Delete object in buffer then insert
  cout << "\nDelete object and try again\n";
  delete p;
  p = new(buffer) HardWired("Good object");
  if (p) cout << "Object in buffer == " << *p << endl;
  delete p;

  return 0;
}

// Output stream operator
ostream & operator<< (ostream &os, HardWired &t)
{
  os << t.s;
  return os;
}
```

continues

Listing 15.3. continued

```
// Construct HardWired object from char pointer S
HardWired::HardWired(const char *S)
{
  s[0] = 0;  // Erase char array in object
  if (S) strncpy(s, S, STRINGSIZE - 1);
}

// Custom new operator uses global buffer for storage
void * HardWired::operator new(size_t, void * bp)
{
  if (objectInBuffer) return 0;
  objectInBuffer = 1;
  return bp;
}

// Custom delete operator empties global buffer
void HardWired::operator delete(void *)
{
  objectInBuffer = 0;
}
```

In the sample listing, class HardWired stores a private string as an array of char values. In addition to constructors and an output stream operator, the class overloads the new and delete operators as

```
void * operator new(size_t, void * bp);
void operator delete(void *);
```

Operator new first declares the required size_t parameter. The operator also declares a pointer of type void *, representing the address at which dynamic HardWired objects are to be stored. Operator delete is declared normally.

Two global variables provide a control value and storage to hold a single instance of the HardWired class:

```
int objectInBuffer = 0;  // If nonzero (true), buffer is full
char buffer[sizeof(HardWired)];  // Big enough for one object
```

If `objectInBuffer` is true, the overloaded new operator assumes that `buffer` already contains an object. If the control value is false, new accepts a request to place a new object into `buffer`. In this sample program, `buffer` can hold only one object—you could expand the technique to store multiple objects, however, in effect converting `buffer` into a private sort of heap. (The programming could also use the concepts demonstrated in the mark-and-release heap techniques in Chapter 14.)

The sample program implements operator new like this:

```
void * HardWired::operator new(size_t, void * bp)
{
  if (objectInBuffer) return 0;
  objectInBuffer = 1;
  return bp;
}
```

If `objectInBuffer` is true, the function returns null, signifying that it could not fulfill the memory allocation request. If `objectInBuffer` is false, then new sets the control value to true (1) and returns the same address passed to new using placement syntax.

Operator delete almost seems too simple to have any useful effect:

```
void HardWired::operator delete(void *)
{
  objectInBuffer = 0;
}
```

Setting the control value to false (0) empties the buffer—or, more correctly, marks the buffer as being available for overwriting with a new object. This action resembles the way that disk files are "deleted" by erasing or modifying their directory entries without actually affecting any data stored on disk. The deleted object isn't erased; it's space is merely marked for reuse.

Note: It would be possible to reset `objectInBuffer` to true and recover the object most recently deleted from the program's buffer. This modification resembles the way disk files can sometimes be "recovered" simply by refreshing their directory entries.

The sample program constructs three objects of the HardWired class. First comes a global object defined outside of main():

```
HardWired global("Global object");
```

The compiler places global in the program's global data area—nothing special here. Function main() constructs another object automatically, probably on the stack:

```
HardWired local("Automatic object");
```

Again, this is straightforward C++ programming. Constructing a dynamic object using new, however, inserts the object directly into a global buffer, effectively bypassing the heap memory manager:

```
HardWired *p = new(buffer) HardWired("Object in buffer");
```

Recall that this version of new simply returns the address passed as an argument. That argument in this case is buffer, thus p is given buffer's address after constructing the object at that location.

At this stage, the buffer is full (it can hold only one object). Attempting to construct a second object in the same buffer causes new to return null:

```
HardWired *bad = new(buffer) HardWired("Bad object");
```

That should set pointer bad to null. To permit another object to be stored in the buffer, the first object must be deleted:

```
delete p;
```

After that step, the buffer is again available to hold another object.

Careful control over objects in buffers, and the actions of new and delete, are critical to the success of this object-placement method. It's your responsibility to ensure that allocated memory is actually available—whether that memory is on the heap or in a global storage location as in this sample.

By the way, it's still possible to construct HardWired objects on the heap (unless you also replace the global new operator). Just preface new with a scope resolution operator:

```
p = ::new HardWired("Object on heap");
```

Variable-Size Objects

For some reason, programming languages never seem to deal very well with variable-size data. Most languages, for instance, have some sort of array capability, but it's unusual to find a language with built-in features that permit programs to adjust the sizes of arrays at will. Surprisingly, BASIC has the capability of "dimensioning" arrays at runtime, but Pascal, C, and C++ have no similar built-in feature.

After programmers gain a bit of experience, they discover how to fool compilers into "thinking" that an array is a certain size when in fact it is another, in effect adding a "dimension" feature at the cost of some risky business. In C and C++, for example, you can define some storage and assign the buffer's address to a pointer:

```
char *array = new char[BUFFERSIZE];
```

You can then use indexing expressions to access values in the dynamic array:

```
array[4] = 123;
cout << "array[9] == " << array[9] << endl;
```

Statements like those are unsafe. Assigning a value to a position outside of the allocated memory might poke bytes directly into another variable, or worse, destroy instructions in the program's compiled code. On systems that provide protected memory areas, an out-of-range index expression might even halt the program unexpectedly.

C++ has all the necessary elements for constructing safe, variable-size arrays, but the technique is not widely known, and many programmers continue to use the dangerous old-style dynamic array method just described.

Listing 15.4 demonstrates a safer solution by creating two variable-sized vectors (arrays). When you compile and run VARY.CPP, you see the values of the two vectors holding long integer values (they could hold any other object). One vector has four values; the other has eight. Though the program's output is simple, the techniques demonstrated in the listing have dozens of possible applications.

Listing 15.4. VARY.CPP.

```cpp
#include <iostream.h>
#include <memuse.h>

// Class for constructing variable-size objects
class vary {
  friend class LongVector;
private:
  vary(int n);    // For use only by LongVector!
  void * operator new(size_t classSize, size_t vectorSize);
private:
  int length;       // Number of long values in vector
  long vector[1];  // Dummy start of long vector
};

// Example of a dynamic vector
class LongVector {
public:
  LongVector(): vp(0) { }
  LongVector(int size);
  ~LongVector() { delete vp; }
  int Length() const { return vp->length; }
  long & operator[](int index);
private:
  vary *vp;  // Pointer to variable-sized object
};

// Function prototypes
void ShowLongVector(const char *s, LongVector &v);
void PerformTest();

int main()
{
  HeapReport("Initial memory use");
  PerformTest();
  HeapReport("\nFinal memory use");
  return 0;
}
```

```
void PerformTest()
{
  LongVector v1(4);
  LongVector v2(8);
  ShowLongVector("v1", v1);
  ShowLongVector("v2", v2);
}

// Display contents of a vector
void ShowLongVector(const char *s, LongVector &v)
{
  cout << "\nvector " << s << ':' << endl;
  for (int i = 0; i < v.Length(); ++i)
    cout << s << '[' << i << "] == "
      << v[i] << endl;
}

// Constructor for vary class
vary::vary(int n)
{
  length = n;
  if (vector) memset(vector, 0, length * sizeof(long));
}

// Overloaded new operator for vary class
void * vary::operator new(size_t classSize, size_t vectorSize)
{
  return new char[classSize + (vectorSize - 1) * sizeof(long)];
}

// Construct LongVector object with size elements
LongVector::LongVector(int size)
{
  vp = new(size) vary(size);
  if (vp)
    for (int i = 0; i < size; ++i)
      vp->vector[i] = i;
}
```

continues

437

Listing 15.4. continued

```
// Index operator
long & LongVector::operator[](int index)
{
  if (0 <= index && index < vp->length)
    return vp->vector[index];
  static long bad = -1;  // Bad value to return for errors
  return bad;
}
```

Class vary declares LongVector as a friend class, giving LongVector full access to vary's private members. All of vary's members are private, including the class constructor. The friend class LongVector is therefore the only class that can construct and use objects of the vary class—a technique that might come in handy in other circumstances where you need to restrict the use of one class to another.

The vary class has two private data members. An integer length records the number of values in the vector—in other words, the vector's range. A second member, vector, is declared as

```
long vector[1];
```

The actual vector begins at this location and expands "below" (toward higher addresses), a trick that relies on the lack of index range checking in C++. Figure 15.6 shows how an object of type vary appears in memory. In the figure, vector is expanded at runtime to hold four long values. The shaded portion shows the declared portion of the object. The actual object extends into the reserved space beyond.

The program's second class, LongVector, contains a private pointer vp to an object of type vary. The class constructor initializes this pointer to address a vary object with a vector of size elements. The problem to solve in LongVector is to construct a vary class object that expands to the desired size.

Closely examine the statement in the LongVector constructor that accomplishes that goal:

```
vp = new(size) vary(size);
```

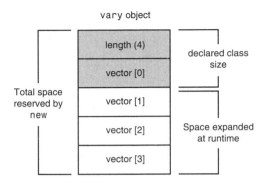

Figure 15.6. The vary object expanded to hold a vector of four long values.

This is another example of new's placement syntax. The statement assigns to pointer vp the address of a vary class object, passing the size parameter both to new and to the vary constructor. The two arguments are the keys to unlocking this technique. Operator new uses size to allocate enough memory for a vector of that many elements plus any extra bytes needed by the vary class. The constructor uses the same size to initialize the vector.

In the sample program, unless new returns null, the vector is filled with sequential values. (If you don't want the program to do that, delete the if and for statements in the LongVector constructor.) Notice how the LongVector constructor accesses the vector:

```
vp->vector[i] = i;
```

Pointer vp is not a vector; it's a pointer to an object of type vary. Because LongVector is a friend of vary, C++ allows this statement inside the class. Statements outside of the class must use LongVector's index operator to access vector values (see function ShowLongVector() for example). In this way, the inner vector is safely hidden inside the classes.

The vary class constructor and overloaded new operator show how variable-size objects of the vary class are sized at runtime. Or, in keeping with object-oriented principles, perhaps I should say that vary objects *size themselves*.

The secret to having vary reserve a variable amount of space for objects of vary's class type is in the overloaded new operator. That operator calls the global new to reserve a requested amount of room. Examine new's only statement:

```
return new char[classSize + (vectorSize - 1) * sizeof(long)];
```

Parameter classSize equals the size of the vary class *as declared.* Parameter vectorSize equals the number of vector elements requested. The class already has a vector with a single element declared as

```
long vector[1];   // Dummy start of long vector
```

For that reason, the program subtracts 1 from vectorSize, accounting for this element. The resulting value times the size of the long data type equals the expanded byte size of the requested vector. Adding to that product the size of the declared class computes the total number of bytes needed for the variable-size object—a computation that is completely portable, by the way.

The technique might take some effort to put into practice, but the end result is an easy-to-use, and *safe,* variable-size vector. To allocate space for an 8-element LongVector object, for example, the program simply executes the statement

```
LongVector v2(8);
```

Duplicate Object References

Like some kind of sneaky, plagiaristic thief, C++ often seems to make numerous copies of objects when you are not looking. Passing objects by value to functions, copying one object to another, returning objects from functions, and similar tasks might cause many wasteful duplications of data in memory. Worse, you might not even be aware that these copies are taking up valuable space.

The problem frequently shows up in string and vector classes. For example, using the vary and LongVector classes in the preceding section, you might want to add code to permit assigning one object to another. The goal is to be able to write statements like these:

```
LongVector copy1(10);      // Construct copy1
LongVector copy2 = copy1;  // Construct copy2 and assign copy1
LongVector copy3;          // Construct default copy3
copy3 = copy2;             // Assign copy2 to copy3
copy2 = copy1;             // Assign copy1 to copy2
```

We also want to pass LongVector objects efficiently to functions. Consider this statement:

```
ShowLongVector("copy1", copy1);
```

If the second LongVector argument is passed by value, C++ passes a copy of the object to the function. If the object is large, that copy might take more than its fair share of RAM. It might even lead to a stack overflow.

The traditional approach to safe object copying uses a copy constructor and an overloaded operator= function. You've seen several examples of this technique in this book (see the Vector class template in Chapter 9, for example, or the String class in Chapter 10).

The standard solution permits safe object copying, but does nothing to prevent *unnecessary* copies of duplicated data. If a program makes three copies of the same string object, for example, it gives birth to triplets in the form of three identical character strings (see Figure 15.7).

Figure 15.7. These objects address wasteful copies of the identical string.

Because the strings in Figure 15.7 are identical, only one copy of the string is needed. Rather than store multiple strings, a single string might instead maintain a *reference count* that indicates how many other objects refer to the string. Figure 15.8 shows how this new arrangement saves space.

In Figure 15.8, the string's reference count of 3 in effect states that "three objects refer to this string." Suppose the program deletes one of those objects. Figure 15.9 shows the result.

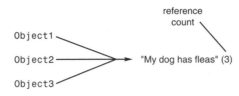

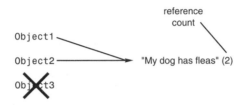

Figure 15.8. A reference count eliminates duplicated information.

Figure 15.9. Deleting an object reduces the reference count.

Deleting one object that refers to duplicated data simply reduces the data's reference count by one—the referenced data can't actually be deleted because two other objects still refer to it. If the program deleted Object2 from Figure 15.9, the reference count would be reduced to 1, and the string still could not be deleted.

When only one object refers to the string, deleting that object finally requires the string also to be deleted. This fact leads to the key rule: Delete potentially duplicated information only if the reference count equals 1, indicating that no other objects refer to the data.

It takes careful planning to program a class that uses reference counts to reduce duplications. The technique is often used in conjunction with variable-size objects as described in the preceding section, so rather than write a new example, I modified VARY.CPP (Listing 15.4) to permit efficient copying of LongVector objects. The result is Listing 15.5, REF.CPP.

Note: REF.CPP has an intentional problem that prevents full use of the operator[] indexing function. After I describe this listing, I'll show you how to fix this problem.

Listing 15.5. REF.CPP.

```cpp
#include <iostream.h>
#include <mem.h>
#include <memuse.h>

// Class for variable-size objects with reference count
class vary {
  friend class LongVector;
private:
  vary(int n);    // For use only by LongVector!
  void * operator new(size_t classSize, size_t vectorSize);
private:
  int length;        // Number of long values in vector
  int refs;          // Number of duplicate references
  long vector[1];    // Dummy start of long vector
};

// Example of a dynamic vector
class LongVector {
public:
  LongVector(): vp(0) { }
  LongVector(int size);
  LongVector(const LongVector &copy);   // Copy constructor
  ~LongVector();   // Destructor
  int Length() const { return vp->length; }
  const long & operator[](int index);
  LongVector & operator=(const LongVector &copy);
private:
  vary *vp;   // Pointer to variable-sized object
};

// Function prototypes
void ShowLongVector(const char *s, LongVector v);
void PerformTest();
```

continues

443

Listing 15.5. continued

```cpp
int main()
{
  HeapReport("Initial memory use");
  PerformTest();
  HeapReport("\nFinal memory use");
  return 0;
}

void PerformTest()
{
  LongVector copy1(10);
  LongVector copy2 = copy1;  // Uses copy constructor
  LongVector copy3;          // Uses default constructor
  copy3 = copy2;             // Uses operator=() function
  copy2 = copy1;             // Uses operator=() function
  ShowLongVector("copy1", copy1);  // Passed by value!
  ShowLongVector("copy2", copy2);  // But does not cause
  ShowLongVector("copy3", copy3);  // duplicated vector.

// The following statement fails to compile because
// operator= returns a const reference. See REF2.CPP
// for the solution to this problem.

//   copy3[7] = 77;  // ???

}

// Display contents of a vector
// NOTE: Rather than pass a LongVector reference, we pass
// the object by value. Even so, the vector is not
// duplicated; only its reference count is increased.
void ShowLongVector(const char *s, LongVector v)
{
  cout << "\nvector " << s << ':' << endl;
  for (int i = 0; i < v.Length(); ++i)
    cout << s << '[' << i << "] == "
      << v[i] << endl;
}
```

```
// Constructor for vary class
vary::vary(int n)
{
  length = n;
  refs = 1;
  if (vector) memset(vector, 0, length * sizeof(long));
}


// Overloaded new operator for vary class
void * vary::operator new(size_t classSize, size_t vectorSize)
{
  return new char[classSize + (vectorSize - 1) * sizeof(long)];
}


// Construct LongVector object with size elements
// Creates new vary object and fills vector for demonstration
LongVector::LongVector(int size)
{
  vp = new(size) vary(size);
  if (vp) {
    for (int i = 0; i < size; ++i)
      vp->vector[i] = i;
  }
}


// Copy constructor
// Updates reference count in duplicate vector
LongVector::LongVector(const LongVector &copy)
{
  vp = copy.vp;
  if (vp)
    vp->refs++;
}


// Destructor
// Destroys vector only if this is the only copy
LongVector::~LongVector()
```

continues

445

Listing 15.5. continued

```
{
  if (vp && --vp->refs < 1)
    delete vp;
}


// Index operator
// This function has a problem: It works okay, but it
// must return a const reference; otherwise, an assignment
// to a vector element would be made for *multiple* vectors!
// See REF2.CPP for the solution.
const long & LongVector::operator[](int index)
{
  if (0 <= index && index < vp->length)
    return vp->vector[index];
  static long bad = -1;  // Value to return for errors
  return bad;
}


// Assignment operator
LongVector & LongVector::operator=(const LongVector &copy)
{
  if (this == &copy)           // Can't assign self to self
    return *this;
  if (vp && --vp->refs < 1)    // Delete current vector if
    delete vp;                 // it is the only copy
  vp = copy.vp;                // Copy vector *pointer*
  if (vp)                      // If pointer is not null,
    vp->refs++;                // update reference count.
  return *this;
}
```

You might want to compare REF.CPP with VARY.CPP. The differences reveal several important aspects of the reference-count technique. I highlighted key differences in bold.

Class vary is almost identical in both programs, but the class now sports a refs integer member. This value indicates the number of *other* objects that refer to identical instances of the vary class. Notice that vary does not have a destructor, and its constructor is still private. Objects of the class are constructed and deleted solely by vary's friend class, LongVector.

Class LongVector adds three new elements, also highlighted in bold. A copy constructor and operator= function perform the usual duties of copying one object to another—but with the added twist of using reference counts rather than actually duplicating entire vectors (more on this later).

I also redeclared operator[] function to return a const reference to a long value—the intentional problem that I mentioned. Because operator[] now returns a const reference, index expressions are "read-only." In other words, assignments to vectors are no longer allowed. Obviously, that problem will need correcting. In the program's PerformTest() function, the following statement is turned into a comment because assignments to vectors are temporarily not allowed:

```
copy3[7] = 77;  // ???
```

> **Note:** Although you might view the inability to assign values to vectors as a bug, the problem described here might have a beneficial side. You could use similar programming to disallow modifications to a vector's elements (characters in a constant string, for example). To do that, just preface operator= with const as shown in LongVector's declaration.

One other significant, but subtle, change is in the ShowLongVector() function. In the original VARY.CPP program, the second parameter in that function was a LongVector reference—in other words, the address of an object. Now, the parameter is a LongVector value.

Usually, potentially large value parameters can waste tons of RAM when C++ copies a class object to be passed as an argument to a function. In REF.CPP, although C++ still makes the copy, potential waste is eliminated by updating the duplicated vector's reference count rather than actually copying the information. One benefit of using duplicate reference counts is that even large objects can be passed by value to functions without taking more than a few bytes of stack space.

Only a few other changes appear in the class implementations. To vary's constructor, I added a statement to initialize the reference count to 1:

```
refs = 1;
```

This is the only change needed to the vary class implementation.

LongVector's new copy constructor is much simpler than other copy constructors in this book. The constructor has only two statements:

```
vp = copy.vp;
if (vp)
  vp->refs++;
```

Be sure to understand how these statements work. First, the copy object's vp pointer is assigned to the newly constructed object's vp pointer. Next, this duplication is recorded by incrementing the duplicated vector's reference count by one.

If myVector is an existing LongVector object, you can construct a copy of that object with the statement

```
LongVector temp(myVector);
```

In LongVector's copy constructor, parameter copy refers to myVector. The this pointer addresses the temp object under construction. Figure 15.10 shows how the copy constructor causes temp and myVector to refer to the same vary object (via their vp pointers). The duplicated vector's reference count now equals two, indicating that two objects refer to this identical vector.

Figure 15.10. The duplicated vary object has a reference count of 2.

LongVector's destructor reveals another key characteristic of this technique. The destructor executes this if statement:

```
if (vp && --vp->refs < 1)
  delete vp;
```

Literally, that states "if vp is not null, then if subtracting one from the object's refs count is less than one, delete the object." In short, the destructor deletes vp *only if the pointer addresses the only copy of the object.*

There are two other member functions to consider. Take the last one first. The operator= function is called to assign one LongVector object to another. First, the function checks whether the program is attempting to assign the *same* object to itself—a mistake that is easily disallowed by returning a reference to the object.

Next, the current vector addressed by vp is deleted, but again, only if reducing the vector's reference count causes refs to become less than one. Following that step, the source vector pointer (copy.vp) is assigned to this object's vp, and because this results in two pointers addressing the identical object, the object's refs counter is incremented by one.

All of the programming so far works as ordered, but the program suffers from its const operator[] function. The operator must return a const reference for a simple reason: If two or more LongVector objects refer to the identical vector, this innocent looking statement:

```
myVector[5] = 123;   // ???
```

would set the sixth element in myVector *and in all duplicate vectors* to 123. A similar problem would occur in Figure 15.8 if *dog* were changed to *cat.* Because of the duplicate references, any changes would affect all objects that use the string.

The solution to this puzzle is to revise functions like operator[] to construct another copy (a real one this time) of the vector being modified. The program can then safely modify that fresh copy. Again referring to Figure 15.8, to modify Object2's string, changing *dog* to *cat,* the program would:

1. Proceed to step 5 if the string is the only copy.

2. Copy the string to a fresh string.

3. Assign the fresh string's address to Object2.

4. Reduce the original string's reference count by one.

5. Modify the string addressed by Object2.

Object2 ends up with the only copy of the modified string, now equal to *My cat has fleas.* That string might exist somewhere else in memory—the technique doesn't search for *all* possible duplications. But at least obvious duplications—copying one string to another or passing an object by value to a function—are limited, and as a result, usually save a great deal of memory and also increasing performance.

Listing 15.6 puts these ideas into practice, modifying the preceding listing so that operator[] is no longer const. Rather than list the entire program, I included only new elements.

Note: The complete REF2.CPP listing is on disk in the PART3 directory.

Listing 15.6. REF2.CPP (partial).

```
// Example of a dynamic vector
class LongVector {
public:
  LongVector(): vp(0) { }
  LongVector(int size);
  LongVector(const LongVector &copy);
  ~LongVector();
  int Length() const { return vp->length; }
  long & operator[](int index);  // No longer const!
  LongVector & operator=(const LongVector &copy);
private:
  vary *vp;  // Pointer to variable-sized object
};


...


// Improved (non const) index operator
// Constructs duplicated vector unless this
// is the only copy. Returns reference to vector
// element.
```

```
long & LongVector::operator[](int index)
{
  static long bad = -1;          // Value to return for errors
  if (!vp || index < 0 || index >= Length())
    return bad;                  // No vector or bad index
  if (vp->refs > 1) {            // Catch duplicate vectors
    vary *t = new(Length()) vary(Length());  // Make new one
    if (!t) return bad;          // And/or call error function
    memmove(t->vector, vp->vector, Length() * sizeof(long));
    if (vp && --vp->refs < 1)    // Delete vary object if
      delete vp;                 // it's the only copy.
    vp = t;                      // Assign new vary pointer
  }
  return vp->vector[index];  // Return safe reference
}
```

The LongVector class has only one change—the removal of const from the operator[] declaration. Now, the operator permits assignments to vectors using indexing expressions such as

```
myVector[5] = 123;
```

If myVector refers to a duplicated vector, this operation causes the entire vector to be copied. Obviously, that must be done because the modified vector is no longer an exact duplicate. The revised operator[] function handles the copying chore by first examining the vector's refs counter. If greater than one, a new vary object is created, using that class's overloaded new operator. After this step, the standard memmove function (declared in mem.h on my system) makes a fresh copy of the duplicated vector. The formerly duplicated vector's reference count is then reduced, and if that count is then less than one, vp is deleted.

Note: The call to memmove() in the operator[] function might fail if the vector stores class objects. In that event, you might need to use a for loop to perform the copy, ensuring that any class constructors are properly called. Function memmove() is faster, however, and is safe to use on vectors of simple values—int, long, double, and so on.

With its revised operator[] function, the LongVector class neatly handles statements that attempt to modify duplicated vectors. For example, suppose that copy3 is a LongVector object that refers to one of several duplicate vectors. The following two statements look similar, but they have deceptively different effects when executed:

```
copy3[7] = 77;  // Creates new vector!
copy3[8] = 88;  // Does *not* create new vector
```

The first statement assigns 77 to the eighth vector element. Inside operator[], the program notices that copy3 refers to a duplicated vector, and the function therefore makes a fresh copy of that vector before carrying out the assignment. This freshly minted vector starts out with a reference count of one, so the second statement does *not* cause operator[] to make another copy.

Other functions that cause changes to possibly duplicated vectors must take similar precautions. Writing these functions requires careful programming and painstaking debugging, but the results are highly efficient, permitting objects to be passed by value to functions and copied in other ways without causing needless waste.

Note: The technique described here has one potential flaw that limits its usefulness. Because operator[] cannot determine whether an assignment will be made to a referenced vector element, the operator always makes a fresh copy of duplicate vectors even when called only to examine a value. The simple statement cout << v[i];, for instance, causes the entire vector at v to be freshly copied, effectively destroying any advantage gained! One way to solve this new problem is to provide a GetAt(int i) function that returns a const reference to a vector element. You can then write cout << v.GetAt(i);, which is not as concise, but prevents the vector from being needlessly copied for "read-only" operations.

Final Words

As this chapter shows, there's more to storing objects efficiently than just making your classes as small as possible. Highly efficient code requires careful planning and a good awareness of how, when, and where objects are constructed.

The next chapter expands this theme with a technique that makes it possible for arrays to appear larger than they actually are. Using *sparse matrices,* you can actually create arrays of objects that couldn't possibly fit in memory—a statement that might seem incredible until you examine the simple secret behind the solution.

Gaining Space with Sparse Matrices

W hen the Beatles wondered in a song how many holes it would take to fill the Albert Hall, they could have been singing about sparse matrices. These intriguing data structures make it possible to construct super size arrays that are seemingly larger than could possibly fit into a computer's memory.

A *sparse matrix,* one of a class of sparse data structures, is mostly filled with holes—that is, with zeros, null pointers, or with nothing at all. That description may seem like smoke and mirrors, but sparse data structures have dozens of practical uses. Spreadsheets, databases, and other applications in which most of an object's elements are inactive can all use sparse data structures to save oodles of RAM.

I'll cover three sparse structures in this chapter: arrays, triangular matrices, and rectangular matrices. Sample programs show how to take advantage of these "holesome" techniques to create huge sparse structures in relatively small spaces.

Sparse Arrays

The simplest kind of sparse data structure is an array where most slots are unfilled. Consider, for example, how you might create an array of strings. If only some entries have values, unused array slots needlessly throw away space.

Despite the obvious waste in a partially filled array, many programmers continue to create string arrays that squander memory, as demonstrated in Listing 16.1, WASTEFUL.CPP.

Listing 16.1. WASTEFUL.CPP.

```
#include <iostream.h>
#include <string.h>

#define STRINGSIZE 40
#define ARRAYSIZE 10

char array[ARRAYSIZE][STRINGSIZE];

int main()
{
  cout << "sizeof(array) == " << sizeof(array) << " bytes\n\n";
  strcpy(array[2], "Waste not");
  strcpy(array[7], "Want not");
```

```
   for (int i = 0; i < ARRAYSIZE; ++i)
     cout << '[' << i << "] == " << array[i] << endl;
   return 0;
 }
```

The program's two-dimensional array reserves space for ten forty-character strings, including null terminators. Despite the fact that only slots 2 and 7 are assigned string values, the structure squats on 400 bytes of memory—an absurd amount of waste. I should fire myself for writing such boneheaded code.

Rather than store characters directly in an array, an array of char pointers makes better use of available space. As Figure 16.1 illustrates, you can assign the addresses of character strings to active slots and leave the others set to null. That way, only active entries take up room.

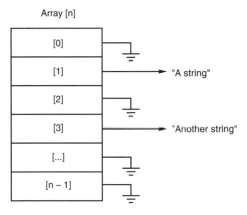

Figure 16.1. A sparse array of char pointers.

An array of char pointers is not perfectly efficient—after all, the pointers still occupy *some* space. But the results are much improved, as Listing 16.2, SPARRAY.CPP, shows.

Listing 16.2. SPARRAY.CPP.

```cpp
#include <iostream.h>
#include <iomanip.h>
#include <string.h>
#include <stdlib.h>
#include <memuse.h>

#define SIZE 100     // Size of array
char * array[SIZE];  // All pointers are null by default

// Function prototypes
void InsertAt(int index, const char *s);
void ShowArray();
void DeleteArray();
void CheckIndex(int index);
void PerformTest();

int main()
{
  HeapReport("Initial memory use");
  PerformTest();
  HeapReport("\nFinal memory use");
  return 0;
}

// Insert string s at array[index]
void InsertAt(int index, const char *s)
{
  CheckIndex(index);               // Test index range
  char *p = array[index];          // Get pointer from array
  delete p;                        // Delete current string if any
  p = new char[strlen(s) + 1];     // Allocate space for new string
  if (p) strcpy(p, s);             // Copy string to memory
  array[index] = p;                // Assign pointer to array
}

// Display non-null strings in array
void ShowArray()
```

```
{
  int count = 0;
  for (int i = 0; i < SIZE; ++i)
    if (array[i]) {
      ++count;
      cout << '[' << setw(2) << i << "] == "
        << array[i] << endl;
    }
  cout << "Number of entries == " << count << endl;
}

// Delete all memory allocated to array
void DeleteArray()
{
  for (int i = 0; i < SIZE; ++i)
    delete array[i];
}

// Halt if index is out of range
void CheckIndex(int index)
{
  if (index >= SIZE || index < 0 ) {
    cout << "\nError: index out of range";
    exit(-1);
  }
}

// Test procedure
void PerformTest()
{
  cout << "-----------\n";
  cout << "Test: Insert strings into sparse array\n";
  InsertAt(4, "Atlantic Ocean");
  InsertAt(10, "Pacific Ocean");
  InsertAt(25, "Caribbean Ocean");
  InsertAt(99, "Red Sea");
  ShowArray();
```

continues

459

Listing 16.2. continued

```
HeapReport("Memory use after insertions");
DeleteArray();
cout << "----------";
}
```

The sample program's 100-element array occupies only 112 bytes of memory after function `PerformTest()` inserts four strings at index positions 4, 10, 25, and 99. If this array were defined as in Listing 16.1, the structure would be a whopping 4,000 bytes long.

Even so, all those null pointers are bothersome. If we could do away with these do-nothing pointers, the array would shrink even more. That notion may seem radical, but with careful programming, it's possible to squeeze out the last drop of waste from some kinds of arrays, leaving only substance behind.

Sparse Triangular Matrices

Triangular matrices are sparse structures that take only about half as much space as they seem to use. Figure 16.2 illustrates a triangular matrix as it might appear if you could see one in RAM.

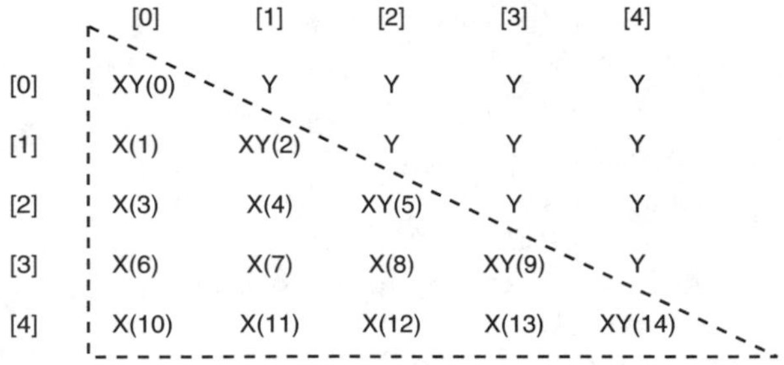

	[0]	[1]	[2]	[3]	[4]
[0]	XY(0)	Y	Y	Y	Y
[1]	X(1)	XY(2)	Y	Y	Y
[2]	X(3)	X(4)	XY(5)	Y	Y
[3]	X(6)	X(7)	X(8)	XY(9)	Y
[4]	X(10)	X(11)	X(12)	X(13)	XY(14)

Figure 16.2. Sparse triangular matrix.

In the figure, only values labeled with an X or XY are stored in the matrix. Values labeled Y are redundant, and therefore, do not need to exist. The matrix *appears* rectangular—or *orthogonal*, if you want to be fancy—but its data is triangular in form.

A mileage chart, as typically printed in tourist books and road maps, is an excellent example of a triangular sparse matrix. If the index values in Figure 16.2 are cities, the matrix needs to be only half of its apparent size. Obviously, the distance from New York to Los Angeles is the same as the mileage from Los Angeles to New York—unless, that is, you return by way of Japan. Each pair of cities therefore needs only one mileage value in the matrix.

To program a triangular sparse matrix, construct a single-dimension array with enough space to store the entries outlined inside the dotted-line triangle in Figure 16.2. In this case, the array needs 15 entries. You could save even more space by cutting out the five entries labeled XY—these are all zero anyway, because of course, the distance "between" the same two cities is zero. Including these values simplifies the program, however, and results in only a small amount of waste in triangular matrices much larger than the small sample shown here.

Given a maximum dimension N for a square matrix having $N+1$ rows and columns, the number of elements needed by its triangular sparse equivalent is

```
S = N * (N + 1) / 2 + N + 1
```

Contrast that with the formula for a normal two-dimensional matrix, with a value at every position. In that case, the size S is calculated by

```
S = (N + 1) * (N + 1)
```

If each matrix element takes eight bytes, a normal rectangular 5x5 matrix occupies 200 bytes. The equivalent triangular matrix takes a relatively sparse 120 bytes.

Another formula calculates the location for any row and column. If R is a row index and C is a column, a simple formula calculates the location of the triangular array element $A[R, C]$. First, the indexes must be swapped if the column is greater than the row:

```
if (C > R) { T = R; R = C; C = T; }
```

Swapping the row and column indexes ensures that they refer only to the triangular portion of the array outlined in Figure 16.2. Given corrected *R* and *C* indexes, another formula calculates index *I* for the triangular array:

```
I = R * (R + 1) / 2 + C;
```

You can now use *I* as an index into a single-dimension array that is used to represent the sparse triangular matrix.

Listing 16.3, TRIANGLE.CPP, collects these formulas into a demonstration that stores sample city mileages in a triangular matrix, represented by a class named `Triangle`.

Note: TRIANGLE.CPP requires a header file sparse.h and SPARSE.CPP, listed later in this chapter, and stored on disk in the PART3 directory. Using Borland C++, compile the program with a command such as

```
bcc -ml triangle sparse secrets.lib
```

See Appendix A for additional instructions if you have trouble compiling this or other programs in this chapter.

Listing 16.3. TRIANGLE.CPP.

```
#include <iostream.h>
#include <iomanip.h>
#include <memuse.h>
#include "sparse.h"

enum Cities {
  baltimore,
  chicago,
  losangeles,
  newyork,
```

```
  sanfrancisco,
  lastCity              // Must be last
};

const char * cityNames[lastCity] = {
  "Baltimore",
  "Chicago",
  "Los Angeles",
  "New York",
  "San Francisco"
};


//----------------------------------------------------------------
// Triangle class declaration
//----------------------------------------------------------------

class Triangle {
public:
  Triangle(int N);
  ~Triangle() { delete matrix; }
  int GetNRows() const { return nrows; }
  unsigned GetAt(int row, int col) const;
  void PutAt(int row, int col, unsigned v);
protected:
  int loc(int row, int col) const
    { return row * (row + 1) / 2 + col; }
  void CheckIndexes(int &row, int &col) const;
private:
  int nrows;            // Number of rows (and columns)
  unsigned * matrix;    // Pointer to triangular matrix
};


//----------------------------------------------------------------
// Function prototype and main test program
//----------------------------------------------------------------

void PerformTest();
```

continues

463

Listing 16.3. continued

```cpp
int main()
{
  HeapReport("Initial memory use");
  PerformTest();
  HeapReport("\nFinal memory use");
  return 0;
}


//-----------------------------------------------------------------
// Triangle class member functions
//-----------------------------------------------------------------

// Construct a triangular matrix of size [N,N]
Triangle::Triangle(int N)
  : nrows(N)
{
  int size = N * (N + 1) / 2 + N + 1;
  matrix = new unsigned[size];
  if (!matrix) Error(err_memory);
  for (int i = 0; i < size; ++i)
    matrix[i] = 0;
}

// Return value in triangular matrix at [row, col]
unsigned Triangle::GetAt(int row, int col) const
{
  CheckIndexes(row, col);
  return matrix[loc(row, col)];
}

// Insert value into triangular matrix at [row, col]
void Triangle::PutAt(int row, int col, unsigned v)
{
  CheckIndexes(row, col);
  matrix[loc(row, col)] = v;
}
```

```
// Verify or modify index ranges; halt on any errors
void Triangle::CheckIndexes(int &row, int &col) const
{
  if (!inrange(row, 0, nrows - 1))
    Error(err_rowindex);
  if (!inrange(col, 0, nrows - 1))
    Error(err_colindex);
  if (col > row) {
    int t = row;
    row = col;
    col = t;
  }
}


//---------------------------------------------------------------
// Miscellaneous functions
//---------------------------------------------------------------

// Display matrix values
void ShowMatrix(Triangle &matrix)
{
  int row, col;
  cout << "    ";
  for (col = 0; col < matrix.GetNRows(); ++col)
    cout << setw(6) << "[" << col << ']';
  for (row = 0; row < matrix.GetNRows(); ++row) {
    cout << "\n[" << row << ']';
    for (col = 0; col < matrix.GetNRows(); ++col)
      cout << setw(8) << matrix.GetAt(row, col);
  }
  cout << endl;
}

// Display city names and corresponding index values
void ShowCities()
{
  for (int i = 0; i < lastCity; ++i)
```

continues

Listing 16.3. continued

```cpp
    cout << '[' << i << "] == " << cityNames[i] << endl;
}

// Create and use a triangular sparse matrix
void PerformTest()
{
  cout << "----------\n";
  Triangle miles(lastCity);
  miles.PutAt(baltimore,   chicago,          705);
  miles.PutAt(baltimore,   losangeles,      2701);
  miles.PutAt(baltimore,   newyork,          197);
  miles.PutAt(baltimore,   sanfrancisco,    2821);
  miles.PutAt(chicago,     losangeles,      2047);
  miles.PutAt(chicago,     newyork,          807);
  miles.PutAt(chicago,     sanfrancisco,    2145);
  miles.PutAt(losangeles,  newyork,         2787);
  miles.PutAt(losangeles,  sanfrancisco,     384);
  miles.PutAt(newyork,     sanfrancisco,    2923);
  ShowCities();
  ShowMatrix(miles);
  cout << "----------";
}
```

Running the program displays a sample mileage chart for a few selected cities. The output is simplistic, but it demonstrates how the triangular matrix works. Here's what my screen showed when I ran the program:

```
[0] == Baltimore
[1] == Chicago
[2] == Los Angeles
[3] == New York
[4] == San Francisco
          [0]     [1]     [2]     [3]     [4]
[0]         0     705    2701     197    2821
[1]       705       0    2047     807    2145
[2]      2701    2047       0    2787     384
[3]       197     807    2787       0    2923
[4]      2821    2145     384    2923       0
```

Only half of these values are actually stored in memory. The top-right triangular portion of the chart is identical (though flopped) in relation to the bottom-left part. As the chart shows (see the bold numbers), Chicago to San Francisco at [1][4] is the same distance as San Francisco to Chicago at [4][1], or 2145 miles.

The program is straightforward, and you should have no trouble understanding how it works. The Triangle class constructs an array of one dimension, assigning its address to a pointer named matrix. The formula in the constructor (see Triangle::Triangle()) is the same as given earlier for computing the size of a triangular matrix. The inline protected function, loc(), returns the location of an indexed entry in the array.

PerformTest() demonstrates how to construct and use a triangular matrix as an object of the Triangle class. After constructing the object, miles, the program calls the class's PutAt() function to insert mileage values into the array. The enumerated city-name symbols such as baltimore and newyork are used as matrix index values. Each mileage is inserted only once.

TRIANGLE.CPP uses a simple Error() function, prototyped in Listing 16.4, sparse.h, and implemented in Listing 16.5, SPARSE.CPP. The header file, sparse.h, also includes a function template, inrange(), used by the program to detect index range errors. Unless you are typing the listings manually, you can skip to the next part, which explains the sparse matrix to beat all sparse matrices—one that in some cases can save megabytes of RAM.

Listing 16.4. sparse.h.

```
#ifndef __SPARSE_H
#define __SPARSE_H    // Prevent multiple #includes

// Function template returns true if b <= a <= c
template<class T>
int inrange(T a, T b, T c)
{
  return (b <= a) && (a <= c);
}
```

continues

Listing 16.4. continued

```
// Error flag values (see Sparse::Error())
enum ErrorFlag {
  err_index,          // Bad row or column index
  err_memory,         // Out of memory
  err_rowindex,       // Row index out of range
  err_colindex        // Column index out of range
};

// Simple error function (halts program)
void Error(ErrorFlag ef);

#endif  // __SPARSE_H
```

Listing 16.5. SPARSE.CPP.

```
#include <iostream.h>
#include <stdlib.h>
#include "sparse.h"

// Display error message and halt program
void Error(ErrorFlag ef)
{
  char *s;
  switch (ef) {
    case err_index:
      s = "Index out of range";
      break;
    case err_memory:
      s = "Out of memory";
      break;
    case err_rowindex:
      s = "Row index out of range";
      break;
    case err_colindex:
      s = "Column index out of range";
      break;
```

```
  default:
    s = "Unknown cause";
  }
  cout << "Error: " << s << endl;
  cout << "Halting program\n";
  exit(-1);
}
```

Sparse Rectangular Matrices

The triangular matrix in Figure 16.2 isn't perfectly efficient. In the case of the mileage chart, for example, the zero entries are wasteful (entries marked XY in the figure). Also, what if some distances aren't known? Maybe that's unlikely, but these entries would still take up space.

Or, consider a more practical example. In a spreadsheet, users might enter values at any "cell," leaving many surrounding spaces empty. What's the best way to represent a spreadsheet and other two-dimensional matrices to store only the bare minimum amount of information?

Figure 16.3 illustrates one possible answer. Using linked lists, and storing the row and column numbers inside the list nodes, it's possible to strip a matrix to the bone, turning it into a *sparse matrix.* Representing the nodes as shown here makes the structure easy to see, but of course, in memory the nodes might be stored anywhere.

Figure 16.3 shows only one of several possible ways to represent a sparse rectangular matrix. To make deletions easier, I used two pointers in each node, labeled *L* and *R* for left and right. If you don't need to delete nodes, or at least not frequently, you can remove the left pointers and instead use singly-linked lists to save even more space.

I also used a bank of header nodes, shaded in the figure. Each header serves as an anchor for that row. Here, rows 0, 1, 2, and 4 have one or more data nodes. Row 3 is empty, so this header's L and R pointers are both null.

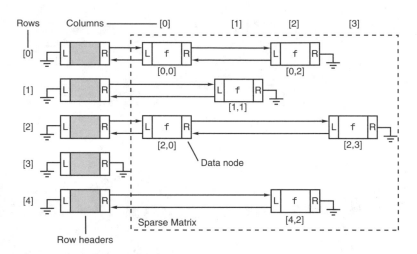

Figure 16.3. Sparse rectangular matrix.

Another possible arrangement is to add other pointers to link each node in two directions. In that design, each column would also have a header node, and the data nodes would each be linked into two lists at once. You could even push the idea to its outer limits, implementing the row headers as a sparse linked list. In that case, an empty sparse matrix would take up only as much room as a null pointer!

Listing 16.6, SPMATRIX.CPP, puts the somewhat less ambitious sparse matrix in Figure 16.3 into action. The program runs several tests, including one that creates a massive 1000-by-2000 matrix of float values that normally would occupy about 8 megabytes of RAM—more than many PCs have available. The empty sparse equivalent takes only about 32K, most of which is taken up by the row headers.

Note: To see SPMATRIX's full output, direct it to a file. Using Borland C++, compile the program with a command such as

```
bcc -ml spmatrix sparse secrets.lib
```

Run it by typing

```
spmatrix >results.txt
```

then use a text editor to view the file RESULTS.TXT.

Listing 16.6. SPMATRIX.CPP.

```cpp
#include <iostream.h>
#include <iomanip.h>
#include <memuse.h>
#include "sparse.h"


//------------------------------------------------------------
// Node class for header and data nodes
//------------------------------------------------------------

class Node {
  friend class Sparse;     // Sparse can use private members
private:
  Node();                  // Default constructor
  Node(int Row, int Col);  // Alternate constructor
  ~Node();                 // Recursive destructor
  void Link(Node *p);      // Link node to right of p
  void Unlink();           // Unlink this node from list
private:
  int row;       // This node's row number (-1 if header)
  int col;       // This node's column number (-1 if header)
  Node *left;    // Points to node in row to "left" of this one
  Node *right;   // Points to node in row to "right" of this one
  float f;       // Data in node (replace with your data)
};
```

continues

Listing 16.6. continued

```cpp
//----------------------------------------------------------------
// Sparse matrix class
//----------------------------------------------------------------

class Sparse {
  static const float spare;
public:
  Sparse(int NRows, int NCols);
  ~Sparse() { delete[] rows; }
  int GetNRows() const { return nrows; }
  int GetNCols() const { return ncols; }
  float GetAt(int row, int col) const;
  void PutAt(int row, int col, float f);
  float DeleteAt(int row, int col);
protected:
  void CheckIndexes(int row, int col) const;
  Node * NodeAt(int row, int col) const;
  Node * InsertAt(int row, int col);
private:
  int nrows;    // Number of rows in sparse matrix
  int ncols;    // Number of columns in sparse matrix
  Node *rows;   // Points to array of row headers
};


//----------------------------------------------------------------
// Function prototypes and main test program
//----------------------------------------------------------------

void PerformTests();
void ShowMatrix(Sparse &matrix);

int main()
{
  HeapReport("Initial memory use");
  PerformTests();
  HeapReport("\nFinal memory use");
  return 0;
}
```

```
//--------------------------------------------------------------
// Node class member functions (private)
//--------------------------------------------------------------

// Default constructor (constructs header nodes)
Node::Node()
  : row(-1), col(-1), left(0), right(0), f(0)
{
}

// Alternate constructor (constructs data nodes)
Node::Node(int Row, int Col)
  : row(Row), col(Col), left(0), right(0), f(0)
{
}

// Destructor (deletes nodes recursively)
Node::~Node()
{
  delete right;
}

// Link this node to the right of p
void Node::Link(Node *p)
{
  right = p->right;
  left = p;
  p->right = this;
  if (right) right->left = this;
}

// Unlink this node from list
void Node::Unlink()
{
  left->right = right;
  if (right) right->left = left;
```

continues

Listing 16.6. continued

```cpp
    right = 0;
    left = 0;
}


//-------------------------------------------------------------
// Sparse class member functions (public)
//-------------------------------------------------------------


// Define value for nonexistent matrix elements
const float Sparse::spare = 0.0;

// Construct a sparse matrix of NRows and NCols
Sparse::Sparse(int NRows, int NCols)
  : nrows(NRows), ncols(NCols)
{
  if (nrows <= 0 || ncols <= 0)
    Error(err_index);
  rows = new Node[nrows];  // Construct array of row headers
  if (!rows)
    Error(err_memory);
}

// Return data in matrix at [row, col]
float Sparse::GetAt(int row, int col) const
{
  CheckIndexes(row, col);
  Node *p = NodeAt(row, col);    // Search for node
  if (p) return p->f;            // If found, return value
  return spare;                  // If not found, return spare
}

// Store data in matrix at [row, col]
void Sparse::PutAt(int row, int col, float f)
{
  CheckIndexes(row, col);
  Node *p = InsertAt(row, col);  // Search or insert node
  if (!p) Error(err_memory);     // If null, report error
```

```
   p->f = f;                        // Store value in node
}


// Delete node at [row, col] and return its value
// Returns spare value if node did not exist
float Sparse::DeleteAt(int row, int col)
{
  CheckIndexes(row, col);
  Node *p = NodeAt(row, col);      // Search for node
  if (!p) return spare;            // If not found, return spare
  p->Unlink();                     // Unlink node at p
  float f = p->f;                  // Save value in node
  delete p;                        // Delete the node
  return f;                        // Return value
}


//-------------------------------------------------------------
// Sparse class member functions (protected)
//-------------------------------------------------------------


// Verify index ranges; halt on any errors
void Sparse::CheckIndexes(int row, int col) const
{
  if (!inrange(row, 0, nrows - 1))
    Error(err_rowindex);
  if (!inrange(col, 0, ncols - 1))
    Error(err_colindex);
}


// Return pointer to node at [row, col]
// Assumes that row and col are in range
Node * Sparse::NodeAt(int row, int col) const
{
  Node *p = rows[row].right;  // Begin search to right of header
  while (p && p->col < col)   // Search for node or end of list
    p = p->right;             // Move to next node
```

continues

Listing 16.6. continued

```cpp
    if (p && p->col == col)      // If node column number matches,
       return p;                 // return node at p.
    return 0;                    // Node not found; return null
}

// Insert or return pointer to node at [row, col]
// Assumes that row and col are in range
Node * Sparse::InsertAt(int row, int col)
{
  Node *t = &rows[row];          // Node "behind" p
  Node *p = rows[row].right;     // Node row pointer
  while (p && p->col < col) {    // Search for node
    t = p;                       // Remember this node
    p = p->right;                // Move to next node
  }
  if (!p || p->col > col) {      // Node found?
    Node *q = new Node(row, col); // Construct new node
    if (!q) Error(err_memory);   // Report any error
    q->Link(t);  // Link node q to right of t
    p = q;       // Prepare to return new node
  }
  return p;      // Return existing or new node pointer
}


//----------------------------------------------------------------
// Miscellaneous functions
//----------------------------------------------------------------

// Display matrix elements (up to 10x10 matrices only)
void ShowMatrix(Sparse &matrix)
{
  int row, col;
  cout << "Matrix of [" << matrix.GetNRows() << ','
    << matrix.GetNCols() << "] elements:\n" << "    ";
  for (col = 0; col < matrix.GetNCols(); ++col)
    cout << setw(4) << '[' << col << ']';
  for (row = 0; row < matrix.GetNRows(); ++row) {
    cout << "\n[" << row << ']';
```

```
      for (col = 0; col < matrix.GetNCols(); ++col)
        cout << setw(6) << matrix.GetAt(row, col);
    }
    cout << endl;
}


// Construct several sparse matrices
void Test1()
{
    cout << "----------\n";
    cout << "Test1: Construct a sparse matrix\n";
    HeapReport("Initial memory use");
    cout << "Sparse m1(10, 20);\n";
    Sparse m1(10, 20);
    HeapReport("Memory after creating 10 x 20 matrix");
    cout << "Sparse m2(100, 100);\n";
    Sparse m2(100, 100);
    HeapReport("Memory after creating 100 x 100 matrix");
    cout << "Sparse m3(1000, 2000);\n";
    Sparse m3(1000, 2000);
    HeapReport("Memory after creating 1000 x 2000 matrix");
}


// Construct and use a sparse matrix
void Test2()
{
    cout << "----------\n";
    cout << "Test2: Construct and use a sparse matrix\n";
    cout << "Constructing matrix\n";
    Sparse matrix(5, 4);
    cout << "Inserting values into matrix\n";
    matrix.PutAt(0, 0, -9.9);
    matrix.PutAt(0, 2, 0.2);
    matrix.PutAt(1, 1, 1.1);
    matrix.PutAt(2, 0, 2.0);
    matrix.PutAt(2, 3, 2.3);
    matrix.PutAt(4, 2, 4.2);
    ShowMatrix(matrix);
```

continues

Listing 16.6. continued

```
    cout << "Searching for values in matrix";
    cout << "\nvalue at [0,0] == " << matrix.GetAt(0,0);
    cout << "\nvalue at [1,1] == " << matrix.GetAt(1,1);
    cout << "\nvalue at [2,2] == " << matrix.GetAt(2,2);
    cout << "\nvalue at [4,2] == " << matrix.GetAt(4,2);
    cout << "\nDeleting values at [2,0], [3,3], [4,2]";
    cout << "\nvalue at [2,0] == " << matrix.DeleteAt(2,0);
    cout << "\nvalue at [3,3] == " << matrix.DeleteAt(3,3);
    cout << "\nvalue at [4,2] == " << matrix.DeleteAt(4,2);
    cout << "\nMatrix after deletions\n";
    ShowMatrix(matrix);
}

// Call test procedures
void PerformTests()
{
  cout.setf(ios::showpoint);  // Always show decimal point
  cout.precision(1);          // Display floats as n.m
  Test1();
  Test2();
  cout << "----------";
}
```

As implemented here, each node in a sparse matrix is an object of the Node class, which specifies the Sparse class as a friend. All of Node's members are private, so only Sparse may construct and use Node objects. As a direct benefit of this design, users of the Sparse class do not need to manipulate nodes or deal with list pointers.

Node objects store five pieces of information. Two int values, row and col, record a node's index locations in the matrix. Two Node * pointers, left and right, link nodes onto lists as Figure 16.3 illustrates. The last member, a float value f, stores data in each node. You can replace this member with your own data, or use a pointer to address strings or other objects.

In addition to its constructors and destructor, the Node class has two member functions. Link() attaches a Node object to another node addressed by p. Unlink() detaches a node from a list so it can be deleted.

The other class in the sample listing, Sparse, constructs and maintains the sparse matrix. The class declares a static, constant, float value named spare for nonpresent matrix elements. Every location in a sparse matrix has a value, but only active nodes occupy space. Nonpresent nodes simply return the value of spare, defined later in the listing as

```
const float Sparse::spare = 0.0;
```

You can assign a different value to spare—use whatever value you want for nonpresent nodes.

Use the Sparse class constructor to create a sparse matrix with the potential to have a specified number of rows and columns. To construct a 10-by-20 matrix, for example, use the statement

```
Sparse m1(10, 20);
```

Insert values into the matrix by calling the PutAt() member function. This inserts 3.14159 at m1[4, 12] (row 4, column 12):

```
m1.PutAt(4, 12, 3.14159);
```

If a Node object exists at that location, Sparse replaces its value with the new one. If no Node exists, Sparse adds one. If that depletes the heap, the sample program halts with an error message. (A more sophisticated program could use one of the memory management techniques described elsewhere in Part 3 to deal with out-of-memory errors—always a concern with sparse structures, which after all, might not fit into RAM if they become less sparse.)

To read the value of an existing node, call GetAt() like this:

```
cout << m1.GetAt(4, 7) << endl;
```

If there's no active node at these index coordinates, GetAt() returns the static sparse value. You can always read a node's value, even if that node doesn't actually exist. To delete a Node, call DeleteAt():

```
m1.DeleteAt(4, 7);
```

Or, you can read and delete a node in one easy motion:

```
cout << m1.DeleteAt(4, 7) << endl;
```

With these three member functions, any array-like operations are possible. You could even multiply two sparse matrices or perform any other two-dimensional matrix algorithm. As the program demonstrates (see function ShowMatrix()), a nested for loop accesses all elements in a sparse matrix. For example, these sample statements display every value in the matrix m1:

```cpp
cout << "Sparse matrix m1:\n";
for (int row = 0; row < m1.GetNRows(); ++row) {
  for (int col = 0; col < m1.GetNCols(); ++col)
    cout << setw(8) << m1.GetAt(row, col);
  cout << endl;
}
```

The Node and Sparse class member functions are well commented in the listing. The two classes spend most of their energy managing the lists of nodes, searching through lists for nodes at specified rows and column, and inserting or deleting Node class objects.

To hide the use of the Node class, Sparse calls three protected functions to perform some key services. CheckIndexes verifies that row and column indexes are within range. NodeAt() returns the address of a Node object for any row and column, or the function returns null if there is no node at that spot. Function InsertAt() inserts a new node.

These last two functions, NodeAt() and InsertAt(), are protected to prevent their misuse (only Sparse members, derived classes, and friends can call the protected functions). The functions assume that row and col arguments are within bounds. InsertAt() also assumes that the node to be inserted does not already exist at the specified row and column.

Two test functions (imaginatively named Test1() and Test2()) demonstrate some ways to use sparse matrices. The first test function constructs matrices of various sizes, showing in each case how much memory remains. The second test function creates a small sample matrix (small so its output fits on-screen), displayed by ShowMatrix():

```
Matrix of [5,4] elements:
      [0]   [1]   [2]   [3]
[0]  -9.9   0.0   0.2   0.0
[1]   0.0   1.1   0.0   0.0
[2]   2.0   0.0   0.0   2.3
[3]   0.0   0.0   0.0   0.0
[4]   0.0   0.0   4.2   0.0
```

The 0.0 entries are sparse—they don't actually exist. The other entries are stored in list nodes, but despite the use of linked lists, the final result has the look and feel of a plain old two-dimensional array. That's one of the best aspects of sparse matrices. You use them much as you do any other *NxM* arrays.

Final Words

Sparse data structures take advantage of the "holes" in data, eliminating waste caused by duplications or unused information. Spreadsheets, databases, and other applications that use large, but sparsely populated matrices, can use the techniques described in this chapter to save huge amounts of memory.

Until now, the chapters in this part have been concerned with object storage in RAM. The next, and final, chapter in this book turns to a different data storage problem: how to store persistent objects of varying sizes and types in disk files.

Preserving
Persistent Objects

An indifferent world rewards persistence, or as my mother always says, "the squeaky wheel gets the grease." But there's more than one kind of persistence. In C++, persistence refers to objects that survive, or *persist,* beyond the runtime lives of their programs.

Most often, persistent objects are preserved in files. Unlike common file data, however, persistent objects *retain their identities,* making it possible for a program to read the objects back into memory without foreknowledge of what kinds of objects the file contains. Doing that might seem only moderately difficult until you consider several complications that arise when storing different objects of related classes in the same file. It takes more than a little personal persistence to unlock the secrets of object persistence in C++.

Objects in Files

In general terms, a persistent object is one that survives outside of the process that created the object. An object on the heap, for example, persists relative to its creating function (see Figure 17.1). Persistent objects might also be stored in a global buffer.

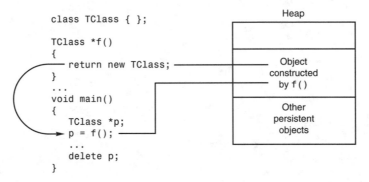

Figure 17.1. Persistent objects on the heap.

Objects that persist in memory are relatively easy to manage because their classes are automatically known—even if the internal methods for relating objects and classes are undocumented by a specific compiler vendor. Of course not every compiler uses the same methods. For example, to link objects to virtual class member functions, it's safe to assume that C++ stores function addresses in a table or in some other structure that is somehow associated with objects of the class. Exactly how that's accomplished shouldn't matter to a well-written program—or to a programmer who writes one.

File-based objects, however, are horses of a different feather. Storing a persistent object in a file does not preserve any internal facts about the object's makeup. Reading the object back into RAM is therefore complicated by the need to reconstruct internal data structures about which you and the program have no direct knowledge! Horses may as well grow wings and *still* not be able to fly.

But don't give up yet. There's a way to accomplish this seemingly impossible task using only familiar—and portable—C++ techniques.

The Problem

The key to understanding how to store persistent objects safely and in a portable mannner is to understand fully the scope of the problem. Imagine a file with objects of different types and sizes (see Figure 17.2), then consider these facts about any single object:

● There is nothing inside the object that identifies its class.

● The size of the object is not saved, nor are the objccts casily distinguished from one another.

● The object's links to its class members and any other internal storage details also are not saved.

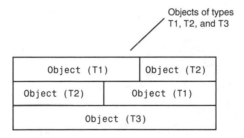

Figure 17.2. A file of objects of different sizes and class types.

It's easy to solve the first two of these problems. Along with each object, a program can store a unique value that identifies the object's class. (Some class libraries use an integer for this purpose; others use a string. The exact nature of the value doesn't matter, only that it uniquely identify the class to which each object belongs.) Figure 17.3 shows this new arrangement of objects prefaced by unique identifiers.

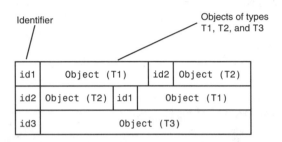

Identifier   Objects of types
                              T1, T2, and T3

id1	Object (T1)		id2	Object (T2)
id2	Object (T2)	id1	Object (T1)	
id3	Object (T3)			

Figure 17.3. A file of objects identified by unique values that preface each object.

Note: You don't have to store object sizes in the file. After the program reads an object's identifier and determines its class *T*, the expression *sizeof(T)* gives the object's size in bytes.

Unique identifiers provide only part of the solution. Another more difficult problem remains—how to handle the loss of the relationship between an object and its class. As I mentioned, C++ probably links objects and class member functions using pointers of some kind. Even if you had access to those pointers, you couldn't store them in a file and expect their address values to remain valid when reloaded into RAM.

That same fact is true for your own pointers declared in a class. Saving pointer address values to a file and leaving the addressed data in memory would be senseless. You may as well throw away your paycheck and deposit the envelope. Obviously, the program must store data addressed by pointers, not the pointer values themselves.

An even more perplexing problem is the inability of C++ classes to identify themselves. Even after you decide to store unique identifiers along with objects, you are still faced with the problem of maintaining a database of identifiers and their related classes. But what is a class? It's not an object that can be stored in an array or on a list with associated identifiers. There's no "class type of classes" in C++, so how can a program use an identifying value to determine the object's class type for the purpose of reconstructing persistent objects in memory?

If you examine various class libraries and read published accounts of persistence, you might believe that the solutions to these problems require fiddling with system-dependent address tables and studying internal object storage details. You might even be misled into believing that saving data addressed by pointers is impossible, or that doing so requires intimate knowledge about the computer's hardware addressing scheme—all surefire ways to destroy portability.

These popular myths deserve a place right next to astrology and palm reading. Despite claims to the contrary, it is possible to read and write persistent objects in a completely portable way. It also is possible to preserve data addressed by pointers—even variable-length strings—without using a single byte of system-dependent code. Before examining the technique, however, let's clarify a few goals to achieve.

The Goals

Complex programming problems are best solved using the top-down method, a fact that remains true even with object-oriented code. So, let's start, not at the beginning, but at the end result. (I followed a similar course when designing the sample statements for this section, but I extracted the actual code from a program listed in full later in this chapter.)

Imagine a hypothetical program that has a few classes representing information to be stored in persistent objects. All classes derive from the same base class:

```
class Base { };                  // Base class
class Derived1: public Base { }; // Derived class
class Derived2: public Base { }; // Another derived class
```

The class details don't matter—just assume that each class has one or more data members, and perhaps, a pointer or two. To store multiple objects, the program defines an array of Base class pointers:

```
Base *array[6];
```

Then, other statements construct objects of `Base`, `Derived1`, and `Derived2` classes, storing their addresses in the array:

```
array[0] = new Base();
array[1] = new Derived1();
array[2] = new Derived2();
array[3] = new Derived1();
array[4] = new Base();
array[5] = new Derived2();
```

A real program would pass arguments of various types to the class constructors, initializing object data with numeric values, strings, pointers, and so on. Because base-class pointers may address objects of that class or of any derived class, you can use the array to address any objects of the `Base` class family.

Suppose that you next want to save this array of objects in a file—in other words, you want to have the objects *persist* so the same or another program can reload the objects into memory. For the output file, you can use the `bofstream` (binary output file stream) class from Chapter 6:

```
#include "bstream.h"
bofstream ofs("TEST.DAT");
if (!ofs) {
  cout << "Error creating TEST.DAT";
  exit(-1);
}
```

The `bofstream` class writes data in binary form to a file stream—exactly what we need to store a persistent object as a mirror of its RAM-based image. Constructing the object `ofs` as shown here creates, or prepares to overwrite, a data file named TEST.DAT. In order to record how many objects are stored in the file, the program probably should store that number (n) in a header record. A simple statement writes n's value to the output stream:

```
ofs << n;  // Store number of records in file
```

Storing simple objects like n requires no special programming. The bytes in n are transferred directly to the file—provided, that is, you follow the binary-file techniques explained in Chapter 6. Unfortunately, however, storing class objects is not so simple. You can't use a `for` loop to write the array of object pointers directly:

```
for (i = 0; i < n; ++i)
  ofs << array[i];   // ???
```

That won't work because the output statement writes the *pointers* to the file. We don't want to save the pointers; we want to save the information that the pointers address. Dereferencing the pointers provides only a partial solution:

```
for (i = 0; i < n; ++i)
  ofs << *array[i];   // ???
```

This stores the objects to a file as illustrated in Figure 17.2. Unfortunately, however, all the problems discussed previously now come into play. The objects lack identity, and any pointers are written directly to the file, leaving any addressed data behind.

Worse, reading the objects back is apparently impossible. First, you might attempt to create a bifstream (binary input file stream) object as explained in Chapter 6:

```
bifstream ifs("TEST.DAT");
if (!ifs) {
  cout << "Error opening TEST.DAT";
  exit(-1);
}
```

The first item in the file indicates the number of objects that follow. You can use the input file stream to read back that information:

```
ifs >> n;
```

That seems clean enough, but the program is now firmly stuck in the mud. Consider what happens if you define another array of uninitialized Base * pointers, then use a for loop to reload the objects from the input stream:

```
Base *newarray[6];
for (i = 0; i < n; ++i)
  ifs >> newarray[i];   // ???
```

Oops. The last line attempts to reload *pointers,* not *objects.* Unfortunately, dereferencing the pointers only makes matters worse:

```
for (i = 0; i < n; ++i)
  ifs >> *newarray[i];   // ???
```

The pointers aren't initialized, so dereferencing them causes the program to refer to random memory locations. Apparently, the program has to call new to initialize each pointer *before* reading objects from the file. But that's not possible—the program doesn't have any knowledge of what those objects are. To read the objects seems to require the foresight of a fortune teller, able to predict in advance object classes before reading the actual objects.

And that's the nub of the problem. Ideally, a program should be able to read persistent objects regardless of order or type. Even better, it should be possible to accomplish that goal using a simple unique identifier stored with each object as illustrated in Figure 17.3.

To demonstrate that idea, using some hypothetical classes, assume you have a list of objects addressed by a pointer named listp. The objects are arranged in no particular order, and all are of Base, Derived1, and Derived2 classes. Ideally, a program should be able to write the list of objects to a file with a few simple statements:

```
if (listp->Count() == 0) return;   // Exit if list is empty
ofs << listp->Object();            // Write first object
while (listp->Next())              // Move to next object
  ofs << listp->Object();          // Write other objects
```

The while loop writes objects by address as returned by the hypothetical listp->Object() function. The *objects,* not their addresses, are written to the output stream. A similar while loop should be able to read the objects back using an input file stream:

```
Base *p;                // Pointer to Base or derived objects
listp = new ListClass;  // Construct a new list
while (!ifs.eof()) {    // Repeat until reaching end of file
  ifs >> p;             // Read and construct object!
  listp->Insert(p);     // Insert object into list
}
```

The statement ifs >> p is a workaholic in disguise. Its many responsibilities include:

● Reading the object's unique identifier

● Determining the object's data type

- Allocating memory for the object

- Reading bytes from the file into the object's reserved memory

- Reallocating memory for any pointers, and loading addressed data

- Properly linking the object to its class so statements can call virtual member functions for the object.

That's a load and a half plus a little more. How is it possible to program a class and file streams to do all those tasks? The answer is a true exercise in object-oriented programming: you don't read file data into objects; *you devise objects that can read and write themselves.*

The Solution

It's highly inconvenient to require all classes to perform duplicate tasks—in this case, the task of reading and writing persistent class objects. Instead, it makes more sense to write another class to handle chores that are common to other classes. To give any class persistence, you can then simply inherit the common class. The goal is to have any class acquire persistence simply through inheritance.

A simple example demonstrates how to use inheritance this way. Ignoring persistence for the moment, consider the simpler but related problem of providing text-stream capabilities to classes.

In Chapter 5 you examined how to do that by overloading the input and output stream operators << and >>. An interesting way to accomplish the same task *without* having to overload the operators for each and every class is to invent another abstract class that provides the necessary items—let's call it TextObject. To bestow *streamability* upon any other class, simply inherit TextObject and provide one or more required member functions.

Listing 17.1, TEXTOBJ.CPP, demonstrates how to write an abstract TextObject class that can provide output stream capabilities to any class. To keep the code simple, I did not implement input streams, but you could use the same techniques demonstrated here for both input and output.

Listing 17.1. TEXTOBJ.CPP.

```cpp
#include <iostream.h>

class TextObject;

typedef TextObject * PTextObject;
typedef TextObject & RTextObject;

class TextObject {
  friend ostream & operator<< (ostream &os, RTextObject r);
  friend ostream & operator<< (ostream &os, PTextObject p);
protected:
  virtual void Print(ostream &os) = 0;
};

class Base: public TextObject {
public:
  Base(int X, int Y): x(X), y(Y) { }
protected:
  virtual void Print(ostream &os);
private:
  int x, y;
};

class Derived: public Base {
public:
  Derived(int X, int Y, double D): Base(X, Y), d(D) { }
protected:
  virtual void Print(ostream &os);
private:
  double d;
};

int main()
{
  Base *bp = new Base(12, 34);
  Base *dp = new Derived(56, 78, 3.14159);
  cout << "*bp == " << *bp << endl;
  cout << "*dp == " << *dp << endl;
```

```
    return 0;
}

// Prints a TextObject or derivative by reference
ostream & operator<< (ostream &os, RTextObject r)
{
  r.Print(os);
  return os;
}

// Prints a TextObject or derivative by pointer
ostream & operator<< (ostream &os, PTextObject p)
{
  p->Print(os);
  return os;
}

// Prints object in text to an output stream
void Base::Print(ostream &os)
{
  os << "x==" << x << ", y==" << y;
}

// Prints object in text to an output stream
void Derived::Print(ostream &os)
{
  Base::Print(os);
  os << ", d==" << d;
}
```

Compiling and running the sample program displays the values of two objects addressed by pointers of type `Base *`. On-screen you see the lines

```
*bp == x==12, y==34
*dp == x==56, y==78, d==3.14159
```

The statements in `main()` that produce this output write `Base *` pointers to cout. Obviously, then, because the pointers are each of the same type, something is causing the code to select the proper object to display. Of course, you probably recognize this action as the key characteristic in *polymorphism*—the capability of calling virtual member functions for objects addressed by base-class pointers.

The virtual member function in this example is named `Print()`, and is inherited from the abstract `TextObject` class. Take a close look at the class's declaration:

```
class TextObject {
  friend ostream & operator<< (ostream &os, RTextObject r);
  friend ostream & operator<< (ostream &os, PTextObject p);
protected:
  virtual void Print(ostream &os) = 0;
};
```

The class has no constructor or destructor, nor any data members. It has only two friend `operator<<` functions, one for a reference to a `TextObject` and another that operates on a `TextObject` pointer. (To add input streams to the class, you could insert `operator>>` friend functions of similar design into the class.)

`TextObject` is abstract because it nulls the virtual `Print()` member function. That function requires a reference to an output stream. Because of `Print()`'s protected status, only members of `TextObject` and derived classes, or friends, may call the function.

One of those friend functions is the overloaded `operator<<` function. Here it is again:

```
ostream & operator<< (ostream &os, RTextObject r)
{
  r.Print(os);
  return os;
}
```

The function calls the virtual `Print()` for the `TextObject` passed by reference in r. The other operator function works similarly, but executes the statement `p->Print()`. To write an object to an output stream, the program can therefore pass the object *or a pointer to an object*. To see this feature in action, change `main()`'s stream statements to

```
cout << "bp == " << bp << endl;
cout << "dp == " << dp << endl;
```

Normally, given these statements, C++ would write pointer address values. Due to the overloaded operators, however, the code now writes the addressed data. (If you really want to write addresses, use a case expression such as (void *)bp.)

To provide some data to write, the program declares two classes, Base and Derived. These classes do not overload operator<<; instead, the Base class inherits TextObject and provides a virtual Print() member function. Here's the class declaration:

```
class Base: public TextObject {
public:
  Base(int X, int Y): x(X), y(Y) { }
protected:
  virtual void Print(ostream &os);
private:
  int x, y;
};
```

Elements that provide streamability to the class are printed in bold. Inheriting TextObject gives the class an output stream operator for Base class references and pointers. The class provides a completed Print() member function, implemented as

```
void Base::Print(ostream &os)
{
  os << "x==" << x << ", y==" << y;
}
```

A stream statement that writes a Base object or pointer calls one of the operator<< functions in TextObject. That function in turn calls the virtual Print() function to write the object's data members—x and y and labels in this example.

Other classes derived from Base simply add their own Print() function to the works. Here's Derived's declaration:

```
class Derived: public Base {
public:
  Derived(int X, int Y, double D): Base(X, Y), d(D) { }
protected:
  virtual void Print(ostream &os);
```

```
private:
  double d;
};
```

The class adds a `double` data member, d, and a virtual `Print()` function. To write `Derived` objects, this version of `Print()` calls the `Base` function, then writes the new class's data member:

```
void Derived::Print(ostream &os)
{
  Base::Print(os);    // Call Base Print() to write x & y
  os << ", d==" << d; // Write this class's data
}
```

The `TextObject` operators call this new `Print()` function for any `Base *` pointers that happen to address `Derived` objects. You could extend this scheme to other classes, inheriting `Base` or starting anew by inheriting `TextObject`. Simply add a virtual `Print()` member function and you're done—there's no need to overload the operators << or >> in each and every class you write.

Now that you've seen the basic mechanism at work, you're ready to apply a similar concept to persistent objects. The goal is to design a *persistence class*—I'll call it `FileObject`—that provides the necessary elements for reading and writing persistent objects, similar to the way `TextObject` provided for text output. To add persistence to a class, a class can inherit `FileObject` and replace a couple of virtual member functions. Actually, there are one or two other details, but I'll explain those as you examine the final program in the next section.

Persistence Pays Off

Listing 17.2, PERSIST.CPP, demonstrates how to create a persistence class, `FileObject`, and use it to read and write objects of different sizes and types in a file. The program also includes the same `TextObject` class from TEXTOBJ.CPP (Listing 17.1). PERSIST.CPP is longer than usual, so I'll describe it in chunks.

Note: On disk, you can find the "unchunked" Listing 17.2 in directory PERSIST. The program uses the bstream.h and BSTREAM.CPP files described in Chapter 6. Copies of these files are also included in the PERSIST directory. To compile the program with Borland C++, enter the commands

```
bcc -c -ml bstream
bcc -ml persist bstream.obj secrets.lib
```

Listing 17.2. PERSIST.CPP.

```cpp
#include <stdlib.h>
#include <iostream.h>
#include <fstream.h>
#include <string.h>
#include <memuse.h>
#include "bstream.h"


//--------------------------------------------------------------
// Miscellaneous definitions
//--------------------------------------------------------------


// File objects are identified by a unique ObjectID value
typedef unsigned ObjectID;

// This flag is used to construct uninitialized objects
enum BuildFlag {build};

// All object ID values begin with this value
const ObjectID FID_USER = 0;

// Object ID values for each class of file objects
const ObjectID FID_BASE = FID_USER + 0;
```

continues

Listing 17.2. continued

```
const ObjectID FID_DERIVED1 = FID_USER + 1;
const ObjectID FID_DERIVED2 = FID_USER + 2;

// Total number of Object ID values
const ObjectID NUM_IDS = 3;
```

After including necessary header files, the program begins with a few miscellaneous definitions. Values of type ObjectID identify persistent objects in files—these are the "ID" values shown in Figure 17.3. I used unsigned as the base type for ObjectID, but you could use another type. (Identifying objects with strings would require extra programming. If you want to make this change, I suggest trying the program as written before attempting the modification.)

The enumerated BuildFlag might seem an odd fellow, having only one symbol named build. The purpose of this type is to make it possible for a class to provide a special constructor taking one argument of type BuildFlag, the only value of which must be build. In other words, a class TClass might have these constructors:

```
class TClass {
public:
  TClass();              // Default constructor
  TClass(BuildFlag) { } // "Build" constructor
  ...
};
```

This class has two constructors (it could have others). The default constructor is an example of a normal constructor. The other one—call it the *build constructor*—declares a BuildFlag parameter and has an empty inline body. The constructor's job is to build raw, uninitialized class objects into which the program deposits persistent objects. How that process works will become clear later in the listing.

Four constants in PERSIST.CPP provide unique values for identifying persistent objects of the program's three classes. FID_BASE identifies objects of type Base, FID_DERIVED1 identifies Derived1 objects, and FID_DERIVED2 identifies Derived2 objects. Constant NUM_IDS represents the total number of class types for which the program stores objects in a file.

There's nothing sacred about the values or the constant names that I used here, but due to the sample program's design, the first object must be identified by the number 0, the second as 1, the next as 2, and so on. Later in this chapter, I'll suggest a way to remove this restriction.

Listing 17.2. PERSIST.CPP (continued).

```
//---------------------------------------------------------------
// TextObject abstract class declaration
//---------------------------------------------------------------

class TextObject;  // Incomplete class declaration

typedef TextObject * PTextObject;
typedef TextObject & RTextObject;

class TextObject {
  friend ostream & operator<< (ostream &os, RTextObject r);
  friend ostream & operator<< (ostream &os, PTextObject p);
protected:
  virtual void Print(ostream &os) = 0;
};
```

Next in the listing is the TextObject class introduced in Listing 17.1. The incomplete class declaration just under the second row of dashes makes it possible for two typedef statements to define handy symbols: PTextObject as a pointer to a TextObject and RTextObject as a reference to a TextObject.

If you skipped the discussion of TextObject, you might want to go back and read that section now. The next part of the listing declares a similar class, FileObject, that provides persistence capabilities much in the way TextObject provides text output services.

Listing 17.2. PERSIST.CPP (continued).

```
//---------------------------------------------------------------
// FileObject abstract class declaration
```

continues

Listing 17.2. continued

```
//--------------------------------------------------------------

class FileObject;

typedef FileObject * PFileObject;
typedef FileObject & RFileObject;
typedef PFileObject & RPFileObject;

class FileObject {
  friend bofstream & operator<< (bofstream &os, RFileObject r);
  friend bofstream & operator<< (bofstream &os, PFileObject p);
  friend bifstream & operator>> (bifstream &is, RPFileObject rp);
private:
  virtual ObjectID Identity() const = 0;
public:
  virtual ~FileObject() { }
protected:
  virtual void * Read(bifstream &is) = 0;
  virtual void Write(bofstream &os) = 0;
};

// Object class Build() function pointer type
typedef PFileObject (*BuildFunction)();
```

Compare the FileObject and TextObject classes—they are similar in purpose and form, but different in content. Several typedef statements provide synonyms for a FileObject pointer (PFileObject), a reference (RFileObject), and a reference-to-pointer (RPFileObject). See the sidebar, "References to Pointers," if you are not familiar with this third type.

The FileObject class declares three overloaded stream operators. Two output operators write to a bofstream (binary output file stream) object, and require either a FileObject reference or a pointer. The input stream operator reads from a bifstream (binary input file stream) object, and requires a reference-to-pointer argument. Programs can use these operators to read and write persistent objects of any class derived from FileObject.

Sidebar: References to Pointers

Use a *reference-to-pointer* as a parameter in functions that need to pass back new address values in pointer arguments. C programmers would employ a double-indirect pointer (`T**`) for this purpose—in other words, a *pointer-to-pointer*. References to pointers (`T*&`) work similarly, but are easier to use.

An example demonstrates how to create references to pointers. Start with a few `typedef` statements:

```
typedef char * Pchar;      // Pointer to char
typedef char & Rchar;      // Reference to char
typedef Pchar & RPchar;    // Reference to char pointer
```

These symbols provide synonyms for a `char` pointer (`Pchar`), a `char` reference (`Rchar`), and a `char` reference-to-pointer (`RPchar`). You don't need to use these definitions, but they are easier to read than cryptic `*`, `&`, and `*&` symbols strewn throughout code.

After these steps, you can write a function that declares a reference-to-pointer parameter. Here's a sample:

```
void f(RPchar rcp)
{
  rcp = "New string";
}
```

The function assigns the address of a string constant to the reference-to-pointer `rcp`. Elsewhere, the program can define a `char` pointer `p`, and initialize the pointer to address a string:

```
char *p = "Original string";
```

Calling function `f()` modifies `p` to address a new string:

```
f(p);   // Modifies p!
```

That statement passes `p` *by reference* to `f()`—that is, it passes the pointer variable's address, not the address value the pointer holds. The function assigns a new address value to `p`, causing it to point to a different location. After this statement, `p` addresses the string `"New string"`.

By the way, there is no such animal as a *pointer-to-reference*. The compiler does not permit defining a type as `T&*`. You also cannot define a reference-to-reference `T&&`. The proper form is `T*&` (literally, a reference to `T*`).

The class also declares four virtual member functions. Except for the destructor, the functions are nulled, making `FileObject` an abstract class. Because it's abstract, you can't define objects of type `FileObject`. Instead, another class must inherit `FileObject` and provide replacements for the nulled member functions, and if necessary, a virtual destructor.

In a class derived from `FileObject`, the private `Identity()` function should return a value that uniquely identifies class objects. This value is stored in the file ahead of each object (see Figure 17.3). The function is declared const because it makes no changes to its object, and can therefore be called for const objects of type `FileObject` (or of a derived class).

The virtual destructor ensures that objects addressed by `PFileObject` pointers can be properly deleted.

Two other virtual member functions read and write object data members. In a class derived from `FileObject`, simply replace `Read()` with your own function that reads data members from the `bifstream` reference is. Also provide a `Write()` function to write data members to the `bofstream` reference os. The two functions must read and write the same data members in the same order.

Finally in this section is another `typedef` statement that defines the symbol `BuildFunction` as a pointer to a function that returns `PFileObject` (a pointer to a `FileObject`), and requires no arguments. The program uses this type to construct a database of object identifiers and classes—but more on that later. First, we need some classes for creating persistent objects to be stored in a file.

Listing 17.2. PERSIST.CPP (continued).

```
//--------------------------------------------------------------
// Base class declaration (sample file object)
//--------------------------------------------------------------

class Base;

typedef Base * PBase;
typedef Base & RBase;
```

```
typedef PBase & RPBase;

class Base: public TextObject, public FileObject {
  virtual ObjectID Identity() const { return FID_BASE; }
public:
  Base(): x(0), y(0) { }
  Base(int X, int Y): x(X), y(Y) { }
  Base(BuildFlag) { }
  virtual ~Base() { }
  static PFileObject Build();
protected:
  virtual void Print(ostream &os);
  virtual void * Read(bifstream &is);
  virtual void Write(bofstream &os);
private:
  int x, y;   // Sample data in Base class objects
};

inline bifstream & operator>> (bifstream &is, RPBase rp)
  { return is >> (RPFileObject)rp; }
```

Class Base is the first of three classes to be used for constructing, reading, and writing persistent objects. Here again, I used typedef to define three synonyms for a Base pointer, a reference, and a reference-to-pointer.

The class inherits two other classes, demonstrating a practical use for multiple inheritance. TextObject provides text output stream services, and requires the class to provide a Print() member function—a demand that Base fulfills in its protected part. The second inherited class, FileObject, provides persistence services. This class requires Base to provide three functions: Identity(), Read(), and Write().

The class must also include two other features. The first of these is a *build constructor,* in this case declared as

```
Base(BuildFlag) { }
```

Every class that inherits FileObject must have a similar build constructor. The constructor's body is empty—its only purpose is to construct a raw, uninitialized class object.

The last and final required element is a static Build() member function that returns PFileObject. Recall from earlier the typedef symbol BuildFunction. The class's Build() member function corresponds to that symbol's design, and therefore, *the address of the static Build() function may be assigned to a variable of type BuildFunction.* As you will see in a moment, it is this relationship that provides the means to build a database of object identifiers and classes, and therefore to reconstruct persistent objects loaded from a file.

Finally in this section is an inline definition of an overloaded operator>> function. The definition is needed because we eventually want to read persistent objects using a statement such as

```
ifs >> p;
```

where ifs is an input file stream object of type bifstream, and p is a PBase pointer. When used to address objects of derived classes, references are not exactly like pointers. A base-class pointer, as you know (and might be tired of my repeating), may address an object of that class or of any derived class. A reference, however, cannot do the same—it can address *only* a object of the reference's class type. So, it's necessary to provide an explicit inline operator>> function that casts an RBase reference to an RFileObject reference, thus permitting the preceding statement to compile correctly. (Disable the inline definition and recompile the program to see the resulting error message or warning on your compiler.)

Other than those requirements, the Base class may have any other data members and member functions. The class may inherit other classes, it can declare other constructors, and so on. Next are two more sample classes derived from Base.

Listing 17.2. PERSIST.CPP (continued).

```
//----------------------------------------------------------------
// Derived1 class declaration (sample file object)
//----------------------------------------------------------------
```

```
class Derived1;

typedef Derived1 * PDerived1;
typedef Derived1 & RDerived1;
typedef PDerived1 & RPDerived1;

class Derived1: public Base {
  virtual ObjectID Identity() const { return FID_DERIVED1; }
public:
  Derived1(): Base(), d(0.0) { }
  Derived1(int X, int Y, double D): Base(X, Y), d(D) { }
  Derived1(BuildFlag) { }
  virtual ~Derived1() { }
  static PFileObject Build();
protected:
  virtual void Print(ostream &os);
  virtual void * Read(bifstream &is);
  virtual void Write(bofstream &os);
private:
  double d;  // Sample data in Derived1 class objects
};

inline bifstream & operator>> (bifstream &is, RPDerived1 rp)
  { return is >> (RPFileObject)rp; }


//---------------------------------------------------------------
// Derived2 class declaration (sample file object with pointer)
//---------------------------------------------------------------

class Derived2;

typedef Derived2 * PDerived2;
typedef Derived2 & RDerived2;
typedef PDerived2 & RPDerived2;

class Derived2: public Base {
  virtual ObjectID Identity() const { return FID_DERIVED2; }
```

continues

Listing 17.2. continued

```
public:
  Derived2(): Base(), len(0), string(0) { }
  Derived2(int X, int Y, const char *s);
  Derived2(BuildFlag) { }
  virtual ~Derived2();
  static PFileObject Build();
  void Init(int start = 0);
protected:
  virtual void Print(ostream &os);
  virtual void * Read(bifstream &is);
  virtual void Write(bofstream &os);
private:
  int len;       // Length of string in characters
  char *string;  // Pointer to string
};

inline bifstream & operator>> (bifstream &is, RPDerived2 rp)
  { return is >> (RPFileObject)rp; }
```

The Derived1 and Derived2 classes demonstrate how to create class families for constructing persistent objects. Each of the two classes listed here inherits Base, and therefore, also inherits TextObject and FileObject. Each derived class provides Print(), Identity(), Read(), and Write() member functions as described for the Base class. Each class also provides a static Build() function and an empty-bodied inline build constructor with a single parameter of type BuildFlag.

Class Derived2 includes a char * data member named string. Later in the listing, I'll explain complications that this data member causes. Reading and writing variable-length objects addressed by pointers—in this case, character strings—is difficult, but with a little care, is easily managed.

The two classes also define overloaded operator>> inline functions for reference-to-pointer arguments of the class types. In each case, the inline functions merely cast the reference-to-pointer argument to RPFileObject, just as Base did. You must supply a similar overloaded operator>> function for each class derived from FileObject.

In the next section, the program builds a database of object identifiers and classes. Hang on—we're almost done with the program's declarations and global variables.

Listing 17.2. PERSIST.CPP (continued).

```
//-------------------------------------------------------------
// Database of Build() function addresses
//-------------------------------------------------------------

BuildFunction Builders[NUM_IDS] = {
  Base::Build,          // Points to Base class Build()
  Derived1::Build,      // Points to Derived1 class Build()
  Derived2::Build       // Points to Derived2 class Build()
};


//-------------------------------------------------------------
// Function prototype and main test program
//-------------------------------------------------------------

void PerformTests();

int main()
{
  HeapReport("Initial memory use");
  PerformTests();
  HeapReport("\nFinal memory use");
  return 0;
}
```

The BuildFunction database defined here is the key element that permits reconstruction of persistent objects loaded from a file into memory. For the demonstration program, I used a simple array, named Builders, of BuildFunction values. The array has room for NUM_IDS entries, each of which holds the address of a class Build() function. The array indexes are the unique object identifiers defined at the beginning of the listing. The following statement, then, locates the Build() function for the Base class:

```
Builders[FID_BASE];  // Address of Base::Build() function
```

The other Build() member functions in classes Derived1 and Derived2 also are stored in the array, indexed by the constants FID_DERIVED1 and FID_DERIVED2.

A more sophisticated program might create the Builders database using a different technique. Some class libraries, for example, store object identifiers and classes (actually, the addresses of class member functions like Build()) in a linked list, or even better, in a container class. I elected to take a simpler route and use an array. After you are familiar with the demonstration program, you might want to replace Builders with a list or other structure, and in the process, eliminate the current requirement that object identifiers (used as array indexes) begin with zero.

The main() test program follows the definition of the Builders array. The program reports before and after heap memory levels as a check that all objects are properly deleted. Function PerformTests() calls two other functions to read and write persistent objects in a file.

The listing continues with the implementations of the operator functions responsible for the program's input and output.

Note: Assuming you are not blessed with a photographic memory, now would be an excellent time to review the listing, starting at "Persistence Pays Off." There's a lot to bite off and chew in this chapter, and the better you understand the program's class declarations and other items, the easier the following code will be to comprehend.

Listing 17.2. PERSIST.CPP (continued).

```
//-----------------------------------------------------------------
// Friend operator functions
//-----------------------------------------------------------------

// Prints a TextObject or derivative by reference
ostream & operator<< (ostream &os, RTextObject r)
```

```
{
  r.Print(os);
  return os;
}

// Prints a TextObject or derivative by pointer
ostream & operator<< (ostream &os, PTextObject p)
{
  p->Print(os);
  return os;
}

// Writes a FileObject or derivative to disk by reference
bofstream & operator<< (bofstream &os, RFileObject r)
{
  os << r.Identity();
  r.Write(os);
  return os;
}

// Writes a FileObject or derivative to disk by pointer
bofstream & operator<< (bofstream &os, PFileObject p)
{
  os << p->Identity();
  p->Write(os);
  return os;
}

// Constructs and reads a FileObject from disk
bifstream & operator>> (bifstream &is, RPFileObject pr)
{
  ObjectID id;    // Unique object identifier
  PFileObject p;  // Pointer to constructed object

  is >> id;                         // Read object ID
  p = Builders[id]();               // Build raw object
  pr = (PFileObject)p->Read(is);    // Read and return object
  return is;                        // Return stream reference
}
```

You already saw the `operator<<` functions for the `TextObject` class. These merely call the virtual `Print()` member functions provided by classes derived from `TextObject`. Together, the functions permit statements such as

```
cout << myObject;
```

where `myObject` is an object of a class derived from `TextObject`. The class simply provides a `Print()` member function to write its data to a text output stream.

The three binary stream operators work similarly. The first two provide overloaded `operator<<` functions for `FileObject` references and pointers. Each operator performs the actions that write persistent objects to a file. In the first `operator<<` function, for instance, this statement writes the object's unique identifier:

```
os << r.Identity();
```

If you do not use a simple integer or other built-in type to identify objects, you will need to modify that statement. For example, to identify objects using strings, you might call a function that writes the string (perhaps with its length or a null terminator) to the file. You would also have to modify the `Identity()` function to return the type `const char *`.

The second action in the overloaded `operator<<` function calls the virtual `Write()` member function. This statement:

```
r.Write(os);
```

calls `Write()` for the object referred to by `r`. The function writes the class's data members to the binary stream identified by `os`. In that way, `Write()` works as `Print()` does for classes derived from `TextObject`. The `operator<<` functions cannot be virtual, but they can call *other* virtual functions like `Write()` to perform actions for objects of derived classes.

The pointer version of the overloaded `operator<<` function performs the same actions, but uses a pointer `p` rather than a reference:

```
os << p->Identity();
p->Write(os);
```

Next in the listing is the overloaded input-stream `operator>>` function, which constructs and reads persistent objects from a file. If there is a heart to the technique of object persistence, this overloaded operator function is the primary pump.

First, the function defines two local variables: id holds an object's unique identifier; p is a pointer to a FileObject. Because all persistent objects are of classes derived from FileObject, p may address any conforming object stored in a file by one of the two operator<< functions just described.

The operator>> function's first statement reads the value of an object's identifier:

```
is >> id;
```

To use non-native identifiers (strings, for example) you would have to modify this statement, perhaps calling another function to read object ID names.

Using the object's identifier, the operator>> function next constructs a raw object of the correct type. It does this by calling the Build() member function stored in the Builders database. This statement plays a leading role in object reconstruction:

```
p = Builders[id]();
```

Peek ahead to the Base::Build() member function implementation later in the listing. The preceding statement calls Build(), using the address stored in the Builders database, indexed by the object's unique identifier. Build() in turn calls the class's build constructor (the one that takes an argument of type BuildFlag), constructing a raw, uninitialized object of the proper type. The address of that object is assigned to p.

It's important for the build constructor not to initialize the object, nor to assign values to any pointers. At this point, the program needs only to dig a hole in memory big enough to hold the object's data. After completing that step, the program can load the object from the file stream, and deposit the information into the excavated hole. This statement performs all the necessary actions:

```
pr = (PFileObject)p->Read(is);  // Read and return object
```

The raw, uninitialized object addressed by p literally reads itself into memory! The pointer returned by Read() is of type void *, and it must be cast to PFileObject before assigning to pr.

Recall that pr is a reference-to-pointer of type RPFileObject. The preceding statement, then, reads a persistent object into the space allocated by the build constructor, and then *modifies the pointer passed to the operator>> function.* When the program executes a statement such as

```
ifs >> p;
```

assuming that ifs is the binary input file stream and p is a FileObject or Base class pointer, the statement modifies p to address a newly constructed object loaded from a file.

It is especially important that p be null or uninitialized when used this way. The program does not read data into *existing* objects—that would require knowing in advance what those objects are, the very requirement we are attempting to avoid. Instead, the program reads to an *uninitialized* pointer, causing the object to read itself from the file, and then assign its address back to the pointer. You can then save the pointer or copy the loaded object for safe keeping.

> **Note:** I did not take great pains to provide extensive error checking in the sample program, particularly in the preceding section. The functions are therefore shorter and easier to understand, but before using the code, you might want to add checks for errors following disk reads and writes. It would also be a good idea to test pointers for null, or to use one of the other memory management techniques discussed elsewhere in Part 3 to guard against object construction errors.

That completes the programming needed to read and write persistent objects. The remaining portions of the listing implement the Base, Derived1, and Derived2 classes, and include test functions that demonstrate how to read and write objects in a file.

Listing 17.2. PERSIST.CPP (continued).

```
//-------------------------------------------------------------
// Base class implementation
//-------------------------------------------------------------

// Constructs raw (uninitialized) object
PFileObject Base::Build()
{
```

```
    return new Base(build);
}

// Prints object in text to an output stream
void Base::Print(ostream &os)
{
  os << "x==" << x << ", y==" << y;
}

// Reads object from a binary file stream
void * Base::Read(bifstream &is)
{
  is >> x >> y;
  return this;
}

// Writes object to a binary file stream
void Base::Write(bofstream &os)
{
  os << x << y;
}
```

First in this part is the implementation of the Base class. The class Build() member function provides the capability of constructing a raw, uninitialized Base class object, into which a persistent object of this type is deposited. The statement

```
return new Base(build);
```

returns a newly constructed Base class object, using the build constructor. That constructor is called by supplying an argument of type build. In a sense, this is a *phony* argument—its value isn't saved or used in any way. The only purpose of the argument is to force the program to select the proper constructor. This is why the enumerated BuildFlag type requires only one symbol (build).

The Print() member function, called by the TextObject overloaded operator<< functions, writes the object's data in text form to an output stream. You saw a similar function in TEXTOBJ.CPP (Listing 17.1).

The Read() member function reads object data from a binary input stream. Write() writes the same data, in the same order, to an output stream. Only Read() returns a value—a void * pointer to the object, now fully initialized with data loaded from a file.

Notice how simple these functions are. Read() and Write() merely transfer the object's data members to and from binary file streams, using the programming declared in bstream.h as explained in Chapter 6. The implementation for class Derived1 is equally simple, as the next section of the listing shows.

Listing 17.2. PERSIST.CPP (continued).

```
//-----------------------------------------------------------
// Derived1 class implementation
//-----------------------------------------------------------

// Constructs raw (uninitialized) object
PFileObject Derived1::Build()
{
  return new Derived1(build);
}

// Prints object in text to an output stream
void Derived1::Print(ostream &os)
{
  Base::Print(os);
  os << ", d==" << d;
}

// Reads object from a binary file stream
void * Derived1::Read(bifstream &is)
{
  Base::Read(is);
  is >> d;
  return this;
}

// Writes object to a binary file stream
```

```
void Derived1::Write(bofstream &os)
{
  Base::Write(os);
  os << d;
}
```

Compare `Derived1::Build()` to `Base::Build()`. Each function returns a newly constructed object of its class type by calling the class's build constructor. The `Build()` functions are the ones stored in the `Builders` database, and are called to construct raw, uninitialized objects for loading persistent objects from a file.

Because `Derived1` is a derived class, its other functions differ slightly from those in the `Base` class. For example, the `Derived1::Print()` member function executes the following two statements:

```
Base::Print(os);
os << ", d==" << d;
```

The first statement calls the ancestor class's `Print()` function, writing the inherited portion of the object to an output stream. The second statement writes data belonging to `Derived1`. Passing a `Derived1` object to an output stream, then, writes the entire object's value:

```
Derived1 d1(8, 9, 3.14159);
cout << d1;
```

`Derived1`'s `Read()` and `Write()` member functions also begin by calling their ancestor class functions. Examine `Write()` first. It executes the two statements

```
Base::Write(os);   // Write inherited members
os << d;           // Write Derived1 member
```

The first statement calls the `Base` class `Write()` function, transferring the inherited portion of the object to the output file stream. The second statement writes `Derived1`'s own data. Here a single `double` value named d. `Read()` works similarly, but also returns a pointer to the loaded object:

```
Base::Read(is);    // Read inherited members
is >> d;           // Read Derived1 member
return this;       // Return pointer to object
```

In other derived classes, you simply continue to supply `Read()` and `Write()` member functions. In each case, call the ancestor function, then read or write the new class's members. Together, these functions can read and write any persistent object no matter how complex. Always end `Read()` with the statement `return this;`.

A minor complication arises when objects have pointers that address data, perhaps stored on the heap. The program must take extra steps to write the data addressed by pointers, not the pointer address values. `Derived2`'s implementation demonstrates how to handle this tricky situation.

Listing 17.2. PERSIST.CPP (continued).

```
//--------------------------------------------------------------
// Derived2 class implementation
//--------------------------------------------------------------

// Constructs object of Derived2 class
Derived2::Derived2(int X, int Y, const char *s)
  : Base(X, Y)
{
  if (s == 0) {
    len = 0;
    string = 0;
  } else {
    len = strlen(s);
    string = new char[len + 1];
    if (string) strcpy(string, s);
  }
}

// Destroys object of Derived2 class
Derived2::~Derived2()
{
  delete string;
}

// Constructs raw (uninitialized) object
PFileObject Derived2::Build()
```

```
{
  return new Derived2(build);
}

// Prints object in text to an output stream
void Derived2::Print(ostream &os)
{
  Base::Print(os);
  os << ", string==\"" << string << '"';
}

// Reads object from a binary file stream
void * Derived2::Read(bifstream &is)
{
  Base::Read(is);
  is >> len;
  if (len == 0)
    string = 0;
  else {
    char c;
    string = new char[len + 1];
    for (int i = 0; i < len; ++i) {
      is >> c;
      if (string) string[i] = c;
    }
    string[len] = 0;
  }
  return this;
}

// Writes object to a binary file stream
void Derived2::Write(bofstream &os)
{
  Base::Write(os);
  os << len;
  if (string)
    for (int i = 0; i < len; ++i)
      os << string[i];
}
```

Though somewhat more complex than the implementations of the `Base` and `Derived1` classes, `Derived2`'s member functions generally follow the same pattern outlined in the preceding sections.

First, however, are two new functions—a constructor and a virtual destructor. The constructor prepares a `Derived2` object, copying a string argument to newly allocated memory on the heap. Pointer member `string` addresses this memory. The destructor deletes the addressed `string`, reclaiming any memory used by the object, as all good destructors should do.

`Derived2`'s `Build()` function is similar to the other two you examined. Again, using the `build` argument selects the class's build constructor, the one with the single parameter of type `BuildFlag`. The resulting object is in a raw, uninitialized state, ready to receive data loaded from a file. Be especially aware of the fact that any pointers in the object also are uninitialized, and probably do not address valid locations. Obviously, the object must not be used in this condition.

Skip to the `Write()` function. After calling the ancestor function, `Write()` writes the string's `len` value (another data member in the `Derived2` class). If the string is not null, a `for` loop transfers the characters from the string one by one to the output stream. In this way, the string's length precedes its characters, giving `Read()` the means to rebuild a string of that same length. The null at the end of the string is redundant, and is therefore not saved. (You could also save the terminating null if you want to mark the end of the string in the file, but not storing the length value would complicate the job of reading the string, so the null isn't strictly needed.)

Next, examine how `Read()` loads and reconstructs the string data. First, `Read()` calls the ancestor's `Read()` function. Then it reads the string's length value:

```
is >> len;
```

If `len` is zero, there isn't any string in the file, and the function sets the `string` pointer to null. If `len` is nonzero, the function calls `new` to construct a new string into which characters are loaded one by one. In this way, the variable-length, addressed data is reconstructed exactly as it was saved, although probably not in the same location in memory.

Note: An out-of-memory error does not eliminate the need to read variable-length data completely. In this case, for example, even if `string` is null following the call to new, it is still necessary to read the entire string from disk, although the characters are not saved. As in other portions of the sample program, I decided not to clutter the code with a lot of error checking. The function shown here, however, reads addressed data correctly even if the program runs out of heap space. You could optimize the sample `Read()` and `Write()` functions by using a system function to read blocks of bytes rather than using a `for` loop as shown here.

The final section of the listing shows how to use the classes and other definitions to read and write persistent objects in a file.

Listing 17.2. PERSIST.CPP (continued).

```
//-------------------------------------------------------------
// Test functions called by main() and PerformTests()
//-------------------------------------------------------------

void WriteObjects()
{
  int i, n = 6;
  PBase array[6];

  cout << "----------\n";
  cout << "Test: Write objects to TEST.DAT\n";
  array[0] = new Base(1,2);
  array[1] = new Derived1(3,4,3.14159);
  array[2] = new Derived2(5,6,"First String");
  array[3] = new Derived1(99,88,1234.5678);
  array[4] = new Base(-7,-8);
  array[5] = new Derived2(7,8,"Second String");

  bofstream ofs("TEST.DAT");
```

continues

Listing 17.2. continued

```
    if (!ofs) {
      cout << "Error creating TEST.DAT";
      exit(-1);
    }
    ofs << n;   // Number of records
    for (i = 0; i < n; ++i)
      ofs << array[i];
    cout << n << " objects written:\n";
    for (i = 0; i < n; ++i) {
      cout << "array[" << i << "]:";
      cout << array[i] << endl;
      delete array[i];
    }
}

void ReadObjects()
{
  int i, n = 6;
  PBase array[6];

  cout << "----------\n";
  cout << "Test: Read objects from TEST.DAT\n";
  // Set all array pointers to null
  // just to prove that objects are read from disk
  for (i = 0; i < n; ++i)
    array[i] = 0;
  bifstream ifs("TEST.DAT");
  if (!ifs) {
    cout << "Error opening TEST.DAT";
    exit(-1);
  }
  // Set n to 0 just to prove that it is loaded from disk
  n = 0;

  // Read objects from file
  ifs >> n;
  for (i = 0; i < n; ++i)
    ifs >> array[i];
```

```
  cout << n << " objects read:\n";
  for (i = 0; i < n; ++i) {
    cout << "array[" << i << "]:";
    cout << array[i] << endl;
    delete array[i];
  }
}

void PerformTests()
{
  WriteObjects();
  ReadObjects();
}
```

For simplicity, I used an array of PBase pointers to address several objects of types Base, Derived1, and Derived2. Another program might use a list or a container class to store a family of objects.

Function WriteObjects() constructs a few objects and assigns their addresses to array slots. The function then creates an output stream, using the statement

```
bofstream ofs("TEST.DAT");
```

Next, the function writes the number of objects to the stream and then uses a simple for loop to store persistent object data to the file:

```
ofs << n;  // Number of records
for (i = 0; i < n; ++i)
  ofs << array[i];
```

The last line is only the tip of an iceberg. Below its seemingly simple shape is a small mountain of code that saves object data, identified by the unique values supplied by the objects' classes.

The final function in the test program, ReadObjects(), completes the other half of the picture, reading the objects from the test file. Again, I used an array to hold PBase pointers, but you could also use a list or another structure.

To prepare for reading the objects, the program constructs an input file stream with the statement

```
bifstream ifs("TEST.DAT");
```

Reading the objects from the file is then a simple matter of loading the number of objects, and then using a `for` loop to load *and reconstruct* the persistent objects saved in the file:

```
ifs >> n;
for (i = 0; i < n; ++i)
  ifs >> array[i];
```

As in `WriteObjects()`, the last line hides its complexity. That single statement reads each object's unique identifier, uses the `Builders` database to construct raw, uninitialized objects of the correct type, calls the proper build constructor, and uses the `FileObject`'s `Read()` member function to load data from disk, also reallocating memory for the variable-length strings addressed by pointers in `Derived2` objects. The pointers at `array[i]` are initialized by the persistent objects themselves to address their images reconstructed in memory.

Final Words

Programming persistent objects takes more than a little personal persistence, but the results are well worth the effort. With the techniques in this chapter, you can store objects of different sizes and shapes in a file, then reconstruct those objects at a later time.

The method has many potential uses. A graphics program could store different shape objects in a file, creating a picture. A database program could store variable-size records, even records having different fields. A text editor could store more than just text—it might also save graphics, formatting information, and other items. Although longer than most of the chapters in this book, this chapter only scratches the surface of persistent objects and database management using C++. If you are looking for a programming subject to pursue, this one could occupy a lifetime.

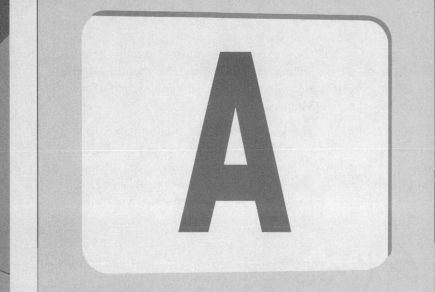

Compiling
the Listings

I receive a great many letters from readers, often asking for advice about compiling a listing in one of my books or articles. In almost all cases, problems are caused by not configuring the compiler correctly, by specifying a faulty pathname, by using a different compiler version, or by choosing the wrong set of compiler or linker options.

This appendix explains in detail how to compile all of the programs in this book and on disk (except for the shareware bonus programs mentioned in Appendix C). You can also use this appendix as a guide to compiling C and C++ listings published in my other books and articles.

Borland C++ and Turbo C++ give you several ways to compile and link programs. If you are using a different brand of compiler, you can probably use similar commands, but you'll have to alter pathnames and select different options from those listed here. Detailed step-by-step instructions follow. First, however, let's examine some of the most common problems that you might encounter.

Common Errors

The most common mistake is to configure your system for more than one C or C++ compiler at a time. *Never do that!* Compilers use many files of the same names but not of the same content. For example, Borland C++, Microsoft C/C++, Zortech C++, and the compiler in my book, *Learning C++,* all read a header file named stdio.h. Unfortunately, however, that file differs in content in each of those products. If you install more than one C or C++ compiler on your system, you must be absolutely certain that each compiler can find its own files.

The best way to do that is to prepare batch files to switch between compiler configurations. Make sure each batch file sets the proper environment variables (LIB, INCLUDE, PATH, and so on) according to your compiler's instructions. Be especially careful to have only one C or C++ compiler on the system PATH at a time. Run the appropriate batch file to use a selected compiler. (I program my AUTOEXEC.BAT file to configure my system for Borland C++, then I run other batch files to switch between Microsoft C/C++, Zortech C++, Turbo C++, and others.)

The second most common mistake is neglecting to link a program to its supporting modules. Many of the programs in this book, for instance, call functions stored in other files. If A.CPP calls a function in B.CPP, you must link A to B before you can run the finished code. In Borland C++, do that by entering a command such as

```
bcc a.cpp b.cpp
```

You don't have to type the .CPP extensions. Given this command, the compiler translates A.CPP to A.OBJ, and B.CPP to B.OBJ, storing the raw compiled object-code instructions along with other information in each .OBJ file. Then, the linker joins A.OBJ and B.OBJ to create A.EXE, containing the finished program, ready to run. If you already have compiled B.CPP to B.OBJ, you don't have to recompile B.CPP. Just specify the compiled object-code filename:

```
bcc a.cpp b.obj
```

The compiler understands that it should compile A.CPP to produce A.OBJ, then link A.OBJ and B.OBJ to create A.EXE. You might also need to link the program to a library file ending in .LIB and containing multiple object-code modules:

```
bcc a.cpp b.cpp c:\mylibs\mystuff.lib
```

There are many other ways to compile and link multifile programs and libraries, some of which are explained later in this appendix.

The third most common mistake is not using the correct memory model. I recommend that all programs in this book be compiled with the large model, but you can use other models if you want. Borland C++ defaults to the small memory model, so to use the large model, you must include the -ml (large-memory-model) option when compiling:

```
bcc -ml a.cpp b.cpp
```

All object-code modules must use the same memory model. If you compiled B.CPP to produce B.OBJ using the small model, the following command would be a serious mistake:

```
bcc -ml a.cpp b.obj ..\lib\secrets.lib
```

If you are unsure whether B.OBJ was compiled with the large memory model, recompile the module by specifying its .CPP source code filename:

```
bcc -ml a.cpp b.cpp ..\lib\secrets.lib
```

Note: Be sure to install your compiler's large memory model files. If you didn't do this, plan to reinstall your compiler as soon as possible. At a minimum, you should install at least the large and small models. If you don't want to install the large memory model, or if you want to use a different model, you must recompile this book's precompiled function library, SECRETS.LIB. See "Building the Library" later in this appendix.

The fourth most common error is misunderstanding how to compile and run programs in an integrated development environment, or IDE. In general, when compiling multifile programs, you must create a project file that specifies the program's components and other information. (See "Borland C++ IDE" and "Turbo C++ IDE" later in this appendix.) Running a program in an IDE might seem to have no effect because, when the program ends, the editor reappears, obscuring the program's output. Borland's IDEs permit you to switch to the other display by pressing Alt+F5. To return to the editor, press that key combination again, or press any other key.

The fifth most common problem arises from attempting to mix the IDE and command-line compilers. Some programmers like to enter and view program listings in the IDE's editor, then shell out to DOS to compile and run the code. There's nothing wrong with that approach, except that is, for a bug in the Borland C++ and Turbo C++ IDEs that prevents running programs like MAKE from a DOS shell. The IDEs are protected-mode applications, and apparently, they are not able to start *another* protected mode program like MAKE. You are supposed to be able to use RMAKE (real-mode MAKE) for this purpose, but that doesn't work either. Borland has acknowledged this problem, but was unable to offer a solution. The only fix is to exit the IDE completely, and then compile and run. Unfortunately, this means you have to reload the IDE to continue editing. (By the way, I use the Brief and Codewright editors, which don't have these problems.)

Finally, many readers attempt to use a Windows-hosted environment to compile and run program examples. That may or may not work, even though your compiler manufacturer advertises 100% compatibility between Windows and DOS. If you can't get a program to run in a graphical window, open a DOS prompt box, and compile and run the program as a DOS application. Microsoft Windows has special programming requirements. This book explains concepts that apply generally to all environments, including but not limited to Windows. The example listings, however, might be easier to run and use under plain DOS.

Most readers having trouble will find a solution in one or more of the preceding notes. The following detailed instructions explain how to use the supplied automated MAKE files to compile the book's listings, how to rebuild the precompiled function library, how to run the command-line Borland C++ and Turbo C++ compilers, and how to create projects for integrated development environments.

Note: If you are just getting started with this book, you don't have to memorize the following information now, though you might want to read it eventually for tips about compiling programs. Instead, I suggest that you attempt to compile and run this book's examples as you read about them in the chapters. If you experience trouble with a specific listing, return here for help.

Using Automated MAKE Files

Installing this book's disk creates a file named MAKEFILE.INC in the installation directory, usually C:\SECRETS. Listing A.1 shows the contents of this file, which specifies compiler and linker options for compiling from the DOS command line, using automated MAKE files. These are always named MAKEFILE with no extension. (See the end of this appendix for MAKEFILE listings.)

Listing A.1. MAKEFILE.INC.

```
# Code Secrets - MAKE file global declarations
# Compiler: Borland C++ 3.1
# (c) 1993 by Tom Swan. All rights reserved.

#- You MUST supply the following three path names!
#  The pathnames must NOT end with backslashes

BCCPATH = C:\borlandc
LIBPATH = C:\secrets\lib
INCPATH = C:\secrets\include


#- Various symbols
#  BCCPATH   Pathname to Borland C++ outer directory
#  CC        Compiler or executive name
#  CCLL      Compiler and linker executive program
#  INCPATH   Pathname to Code Secrets include files
#  LIB       Library manager utility (tlib usually)
#  LIBPATH   Pathname to Code Secrets library
#  OPTS      Optimizations (-Od = none for fastest compilation)
#  WARN      Warning level (-w == all warnings enabled)
#  MODEL     Memory model (s, m, l, etc.)
#  CDEBUG    Debugging flag (-v == debug info; -vi inline expansion)
#  CSLIB     Filename of Code Secrets library
#  CSPLIB    Path and file name to CSLIB library
#  CLFLAGS   Compile and link flags (e.g. .CPP -> .EXE)
#  CFLAGS    Compile-only flags (e.g. .CPP -> .OBJ)


#- Some of the following declarations are position dependent

CC = bcc
CCLL = bcc
LIB = tlib
OPTS = -Od
WARN = -w
MODEL = l
CDEBUG = -v -vi
CSLIB = secrets.lib
```

```
CSPLIB = $(LIBPATH)\$(CSLIB)
CLFLAGS = $(OPTS) $(WARN) -m$(MODEL) $(CDEBUG)
CFLAGS = -c $(CLFLAGS)
```

Load MAKEFILE.INC into your text editor, and modify the three macros near the beginning of the listing as follows:

- BCCPATH must specify the pathname where you install Borland C++ or Turbo C++. For example, if you installed Borland C++ to D:\BC, change BCCPATH to that drive and directory name. Do *not* end the pathname with a backslash.

- LIBPATH must specify the pathname to this book's SECRETS.LIB file. *Do not specify your compiler's LIB subdirectory in LIBPATH.* The current setting, C:\SECRETS\LIB, assumes that you installed the book's disk to C:\SECRETS.

- INCPATH must specify the pathname to this book's header files (ending in .h). *Do not specify your compiler's INCLUDE subdirectory in INCPATH.* The current setting, C:\SECRETS\INCLUDE, assumes that you installed the book's disk to C:\SECRETS.

After setting these three pathnames, you can adjust various other options in MAKEFILE.INC, but you don't have to. Most readers will not need to change any of the default options.

Note: If you are using Turbo C++, make these additional changes to MAKEFILE.INC. Change BCCPATH to

```
BCCPATH = C:\tc
```

or to another installation directory. Also set CC (compiler name) and CCLL (compiler and linker name) to tcc (both are currently set to bcc):

```
CC = tcc
CCLL = tcc
```

Finally, set the OPTS variable to null by deleting the text to the right of the equal sign:

```
OPTS =
```

You might want to preserve a copy of the original MAKEFILE.INC in case you decide to use the full Borland C++ compiler in the future.

Skip to the section "Building the Library," and follow instructions to build the library file SECRETS.LIB for Turbo C++. When you are done, come back here and continue.

Next, from a DOS prompt, type **path** and verify that your compiler's code-file directory is on the current system PATH. Your path should look something like this:

```
PATH=C:\WINDOWS;C:\DOS;C:\BORLANDC\BIN
```

Notice that C:\BORLANDC\BIN specifies the path to the "binaries" directory—that is, the directory where the compiler stores its binary code files such as BCC.EXE and TASM.EXE.

Note: The system PATH must specify the BIN subdirectory for the compiler. The BCCPATH macro in MAKEFILE.INC (Listing A.1) must specify only the outer installation root directory such as C:\BORLANDC. *Do not specify a subdirectory name such as BIN in BCCPATH.*

Type **bcc** to verify that you can run the compiler. (If you are using Turbo C++, type **tcc**.) You should see a copyright notice and a list of compiler options. If not, PATH is not set correctly or the compiler is improperly installed.

You should now be able to compile the book's listings using the automated MAKEFILEs in various directories. To try this, enter the following commands:

```
cd c:\secrets\part1
make
```

That compiles and links all programs in the PART1 directory. (This will take several minutes.) If you receive error messages, you probably did not modify MAKEFILE.INC correctly, or you did not install the large memory model for your compiler. Reinstall the compiler, edit MAKEFILE.INC, and try again. Similar MAKEFILEs are supplied in the PART2, PART3, and other directories. Use them identically—change to a directory and type **make** to compile.

After you compile all listings in a directory, you can load individual files into your editor, make changes as suggested in the chapters, or add your own modifications. You might, for example, enter an output statement to display the value of a variable. Make the change, save the file to disk, then return to the DOS prompt. (If you are using an IDE, exit to DOS.) To compile your changes, simply type **make**. The MAKE utility figures out which files were changed, then compiles only the minimum number of modules.

> **Note:** If you type **make** and nothing seems to happen, it means that all programs are currently up to date. MAKE issues compiler commands only if necessary. If all programs are already compiled, MAKE simply ends without taking any action.

After compiling with MAKE, you might notice a new file named TURBOC.CFG in the directory. The supplied MAKEFILEs store the current set of options and pathnames in this file for the compiler to use.

If this is your first exposure to MAKE, these steps might seem more complex than they really are, especially until you try them a few times. Here's a quick review of what we've covered so far:

1. Install the large memory model for your compiler

2. Edit the pathnames in MAKEFILE.INC

3. Make sure your system PATH is set correctly

4. Change to any directory

5. Type `make` to compile and to recompile program listings

Here are some other hints for using my automated MAKEFILEs along with the MAKE utility:

● To delete .BAK, .OBJ, and .EXE files in the current directory, type `make` `clean`. *Don't enter this command unless you are sure you want to delete all files ending in those three extensions.* Use this command to conserve disk space, or as a prelude to rebuilding all programs in the current directory. For example, after typing `make clean`, type `make` to recompile all programs.

● To create a TURBOC.CFG configuration file in the current directory, type `make config`.

● To compile a specific program, feed its .EXE filename to MAKE. You must have created a TURBOC.CFG configuration file for this to work. For example, change to the PART1 directory, and type `make config` followed by `make newio.exe` to compile only the NEWIO.CPP program, creating NEWIO.EXE. When you know the target .EXE filename, this is the fastest method to compile individual programs without having to compile all other programs in the current directory.

You can also compile all programs in all directories at once with a single command. First, modify the pathnames in MAKEFILE.INC (Listing A.1) as explained, and verify that the system PATH is set correctly. Then, change to C:\SECRETS and run the MAKEALL.BAT batch file in Listing A.2. The batch file changes to each subdirectory and calls MAKE to perform the actual compilations. Before starting this operation, you might want to plan to do the laundry, walk the dog, and paint the living room. Depending on your system's speed, compiling everything will take some time. (It actually takes only about ten or twenty minutes or so, but don't run this batch file if you need to use your system right now for other tasks.)

Listing A.2. MAKEALL.BAT.

```
@echo off
rem
rem Code Secrets - Build all programs (but not library)
rem Compiler: Borland C++ 3.1
rem  (c) 1993 by Tom Swan. All rights reserved.
rem
cd part1
make
if errorlevel == 1 goto ERROR
cd ..\part2
make
if errorlevel == 1 goto ERROR
cd ..\part3
make
if errorlevel == 1 goto ERROR
cd ..\persist
make
if errorlevel == 1 goto ERROR
cd ..
echo.
echo Done making programs
echo.
goto END
:ERROR
echo MAKE aborted due to error
:END
```

Building the Library

SECRETS.LIB in the C:\SECRETS\LIB directory contains compiled object-code modules required by many of the book's listings. All library source code is provided in one of these three directories:

● LIB\CLASSLIB contains the source code files for the book's container class library.

● LIB\MEMUSE contains a memory utility used to display information about a program's use of heap space.

● LIB\STRING contains the source code files for the book's String class.

These modules are supplied in precompiled form inside SECRETS.LIB to make it easier to compile programs that require one or more of the modules. If you are using Borland C++ and the large memory model, you do not have to rebuild the library. You must rebuild SECRETS.LIB for Turbo C++, or if you want to use a different memory model, or if you upgrade your compiler.

As with other directories, automated MAKEFILES are supplied to compile the individual library components. It's usually best, however, to rebuild the entire library. To do that, change to the LIB directory, and run the BUILD.BAT file, Listing A.3. This batch file changes to each library subdirectory, runs MAKE, copies .h header files to the INCLUDE directory, and uses the TLIB.EXE utility (supplied with Borland C++ and Turbo C++) to update SECRETS.LIB with the compiled .OBJ code files.

Note: Before building the library, you must modify MAKEFILE.INC and set your system's PATH as explained in this appendix.

Listing A.3. BUILD.BAT.

```
@echo off
rem
rem Code Secrets - Build common library batch file
rem Compiler: Borland C++ 3.1
rem (c) 1993 by Tom Swan. All rights reserved.
rem
echo.
echo This program:
echo  - deletes secrets.lib
echo  - deletes *.obj, *.exe, *.bak files in subdirectories
```

```
echo  - recompiles all *.obj, *.exe files in subdirectories
echo  - rebuilds secrets.lib
echo.
echo If you do NOT want to rebuild the library,
echo press Ctrl+Break now and answer Yes to the prompt
echo asking whether to end the batch file.
echo.
echo If you DO want to rebuild, press Enter. (Ignore any warnings
echo about symbols "not found" in the library.)
echo.
pause.
echo.
del secrets.lib
del secrets.txt
rem
rem *** Following sections are position dependent, meaning they
rem     must be compiled in the order shown. Do not rearrange
rem     without careful thought!
rem
rem *** MEMUSE
rem
cd memuse
make clean
make
if errorlevel == 1 goto ERROR
copy *.h ..\..\include
cd ..
rem
rem *** STRING
rem
cd string
make clean
make
if errorlevel == 1 goto ERROR
copy *.h ..\..\include
cd ..
rem
```

continues

Listing A.3 continued

```
rem *** CLASSLIB
rem
cd classlib
make clean
make
if errorlevel == 1 goto ERROR
copy *.h ..\..\include
cd ..
rem
rem *** SECRETS.TXT (documents library contents)
rem
tlib secrets.lib, secrets.txt
rem
echo.
echo Done building library
echo.
goto END
:ERROR
echo MAKE aborted due to error
:END
```

In addition to recompiling library components and updating SECRETS.LIB, the batch file also creates a file named SECRETS.TXT listing the library's public functions (those that other programs can call by linking to SECRETS.LIB). You might want to print a copy of this file for reference.

Note: If you make *any* change to *any* library component in the CLASSLIB, MEMUSE, or STRING directories, or if you modify any of the options in MAKEFILE.INC, you should rebuild the entire library by running BUILD.BAT.

Borland C++ IDE

If you suspect that I'm not overly fond of integrated development environments, also called IDEs, you are correct. I don't use the Borland C++ or Turbo C++ IDEs for my programming. Instead, I use the Brief and Codewright editors, and I compile programs from the command line. (I suppose this makes me the old fashioned type.)

I realize, however, that some people like chocolate; others are crazy about vanilla. Everybody has their favorite editors, and you can certainly use the IDEs with all of the programs in this book. Here's how.

For simple, single-file programs, load the listing into the IDE and press F9 to run, or press Ctrl+F9 to compile and run. If you receive errors, try these suggestions:

● Edit the pathnames in MAKEFILE.INC as explained in this appendix.

● Change to a directory such as PART1 or PART2.

● From a DOS prompt, type `make config` to create a configuration file TURBOC.CFG in the current directory.

● Get back to the IDE, select the large memory model, and try compiling again.

Multifile programs are not as simple to compile. When a program A.CPP calls functions in another program B.CPP, you have to create a *project file,* listing each of the program's components. With a project open, the compiler compiles the individual program components, then links them to create the finished .EXE code file, ready to run.

Unfortunately, you have to create these project files for each and every multifile program in this book. I did not supply these files for two compelling reasons:

● Your directory names are probably different from mine. If I supplied project files, you would have to modify all of the directories in each project.

● Project files for Borland C++ and Turbo C++ are compatible, but the directories for the two compilers are different. Again, to switch compilers requires modifying every directory setting in each project.

Modifying directories in dozens of project files is much more difficult than simply creating your own project files in the first place. Like many seemingly complex tasks, this one is easiest to learn by following a step-by-step demonstration. Install the book's disk if you haven't done so already, then follow these numbered steps:

1. Start the Borland C++ IDE and close any open files.

2. Use **F**ile|**C**hange dir... to make C:\SECRETS\PART3 the current directory.

3. Select **P**roject|**O**pen project... and enter `triangle` as the project file name. A project can have any name, but it's best to name it the same as the main program, in this case TRIANGLE. The IDE automatically adds the extension .PRJ to the project filename.

4. You now see a project window. Select **P**roject|**A**dd item... and enter the name of the project's main module, TRIANGLE.CPP, if you are following along.

5. Note that after you press Enter or select the **A**dd button, the "Add to Project List" dialog closes briefly, then pops back into view. It does this so you can add multiple files to the project without reselecting the menu command. Enter the other modules one by one. For this example, you have to enter two more: SPARSE.CPP and SECRETS.LIB. After you are finished, select the **D**one button. The project window should now list three files: TRIANGLE.CPP, SPARSE.CPP, and SECRETS.LIB.

6. Select **O**ptions|**D**irectories and modify the pathnames in the resulting dialog. Set **I**nclude Directories to

   ```
   C:\BORLANDC\INCLUDE;C:\SECRETS\INCLUDE
   ```

   and set **L**ibrary Directories to

   ```
   C:\BORLANDC\LIB;C:\SECRETS\LIB
   ```

Modify the drive letters and directory names as needed for your installation. Separate multiple pathnames with semicolons and no spaces. Leave the **O**utput and **S**ource directory settings blank.

7. Select **O**ptions**A**pplication and choose the DOS **S**tandard button (simply named **S**tandard in Turbo C++). As I mentioned elsewhere in this appendix, most simple programs work best when run as plain DOS applications. Attempting to run some examples may or may not work correctly if compiled as Windows graphical programs. (Because most example programs generate plain text output, there's no advantage to be gained in running them under Windows.)

8. Finally, in the **O**ptions menu, select **C**ompiler and **C**ode generation..., and change Model to **L**arge.

9. That completes the creation of a project file for the TRIANGLE program. For unknown reasons, the only way to save the project is to close it. I suggest you always do this by selecting **P**roject**C**lose project before compiling and running the program. Otherwise, if something goes wrong and you have to reboot, you will have to recreate the unsaved project from scratch.

10. If you just closed the project, select **P**roject**O**pen project... to reopen TRIANGLE.PRJ.

11. Press Ctrl+F9 to compile and run the program. After compiling and running, press Alt+F5 to view the program's output. Or, get to a DOS prompt and type **triangle** to run the compiled program.

> **Tip:** If you have a mouse, double-click on any filename ending in .CPP in the project window to open that file. If you don't have a mouse or just prefer the feel of a keyboard, select the file name and press Enter.

You must carry out these same eleven steps for every multifile program. You may also create projects for single-file programs—to specify pathnames and other options, for example. In those cases, the project files simply list the program's name (and, perhaps, SECRETS.LIB).

Table A.1 alphabetically lists programs that require projects before compiling with Borland's IDEs. All other programs can be compiled directly (though you still have to set directories, select options, and set the memory model to large as described in this section). To compile these multifile programs, create project files by following the above steps, but specify the component filenames in the table.

Tip: Close all files and projects, then specify global directory pathnames and compiler options. Save those settings with **O**ptions\|**S**ave. By doing this, you no longer have to reenter the same settings for each new project. This will make creating new projects faster.

Table A.1. Multifile Components.

Target Filename	C:SECRETS Subdirectory	Component Project Filenames
ADTDEMO1.EXE	PART2	ADTDEMO1.CPP, SECRETS.LIB
ADTDEMO2.EXE	PART2	ADTDEMO2.CPP, SECRETS.LIB
ADTDEMO3.EXE	PART2	ADTDEMO3.CPP, SECRETS.LIB
ADTDEMO4.EXE	PART2	ADTDEMO4.CPP, SECRETS.LIB
ADTDEMO5.EXE	PART2	ADTDEMO5.CPP, SECRETS.LIB
BFSTEST.EXE	PART1	BFSTEST.CPP,

Target Filename	C:SECRETS Subdirectory	Component Project Filenames
		BFSTREAM.CPP
CLONE.EXE	PART3	CLONE.CPP, SECRETS.LIB
FLAG.EXE	PART3	FLAG.CPP, SECRETS.LIB
PERSIST.EXE	PERSIST	PERSIST.CPP, BSTREAM.CPP, SECRETS.LIB
PLACE.EXE	PART3	PLACE.CPP, SECRETS.LIB
REF.EXE	PART3	REF.CPP, SECRETS.LIB
REF2.EXE	PART3	REF2.CPP, SECRETS.LIB
SPARRAY.EXE	PART3	SPARRAY.CPP, SECRETS.LIB
SPMATRIX.EXE	PART3	SPMATRIX.CPP, SPARSE.CPP, SECRETS.LIB
STRING.EXE	PART2	STRING.CPP, SECRETS.LIB
STRMAX.EXE	PART2	STRMAX.CPP, SECRETS.LIB
STRVECT.EXE	PART2	STRVECT.CPP, SECRETS.LIB
STRVECT2.EXE	PART2	STRVECT2.CPP, SECRETS.LIB
SVECTOR.EXE	LIB\CLASSLIB	SVECTOR.CPP,

continues

Table A.1. continued

Target Filename	C:SECRETS Subdirectory	Component Project Filenames
		TCLASS.CPP, SECRETS.LIB
TBCLASS.EXE	PART1	TBCLASS.CPP, BSTREAM.CPP
TBDOUBLE.EXE	PART1	TBDOUBLE.CPP, BSTREAM.CPP
TBSTREAM.EXE	PART1	TBSTREAM.CPP, BSTREAM.CPP
TCONTAIN.EXE	LIB\CLASSLIB	TCONTAIN.CPP, CONTAIN.CPP, TCLASS.CPP, SECRETS.LIB
TFIELD.EXE	PART1	TFIELD.CPP, LABEL.CPP, FIELD.CPP
TLABEL.EXE	PART1	TLABEL.CPP, LABEL.CPP
TLIST.EXE	LIB\CLASSLIB	TLIST.CPP, TCLASS.CPP, SECRETS.LIB
TLIST.EXE	PART2	TLIST.CPP, SECRETS.LIB
TRIANGLE.EXE	PART3	TRIANGLE.CPP, SPARSE.CPP, SECRETS.LIB
TTREE.EXE	PART2	TTREE.CPP, SECRETS.LIB
TVECTOR.EXE	LIB\CLASSLIB	TVECTOR.CPP,

Target Filename	C:SECRETS Subdirectory	Component Project Filenames
		TCLASS.CPP, SECRETS.LIB
VARY.EXE	PART3	VARY.CPP, SECRETS.LIB

Turbo C++ IDE

Edit MAKEFILE.INC, changing the BCCPATH, LIBPATH, INCPATH, CC, CCLL, and OPTS macros as explained in this appendix. Make sure your PATH settings include C:\TC\BIN (if that's the name of your Turbo C++ installation directory). Then, follow instructions under "Building the Library" in this appendix to create SECRETS.LIB for Turbo C++.

After rebuilding the library, you can follow the steps for the "Borland C++ IDE" to compile programs with the Turbo C++ IDE.

MAKEFILE Files

Following are the MAKEFILE listings, A.4 through A.10, stored in various directories. See "Using Automated MAKE Files" earlier in this appendix for instructions on running the MAKE utility with these automated compilation scripts. If you are not using Borland C++ or Turbo C++, you can use these MAKEFILEs as guides to compiling the book's programs with other compilers and MAKE utilities.

Note: Because all MAKEFILEs have the same filename, they are identified in the following listings by subdirectory and name.

Listing A.4. LIB\CLASSLIB\MAKEFILE.

```
# Code Secrets - MAKE file for container class library
# Compiler: Borland C++ 3.1
# (c) 1993 by Tom Swan. All rights reserved.

!include "..\..\makefile.inc"

depends: config\
         tclass.obj\
         tvector.exe\
         svector.exe\
         tlist.exe\
         ttree.exe\
         contain.obj\
         tcontain.exe\

TEMPHEAD = array.h contain.h deque.h listiter.h list.h minmax.h queue.h \
set.h stack.h vector.h vectiter.h

tclass.obj: tclass.h tclass.cpp
  $(CC) $(CFLAGS) tclass

tvector.exe: vector.h tvector.cpp tclass.obj
  $(CCLL) $(CLFLAGS) tvector tclass.obj $(CSLIB)

svector.exe: vector.h svector.h svector.cpp tclass.obj
  $(CCLL) $(CLFLAGS) svector tclass.obj $(CSLIB)

tlist.exe: list.h tlist.cpp tclass.obj
  $(CCLL) $(CLFLAGS) tlist tclass.obj $(CSLIB)

ttree.exe: tree.h ttree.cpp
  $(CCLL) $(CLFLAGS) ttree $(CSLIB)

contain.obj: contain.h contain.cpp
  $(CC) $(CFLAGS) contain
  $(LIB) $(CSPLIB) -+contain.obj
```

```
tcontain.exe: $(TEMPHEAD) tcontain.cpp contain.obj tclass.obj
  $(CCLL) $(CLFLAGS) tcontain contain.obj tclass.obj $(CSLIB)

#- Delete backups, object code, and executables
#  Enter MAKE CLEAN to use

clean:
  del *.bak
  del *.obj
  del *.exe

#- Create turboc.cfg configuration file
#  Enter MAKE CONFIG to use

config: turboc.cfg

turboc.cfg: ..\..\makefile.inc
  echo -I$(INCPATH);$(BCCPATH)\include   >turboc.cfg
  echo -L$(LIBPATH);$(BCCPATH)\lib       >>turboc.cfg
```

Listing A.5. LIB\MEMUSE\MAKEFILE.

```
# Code Secrets - MAKE file for memuse debugging function
# Compiler: Borland C++ 3.1
# (c) 1993 by Tom Swan. All rights reserved.

!include "..\..\makefile.inc"

depends: config memuse.obj

.cpp.obj :
  $(CC) $(CFLAGS) $.
  $(LIB) $(CSPLIB) -+$&.obj

#- Delete backups, object code, and executables
#  Enter MAKE CLEAN to use
```

continues

545

Listing A.5. continued

```
clean:
  del *.bak
  del *.obj
  del *.exe

#- Create turboc.cfg configuration file
#  Enter MAKE CONFIG to use

config: turboc.cfg

turboc.cfg: ..\..\makefile.inc
  echo -I$(INCPATH);$(BCCPATH)\include   >turboc.cfg
  echo -L$(LIBPATH);$(BCCPATH)\lib      >>turboc.cfg
```

Listing A.6. LIB\STRING\MAKEFILE.

```
# Code Secrets - MAKE file for String class
# Compiler: Borland C++ 3.1
# (c) 1993 by Tom Swan. All rights reserved.

!include "..\..\makefile.inc"

OBJ1 = strstats.obj strio.obj strfrnds.obj
OBJ2 = strctor.obj strops.obj strmfs.obj

depends: config str.exe

.cpp.obj :
  $(CC) $(CFLAGS) $.
  $(LIB) $(CSPLIB) -+$&.obj

str.obj : str.cpp str.h dump.inc $(OBJ1) $(OBJ2)
  $(CC) $(CFLAGS) str

str.exe : str.obj $(OBJ1) $(OBJ2)
  $(CCLL) $(CLFLAGS) str.obj $(CSLIB)
```

```
#- Delete backups, object code, and executables
#  Enter MAKE CLEAN to use

clean:
  del *.bak
  del *.obj
  del *.exe

#- Create turboc.cfg configuration file
#  Enter MAKE CONFIG to use

config: turboc.cfg

turboc.cfg: ..\..\makefile.inc
  echo -I$(INCPATH);$(BCCPATH)\include   >turboc.cfg
  echo -L$(LIBPATH);$(BCCPATH)\lib      >>turboc.cfg
```

Listing A.7. PART1\MAKEFILE.

```
# Code Secrets - MAKE file for Part 1
# Compiler: Borland C++ 3.1
# (c) 1993 by Tom Swan. All rights reserved.

!include "..\makefile.inc"

depends: config\
         oldio.exe\
         newio.exe\
         strout.exe\
         strin.exe\
         rwords.exe\
         cmanip.exe\
         repeat.exe\
         phone.exe\
         label.obj\
```

Listing A.7. continued

```
            tlabel.exe\
            field.obj\
            tfield.exe\
            polystr.exe\
            overout.exe\
            overin.exe\
            rchar.exe\
            wchar.exe\
            rline.exe\
            wline.exe\
            wdouble.exe\
            rdouble.exe\
            bstream.obj\
            tbdouble.exe\
            tbstream.exe\
            tbclass.exe\
            bfstream.obj\
            bfstest.exe\

oldio.exe: oldio.cpp
  $(CCLL) $(CLFLAGS) oldio

newio.exe: newio.cpp
  $(CCLL) $(CLFLAGS) newio

strout.exe: strout.cpp
  $(CCLL) $(CLFLAGS) strout

strin.exe: strin.cpp
  $(CCLL) $(CLFLAGS) strin

rwords.exe: rwords.cpp
  $(CCLL) $(CLFLAGS) rwords

cmanip.exe: cmanip.cpp
  $(CCLL) $(CLFLAGS) cmanip
```

```
repeat.exe: repeat.cpp
  $(CCLL) $(CLFLAGS) repeat

phone.exe: phone.cpp
  $(CCLL) $(CLFLAGS) phone

label.obj: label.h label.cpp
  $(CC) $(CFLAGS) label

tlabel.exe: tlabel.cpp label.obj
  $(CCLL) $(CLFLAGS) tlabel label.obj

field.obj: field.h field.cpp
  $(CC) $(CFLAGS) field

tfield.exe: tfield.cpp label.obj field.obj
  $(CCLL) $(CLFLAGS) tfield label.obj field.obj

polystr.exe: polystr.cpp
  $(CCLL) $(CLFLAGS) polystr

overout.exe: overout.cpp
  $(CCLL) $(CLFLAGS) overout

overin.exe: overin.cpp
  $(CCLL) $(CLFLAGS) overin

rchar.exe: rchar.cpp
  $(CCLL) $(CLFLAGS) rchar

wchar.exe: wchar.cpp
  $(CCLL) $(CLFLAGS) wchar

rline.exe: rline.cpp
  $(CCLL) $(CLFLAGS) rline

wline.exe: wline.cpp
  $(CCLL) $(CLFLAGS) wline
```

continues

Listing A.7. continued

```
wdouble.exe: wdouble.cpp
  $(CCLL) $(CLFLAGS) wdouble

rdouble.exe: rdouble.cpp
  $(CCLL) $(CLFLAGS) rdouble

bstream.obj: bstream.h bstream.cpp
  $(CC) $(CFLAGS) bstream

tbdouble.exe: tbdouble.cpp bstream.obj
  $(CCLL) $(CLFLAGS) tbdouble bstream.obj

tbstream.exe: tbstream.cpp bstream.obj
  $(CCLL) $(CLFLAGS) tbstream bstream.obj

tbclass.exe: tbclass.cpp bstream.obj
  $(CCLL) $(CLFLAGS) tbclass bstream.obj

bfstream.obj: bfstream.h bfstream.cpp
  $(CC) $(CFLAGS) bfstream

bfstest.exe: bfstest.cpp bfstream.obj
  $(CCLL) $(CLFLAGS) bfstest bfstream.obj

#- Delete backups, object code, and executables
#  Enter MAKE CLEAN to use

clean:
  del *.bak
  del *.obj
  del *.exe

#- Create turboc.cfg configuration file
#  Enter MAKE CONFIG to use

config: turboc.cfg
```

```
turboc.cfg: ..\makefile.inc
  echo -I$(INCPATH);$(BCCPATH)\include   >turboc.cfg
  echo -L$(LIBPATH);$(BCCPATH)\lib      >>turboc.cfg
```

Listing A.8. PART2\MAKEFILE.

```
# Code Secrets - MAKE file for Part 2
# Compiler: Borland C++ 3.1
# (c) 1993 by Tom Swan. All rights reserved.

!include "..\makefile.inc"

depends: config\
         minmax.exe\
         proto.exe\
         badtemp.exe\
         goodtemp.exe\
         tempsort.exe\
         cltdemo.exe\
         matrix.exe\
         members.exe\
         derived.exe\
         vect1.exe\
         vect2.exe\
         vect3.exe\
         string.exe\
         strmax.exe\
         strvect.exe\
         strvect2.exe\
         tlist.exe\
         ttree.exe\
         adtdemo1.exe\
         adtdemo2.exe\
         adtdemo3.exe\
         adtdemo4.exe\
         adtdemo5.exe\
```

continues

551

Listing A.8. continued

```
minmax.exe: minmax.h minmax.cpp
  $(CCLL) $(CLFLAGS) minmax

proto.exe: proto.cpp
  $(CCLL) $(CLFLAGS) proto

badtemp.exe: badtemp.cpp
  $(CCLL) $(CLFLAGS) badtemp

goodtemp.exe: goodtemp.cpp
  $(CCLL) $(CLFLAGS) goodtemp

tempsort.exe: tempsort.cpp
  $(CCLL) $(CLFLAGS) tempsort

cltdemo.exe: cltdemo.cpp
  $(CCLL) $(CLFLAGS) cltdemo

matrix.exe: matrix.cpp
  $(CCLL) $(CLFLAGS) matrix

members.exe: members.h members.cpp
  $(CCLL) $(CLFLAGS) members

derived.exe: members.h derived.cpp
  $(CCLL) $(CLFLAGS) derived

vect1.exe: vect1.cpp
  $(CCLL) $(CLFLAGS) vect1

vect2.exe: vect2.cpp
  $(CCLL) $(CLFLAGS) vect2

vect3.exe: vect3.cpp
  $(CCLL) $(CLFLAGS) vect3

string.exe: string.cpp
  $(CCLL) $(CLFLAGS) string $(CSLIB)
```

```
strmax.exe: strmax.cpp
  $(CCLL) $(CLFLAGS) strmax $(CSLIB)

strvect.exe: strvect.cpp
  $(CCLL) $(CLFLAGS) strvect $(CSLIB)

strvect2.exe: strvect2.cpp
  $(CCLL) $(CLFLAGS) strvect2 $(CSLIB)

tlist.exe: tlist.cpp
  $(CCLL) $(CLFLAGS) tlist $(CSLIB)

ttree.exe: ttree.cpp
  $(CCLL) $(CLFLAGS) ttree $(CSLIB)

adtdemo1.exe: adtdemo1.cpp
  $(CCLL) $(CLFLAGS) adtdemo1 $(CSLIB)

adtdemo2.exe: adtdemo2.cpp
  $(CCLL) $(CLFLAGS) adtdemo2 $(CSLIB)

adtdemo3.exe: adtdemo3.cpp
  $(CCLL) $(CLFLAGS) adtdemo3 $(CSLIB)

adtdemo4.exe: adtdemo4.cpp
  $(CCLL) $(CLFLAGS) adtdemo4 $(CSLIB)

adtdemo5.exe: adtdemo5.cpp
  $(CCLL) $(CLFLAGS) adtdemo5 $(CSLIB)

#- Delete backups, object code, and executables
#  Enter MAKE CLEAN to use

clean:
  del *.bak
  del *.obj
  del *.exe
```

continues

553

Listing A.8. continued

```
#- Create turboc.cfg configuration file
#  Enter MAKE CONFIG to use

config: turboc.cfg

turboc.cfg: ..\makefile.inc
  echo -I$(INCPATH);$(BCCPATH)\include   >turboc.cfg
  echo -L$(LIBPATH);$(BCCPATH)\lib      >>turboc.cfg
```

Listing A.9. PART3\MAKEFILE.

```
# Code Secrets - MAKE file for Part 3
# Compiler: Borland C++ 3.1
# (c) 1993 by Tom Swan. All rights reserved.

!include "..\makefile.inc"

depends: config\
         global.exe\
         mymem.exe\
         restrict.exe\
         mark.exe\
         handler.exe\
         heap.exe\
         clone.exe\
         noclone.exe\
         place.exe\
         flag.exe\
         vary.exe\
         ref.exe\
         ref2.exe\
         wasteful.exe\
         sparse.obj\
         sparray.exe\
         spmatrix.exe\
```

```
        triangle.exe\
        textobj.exe\

global.exe: global.cpp
  $(CCLL) $(CLFLAGS) global

mymem.exe: mymem.cpp
  $(CCLL) $(CLFLAGS) mymem

restrict.exe: restrict.cpp
  $(CCLL) $(CLFLAGS) restrict

mark.exe: mark.cpp
  $(CCLL) $(CLFLAGS) mark

handler.exe: handler.cpp
  $(CCLL) $(CLFLAGS) handler

heap.exe: heap.cpp
  $(CCLL) $(CLFLAGS) heap

clone.exe: clone.cpp
  $(CCLL) $(CLFLAGS) clone $(CSLIB)

noclone.exe: noclone.cpp
  $(CCLL) $(CLFLAGS) noclone

place.exe: place.cpp
  $(CCLL) $(CLFLAGS) place $(CSLIB)

flag.exe: flag.cpp
  $(CCLL) $(CLFLAGS) flag $(CSLIB)

vary.exe: vary.cpp
  $(CCLL) $(CLFLAGS) vary $(CSLIB)
```

continues

Listing A.9. continued

```
ref.exe: ref.cpp
  $(CCLL) $(CLFLAGS) ref $(CSLIB)

ref2.exe: ref2.cpp
  $(CCLL) $(CLFLAGS) ref2 $(CSLIB)

wasteful.exe: wasteful.cpp
  $(CCLL) $(CLFLAGS) wasteful

sparse.obj: sparse.h sparse.cpp
  $(CC) $(CFLAGS) sparse

sparray.exe: sparray.cpp
  $(CCLL) $(CLFLAGS) sparray $(CSLIB)

spmatrix.exe: spmatrix.cpp sparse.obj
  $(CCLL) $(CLFLAGS) spmatrix sparse.obj $(CSLIB)

triangle.exe: triangle.cpp sparse.obj
  $(CCLL) $(CLFLAGS) triangle sparse.obj $(CSLIB)

textobj.exe: textobj.cpp
  $(CCLL) $(CLFLAGS) textobj

#- Delete backups, object code, and executables
#  Enter MAKE CLEAN to use

clean:
  del *.bak
  del *.obj
  del *.exe

#- Create turboc.cfg configuration file
#  Enter MAKE CONFIG to use

config: turboc.cfg
```

```
turboc.cfg: ..\makefile.inc
  echo -I$(INCPATH);$(BCCPATH)\include    >turboc.cfg
  echo -L$(LIBPATH);$(BCCPATH)\lib       >>turboc.cfg
```

Listing A.10. PERSIST\MAKEFILE.

```
# Code Secrets - MAKE file for Chapter 17
# Compiler: Borland C++ 3.1
# (c) 1993 by Tom Swan. All rights reserved.

!include "..\makefile.inc"

depends: config\
         persist.exe\
         bstream.obj\

persist.exe: persist.cpp bstream.obj
  $(CCLL) $(CLFLAGS) persist bstream.obj $(CSLIB)

bstream.obj: bstream.h bstream.cpp
  $(CC) $(CFLAGS) bstream

#- Delete backups, object code, and executables
#  Enter MAKE CLEAN to use

clean:
  del *.bak
  del *.obj
  del *.exe
  del test.dat
  del turboc.cfg

#- Create turboc.cfg configuration file
#  Enter MAKE CONFIG to use

config: turboc.cfg
```

continues

557

Listing A.10. continued

```
turboc.cfg: ..\makefile.inc
  echo -I$(INCPATH);$(BCCPATH)\include   >turboc.cfg
  echo -L$(LIBPATH);$(BCCPATH)\lib      >>turboc.cfg
```

Disk Directory

F ollowing is a complete inventory of the directories and files created by installing this book's disk. Use this information to locate a specific file mentioned in a chapter, and to verify that your installation is complete. (See the README.TXT file, however, for last-minute changes and updates that might affect this list.)

Directories and Files

```
C:\SECRETS
¦    !
¦    HISTORY.ENG
¦    LHA.EXE
¦    LHA.HLP
¦    LHA213.DOC
¦    MAKEALL.BAT
¦    MAKEFILE.INC
¦    README.TXT
¦
+---INCLUDE
¦        ARRAY.H
¦        CONTAIN.H
¦        DEQUE.H
¦        ITER.H
¦        LIST.H
¦        LISTITER.H
¦        MEMUSE.H
¦        MINMAX.H
¦        MISC.H
¦        QUEUE.H
¦        SARRAY.H
¦        SET.H
¦        SLIST.H
¦        STACK.H
¦        STR.H
¦        SVECTOR.H
¦        TCLASS.H
¦        TREE.H
¦        VECTITER.H
¦        VECTOR.H
¦
+---LIB
¦   ¦    BUILD.BAT
¦   ¦    SECRETS.LIB
¦   ¦    SECRETS.TXT
¦   ¦
```

```
+---CLASSLIB
¦       ARRAY.H
¦       CONTAIN.CPP
¦       CONTAIN.H
¦       DEQUE.H
¦       LIST.H
¦       LISTITER.H
¦       MAKEFILE
¦       MINMAX.H
¦       MISC.H
¦       QUEUE.H
¦       SET.H
¦       STACK.H
¦       SVECTOR.CPP
¦       SVECTOR.H
¦       TCLASS.CPP
¦       TCLASS.H
¦       TCONTAIN.CPP
¦       TLIST.CPP
¦       TREE.H
¦       TTREE.CPP
¦       TVECTOR.CPP
¦       VECTITER.H
¦       VECTOR.H
¦
+---STRING
¦       DUMP.INC
¦       MAKEFILE
¦       STR.CPP
¦       STR.H
¦       STRCTOR.CPP
¦       STRFRNDS.CPP
¦       STRIO.CPP
¦       STRMFS.CPP
¦       STROPS.CPP
¦       STRSTATS.CPP
¦
\---MEMUSE
        MAKEFILE
        MEMUSE.CPP
        MEMUSE.H
```

```
+---PART1
|       BFSTEST.CPP
|       BFSTREAM.CPP
|       BFSTREAM.H
|       BSTREAM.CPP
|       BSTREAM.H
|       CMANIP.CPP
|       FIELD.CPP
|       FIELD.H
|       LABEL.CPP
|       LABEL.H
|       MAKEFILE
|       NEWIO.CPP
|       OLDIO.CPP
|       OVERIN.CPP
|       OVEROUT.CPP
|       PHONE.CPP
|       POLYSTR.CPP
|       RCHAR.CPP
|       RDOUBLE.CPP
|       REPEAT.CPP
|       RLINE.CPP
|       RWORDS.CPP
|       STRIN.CPP
|       STROUT.CPP
|       TBCLASS.CPP
|       TBDOUBLE.CPP
|       TBSTREAM.CPP
|       TFIELD.CPP
|       TLABEL.CPP
|       WCHAR.CPP
|       WDOUBLE.CPP
|       WLINE.CPP
|
+---PART2
|       ADTDEMO1.CPP
|       ADTDEMO2.CPP
|       ADTDEMO3.CPP
|       ADTDEMO4.CPP
|       ADTDEMO5.CPP
```

```
|        BADTEMP.CPP
|        CLTDEMO.CPP
|        DERIVED.CPP
|        GOODTEMP.CPP
|        MAKEFILE
|        MATRIX.CPP
|        MEMBERS.CPP
|        MEMBERS.H
|        MINMAX.CPP
|        MINMAX.H
|        PROTO.CPP
|        STRING.CPP
|        STRMAX.CPP
|        STRVECT.CPP
|        STRVECT2.CPP
|        TEMPSORT.CPP
|        TLIST.CPP
|        TTREE.CPP
|        VECT1.CPP
|        VECT2.CPP
|        VECT3.CPP
|
+---PART3
|        CLONE.CPP
|        FLAG.CPP
|        GLOBAL.CPP
|        HANDLER.CPP
|        HEAP.CPP
|        MAKEFILE
|        MARK.CPP
|        MYMEM.CPP
|        NOCLONE.CPP
|        PLACE.CPP
|        REF.CPP
|        REF2.CPP
|        RESTRICT.CPP
|        SPARRAY.CPP
|        SPARSE.CPP
|        SPARSE.H
|        SPMATRIX.CPP
```

```
¦        TEXTOBJ.CPP
¦        TRIANGLE.CPP
¦        VARY.CPP
¦        WASTEFUL.CPP
¦
+---PERSIST
¦        BSTREAM.CPP
¦        BSTREAM.H
¦        MAKEFILE
¦        PERSIST.CPP
¦
\---BONUS
         PROMODEM.LZH
         OBJEAS2A.LZH
         OBJEAS2B.LZH
         SCRED1.LZH
         SCRED2.LZH
```

Bonus
Programs on Disk

E ven though the accompanying disk holds all of this book's listings plus
several additional files, there was plenty of room on the disk, and it seemed
a shame to let all that delicious space go to waste. So, the publisher provided me
with several bonus programming libraries to include on the disk that you might
find interesting.

Installing the diskette copies the bonus programs into a directory named BONUS. All programs are "try-before-you-buy" shareware, and are provided directly by their authors. The programs are not described elsewhere in this book.

To examine the bonus files, change to the BONUS directory and copy one or more files ending in .LZH to another, empty directory. (This preserves the original .LZH files in case you make a mistake or want to reinstall the programs later.)

To unpack the files, change to the directory containing an archive file and enter a command such as

```
LHA x filename.LZH
```

That extracts the packed files, after which you can delete *filename*.LZH.

> **Note:** The supplied LHA.EXE program must be on the PATH or in the current directory.

After unpacking an archived file, look for additional instructions. You'll find information on what files to read in the sections of this appendix that talk about each included program. Some programs may require you to run an additional utility or to unpack other archives to complete the installation. Contact the shareware authors directly for updates, to register your programs, and to obtain more information.

In the following sections, you'll find more information about each included bonus program, including the name of the documentation file.

ObjectEase

Name of compressed files:
OBJEAS2A.LZH and OBJEAS2B.LZH

Author:
David S. Reinhart Associates
1004 Marticville Road
Pequea, PA 17565
(717) 284-3736

Documentation: DOCS\OBJEASE.DOC

Readme File: README.1ST

ObjectEase is a library of C++ classes and member functions. All of the classes are intuitive—you've been using them in someone else's programs for years, but you may have never have been able to duplicate them on your own. Not because you don't have the programming skill, but because you didn't want to waste time developing tools when you could spend your valuable time developing a completed project.

> **Note:** After you use LHA.EXE to unpack the two ObjectEase .LZH files, you'll find three .LZH files: DOCS.LZH, DEMOS.LZH, and LIBS.ZIP. The author of ObjectEase recommends that you extract each of these .LZH files into its own subdirectory. Use LHA.EXE to extract these files.

You don't have to re-code anything with ObjectEase. Just include the ObjectEase libraries in your project file and use these objects over and over to produce professional quality applications.

The demo programs that are provided are the quickest and easiest way to see what the ObjectEase library can do. The demos are called TUIDEMO.EXE, GUIDEMO.EXE, and VIDDEMO.EXE. These demo programs are located in the DEMO.LZH file.

Turbo Screen Edit

Compressed files:
SCRED1.LZH and SCRED2.LZH

Author:
iHn Systems
P.O. Box 1707
Tulare, CA 93275-1707
(209) 685-8769

Documentation: MANUAL.PT1, MANUAL.PT2, MANUAL.PT3

Readme File: READ.ME

With Turbo ScrEdit, you can quickly design, develop, and fully test menu, help, and data entry screens for use in your programs. After you use LHA.EXE to unpack the two .LZH files, you will run the author's installation program, TSINSTAL.EXE.

The screen editor features:

- A full screen text editor that allows the most complex screens to be designed quickly and tested thoroughly without writing a single line of code.

- Complete online help for every screen editor function.

- Undo.

- Full color control.

- Change cursor direction for typing lines, boxes, borders.

- Line and Box drawing function keys.

- Automatic backup files.

- Keyboard toggles between regular characters and the extended graphics character (line drawing) mode.

- Redefinable key provides access to all (0-255) ASCII characters.

ProModem

Name of compressed file:
PROMODEM.LZH

Author:
Adrian Michaud
93 Linden Ave.
Swampscott, MA 01907
(617) 595-8912

Documentation: PROMODEM.DOC

ProModem is a High Performance Interrupt-Driven RS232 serial communications library that can be used for creating a Computerized Bulletin Board System, a Terminal program, an RS232 Networking Driver, or for RS232 Host-to-Host communications.

ProModem contains the following features:

- Interrupt-driven INPUT directly VIA 8259 Peripheral Interrupt Controller.

- Full 16550 FIFO support with selectable trigger levels.

- Supports user definable Base Addresses using IRQ3 or IRQ4.

- Automatic CTS/RTS Hardware Handshaking for Asynchronous Devices.

- Baud rates up to 115K bits per second.

- Handles unlimited Open Com Ports using IRQ3 and IRQ4.

- Supports both ISA (PC AT) and MCA (PS 2) machines.

The compiled programs BBS.EXE and TERMINAL.EXE are simple examples of what can be done using the ProModem library. Source code is supplied for these example programs as well.

LHA

An additional bonus program is the LHA.EXE utility itself. This remarkable program written by Haruyasu Yoshizaki is the top file compressor and decompressor around. It isn't as fast as some other compression utilities (though it's no slowpoke), but it usually produces the tightest results. Complete instructions for using LHA.EXE are provided in the LHA213.DOC file in C:\SECRETS (if that's where you installed the disk).

Index

C

M

N

O

W

X

Y-Z

Add to Your Sams Library Today with the Best Books for Programming, Operating Systems, and New Technologies!

Yes, please send me the productivity-boosting material I have checked below. Make check payable to Sams Publishing.

☐ **Check enclosed**

Charge to my credit card:

☐ VISA ☐ MasterCard ☐ American Express

Acct: _____

Expiration date: _____

Signature: _____

Name: _____

Company: _____

Address: _____

City: _____

State: _____ ZIP: _____

Phone: _____

The easiest way to order is to pick up the phone and call 1-800-428-5331 between 9:00 a.m. and 5:00 p.m. EST. For faster service please have your credit card available.

ISBN #	Quantity	Description of Item	Unit Cost	Total Cost
0-672-30274-8		Mastering Borland C++	$39.95	
0-672-30168-7		Advanced C (Book/Disk)	$39.95	
0-672-30158-X		Advanced C++ (Book/Disk)	$39.95	
0-672-30200-4		C++ Programming 101 (Book/Disk)	$29.95	
0-672-30137-7		Secrets of the Borland C++ Masters	$44.95	
0-672-30226-8		Windows Programmer's Guide to OLE/DDE	$34.95	
0-672-30248-9		FractalVision (Book/Disk)	$39.95	
0-672-27366-7		Memory Management for All of Us	$29.95	
0-672-30080-X		Moving from C to C++	$29.95	
0-672-30199-7		Moving from Turbo Pascal to Turbo C++	$29.95	
0-672-30249-7		Multimedia Madness! (Book/Disk)	$44.95	
0-672-30138-5		Secrets of the Visual Basic for Windows Masters (Book/Disk)	$39.95	
0-672-30040-0		Teach Yourself C in 21 Days	$24.95	
0-672-30188-1		Tom Swan's C++ Primer (Book/Disk)	$34.95	
0-672-30135-0		Tricks of the Windows 3.1 Masters (Book/Disk)	$44.95	
0-672-30236-5		Windows Programmer's Guide to DLLs and Memory Management	$34.95	
0-672-30280-2		Turbo C++ Programming 101 (Book/Disk)	$29.95	
0-672-30145-8		Visual Basic for Windows Developer's Guide (Book/Disk)	$39.95	
☐ 3 1/2" Disk ☐ 5 1/4" Disk		Shipping and Handling: See information below.		
		TOTAL		

Shipping and Handling: $4.00 for the first book and $1.75 for each additional book. Floppy disk: add $1.75 for shipping and handling. If you need to have it NOW, we can ship product to you in 24 hours for an additional charge of approximately $18.00, and you will receive your item overnight or in two days. Overseas shipping and handling add $20.00 per book and $8.00 for up to three disks. Prices subject to change. Call for availability and pricing information on latest editions.

11711   N. College Avenue,   Suite 140,   Carmel, Indiana   46032

1-800-428-5331— Orders   1-800-835-3202—FAX   1-800-858-7674 — CustomersService

What's on the Disk

The companion disk includes all the source code for Tom Swan's programming examples. As a bonus, the disk also contains three shareware programming tools:

- ObjectEase, a library of C++ classes and member functions.
- Turbo ScrEdit, a tool for designing and developing screens.
- ProModem, a serial communications library.

Installing the Floppy Disk

Follow these steps to install the disk's software to your hard drive. For more detailed instructions, read Appendix B, "Disk Directory," in this book.

1. Create a directory on your hard drive.

2. Copy all files from the disk to the new directory.

3. Change to the new directory and run UNPACK.BAT to complete the installation.

4. After you see the message "Done," you can delete the .LZH compressed files and the UNPACK.BAT batch file.

The bonus shareware tools need further installation before they can be used—see Appendix C, "Bonus Programs on Disk," for more information.

Note: For additional notes and late breaking news, see the README.TXT file (load it into any ASCII text editor). To install all the files, you'll need at least 3.1M of free space on your hard drive.